Iron Age and Roman Setttlement on the Northamptonshire Uplands

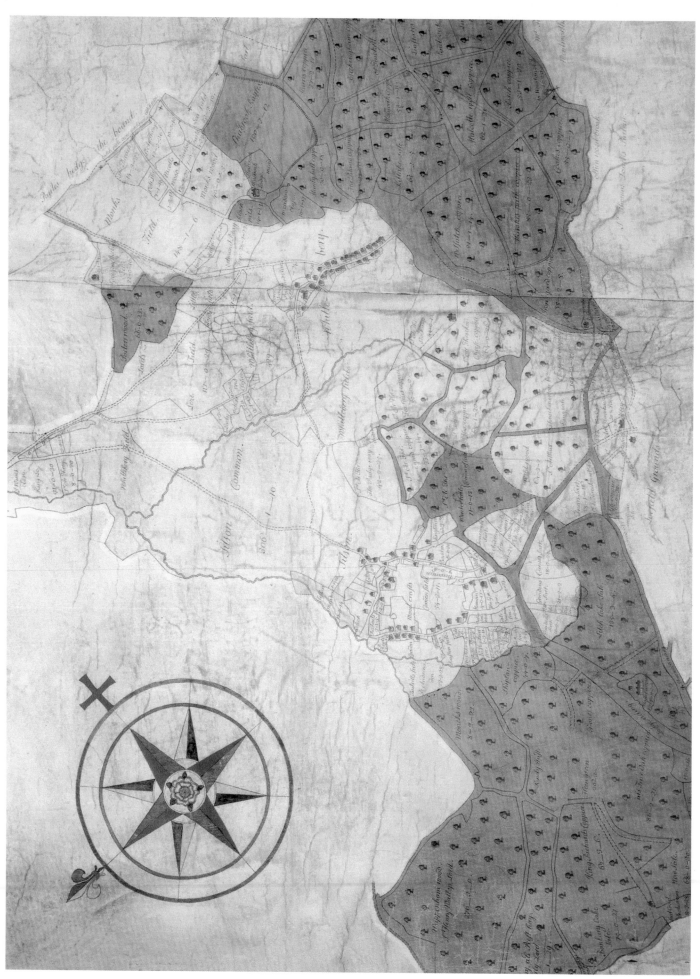

Frontispiece: *Map of Whittlewood Forest c 1608. (Northamptonshire Record Office, Map 4210).*

Iron Age and Roman settlement on the Northamptonshire uplands

Archaeological work on the
A43 Towcester to M40 Road Improvement scheme
in Northamptonshire and Oxfordshire

by

Andrew Mudd

With major contributions by
W J Carruthers, K Deighton, T Hylton, I Meadows,
M Robinson, C Salter and J Timby

Other contributors
A Chapman, P Chapman, H E M Cool, M Curteis,
R Gale, D Mackreth and A Thorne

Illustrations by
J Harding, A Foard-Colby, C Simmonds,
H A Jacklin and A Butler

Northamptonshire Archaeology

Monograph 1

2007

NORTHAMPTONSHIRE ARCHAEOLOGY

NORTHAMPTONSHIRE COUNTY COUNCIL

ISBN 978-0-9555062-0-8

Typesetting and layout by Heritage Marketing & Publications Ltd.

Printed and distributed by Heritage Marketing & Publications Ltd
Great Dunham, King's Lynn, Norfolk.

Northamptonshire County Council are indebted to the Highways Agency, Costain Skanska JV and Walters UK Ltd for their funding of both the fieldwork and the preparation and publication of this volume.

Front cover: Iron Age site at Silverstone Fields Farm, looking north (photograph by Aerial Close-Up Ltd).

Back cover: (from top) Iron Age glass ring from Silverstone Fields Farm; using an Iron Age bloomery iron smelting furnace (illustration by Alex Thorne); geophysical survey results at Tusmore; using a late Iron Age pottery kiln (illustration by Alex Thorne).

CONTENTS

List of contents - iii
List of illustrations - iv
List of plates - v
List of tables - vi
Summary/Résumé/Zusammenfassung - ix
Acknowledgements - x

CHAPTER 1: Introduction

Project location - 1
Geology and topography - 1
Project background - 1
Archaeological background - 3
Archaeological character of the route - 6
Excavation strategy - 7
Archive - 8

CHAPTER 2: Iron Age and Roman periods

Introduction - 9
Earlier prehistoric material - 9
Silverstone 3: Iron Age settlement - 9
Silverstone 2: Iron Age settlement - 25
Silverstone Fields Farm: Iron Age settlement - 30
Silverstone 1: Roman road - 39
Shacks Barn Farm: Iron Age and Roman occupation - 42
Silverstone 4: Iron Age and Roman features - 47
Great Ouse Culvert: Roman midden - 47
Biddlesden Road Bridge: Iron Age iron smelting site - 48
Area G Syresham (Pimlico): Iron Age and Roman occupation - 61
Brackley Hatch 4: Roman pottery producing site - 66
Cottisford Turn, Tusmore: Iron Age pit alignment - 71
Tusmore Drain Outfall and Park: Iron Age and Roman occupation - 76

CHAPTER 3: Medieval and later periods

Introduction - 79
Hazelborough Wood survey and trench excavations - 79
Four field boundaries east of Silverstone - 81
Post-medieval features at Silverstone 3 and Wood Burcote Bridge - 83
Medieval cultivation - 84

CHAPTER 4: The Finds

The flint by A Thorne - 87
The Iron Age and Roman Pottery by J Timby - 88
Post-Roman pottery - 118
Pottery kiln furniture by J Timby and T Hylton - 118
Coins I Meadows and M Curteis - 120
Non-ferrrous metal objects by I Meadows with a contribution by D Mackreth - 122
Iron objects by I Meadows and T Hylton - 125
Iron slag by C Salter with a contribution by A Chapman - 126
Other finds by I Meadows and T Hylton with a contribution by H E M Cool - 133

CHAPTER 5: Human Skeletal Material

Introduction - 137
Infant Burials from Silverstone Fields Farm by T Anderson - 137

CHAPTER 6: Economic and Environmental Evidence

The animal bones by K Deighton - 141
Charred plant remains by W J Carruthers - 147
Charcoal fuel debris from Biddlesden Road Bridge and Brackley Hatch 4 by R Gale - 157
Land snails by M Robinson - 159

CHAPTER 7: General Discussion

Chronology - 163
The nature of the Iron Age settlement - 166
Iron smelting at Biddlesden Road Bridge - 174
Roman pottery production at Brackley Hatch 4 - 176
Settlement and Economy - 177
Conclusions - 181

BIBLIOGRAPHY

APPENDICES

Appendix 1:   Scientific dating - 187
   1.1   Radiocarbon dating
   1.2   Optically Stimulated Luminescence Dating from Cottisford Turn pit alignment

Appendix 2:   Infant burials from Silverstone Fields Farm - 191

Appendix 3:   Bone quantification and measurements - 201

LIST OF ILLUSTRATIONS

Figure

1.1   Project location.

1.2   Geology (Source: British Geological Survey digital mapping. Permit No. IPR/47-19C British Geological Survey. © NERC. All rights reserved).

1.3   Route of A43 road improvement showing locations of excavated sites.

2.1   Iron Age sites Silverstone 3 and Silverstone 2. Magnetometer survey results, including areas outside the road corridor.

2.2   Silverstone 3, overall plan. The magnetometer survey interpretation is shown in grey tone to the west of the excavation.

2.3   Silverstone 3, detail of northern area.

2.4   Silverstone 3, detail of central area.

2.5   Silverstone 3, detail of southern area.

2.6   Silverstone 3, Phase 1 northern area and other potentially early features (grey tone).

2.7   Silverstone 3, northern area Phases 2-4.

2.8   Silverstone 3, northern area, sections 81, 79, 103.

2.9   Silverstone 3, northern area, sections 87, 115, 77.

2.10   Silverstone 3, central area, section 31.

2.11   Silverstone 3, southern area, Structure 1 Phases 1-4.

2.12   Silverstone 3, southern area, section 60.

2.13   Silverstone 3, ditch 2051 (Enclosure 1), sections 78, 114, 52 and 7.

2.14   Silverstone 2, overall plan. The magnetometer survey is shown in grey tone.

2.15   Silverstone 2, detail of southern boundary.

2.16   Silverstone 2, pit sections 10 and 14.

2.17   Silverstone 2, enclosure ditch, sections 33 and 20.

2.18   Silverstone 2, Structure 1, detail of ring ditches 1082 and 1063.

2.19   Silverstone 2, Structure 1, sections 38, 46 and 39

2.20   Silverstone Fields Farm, site plan.

2.21   Silverstone Fields Farm, detail of northern area.

2.22   Silverstone Fields Farm, detail of southern area.

2.23   Silverstone Fields Farm, Enclosure 1 sections 22, 19, 1 and 2.

2.24   Silverstone Fields Farm, Enclosure 1 sections 7 and 10.

2.25   Silverstone Fields Farm, pit sections 30, 31, 43, 8 and 42.

2.26   Location of site Silverstone 1 (SL1) in relation to Silverstone 2, Silverstone Fields Farm and the Roman road from Towcester to Alchester. The road's projected course southward was not confirmed.

2.27   Silverstone 1, site plan. The cobbles of the remnant Roman road (18) lay upslope of a later hollow-way (14).

2.28   Shacks Barn Farm soil disposal area. Geophysical meshes and trial trench locations.

2.29   Shacks Barn Farm, trench 27 plan and sections of Iron Age enclosure.

2.30   Shacks Barn Farm, trenches 31 and 32 plans.

2.31   Shacks Barn Farm, trenches 35 and 36 plans.

2.32   Shacks Barn Farm, trench 39 plan and sections.

2.33   Silverstone 4, site location with surface finds. Inset showing features.

2.34   Great Ouse Culvert, site plan.

2.35   Biddlesden Road Bridge, magnetometer survey results.

2.36   Biddlesden Road Bridge, site plan.

2.37   Biddlesden Road Bridge, Structure 1, ditch 8 and pit and gully groups 9 and 10.

2.38   Biddlesden Road Bridge, Structure 1 sections 134 and 71.

2.39   Biddlesden Road Bridge, Structure 2 and gully 20.

2.40   Biddlesden Road Bridge, Structure 2 sections 151, 108 and 135.

2.41   Biddlesden Road Bridge, Structure 3, Structure 4 and ditch 17.

2.42   Biddlesden Road Bridge, Furnaces 1 and 2, and pit and gully group 18.

2.43   Biddlesden Road Bridge, Furnace 1 sections 22, 23 and 24.

2.44   Biddlesden Road Bridge, Furnace 2 sections 25, 26 and 27.

2.45   Biddlesden Road Bridge, Furnace 3, ditch 25 and 'industrial refuse' deposit 24.

2.46   Biddlesden Road Bridge, Furnace 3 sections 54 and 55.

2.47   Area G Syresham, Field A. Trench locations and magnetometer survey.

2.48   Area G Syresham, Fields B-E. Trench locations and magnetometer survey.

2.49   Area G Syresham, Field A. Iron Age enclosure, trenches 4, 5 and 6. Sections 20-24.

2.50   Area G Syresham, Field C. Roman occupation, trench 10; Roman pottery kiln and iron smelting furnace, trench 23. Sections 14-17.

2.51   Area G Syresham, Magnetometer survey, Fields C and D.

2.52   Brackley Hatch 4, site plan.

2.53   Brackley Hatch 4, extended magnetometer survey.

2.54   Brackley Hatch 4, Phase 1 (early to mid second century AD).

2.55   Brackley Hatch 4, Phase 2 (second to early third century AD).

2.56   Brackley Hatch 4, Phases 2-3 (third century AD).

2.57 Brackley Hatch 4, Ditch 48 and Ditch 35, sections.

2.58 Brackley Hatch 4, Pottery Kiln 66, plan and sections.

2.59 Brackley Hatch 4, Pottery Kiln 61, plan and sections.

2.60 Cottisford Turn, site plan.

2.61 Cottisford Turn, sections 1, 10, 7 and 63.

2.62 Tusmore Drain Outfall, magnetometer survey of Roman settlement east of the drain trench.

3.1 Historical features near Silverstone. Sources: Cropmark and earthwork ridge and furrow from NCCHET Historic Landscape Characterisation; Ancient boundaries from NRO Map 4210 (c 1608) and Silverstone Inclosure Map (c 1825); other ridge and furrow and surface distribution of medieval pottery from present project. (Ridge and furrow not oriented). For detail of Hazelborough Wood trenches see Figure 3.3.

3.2 Historical features south of Syresham. (For key, see Figure 3.1).

3.3 Hazelborough Wood, locations of woodland boundary and trenches HA1 and HA2. Features outside road corridor from Hall (2000, figure 13).

4.1 Pottery from Silverstone Fields Farm, 1–22.

4.2 Pottery from Silverstone 3, 23–35; and Silverstone 2, 36–50.

4.3 Pottery from Biddlesden Road Bridge, 51–58.

4.4 Pottery from Shacks Barn Farm, 59; Tusmore Drain Outfall, 60; WB SL Chainage 7420, 61; Area G Syresham, 62–68; Great Ouse Cuulvert, 69–70.

4.5 Pottery from Brackley Hatch 4, 71–85.

4.6 Pottery from Brackley Hatch 4, 86–103.

4.7 Frequencies of vessels by rim diameter for grog-tempered, shell-tempered and other fabrics. Silverstone Fields Farm, Silverstone 2, Silverstone 3 and Biddlesden Road Bridge.

4.8 Kiln furniture from Brackley Hatch 4, Kiln 61 (1) and (10).

4.9 Copper alloy objects from near Silverstone 2 (43); Brackley Hatch 4 (48); Great Ouse Culvert (4) and (46).

4.10 Iron artefacts from Silverstone Fields Farm (65), (66) and (68).

4.11 Iron artefacts from Area G Syresham (73) and (82).

4.12 Normal sandy and clay refractory fired to terracotta red colour. Showing a mass of small angular and sub-rounded silica grains in clay matrix. The bright grain in centre of field is a monazite (Cerium/ Lanthanum Phosphate). Sample OX463.

4.13 Microstructure of lighter coloured refractory, with higher proportion of large silica grains. Sample OX 440.

4.14 Lighter coloured refractory. Sample OX426.

4.15 A typical microstructure of a furnace slag from context group 2 with large primary fayalite laths and a matrix of hercynite and 'glass'.

4.16 A typical slag of context group 3, with fine, light-coloured free oxide dendrite in a ground mass of fayalite (mid-grey) and hercynite (lighter grey) outlined by dark glass.

4.17 Showing poorly consolidated metal (white) surrounded by slag with high free iron oxide content (midgrey) and fayalite with hercynite with occasional pools of glass.

4.18 Tenary FeO-SiO2 Anorthite plot showing the regions where the slags from composition groups 2 and 3 fall. (After Morton and Wingrove 1972).

4.19 Antler and bone artefacts from Silverstone 3 (88); Silverstone Fields Farm (92) and (93).

4.20 Limestone disc, Silverstone 3 (89) and spindle whorl, Silverstone Field Farm (90).

4.21 Glass ring, Silverstone Fields Farm (91); Jasper intaglio, Area G Syresham (101); Base of glass bowl, Area G, Syresham (104).

6.1 Silverstone 3, Preservation of Bos and Ovicaprid.

6.2 Silverstone Fields Farm, Preservation of Bos and Ovicaprid.

6.3 Silverstone Field Farm, Survival pattern of Ovicaprid based on tooth eruption and wear (from 29 mandibles).

7.1 Silverstone Fields Farm Enclosure 1, Pottery quantification for excavated sections, upper (u), middle (m) and lower (l) fills.

7.2 Possible development from agglomerated settlement at Silverstone 3 to individual pastoral and arable settlements at Silverstone 2 and Silverstone Fields Farm.

LIST OF PLATES

Plate

1 Silverstone 3. Northern terminal of ditch 1051, Enclosure 1. Looking north-west.

2 Silverstone 3. Section through the northern arm of ditch 1051, Enclosure 1.

3 Silverstone 2. Northern arm of enclosure, ditch 1050, looking east.

4 Silverstone Fields Farm. Enclosure 1, entrance between ditch terminals.

5 Silverstone Fields Farm. Infant burial 2 within the ditch of Enclosure 1.

6 Silverstone Fields Farm. Burial of partial cattle carcass within the ditch of Enclosure 1.

7   Silverstone Fields Farm. Pit 166, a possible grain storage pit.

8   Biddlesden Road Bridge. Iron smelting Furnace 1. The partly exposed firing chamber lies within the pit to the fore. The rake-out pit is cut by ditch 17 on the left.

9   Biddlesden Road Bridge. Iron smelting Furnace 2 under excavation.

10   Cottisford Turn. Ditch and pit alignment, looking south from ditch 178.

11   Cottisford Turn. Pit 139.

12   Cottisford Turn. Terminal of ditch 180 and underlying pit 136.

LIST OF TABLES

Table

1.1   Summary of sites examined.

4.1   Worked flint by category and site .

4.2   Summary of pottery from Silverstone Fields Farm.

4.3   Summary of pottery from Silverstone 3.

4.4   Summary of pottery from Silverstone 2.

4.5   Summary of pottery from Biddlesden Road Bridge.

4.6   Summary of pottery from Area G Syresham.

4.7   Summary of pottery from Great Ouse Culvert (★ = less than 1%).

4.8   Summary of Roman fabrics from Brackley Hatch 4 (★ = less than 1%).

4.9   Weight of debris by major class.

4.10   Slag distribution by group.

4.11   Debris type by feature groups (weight in grammes).

4.12   Debris type by feature groups (weight in grammes).

4.13   Composition of normal and lighter coloured furnace lining.

6.1   Animal bone; summary of taxa by site (MinAU).

6.2   Animal bone; summary of taxa present by minimum number of individuals.

6.3   Charred plant remains from Silverstone 2.

6.4   Charred plant remains from Silverstone 3.

6.5   Charred plant remains from Silverstone Fields Farm.

6.6   Charred plant remains from Biddlesden Road Bridge.

6.7   Charred plant remains from Brackley Hatch 4.

6.8   Percentage abundance of cereals. Barley was the dominant crop at Silverstone 2, contrasting with the greater abundance of wheat at the other Iron Age sites, Silverstone 3 and Silverstone Fields Farm, and the Roman site Brackley Hatch 4.

6.9   Percentage of samples where present. Despite the greater abundance of barley compared to wheat at Silverstone 2, barley was present in more samples at the other sites, albeit as a low proportion of cereals present.

6.10   Grain: Chaff: Weed ratios. The two richest samples (Sample 2, Silverstone 2 and Sample 11, Silverstone Fields Farm), with high proportions of chaff, probably represent the charred waste from crop processing.

6.11   Biddlesden Road Bridge: Late Iron Age iron-working fuel debris – charcoal identification.

6.12   Brackley Hatch, BH4: Charcoal analysis of fuel debris from Early Roman pottery kilns.

6.13   Molluscs from Silverstone 2.

6.14   Molluscs from Cottisford Turn.

7.1   Comparison of pit dimensions at Twyell, Silverstone Fields Farm and Pennyland.

APPENDICES

Table

1.1   Radiocarbon dating.

1.2   Results of Optically Stimulated Luminescence Dating.

2.1   Infant burials: age estimation based on diaphyseal bone lengths.

2.2   Infant burials: long bone indices.

2.3   Infant burials: dimensions of the unerupted deciduous teeth.

2.4   Infant burials: sexing criteria: pelvic indices.

2.5   Infant burials: limb bone robusticity.

2.6   Infant burials: the cranial metrics.

2.7   Infant burials: the post-cranial metrics.

3.1   Animal bone: Silverstone 2, species by element.

3.2   Animal bone: Silverstone 3, species by element.

3.3   Animal bone: Silverstone Fields Farm, species by element.

3.4   Animal bone: Brackley Hatch 4, species by element.

3.5   Animal bone: Biddlesdon Road Bridge, species by element.

3.6   Toothwear for cattle from Biddlesden Road Bridge.

3.7   Toothwear for sheep/goat from Silverstone 3.

3.8   Toothwear for sheep/goat at Silverstone Fields Farm.

3.9   Measurements from Silverstone Fields Farm cattle skeleton.

3.10   Percentage survival for Ovicaprids from Silverstone Fields Farm.

3.11   Percentage survival for Ovicaprids from Silverstone 3.

3.12   Percentage survival for cattle from Biddlesdon Road Bridge.

3.13.   Bone elements used in defining fusion stages and ages at which fusion occurs.

SUMMARY

Archaeological excavations in advance of the construction of the new A43 dual carriageway between Towcester and the M40, in both Northamptonshire and Oxfordshire, were carried out by Northamptonshire Archaeology in 2000 and 2001 in accordance with Highways Agency requirements.

Excavations were undertaken on five settlement sites – four dating to the Iron Age/early Roman period, and one to the Roman period. Three of the Iron Age sites, each of a different form, lay within 500 m of each other south of Towcester. There were also investigations on a smaller scale on sites principally of the Iron Age and Roman periods, including a pit alignment. The opportunity has also been taken to present the results of a magnetometer survey at Tusmore Deserted Medieval Village, which included part of a Roman settlement. This report also summarises the more disparate evidence for medieval land-use. The investigations are particularly significant in view of the limited previous archaeological work in this area, much of which lies on Boulder Clay geology.

The finds comprise moderately large collections of pottery (*c* 8000 sherds) and animal bone (77 kg) and small collections of metal and other finds. Of particular importance was the discovery of Iron Age iron smelting at Biddlesden Road Bridge and early Roman iron smelting at Syresham. Detailed analysis indicates that both slag tapping and non-slag tapping technologies were used in the Iron Age. Early Roman pottery kilns were found at Syresham and Whitfield, adding to the picture of a widespread but small-scale industry at this time. A report on a group of infant burials from Silverstone Fields Farm is presented in detail.

The evidence is discussed and set in its regional context. A comparison of the artefactual and economic evidence from the Iron Age sites suggests that there were slight differences in the assemblages which could indicate different economic practices and perhaps social roles for these settlements.

RÉSUMÉ

Des recherches archéologiques préliminaires à la construction de la nouvelle A43 à double voie entre la ville de Towcester et l'autoroute M40, dans les comtés du North-amptonshire et de l'Oxfordshire, ont été effectuées par Northamptonshire Archéology en 2000-2001, selon un cahier des charges établis par la Highways Agency.

Cinq habitats anciens furent fouillés, quatre datant de la charnière Age du Fer/début de la période Romaine, et un cinquième datant de la période Romaine propre. Trois des sites de l'Age du Fer, tous de morphologie différente, gisaient à moins de 500 m les uns des autres au sud de Towcester. Des recherches de moindre envergure furent menées sur d'autres sites, dont un alignement de fosses, de l'Age du Fer et de la période Romaine,. Le présent rapport inclut également les résultats d'une inspection magnétomètrique menée sur les vestiges enfouis du village médiéval abandonné de Tusmore. Le périmètre de l'investigation incluait aussi en partie un habitat d'origine romaine. Le rapport présente enfin l'existence de preuves disparates concernant l'utilisation des terres pendant le Moyen-Age. L'ensemble des résultats est d'autant plus important pour la recherche que la zone concernée a été l'objet de très peu d'investigations jusqu'ici.

Les objets recueillis se composent d'un groupe de fragments de céramique de taille moyenne (8000 tessons), d'un assemblage d'ossements d'animaux (77 kg) , et d'un petit nombre d'objets en fer et autres matériaux. Des traces de métallurgie (fonte de minerais) datant de l'Age du Fer à Biddleden Road Bridge, et du début de la période Romaine à Syresham, présentent un intérêt scientifique particulièrement important. Leur analyse a démontré que les techniques de fonte avec ou sans écoulement de laitier étaient utilisées sans discrimination dès l'Age du Fer. Des fours de potiers découverts à Syresham Whitfield, complètent le tableau d'une activité industrielle modeste certes, mais géographiquement extensive durant les deux périodes historiques concernées. Le présent rapport relate également la découverte d'un groupe d'inhumations d'enfants dans les environs de Silverstone Fields Farm.

L'ensemble des résultats est présenté et interprété dans leur contexte archéologique régional. L'analyse comparative des collections d'objets et l'interprétation de l'activité économique des habitats de l'Age du Fer a mis au jour de légères différences inter-sites qui, bien que ténues, peuvent suggérer des fonctions différenciées et donc peut-être une hiérarchie sociale.

Trans. Michel Audouy

ZUSAMMENFASSUNG

Archäologische Ausgrabungen wurden im Vorlauf der Konstruktion der neuen Schnellstraße A43 zwischen Northamptonshire und Oxfordshire von 'Northampton-shire Archaeology' in 2000 und 2001 entsprechend der Straßen Behörde vorgenommen.

Ausgrabungen wurden auf fünf Siedlungsgebiete ausgetragen – vier aus der Eisenzeit/frühen-römischen Zeitalter, und eins aus dem römischen Zeitalter. Drei der eisenzeitlichen Stätten, jedes in einen anderen Art, liegen innerhalb 500 Metern von einander südlich von Towcester. Es wurden auch Untersuchungen auf einen kleineren Umfang auf Stätten aus der Eisenzeit und des römischen Zeitalters durchgeführt, einschließlich eine Reihe von Gruben. Die Gelegenheit bot sich auch die Resultate der geomagnetische Prospektion bei dem verlassenen mittelalterlichen dorf 'Tusmore' zu präsentieren, welches Teile der römischen Siedlung einschließt. Dieser Bericht fasst auch die disparaten Beweise für die mittelalterlichen

Landnutzung zusammen. Die Untersuchungen sind von besonderer Bedeutung in der Ansicht der bisher begrenzten archäologischen Arbeit in der Gegend, welches zum großen Teil auf dem Geschiebelehm liegt.

Die Funde bestehen aus einer mäßig großen Sammlung von Tonwaren (circa 800 Scherben) und Tierknochen (77 kg) und kleine Sammlungen von Metall und sonstigen Funden. Von Besonderer Bedeutung war die Entdeckung einer eisenzeitlichen Eisenverhütung bei 'Biddlesden Road Bridge' und einer früh-römischen Eisenverhütung bei Syresham. Ausführliche Analysen deuten auf Technologien wo die Schlacke abgelaufen sowohl auch nicht abgelaufen wird. Früh-römische Töpfereien wurden bei Syresham und Whitfield entdeckt, sie ergänzen das Bild eines weiterverbreitetes aber einer klein angelegten Industrie zu diesem Zeitpunkt. Ein Bericht zu einer Gruppe von Säuglingen von Silverstone Fields Farm ist umfangreich hierein berichtet.

Die Beweise sind in einen Regionalen Zusammenhang diskutiert. Ein Vergleich von Artefakten und ökonomischen Beweisen von den eisenzeitlichen Stätten zeigten kleine Unterschiede in ihrer Sammlungen, dies könnte auf verschiedene ökonomische Praktiken und vielleicht sozialen Rollen für diesen Siedlungen deuten.

Trans. *Yvonne Wolframm*

ACKNOWLEDGEMENTS

The archaeological work on the A43 Towcester to M40 Road Improvement scheme owes its success to a large number of people. The project was funded by the Highways Agency, the road building contractor Costain Skanska JV, and the earthmoving contractor Walters UK Ltd, each organisation deserving the utmost gratitude for making the whole enterprise possible. The pre-contract fieldwork was undertaken on behalf of Northamptonshire County Council's Highways Department, with Roger Butterick Head of Project Management, until his retirement towards the end of 2000, and subsequently with Alan Bransby (now of WS Atkins) in that post. Alan Bransby continued his involvement with the archaeology of the scheme after the award of contract upon secondment to White Young Green, the Highways Agency's Agent. The design of the archaeological work owes a great deal to Glenn Foard (then County Archaeological Officer for Northamptonshire) and Myk Flitcroft (then Archaeological Planning Officer), both of NCC's Historic Environment Team. Archaeological advice and monitoring was also undertaken by David Freke of RPS Consultants, appointed as the Highways Agency's Archaeological Adviser, and Paul Smith, County Archaeological Officer for Oxfordshire. English Heritage is also gratefully acknowledged for a grant enabling geophysical survey to be undertaken at Tusmore Deserted Medieval Village.

The integration of the archaeological excavations and watching brief with the civil engineering works resulted from the co-operation of many individuals on the ground. In addition to those mentioned above, particular thanks must be given to Darren James, Costain Skanska's Project Manager, and David Thursfield of Walters UK for providing the time, space and means for archaeological investigations to be carried out. The section managers Tom France, Paul Baker and Ken Jones (Walters UK), and Steve Ricketts, Lee Davis and Paul Swann (CSJV) deserve to be singled out for their help.

With regard to the archaeology itself, staff of Northamptonshire Archaeology merit praise for the efforts made in completing the excavations within time and budget, especially over the wet winter of 2000-1. The individual site managers were Tim Hallam, Chris Jones, Michael 'Tam' Webster, Simon Carlyle and Rowena Lloyd. The excavations were carried out by dedicated professional teams of project archaeologists, too numerous to mention by name. Much of the watching brief during the long hours of the following summer was carried out by David Leigh and Jim Brown. The magnetometer surveys were undertaken by Peter Masters, Erlend Hindmarch, Ian Fisher, Steve Morris and Jim Brown. Thanks also to Steven Critchley for undertaking metal detecting. Of the many farmers inconvenienced at one time or another, we are especially grateful to Anthony Bonner of Whitfield House Farm, Andrew Diment of Silverstone Fields Farm, Richard Cook of Burcote Wood Farm, and Col. Anthony Barkas, Estate Manager at Tusmore, for allowing further magnetometer surveys to be undertaken on sites extending outside the road corridor.

The post-excavation work was also a team effort. The individual specialist authors are credited in this volume, but particular mention must be made of Tora Hylton (Finds and Archives Manager), Pat Chapman (Finds Supervisor) and Karen Deighton (Environmental Supervisor) for valuable support throughout. The illustrations for this publication have been undertaken by Jacqueline Harding, Anne Foard-Colby, Carol Simmonds and Hari Anne Jacklin, with Adrian Butler providing the geophysical plots. Brian Dix commented on the typescript with a diligence beyond the duty of an academic referee, greatly aiding the clarity as well as the balance of the finished product. Final proof reading has been carried out by Pat Chapman and Andy Chapman.

Jane Timby would like to thank Dennis Jackson for looking at a selection of the material and his helpful comments regarding local assemblages.

Karen Deighton would like to thank Dr Helen Keeley for environmental co-ordination and advice on the sampling.

Dr Diana Sutherland, Leicester University, provided identifications of stone.

The infant burials were studied by the late Trevor Anderson, consultant osteoarchaeologist

CHAPTER ONE

INTRODUCTION

PROJECT LOCATION

The archaeological work in connection with the A43 dualling project covered a linear distance of about 18 km between Towcester in South Northamptonshire and the M40 motorway near Ardley in Oxfordshire (Fig 1.1). The work comprised an examination of land within the road corridor, together with a smaller amount of 'off-site' work connected with areas of permanent soil disposal and drainage. The road design mostly entailed the construction of a new dual carriageway, although the existing road was integrated to a limited extent, mostly in the Oxfordshire section. The route was divided into three sections. The northern section runs from just south of Towcester, bypasses the village of Silverstone and rejoins the existing dual carriageway south of Hazelborough Wood. The central section bypasses the village of Syresham, leaving the existing dual carriageway at Brackley Hatch near the Great Ouse crossing and rejoins it again opposite the village of Whitfield. The southern section runs closely parallel with the existing road from the A421 (Barley Mow Roundabout) to a new junction with the M40.

GEOLOGY AND TOPOGRAPHY

The route crosses two broad topographic zones – the predominantly Boulder Clay region of south-west Northamptonshire and the Jurassic limestone uplands of north-east Oxfordshire (Fig 1.2). In detail, the topography of the Northamptonshire section of the route is varied. From the Towcester roundabout to south of Wood Burcote Bridge on Silverstone Brook the geology is predominantly Upper Lias Clay with some river deposits. The new road here was largely within the verge of the existing A43. South of Wood Burcote Bridge the new road takes a straighter route, rising up the ridge of Upper Estuarine Series and Oolitic (Blisworth) Limestone towards Silverstone Fields and the new A413 Whittlebury junction (120 m OD). The route then drops towards Bandbrook Bridge and passes east of Silverstone where the terrain is strongly undulating and formed on Boulder Clay. The main area of soil disposal covers about 30 ha east of Shacks Barn Farm. This area is also strongly undulating on a geology of Boulder Clay and gravel drift.

Around Syresham the rolling terrain is formed on Boulder Clay with superficial deposits of glacial sand and gravel. The route crosses two streams – The Brook and Great Ouse – which cut through the Boulder Clay to expose the underlying limestone. Further areas of soil disposal, covering about 15 ha in total, lie to the south of the new Welsh Lane Interchange, on both sides of The Brook. Blisworth Limestone outcrops here and under the village of Whitfield.

South-east of Brackley, Oolitic Limestone is the dominant substratum. From Barley Mow Roundabout the land rises to the Jurassic Ridge at Juniper Hill. From here the land is flat or gently undulating at an elevation of 120-130 m OD. Minor streams lie close to the route at Cottisford Turn and Tusmore. Around Tusmore spreads of glacial gravel overlie the limestone.

PROJECT BACKGROUND

A programme of archaeological work was undertaken by Northamptonshire Archaeology in advance of and during works associated with the A43 road improvement. The work comprised a staged series of assessments, field evaluations and surveys, followed by archaeological excavations ahead of groundwork. Subsequently, a Watching Brief was maintained along the whole length of the route during earthmoving. The work undertaken ahead of the Design and Build contract was funded by the Highways Agency and the Watching Brief by the construction contractor Costain Skanska JV.

The programme was undertaken between 1993 and late 2001. The early surveys in the Oxfordshire section of the route were undertaken in 1993 by Wessex Archaeology. In September 2000 Northamptonshire Archaeology was appointed the archaeological contractor for the route in both counties.

Archaeological excavations took place on eight sites threatened wholly or in part by the construction of the new road and associated works. These were carried out between autumn 2000 and spring 2001. Several other sites and features of archaeological and historical interest were also recorded. These included historical enclosure boundaries.

The archaeological investigations were in fulfilment of the Highways Agency's requirement for archaeological

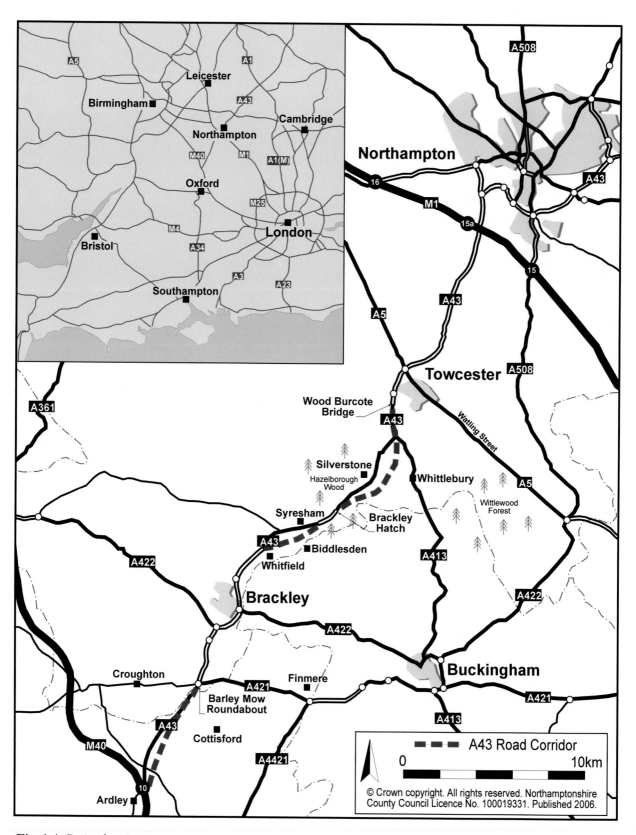

Fig. 1.1: *Project location.*

mitigation both ahead of and during the road construction. The initial surveys and evaluations in Northamptonshire were undertaken on behalf of Northamptonshire County Council (NCC) Highways Department. Subsequent area excavations, and evaluations which could not be completed ahead of compulsory purchase, were conducted in accordance with a Brief for Archaeological Recording Action and a Specification for Outstanding Archaeological Evaluation issued by NCC's Northamptonshire Heritage (which later became the Historic Environment Team) in May 2000 and June 2000 respectively. The Brief also outlined the requirements for post-excavation analysis and reporting, including an assessment and updated project design, and the current publication. It required the work from the other stages of investigation to be incorporated into the assessment (NA 2002).

The archaeological finds made during the Watching Brief were recorded in accordance with the Archaeological Strategy Specification: Level 1 Watching Brief (v2, 30/1/01) prepared by Northamptonshire Archaeology on behalf of Costain Skanska JV. This document incorporated both the requirements of Northamptonshire Heritage and Costain Skanska's terms of contract with the Highways Agency with regard to archaeological matters. There was a requirement for the maintenance of archaeological observation, along with a provision for detailed recording in the event of unexpected archaeological remains coming to light.

Archaeological evaluations were also undertaken, under a separate contract with the earthmoving contractor, Walters UK Ltd, in the two main areas of off-site soil disposal (Shacks Barn Farm and 'Area G' south of Syresham). These were conducted in accordance with mitigation strategies approved by Northamptonshire Heritage and had the aim of identifying and defining archaeological deposits which were to be preserved in situ under the new landscaping. The archaeological work here was therefore limited in scope.

The several elements of the project incorporated in the present report therefore comprise:

- archaeological evaluations and excavations undertaken before the award of the Design and Build contract.
- excavations and observations undertaken during the Level 1 Watching Brief.
- trenches targeting historical boundaries, undertaken in both phases of work.
- geophysical surveys and trial trenching undertaken in the off-site (soil disposal) areas.

ARCHAEOLOGICAL BACKGROUND

Introduction

While in general terms Northamptonshire has a wealth of archaeological sites of all periods, the south-west of the county is relatively poorly represented or understood. This is partly due to the unresponsiveness of the clayland

of the region to aerial survey, in comparison with the permeable geologies of the river gravels and Northampton Sand further north and east – a factor affecting both arable land and, more severely, the relatively high proportion of permanent pasture and woodland. The lower pressure of development here has also been a factor in the lack of archaeological prospection.

The north-east of Oxfordshire is similarly not well-known archaeologically. The paucity of sites in the area can be attributed to the lack of development pressure, perhaps allied to the region's marginality in historical as well as modern times.

Desk-based, fieldwalking and geophysical surveys

Archaeological information was gathered from the Sites and Monuments Records (SMRs) for Northamptonshire and Oxfordshire in the early stages of fieldwork. This was followed by fieldwalking (ie. surface collection) and geophysical surveys, the results of which are summarised below (Fig 1.3). A later desk-based assessment was undertaken as the first stage of mitigation for the soil disposal and landscaping areas (NA 2001a). This included updated SMR information for the whole route and a consideration of historical landscape characterisation for the Northamptonshire section.

Silverstone bypass
A 100 m wide corridor was investigated through surface collection and geophysical survey in 1996-7 (Masters & Shaw 1997). Of the forty-four land parcels on the route, the eleven under arable were suitable for the surface collection survey. This was done on a 20 m sampling grid. Geophysical scanning was undertaken on the remaining fields with detailed gridded survey targeted on 'hot spots' identified by the scan and fieldwalking.

Three new Iron Age/Roman sites were discovered (Fig 1.3). All were later more fully defined by extended geophysical surveys and trial trenching (NA 2000a):

> *Silverstone 2:* a large enclosure with traces of internal houses and a surface scatter of Iron Age and Roman pottery.
>
> *Silverstone 3:* a wide-ditched enclosure with associated smaller enclosures and ditches nearby, and surface scatters of Iron Age and Roman pottery.
>
> *Silverstone 4:* a surface concentration of Roman pottery and a coin, but without recognisable archaeological features.

Syresham bypass
A desk-based study and surface collection survey was undertaken in 1993 (Audouy & Sharman 1993). The surface collection was undertaken on nine suitable fields of the thirty along the route. A corridor about 150 m wide was walked in transects 30 m apart and finds collected in 20 m units.

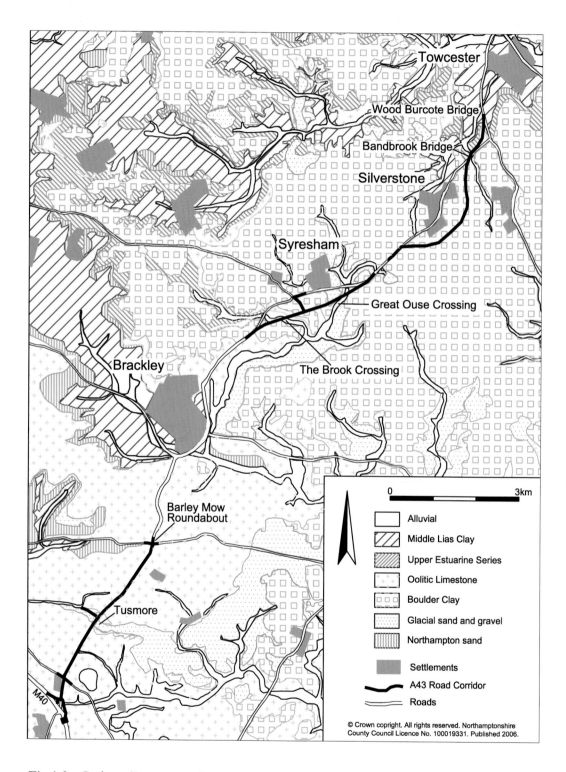

Fig.1.2: *Geology (Source: British Geological Survey digital mapping. Permit No. IPR/47-19C British Geological Survey. © NERC. All rights reserved).*

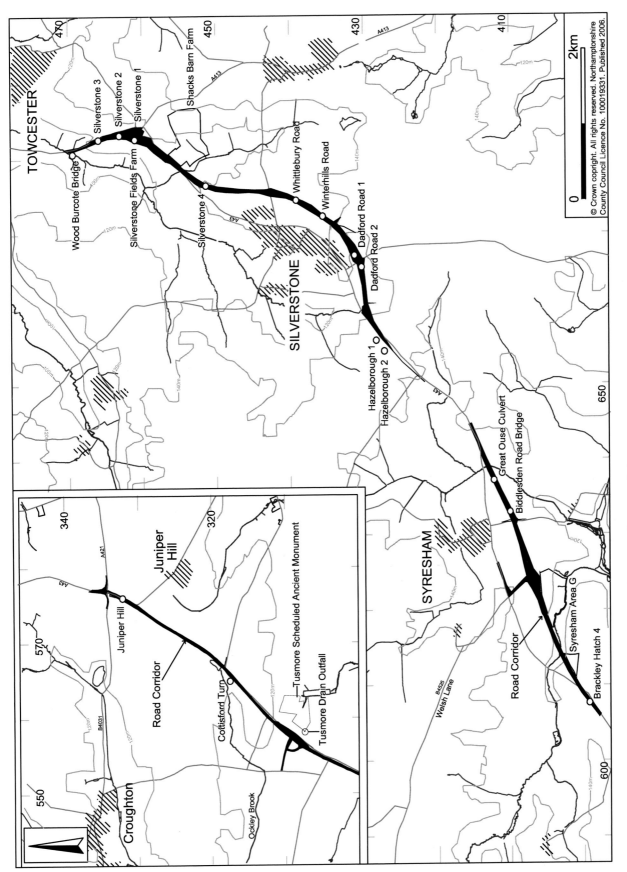

Fig. 1.3: *Route of A43 road improvement showing locations of excavated sites.*

Three potential sites were identified within the road corridor:

Brackley Hatch 2: the assumed course of a Roman road between Wormleighton and Bletchley which has been inferred to enter Northamptonshire via Aston le Walls and Helmdon, and to leave the county at Biddlesden (Margary 1973, Route 166). There was no surface evidence for it.

Brackley Hatch 4: a Romano-British small rural settlement opposite Whitfield Turn, identified by a surface concentration of pottery. The field name 'Big Ditch' was thought to be potentially significant.

Brackley Hatch 5: earthwork remains east of High Cross Farm. These comprise ridge and furrow, a pond or quarry pit, indistinct raised platforms, part of a possible hollow way and a bank or plough headland. A topographic survey was produced.

In early 2000 geophysical reconnaissance was undertaken on land which had not been fieldwalked (NA 2000a). This resulted in the discovery of an Iron Age settlement near the proposed Biddlesden Road Bridge. A detailed survey was then undertaken.

Brackley Hatch 4 and Biddlesden Road Bridge were examined by trial trenching during 2000 (NA 2000a; NA 2000c)

Barley Mow Roundabout to M40 Motorway

A desk-based study, a surface collection survey and a geophysical survey were carried out by the Trust for Wessex Archaeology (WA 1993). The field surveys were undertaken along an 80 m wide corridor spanning the centre line of the route. The surface collection was undertaken in transects 20 m apart and finds collected in 20 m sections (runs). About 1700 m of the 6 km stretch was not suitable or available for fieldwalking. The geophysical survey comprised a gradiometer scan of the whole route on 10 m traverses and detailed survey where anomalies were detected.

The density of surface finds was very low and no sites were identified. The geophysical survey identified curvilinear and other anomalies between Barley Mow and the Juniper Hill road. This site was interpreted as a possible prehistoric enclosure. However, subsequent trial trenching on the part of the site within the later-defined boundary of compulsory purchase showed these features to be natural fissures and solution hollows in the limestone (NA 2000d). The deserted medieval village at Tusmore (National Scheduled Ancient Monument No. 28141) was to be avoided in the design of the new road.

ARCHAEOLOGICAL CHARACTER OF THE ROUTE

The principal features of archaeological interest within the general route corridor and adjacent areas can be summarised as follows (Fig 1.3).

Iron Age and Roman remains south of Towcester (Roman Lactodurum)

The Roman road from Towcester to Alchester ran south-south-east to the A43/A413 junction. Probable traces of the road were found at site Silverstone 1 of the current project. It is thought to have turned south from here, following a course to the east of Shacks Barn Farm. Extra-mural settlement along this road has been investigated in the recent housing developments on the southern side of the town (Brown & Woodfield 1983) and a scatter of Roman finds have been made in the surrounding area. These include a villa and possible temple adjacent to the Roman road near Swinneyford Farm (Turland 1977). Three Iron Age settlements (Silverstone 2, Silverstone 3 and Silverstone Field Farm) were discovered and excavated as part of the current project. Another Iron Age/Roman site (Silverstone 4) probably lay between the new A43 and Pits Farm to the west, although within the road corridor the evidence for it was slight. Further Iron Age and Roman occupation was identified at Shacks Barn Farm in the current investigations.

Medieval settlement south of Shacks Barn Farm

A probable medieval settlement lay at 'Netherends' in the valley south of Shacks Barn Farm. The 1608 Whittlewood Forest map (Frontispiece, NRO Map 4210) shows a group of closes here. A hollow way, running north from the closes coincides with a trackway shown on the map which linked to what was then the road to Towcester (the forerunner of the A43). The Silverstone-Whittlewood parish boundary, also on the 1608 map, existed as a hedgerow following a similar but less direct course. Another ancient hedgerow runs east from 'Netherends' and links to the scheduled medieval moated site at Lordsfields Farm 500 m distant. 'Netherends' and the hollow way lay outside the soil storage area at Shacks Barn Farm. The ancient hedgerows have now been replanted on their original courses following land re-instatement.

Medieval land boundaries east and south of Silverstone

The singular characteristic of this part of the route is the dominance of woodland and woodland clearances in the medieval and early post-medieval periods. A number of existing enclosure boundaries date from this time. The area was part of Whittlewood Forest which was not fully and finally enclosed until the mid 19th century. Four archaeological trenches were targeted on enclosure boundaries here and a further two on woodland boundaries in Hazelborough Wood. No other significant archaeology had been recorded in this section.

Roman and medieval features between Syresham and Whitfield

A scatter of features and finds have been recorded in this section of the route. These include the possible line

Site Name	Site Code	Watching Brief	Strategy	Date
Burcote Bridge	WBB 01	★	Salvage	Post-medieval
Silverstone 3	SL3 00		Excavation	Iron Age
Linnell's Trackway	WB SL Ch 7490	★	Salvage	Roman
Silverstone 2	SL2 00		Excavation	Iron Age
Silverstone 1	SL1 00		Excavation	Roman road
Silvestone Fields Farm	SFF 01	★ notified	Excavation	Iron Age
Shacks Barn Farm	SHB 01		Geophysics and trenching	Iron Age and Roman
Silverstone 4	SL4 01	★	Excavation	Iron Age and Roman
Whittlebury Road	WBR 01		Boundary trench	Post-medieval?
Winterhills Road	WHR 01		Boundary trench	Post-medieval?
Dadford Road 1	DAD1 01		Boundary trench	Post-medieval?
Dadford Road 2	DAD2 00		Boundary trench	Post-medieval
Hazelborough Wood 1	HAZ1 00		Boundary trench	Medieval ?
Hazelborough Wood 2	HAZ2 01	★	Boundary trench	Medieval ?
Great Ouse Culvert	GOC 01	★ notified	Excavation	Roman
Biddlesden Road Bridge	BRB 00		Excavation	Iron Age
Area G Syresham	SYR 01		Geophysics and trenching	Iron Age and Roman
Brackley Hatch 4	BH4 00		Excavation	Roman
Juniper Hill	JH 01	★	Salvage	Iron Age
Juniper Hill to Cottisford Turn	WB M40 Ch 5400-6300	★	Salvage	Post-medieval
Cottisford Turn	TCT 01	★ notified	Excavation	Iron Age
Tusmore Drain Outfall	TDO 01	★ notified	Excavation	Iron Age and Roman

Table 1.1: Summary of sites examined.

of a Roman road between Biddlesden and Welsh Lane; traces of medieval ridge and furrow cultivation; a skeleton possibly associated with Saxon pottery near Welsh Lane; and another skeleton, reported as coming from just north of Whitfield, but likely to have been mislocated. Scatters of medieval and Roman pottery were recovered during the earlier fieldwalking phase of the project. One of these was later shown to be related to a Roman settlement (site Brackley Hatch 4) north of Whitfield (Fig 1.3).

Tusmore Deserted Medieval Village and associated features

The deserted medieval village at Tusmore (Oxfordshire) is a Scheduled Ancient Monument. The protected area was avoided by the road design and soil disposal/landscaping works. The line of the former Tusmore-Souldern Road was expected to cross the road corridor. A bank and ditch associated with the settlement and lying to the north-west was anticipated in or close to the road corridor. Extensive geophysical survey in the evaluation phase had failed to locate either of these features.

EXCAVATION STRATEGY

Excavation and recording strategies were subject to agreements with the appropriate monitoring authority. In the pre-contract phase of excavation, and for the off-site works (except that within the scheduled area at Tusmore), the work was carried out in accordance with the requirements of Northamptonshire Heritage and monitored by Mr Myk Flitcroft, Archaeological Planning Officer. Following the award of the Design and Build contract, monitoring of archaeological work within the boundary of compulsory purchase was undertaken by the Highways Agency's Archaeological Adviser, Mr David Freke. By the terms of the archaeological contract, 'significant' finds made during the Watching Brief were the subject of a notification procedure which allowed time for a specified level of excavation commensurate with the importance of the find. Other less significant finds made during the Watching Brief were recorded without notification with the co-operation of Costain Skanska JV and Walters UK Ltd, either within a demarcated zone of excavation, or on an opportunistic 'salvage' basis. Table

7

1.1 summarises the nature of the mitigation strategy on each site. The exception to these procedures was the work within the scheduled area at Tusmore (Tusmore Drain Outfall) which was subject to the usual consents from English Heritage, Mr Freke monitoring this work on their behalf.

The principal archaeological sites were given individual codes. Less significant finds made during the Watching Brief were coded according to the chainage location in the relevant section of road (eg. WB SL Ch 7490 indicates Chainage 7490 in the Silverstone section). Sometimes finds made during the Watching Brief were related to a nearby site and were later subsumed within it (eg. WB BH 3600 was near the Great Ouse Culvert excavation area).

The excavations undertaken before the Watching Brief phase were conducted with standard methods of overburden removal by machine. There was a certain amount of flexibility in the strategy for soil stripping, due principally to the extremely wet weather during the winter of 2000–1. At Brackley Hatch 4 spoil could not be removed from the site, and as a consequence it had to be excavated in two separate strips. Biddlesden Road Bridge was also excavated in two parts due to the urgent need for a contractor's haul road which was opened up along the southern boundary.

Excavation sampling levels were also standardised for the pre-contract excavations. The base-line sampling level was 'non-intensive' (specifically 5% of linear features, 25% of ring-ditches and 50% by number of pits), but there was provision for the 'intensive' sampling of 10% of each site, which doubled the sampling level (NH 2000).

There was greater variation in the methods and sampling levels for the excavations undertaken as part of the Watching Brief, which were dealt with on a case by case basis, taking into account the financial implications of construction delays. In all cases, however, an appropriate machine with a toothless bucket was made available by the contractor for archaeologically controlled stripping. At Silverstone Fields Farm a sample of 30 pits were excavated (amounting to a little over one third of the total). The discovery of burials within the enclosure ditch during its initial sampling led to its complete excavation by machine under archaeological supervision. At Cottisford Turn the excavation of the pit alignment was undertaken at an 'intensive' sampling level due to its significance, while at Great Ouse Culvert a smaller sample of archaeological deposits were excavated either side of a haul road.

Extended geophysical surveys were later undertaken at Silverstone 2, Silverstone 3 and Brackley Hatch 4 as part of the Highways Agency's 'Environmental Enhancements' scheme, which encouraged environment-linked initiatives beyond the base-line contract requirements. These surveys covered an additional hectare at each of these sites enabling the excavations to be put into better perspective. Geophysical survey was also undertaken at Tusmore Deserted Medieval Village in response to the findings at Tusmore Drain Outfall where Iron Age and Roman settlement was suspected. This work was funded by English Heritage.

ARCHIVE

The project paper archive, including all site records, is to be deposited in the appropriate (Oxfordshire or Northamptonshire) county repository, although at the time of writing there is no appropriate repository for Northamptonshire. Microfilm copies of these records will be made and lodged with the National Monuments Record. Finds made within land defined by the Compulsory Purchase Orders are to be deposited with the relevant county repository, in accordance with the terms of the Highways Agency's contract. Title to finds made before the issue of CPOs, and finds outside the road corridor itself, lie with the individual landowners who are encouraged to donate them to the appropriate repository.

CHAPTER TWO

IRON AGE AND ROMAN PERIODS

Introduction

The most significant archaeological findings relate to the Iron Age and Roman periods. The Iron Age settlements at Silverstone 3, Silverstone 2, Silverstone Fields Farm and Biddlesden Road Bridge were particularly important and their description and analysis form the core of the present report. The Silverstone sites were closely adjacent and are significant for that reason (see Fig 1.3). The discovery of iron smelting at Biddlesden Road Bridge adds to the importance of that site. These were all previously unsuspected sites and are unlikely to have been discovered without the systematic surveys undertaken as part of the archaeological mitigation. The pit alignment at Cottisford Turn, which did not seem to have been associated with settlement, was also relatively invisible. All these sites were fully excavated within the limits of the Compulsory Purchase Order (CPO) boundary. Other Iron Age sites were identified within the soil disposal areas at Shacks Barn and Area G Syresham, and at Tusmore Drain Outfall. These were examined to a more limited extent.

The pottery from Tusmore Drain Outfall suggests a date in the early Iron Age, but elsewhere the sites are securely of the middle to late Iron Age. There is enigmatic evidence of early Roman activity at Silverstone 3, Silverstone 2 and Silverstone Fields Farm, but these sites did not continue long into the Roman period. Roman sites per se were not well defined. The principal site at Brackley Hatch 4 proved to be part of a settlement which engaged in pottery production. Part of a probable midden, with predominantly late Roman material, was examined at Great Ouse Culvert, but the associated settlement seems to have lain a short distance away. Traces of Roman occupation at Shacks Barn Farm and Syresham Area G indicate that settlement here was located in a landscape of ditched fields and enclosures. Evidence of both iron smelting and pottery making were found at Syresham Area G.

Except at Silverstone Fields Farm, none of the excavations uncovered the entire settlement and interpretation is limited for this reason. However, the extended geophysical surveys at Silverstone 2, Silverstone 3 and Brackley Hatch 4 add considerably to the picture of those settlements (Figs 2.1 & 2.53). The opportunity has also been taken to present the results of the geophysical survey on the site of Tusmore Deserted Medieval Village which shows part of a previously unknown rural Roman settlement (Fig 2.62).

Earlier prehistoric material

While no earlier prehistoric sites were discovered, a small collection of worked flint was recovered from the several stages of fieldwork. This was all residual, either as superficial finds from the ploughsoil, or excavated from later features.

The superficial finds have not been characterised in detail and there were no obvious concentrations to indicate more than a background scatter of Neolithic or Bronze Age date. Overall quantities were very low. The Stage 2 fieldwalking resulted in the recovery of just five worked flints from 15 ha or so in the Silverstone bypass section, and a further 61 in the 12 ha in the Syresham bypass section. The far larger area covered in the Barley Mow to M40 section (c 260 ha) yielded just 23 flints from fieldwalking.

The flint from the excavations was examined as part of the formal post-excavation assessment. Seventy-two pieces were recovered. Most did not warrant further consideration, although a report on the largest assemblage (56) from Silverstone 3 has been included (Thorne, Chapter 4). This indicates that the area which was later occupied by the Iron Age settlement may have been a favoured location for transient activity in the earlier prehistoric period, perhaps principally in the earlier Neolithic, although some potentially later Neolithic and Bronze Age material was also found. While there is some debate as to the extent to which flint tools were made and used in the Iron Age, there is absolutely no indication that any flintworking was practised on the Iron Age sites in the present project.

SILVERSTONE 3: IRON AGE SETTLEMENT

General description

The extended geophysical survey (Fig 2.1) gives a good indication of the form of the settlement, to which the excavated part (Fig 2.2) adds some detail. The settlement comprised a group of small enclosures and roundhouse ring ditches, some of which were intercutting, lying on the north-eastern side of a linear boundary that appeared to be represented by a pit alignment within the excavated area. On the south-west side of the boundary lay a large

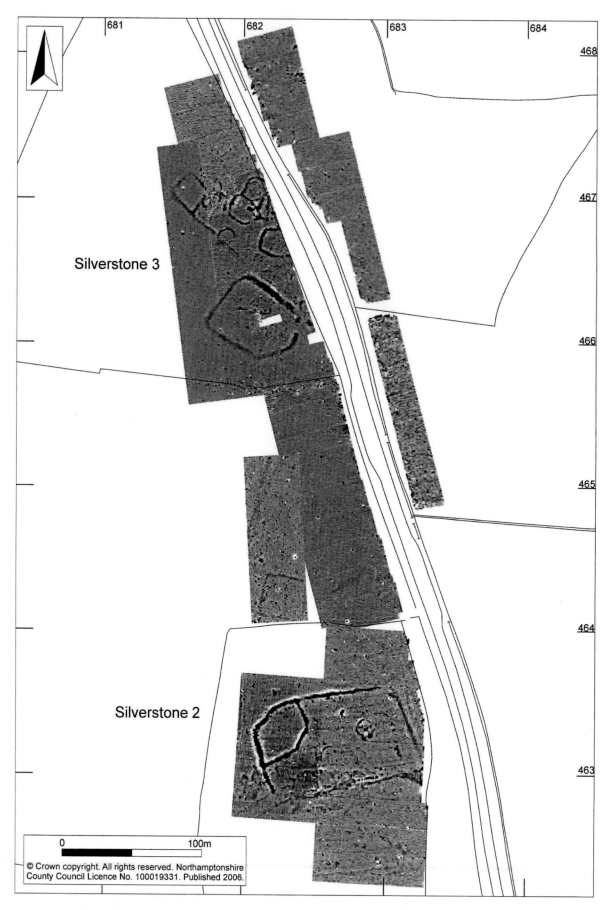

Fig. 2.1: *Iron Age sites Silverstone 3 and Silverstone 2. Magnetometer survey results, including areas outside the road corridor.*

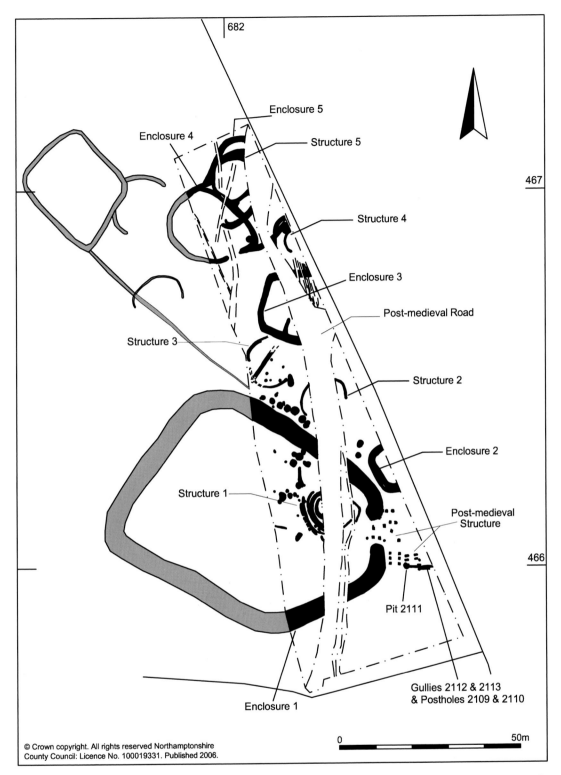

682

467

Enclosure 5

Enclosure 4

Structure 5

Structure 4

Enclosure 3

Post-medieval Road

Structure 3

Structure 2

Enclosure 2

Structure 1

Post-medieval
Structure

466

Pit 2111

Gullies 2112 & 2113
& Postholes 2109 & 2110

Enclosure 1

0   50m

Fig. 2.2: *Silverstone 3, overall plan. The magnetometer survey interpretation is shown in grey tone to the west of the excavation.*

enclosure with few internal features other than a further roundhouse ditch.

It is evident that broadly the same site layout was maintained throughout the occupation, although there was some complexity to the interrelationship of features, particularly in the northern area where up to four phases of enclosures could be recognised. The detailed account of the sequence of enclosures is limited to the northern part of the site (Figs 2.6 & 2.7). Elsewhere, there was little firm evidence of a sequence, either from the stratigraphy, or from the pottery, although some suggestions are made on the basis of site layout. It is probable that the developments in the northern, central and southern areas were more or less synchronous, rather than successive, but there is no way of being sure of this. There are no clearly early or late elements in the pottery to contradict this assumption and a 'short chronology' is preferable to a long one from this point of view. Altogether, the pottery was too limited

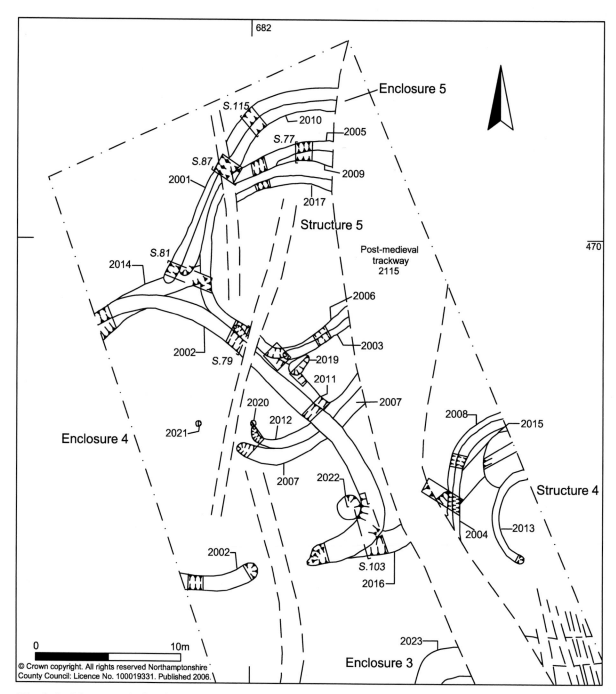

Fig. 2.3: *Silverstone 3, detail of northern area.*

typologically to show any clear trends in the stratigraphic sequences (Timby, Chapter 4).

There was a post-medieval road bisecting the site which was marked by a heavy concentration of wheel-ruts. This, and a post-medieval post-built structure in the southern area, are described elsewhere (Chapter 3).

For descriptive analysis the site has been divided into these three areas.

Northern Area: Enclosure Ditches

The enclosure ditches and gullies here have been divided into four phases. The layout in each phase is not unequivocal and there is more than one phasing option, although only the most likely is given (Figs 2.3 & 2.6).

Phase 1: Ditches 2014, 2011 and 2016

These ditches were stratigraphically early and heavily truncated (Figs 2.3 and 2.6). The overall pattern formed by these features is unclear and the geophysical survey is also unhelpful in this matter. Ditch 2014 ran to an eastern terminal. It was a substantial feature 1.2 m wide and 0.6-1.0 m deep (deepest at the terminal) with steeply sloping sides and a rounded base (Fig 2.8, S.81). The primary deposit (1374) was of compact mixed clay, overlain by a darker grey silty clay (1373) containing animal bones and pottery. The upper fill (1372) was a friable clayey silt.

Ditch 2011 ran from the south-east to a terminal at its north-west end. It was about 1.2 m wide and 0.6-0.7 m deep with steep sides and a rounded base (Fig 2.8, S.79).

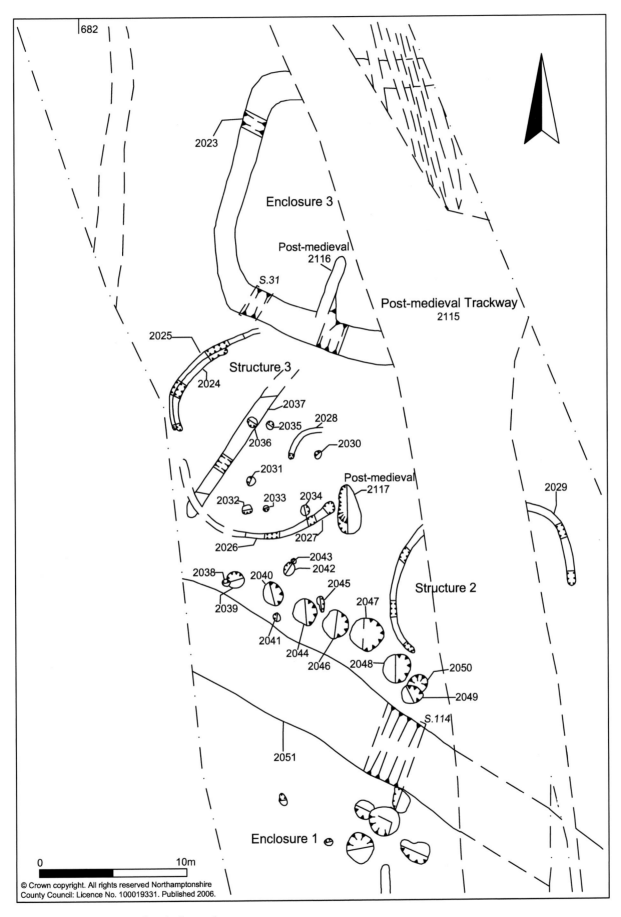

682

2023

Enclosure 3

Post-medieval
2116

S.31

Post-medieval Trackway
2115

2025

Structure 3

2024

2037

2035
2028

2036

2030

2031

2032   2033   2034
Post-medieval
2117

2026   2027

2029

2038   2040
2043
2042

2039
2045

Structure 2

2047

2041
2044

2046   2048

2050

2049

S.114

2051

Enclosure 1

0   10m

Fig. 2.4: Silverstone 3, detail of central area.

13

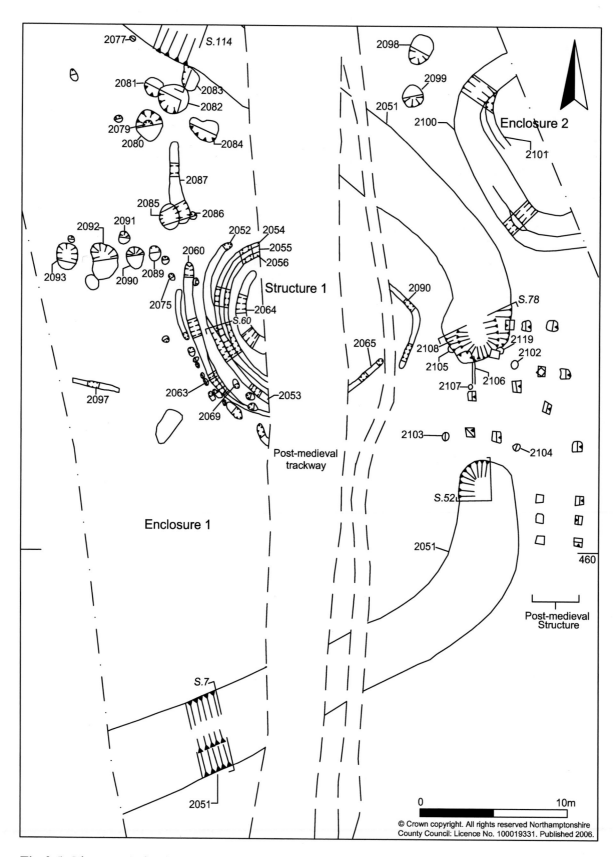

Fig. 2.5: Silverstone 3, detail of southern area.

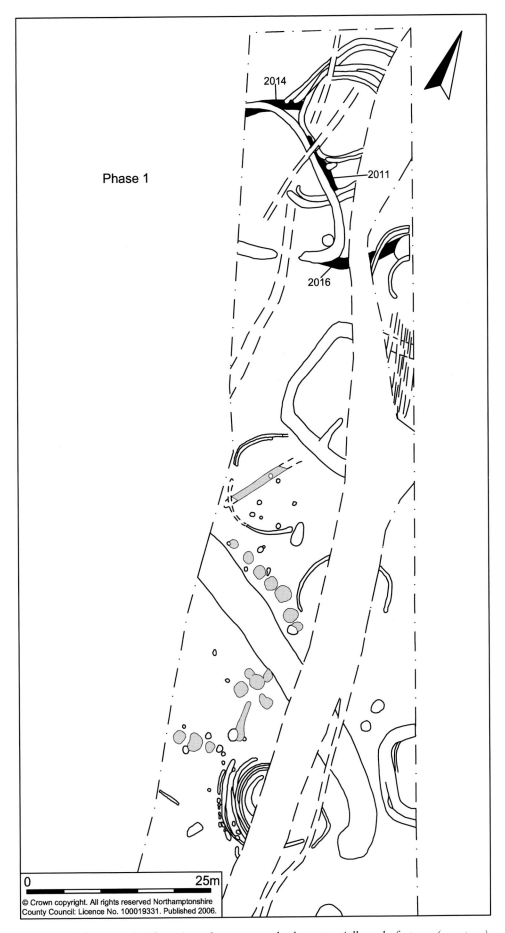

Fig. 2.6: Silverstone 3, Phase 1 northern area and other potentially early features (grey tone).

To the south it is assumed to have turned and followed the same alignment as the later ditches 2012 and 2007 of Enclosure 5.

Ditch 2016 was a substantial early ditch with a terminal 1.4 m wide and 0.87 m deep, and was only slightly shallower elsewhere. The lower fill (1417) was a yellow brown sterile silty clay. The upper fill (1416) was greyish brown containing a large quantity of fire-cracked stones together with a small quantity of animal bones and pottery from the base of the fill.

After having been completely filled, its terminal seems to have been re-cut by ditch 2002, to form the eastern side of a later enclosure entrance (Enclosure 4, Phase 4) (Fig 2.8, S.103). This later respect may suggest that ditch 2016 was later than Phase 2. However, there is a clear sequence of at least three further phases to the east (features 2004, 2008, 2015) and a later phasing would prolong the chronology here to an awkward extent.

Phase 2: Structure 5

An earlier phase ditch, 2009, was almost entirely truncated by the ditches of this structure, 2005 and 2006 (Figs 2.3 & 2.7), which are almost certainly the eaves drainage ditch of a roundhouse, although the complete circuit, including the entrance, was not recoverable due to truncation by the medieval road to the east. Its internal diameter was about 12 m. The ring ditch does not appear to have been within an enclosure, although it is possible that 2012 and 2007 were contemporary with it rather than being part of Enclosure 5 of the later phase.

Ditch 2009 was only partially visible as an earlier cut of 2005 and was recorded as 0.28 m deep (Fig 2.9, S.77). The relationship of ditches 2005 and 2006 was obscured by the later ditch 2010. The ring ditch was a fairly substantial feature, generally 1.1-1.4 m wide and 0.35-0.55 m deep. It had a consistently steeper inner edge and the base was flat or concave. The lower fill was a solid clay-silt. The upper fill was a variable yellow grey to dark brown clayey soil. A small amount of fire cracked stones, animal bones and pottery was recovered throughout.

Phases 2-4: Structure 4

This structure comprised a gully and ditch, 2008 and 2004, around a smaller concentric gully, 2013, which almost certainly surrounded a roundhouse, perhaps with an entrance facing south (Fig 2.3). Gully 2008 was the earliest. It was 0.4 m wide and 0.2 m deep, and its complete circuit would have enclosed an area of about 13 m diameter. Its inner edge was cut by ditch 2004, which appears to have been a later phase of the same circuit. It was 1 m wide and 0.5 m deep with a V-shaped profile and a sharp concave base.

Curvilinear gully 2013 would have enclosed an area 7 m in diameter and had a terminal to the south. It was 0.65 m wide and 0.13 m deep, containing dark brown compact silt. This feature may well have been a roundhouse eaves drip gully.

Phase 3: Enclosure 5

Enclosure 5 was roughly oval in shape and about 20 m long by 12 m wide, with a broad entrance facing south-west (Figs 2.3 & 2.7). The southern arm, ditch 2012, was at least 1m wide, and was 0.55 m deep at the terminal which turned in sharply. The dark primary fill contained burnt clay and charcoal, while the upper fill was greyish.

The northern arm, ditch 2010, was a substantial feature about 1.5 m wide and almost 1.0 m deep. It cut the ditch enclosing Structure 5, although the roundhouse within the ring ditch could still have been standing. Ditch 2010 had varying sequences of fills, which included a dark grey lower fill (Fig 2.9, S.87, 1340) and a middle fill at the southern terminal containing deposits of cultural material and fire-cracked stones (Fig 2.8, S.81, 1369).

The northern arm was re-cut, ditch 2001, to a slightly shallower depth, and the new terminal lay south of its predecessor. The ditch reached its greatest depth and width at this point, 1.2 m wide by 0.68 m deep (Fig 2.8, S. 81, 1367). Here, a compact greyish silt (1366) was overlain by a more friable browner soil (1365). The ditch was generally 1.1 m wide and up to 0.45 m deep (Fig 2.9, S.115), with a lower fill of grey brown silt and a charcoal-rich upper fill (1401).

On the southern arm, ditch 2007 replaced ditch 2012. The terminal was 1.5 m wide and 0.65 m deep. The primary fill was compacted sterile clayey silt. The upper fill was friable and charcoal-rich with some animal bones.

Phase 4: Ditch 2003 and Gully 2017

Ditch 2003 has been interpreted as forming, with ditch 2017, a roundhouse eaves drip gully about 10 m in diameter. It would have been somewhat asymmetrical in relation to the northern arm of Enclosure 5, ditches 2010/2001, and so has been shown as belonging to Phase 4 (Fig 2.7). The terminal would appear to have respected Enclosure 4, although positioned quite close by.

Ditch 2003 was 0.9 m wide and 0.4 m deep, containing a dark grey brown fill with an abundance of fire-cracked stones. Gully 2017 was a shallow curvilinear gully, 0.39 m wide and 0.15 m deep, containing a single dark grey brown fill. The gully was truncated at both ends by post-medieval features.

Phase 4: Enclosure 4

This oval enclosure, ditch 2002, was the final phase of ditch cutting in the northern area. It appears to mark a more significant change in the site layout than the earlier ditch phases, and entailed the replacement of Enclosure 5 (Phase 3) with a new enclosure of similar form and size, with a narrower, south-facing entrance. The ditch was between 0.8 m and 1.6 m wide and 0.5 m to 1 m deep (Fig 2.8, S.79 & S.103). The fills varied, with a grey silt overlain by middle deposit of redeposited clay in the south-west terminal and other sections (Fig 2.8, S.103). The south-east terminal and east ditch by contrast had a homogeneous fill of dark loam with charcoal and cultural material (Fig 2.8, S.79).

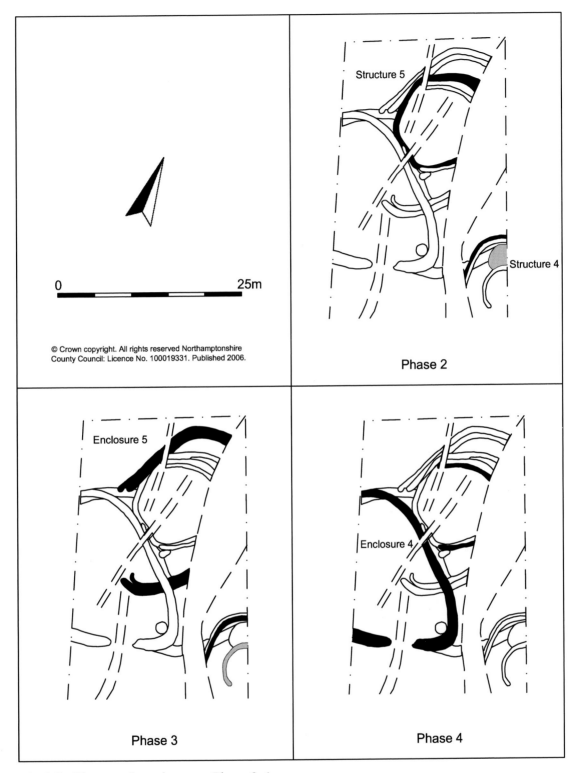

Fig. 2.7: Silverstone 3, northern area Phases 2-4.

Pits 2015, 2018 to 2022

A small number of individual pits, of several phases, lay in the northern area (Fig 2.3). Pit 2015 cut an early ditch, 2016, and was in turn cut by gully 2013 of Structure 4. Pit 2019 cut ditch 2011 but had an undetermined relationship with 2003. Pit 2020 cut the terminal of ditch 2012, Enclosure 5. All the pits were shallow, with unremarkable finds. Their purposes are unclear but the small ones may have been postholes and the larger ones for storage of some sort. A soil sample from pit 2022, which was cut by ditch 2002, yielded a large quantity of chess seeds, presumed to be a weed of arable land (Carruthers, Chapter 6, Table 6.4).

Central Area: Pit Alignment

A series of flat-based, roughly circular pits formed an irregular line or alignment alongside ditch 2051, Enclosure 1 (Fig 2.4; pits 2039, 2040, 2044, 2046 to 2050). Pit 2049 cut pit 2050, but otherwise they were discrete features.

17

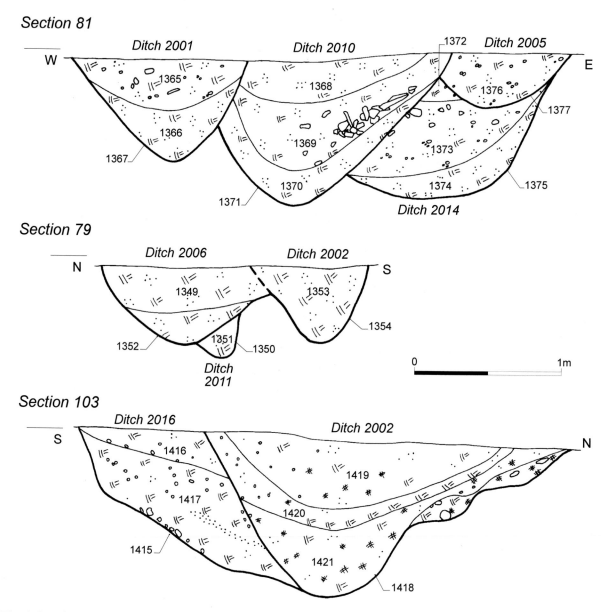

Fig. 2.8: *Silverstone 3, northern area, sections 81, 79, 103.*

The geophysical survey shows the alignment possibly continuing to the north-west, although this may at least partly comprise a ditch rather than pits, and this boundary appears to define the axis of the settlement. The pits are interpreted as a primary feature belonging to Phase 1 and pre-dating the enclosure ditch, 2051, although none of the pits in this group had a relationship with it, nor with any other features.

The pits varied in size, but 2040, 2046, 2047 and 2048 formed a group which were very similar, being 1.6-1.7 m in diameter and 0.45-0.55 m deep. Pit 2039 was narrower (1.17 m) but of a similar depth (0.50 m), while 2044, 2049 and 2050 were shallow (0.20-0.30 m). The single fills varied from grey brown to orange brown silty clay. A small sample of pottery and animal bone was recovered from the pits but they contained very little charcoal and it is difficult to determine whether they were of a domestic character.

Central Area: Circular Structures

Structure 3

This group of gullies appear to be part of a roundhouse eaves drip gully of two phases (Fig 2.4). Structure 3 cannot have been contemporary with Enclosure 3 since the projected gully circuit overlaps, but there is no way of telling which was the earlier.

Gullies 2025 and 2027 formed an approximate circle, about 12 m in diameter, with aan open eastern side and a possible narrow entrance to the west. Gully 2025 had a southern terminal, the outer edge was sharply cut and what could be seen of the inner edge seemed more gradual. The base was fairly narrow and flat and between 0.2 m and 0.28 m deep. Gully 2027 had an eastern terminal, but faded out to the west.

Both gullies were re-cut, 2024 and 2026. Gully 2024 was 0.7-0.8 m wide and 0.15-0.25 m deep, with a gradual incline and rounded base.

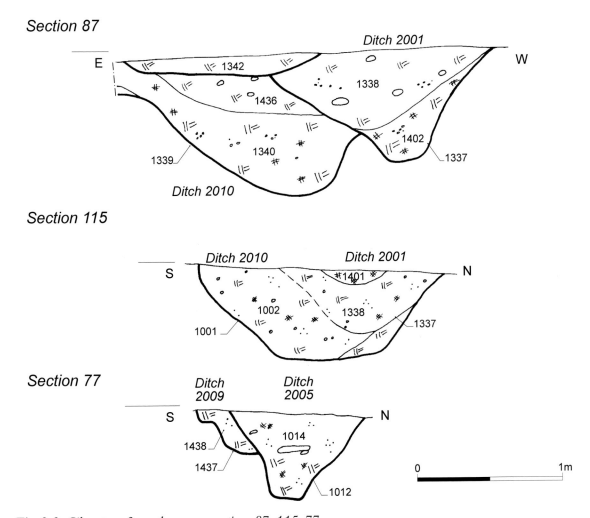

Fig. 2.9: *Silverstone 3, northern area, sections 87, 115, 77.*

An irregularly scatterred group of postholes lay within the area defined by Structure 3. Posthole 2035 was approximately central to the ring gullies and 2030 and 2031 were equidistant from it.

Structure 2
This was a roundhouse eaves drip gully, 11 m in diameter, but open to the south-east. The gully was 0.4 m wide and 0.18 m deep to the west, but was more substantial on the eastern side, where ground incline and greater depth of topsoil provided protection from recent plough damage. The eastern terminal was 1.07 m wide and 0.35 m deep. The profile of the gully varied slightly along its length but generally remained rounded. Much of the interior was lost under the medieval trackway.

Central Area: Enclosures and Gullies

Enclosure 3
Ditch 2023 formed part of a polygonal enclosure. Three sides were exposed in the excavation but the eastern part was heavily truncated by the post-medieval trackway (Fig 2.4). The enclosure measured 12.5 m north to south, but its length could not be determined. The ditch was 2.14 m to 2.39 m wide and from 0.85 m to 1.3 m deep (Fig 2.10, S.31). The profile displayed slight variation, from a more

gradual slope and rounded base to a steeper incline and concave base. The upper fill (1237) was generally dark and contained an abundance of charcoal and fire-cracked stones, and a relatively large assemblage of pottery. There were no features within the excavated part of the enclosure.

Gully 2037
This was a linear feature, of negligible depth, cut by posthole 2036 and probably by Structure 3.

Gully 2028
An isolated arc of gully, which was heavily truncated, is of unknown significance.

Miscellaneous postholes
A scatter of postholes, 2038, 2041-2043, and 2045, lay near the pit alignment. Posthole 2043 contained a small fragment of samian ware, the only piece recovered from the site.

Southern Area: Pit Groups

A group of pits lay just south of the northern arm of Enclosure 1 (Fig 2.5, pits 2079-2084). All were very shallow, up to 0.16 m, and of rather irregular profile. Pit 2083 was truncated by ditch 2051.

Fig. 2.10: *Silverstone 3, central area, section 31.*

To the west of Structure 1, pits 2089-2093 formed a rough east-west alignment, and the geophysical plot shows a distinct linear anomaly running east-west for over 20 m. The most substantial was 2093, which was over 2.0 m wide and 0.3 m deep, with very gently sloping sides.

The most substantial pit in this area was pit 2085, about 1.0 m wide and 0.5 m deep, with moderately sloping sides and a narrow, flat base. It cut a shallow gully 2087 (see below). To the east of Structure 1, pit 2108 was cut by the northern terminal of the enclosure ditch 2051 (Fig 2.13, S.78). It was filled by a deposit of orange brown silty clay (1314) and contained a near-complete vessel in shelly fabric (Fig 4.2, 31).

Southern Area: Structure 1

A complex series of curvilinear and near concentric gullies within Enclosure 1 are related to at least four, and possibly as many as eight, phases of roundhouse usage (Fig 2.5). No definitive interpretation of the sequence is possible, and the phasing presented shows the simplest, four-phase, interpretation assuming that some of the inner gullies were contemporary with near concentric outer gullies (Fig 2.11). This may either imply that the inner examples were wall slots and the outer ones eaves drainage gullies, or that there was a double gully system. An arc of external postholes may relate to a different construction. The gullies were generally small. The widest was 1.1 m (2054) and the deepest 0.4 m (2064). Many had terminals to the north.

The post-medieval trackway truncated the gullies on their eastern side, and only two gullies (2065 and 2090) were recorded east of the trackway. These may have been paired to leave a narrow entrance to the south-east.

Inner gullies Phase 1: gullies 2056 and 2055
Gully 2056 was 0.65-0.75 m wide, and 0.13-0.35 m deep with a flat base (Fig 2.12, S.60). No terminals were evident. It would have enclosed a circle about 8 m in diameter. It may have been contemporary with 2063. Gully 2055 was a recut of 2056, but more heavily truncated and was 0.7 m wide and up to 0.4 m deep with a rounded base. No terminals were evident.

Inner gullies Phase 2: gullies 2053, 2065 and 2090
Gully 2053 was 0.4 m wide and 0.12 m deep (Fig 2.12, S 60). Its terminal would have lain to the north (removed by 2052). It lay on the same arc as 2065, which may indicate another terminal to the south-east. It may have enclosed a circle 12 m in diameter. It had no relationship with 2054 (below) but is unlikely to have been contemporaneous.

Inner gullies Phase 3: gully 2054
This was 1.0 m wide and up to 0.22 m deep with a broad base (Fig 2.12, S 60). It would have enclosed a circle about 9 m in diameter. It is interpreted as being of the same phase as 2060 (below).

Inner gullies Phase 4: gully 2052
This was 0.44 m wide, 0.18 m deep (Fig 2.12, S 60). It appeared to be just a short arc of gully with a clear northern terminal and possibly a southern one near S.60. It may have been contemporary with Gully 2064 whose northern terminal it mirrored.

Inner gullies Phase 4: gully 2064
This, the innermost gully, had a width of 1.0 m and a depth of 0.4 m with a slightly rounded base. Its terminal mirrored that of Gully 2052. The gully would have enclosed an area little more than 5 m in diameter, which is small for a roundhouse. There is no particular indication in the form and the overall size of the gully that it had held a wall-line, rather than being an eaves drainage gully.

Outer gullies Phase 1: gully 2063
This was 0.4 –0.8 m wide and 0.21- 0.25 m deep with a rounded base. It was largely truncated by 2060. It may have been contemporary with gullies 2056 and 2055.

Outer gullies Phase 3: gully 2060
This gully was generally 0.7 m wide and 0.32 m deep with a shallow terminal (1109) which may have been truncated. It would have enclosed a circle about 15 m in diameter, which is on the large side for a roundhouse. It may have been contemporary with inner Gully 2054. To the east of the trackway, Gully 2065 lay approximately on this circumference.

Outer gullies and postholes
A group of short lengths of gully and pits/postholes lay predominantly outside Gully 2060. Most were quite shallow (c 0.15 m deep) and in the form of scoops rather

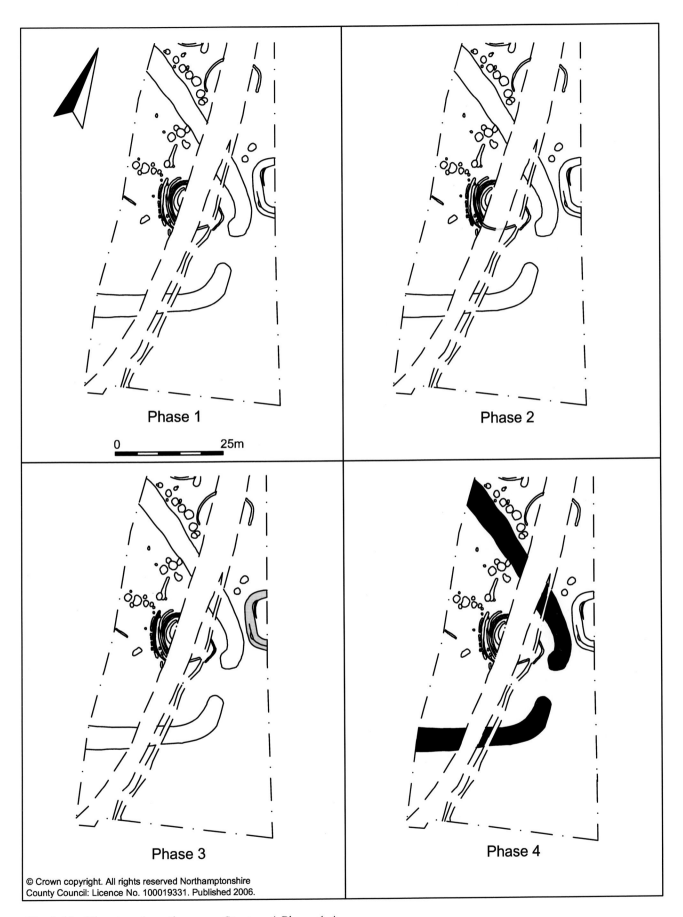

Phase 1

Phase 2

0   25m

Phase 3

Phase 4

Fig. 2.11: *Silverstone 3, southern area, Structure 1 Phases 1-4.*

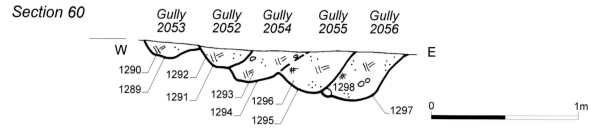

Section 60

Gully 2053   Gully 2052   Gully 2054   Gully 2055   Gully 2056

W

1290   1292
1289   1291   1293   1296
1294   1295
1298
1297

E

0   1m

Fig. 2.12: *Silverstone 3, southern area, section 60.*

than convincing postholes. Postholes 2069 and 2075 were more substantial (c 0.30 m deep). It is likely that they were part of a fence line outside the structure.

Southern Area: miscellaneous gullies (2087 & 2097) and postholes within Enclosure 1

A series of shallow gullies (including 2087 and 2097) and postholes (not numbered) lay to the north and west of Structure 1.

Southern Area: Enclosure 2

This enclosure lay largely outside the area of excavation. The enclosure ditch, 2100, and was 2.0 m wide and 0.7 m deep, with fairly sharp sides, particularly the outer

edge, and a wide flat base. It was re-cut, with the two phases diverging at the south-western corner. A single dark brown fill contained a large quantity of animal bones and some pottery. To the north the enclosure ditch cut a shallow gully, 2101.

The narrow gap of about 1 m between this enclosure and Enclosure 1 implies that it restricted access through this area, or that it was of a different phase. Pits 2098 and 2099, to the north-west, were flat-based and shallow being 0.2 m and 0.15 m deep respectively. Pit 2099 contained part of a grog-tempered jar and other sherds.

Southern Area: Enclosure 1

Enclosure 1 was the most substantial feature on the site (Figs 2.2 & 2.5). The enclosure ditch, 2051, averaged 4

Plate 1: *Silverstone 3. Northern terminal of ditch 1051, enclosure 1. Looking north-west.*

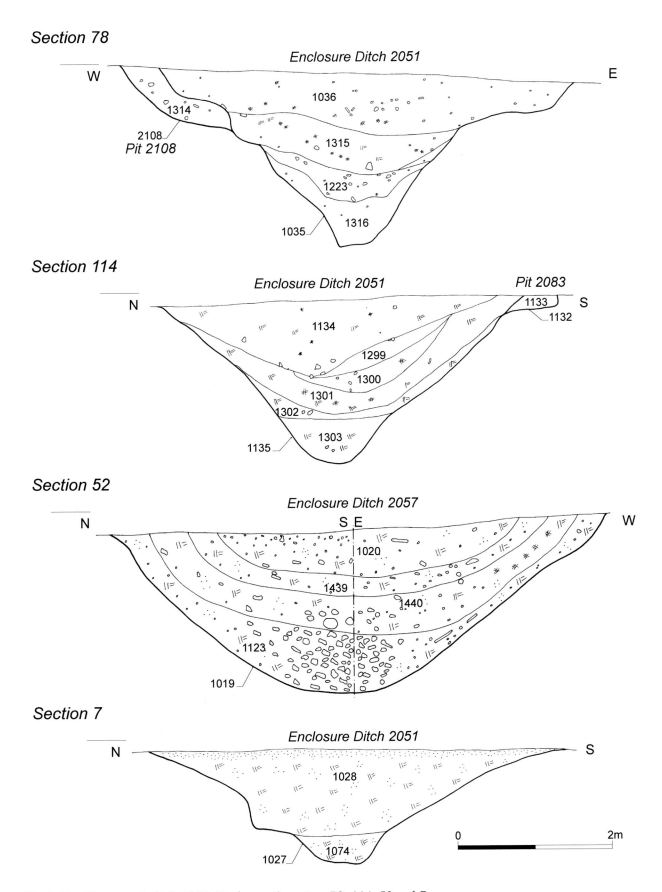

Fig. 2.13: *Silverstone 3, ditch 2051 (Enclosure 1), sections 78, 114, 52 and 7.*

Plate 2: *Silverstone 3. Section through the northern arm of ditch 1051, Enclosure 1.*

- 5 m wide and about 2 m deep. The geophysical survey shows it to have enclosed a space about 40 m wide and 60 m long, with an east-facing entrance 6 m wide.

The ditch had few relationships with other features, but was shown to cut, or to have eroded back through, two pits (2108 and 2083). It is considered likely to have been later than the internal roundhouse gullies as the position of the latter, within 3 m of the lip of the ditch, suggests insufficient space for a contemporaneous internal bank.

Northern terminal
The northern terminal was 2.2 m deep, with a V-shaped profile, 5.8m wide at the surface but narrowing in after about 0.5m of depth (Fig 2.13, S.78; Plate 1).

The primary fill (1316) was a firm, light blue grey mottled silty clay representing natural weathering of the sides: it contained a single flint flake. The secondary fill (1223) was a looser grey brown sandy silt with some pottery and animal bones. Above this was a deposit of sterile orange-brown clay (1315) containing ironstone and pockets of sandy silt. This was re-deposited natural sediment, probably the result of deliberate backfilling. This deposit may have been the original bank material, and there is slight but inconclusive evidence that it was derived from the western (internal) side.

The upper fill (1036) occupied the wider upper depression formed by weathering of the upper ditch edges. It was a dark grey-brown soil containing relatively abundant cultural material and burnt stones, possibly the

result of deliberate infilling. Two Roman sherds from this deposit are among the latest material from the site, although they may be intrusive.

Southern terminal
The southern terminal was 1.7 m deep, but it is possible that the ditch had not been fully bottomed (Fig 2.13, S.52).

The sedimentary sequence was similar to that in the northern terminal. The primary fill (1123) of yellowish silty clay contained a substantial deposit of limestone rubble, probably derived from the ditch edges which here cut through rock. This was overlain by a darker silty fill (1440) containing some burnt material. Above this was a thin, but distinctive band of yellowish brown silty clay (1439) which may represent redeposited bank material. The upper fill (1020) was dark grey brown soil (like 1036) containing a high proportion of the finds from the cut.

Northern arm
The northern arm showed a sequence of deposits which can be interpreted in a similar manner to those in the terminals (Fig 2.13, S. 114; Plate 2). The lower fills (1302 & 1303) were light coloured clay silts derived from the weathering of the ditch edges. The middle fill (1301) was grey-brown with charcoal. This was overlain by a mottled yellow and grey deposit (1300), apparently derived from the

southern side, which again may represent the redeposition of predominantly bank material. The upper fill (1134) was a charcoal-rich grey-brown soil overlying similar, but more clayey material (1299).

Southern arm

The southern arm was broad but comparatively shallow at 1.5 m deep and with gradual sides (Fig 2.13, S.7). Above a clayey primary fill (1074), the ditch was mainly filled by a fairly sterile orange brown silty clay (1028) containing only a small quantity of bones and pottery, that included two Roman sherds.

Gully 2106 and postholes at entrance to Enclosure 1

A group of five circular postholes, which were distinct from the rectangular postholes of the post-medieval structure in the same area, lay within the entrance to Enclosure 1.

Postholes 2103 and 2104 were about 0.6 m wide and shallow, 0.14 m deep, with rounded sides and base. Posthole 2107 was 0.28 m wide and 0.22 m deep, while 2102, at 0.5 m wide and 0.36 m deep, was the largest of the group. Posthole 2105 may have been cut by the enclosure ditch terminal, although this is uncertain and rather it may have been truncated by the weathered edge of the ditch.

Gully 2106 ran partially across the enclosure entrance. It was 0.35 m wide and 0.15 m deep and a length of about 2 m was visible before it faded out.

These features are undated but their position within the enclosure entrance could lead to a tentative interpretation as the remnants of an associated gateway. It can be seen that 2102, 2103, 2104 and 2105 formed an approximate rectangle, about 6 m long by 5 m wide, although this did not lie symmetrically in relation to the enclosure ditch terminals.

Southern Area miscellaneous features

South-east of the entrance to Enclosure 1 were a series of features comprising two linear gullies 2112 and 2113, two postholes 2109 and 2110 and pit 2111 (Fig 2.2). These may all relate to the post-medieval structure rather than the Iron Age occupation, although a sherd of Iron Age pottery came from pit 2111 and this feature may have cut gully 2113. Interpretation of these features remains inconclusive.

SILVERSTONE 2: IRON AGE SETTLEMENT

General Description

This settlement comprised a large sub-rectangular enclosure, measuring 60 m north to south and 105 m east to west (Fig 2.14). A smaller enclosure in the north-west corner and a ditched trackway leading to an entrance in the south-west corner, lay beyond the excavated area. The probable entrance in the south-eastern corner was not investigated due to the presence of a badger sett. Excavation showed the northern and eastern enclosure ditches to have been moderately deep, but the southern boundary comprised three phases of shallow ditch, with an adjacent line of pits. Features within the enclosure were limited to a roundhouse ring ditch, of two phases, and a few pits. The geophysical survey shows that this lack of cut features may be typical of the enclosure as a whole, although an arc of a probably further ring ditch lay to the west.

Most of the pottery recovered was Iron Age in character, although occupation appears to have continued into the first century AD. It is possible that the ring ditch went out of use before the enclosure as a whole.

Pits along the southern boundary

Ten pits formed a line extending for over 20 m inside, and parallel to, the southern boundary (Fig 2.15). They were 2-4 m apart (centre to centre), but not regularly spaced nor precisely aligned. They are considered likely to be among the earliest features on the site, although only pits 1004 and 1086 were stratigraphically related to the southern boundary ditches and were cut by the latest ditch 1023.

All the pits were circular, a little over 1 m in diameter, and generally about 0.7 m deep, although some were shallower. Their fills were unremarkable except for the presence of concentrations of limestone rubble in the central part of four of them, possibly the remains of post-packing although there was no evidence of a post-pipe in any of them, and a small quantity of pottery and animal bone in pit 1004.

Pit 1000 was 1.4 m in diameter and 0.75 m deep with vertical sides and a flat base. It had a light brown silt primary fill (1003) over which were two secondary fills; a dark, relatively stone-free silt (1002) and a much stonier dark greyish brown silt loam (1001) within the central part of the pit (Fig 2.16, S.10). Most of the charred plant assemblages from this site were dominated by grain, however, sample 2 from this pit produced larger amounts of chaff (Carruthers, Chapter 6).

Pit 1034 was 1.8 m in diameter and 0.7 m deep with vertical sides and a flat base. Like 1031, it had a central rubble fill (1035) and an outer less stony dark silt (1036) (Fig 2.16, S.14).

Southern enclosure ditches

A sequence of three shallow ditches, with a progressive northward shift, defined the southern boundary of the enclosure (Fig 2.15).

Phase 1: ditch 1006

Ditch 1006 crossed the entire width of the excavation area. It was 0.85 m wide and about 0.3 m deep with moderately sloping sides and a flattish but irregular base. It was filled with greyish brown silt with limestone fragments which contained a few fragments of pottery and animal bones.

Phase 2: ditch 1021

This ditch was very similar to 1006, at about 0.6 m wide and 0.4 m deep. It was filled with stony light brown silt

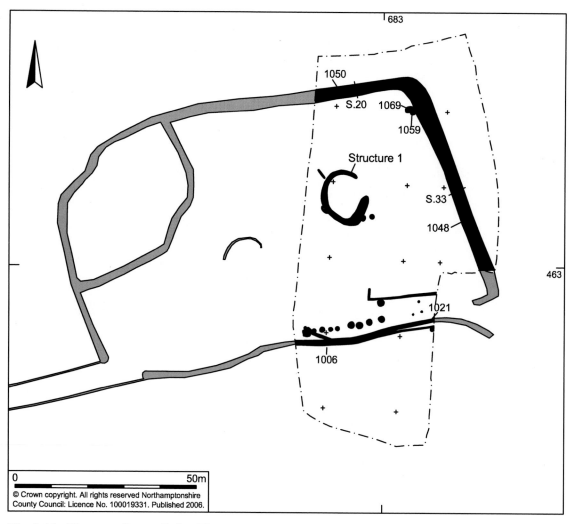

Fig. 2.14: *Silverstone 2, overall plan. The magnetometer survey is shown in grey tone.*

with a few fragments of animal bone. At the western edge of the site it appeared to continue along the line of the earlier cut.

Phase 3: ditch 1023

This ditch was 1.4 m wide, broader than the earlier ditches, but of a similar depth. It had a darker and less stony fill than the others, yielding several sherds of pottery and some animal bones. To the west the ditch curved inward to a terminal, cutting pits 1004, 1041 and 1086 in this area.

Eastern and northern enclosure ditches 1048 and 1050

The eastern side of the enclosure was formed by a substantial ditch up to 3.6 m wide and 1.3 m deep, and generally 2.5-3.0 m wide and 1.1 m deep (Fig 2.17, Sections 20 & 33; Plate 3). It had a characteristic steep-sided V-shaped profile, with the inner edge marginally steeper than the outer edge all the way round. Its relationship with the southern boundary ditches was not examined due to the presence of a badger sett near this corner of the enclosure.

The primary ditch fills (1058 and 1055) were light orange brown clayey silts with blue clay mottles and sparse lumps of limestone. Several sherds of pottery, daub and

some animal bone were retrieved. This was overlain by a darker greyish brown clayey silt (1049 and 1051) with more abundant limestone fragments and some pottery and animal bone and high concentrations of snail shell from (1049) (Robinson, Chapter 6). In places intervening layers of dark brown clay and redeposited natural blue clay were recorded. The deposit of natural clay would appear to be deliberate dumping in the ditch.

Structure 1

The only structure within the enclosure was a sub-circular ring ditch, with an internal diameter of 9 m east to west and 11 m north to south, with a 5 m wide entrance facing north-east (Fig 2.18). It could have accommodated a roundhouse of up to 8 m in diameter. No internal features were identified. The ditch was of two phases.

Phase 1: ditch 1082

The first phase ditch was broader to the south, measuring 2.2 m wide and 0.6 m deep (Fig 2.19, S.39). Elsewhere, it was 1.2 – 1.5 m wide. It generally had steep or moderately steep sides and a narrow, rounded base. There was evidence of weathered edges in the shallower upper slopes, and in all sections a shallower ledge on the outside, except in the

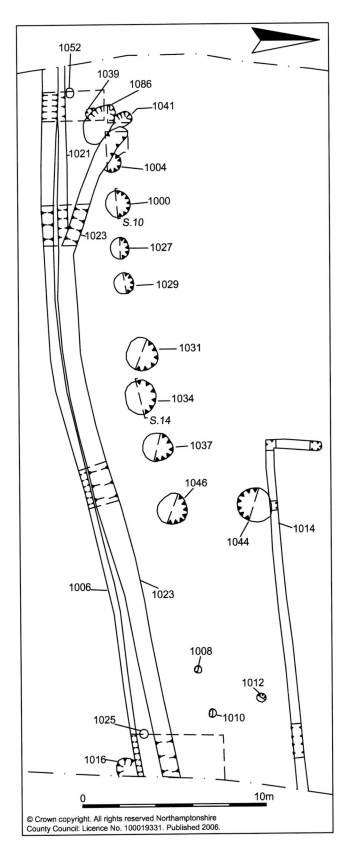

Fig. 2.15: *Silverstone 2, detail of southern boundary.*

north-east, where it was on the inside (Fig 2.19, S. 46). This suggests that there had been a still earlier phase of shallow ditch (0.2-0.5 m deep), although there was no discernible distinction in the fill.

The fill was a uniform light brown clayey silt, with abundant limestone fragments, particularly at the base of the ditch. To the east there was a band of redeposited weathered limestone in the central part of the fill, but there was no sign that there had been a bank on one or other side (Fig 2.19, S.38). A small quantity of pottery and animal bone was retrieved from fill 1083 and Evaluation Trench 1/11.

Phase 2: ditch 1063
The second phase comprised a recut along the length of the earlier ditch, and it was substantially deeper on the southern side. The southern terminal, which was 2.4 m wide and 0.7 m deep, had completely removed the earlier ditch. In the south-east the re-cut was of similar size to the earlier ditch (Fig 2.19, S 39), but elsewhere it was shallower at 0.4 m. The northern terminal was just 0.1 m deep.

The ditch was filled with dark brown silt (1064) with moderately abundant limestone inclusions. The soil was darker with considerably more burnt material in the north-west side, apparently representing a deliberate dumping of hearth debris. There were relatively large quantities of pottery and animal bone from 1064.

Gullies 1084 and 1080
Gully 1084, on the west side of Structure 1, was a narrow slot 0.4 m wide, running on a slightly curving alignment for 2.5 m appearing to cut ditch 1082 (Fig 2.19, S. 38). The fill was a light brown clayey silt (1085) with some animal bone. The purpose of this feature is uncertain. On the north-east side of Structure 1, gully 1080 was a 3 m long, V-shaped slot 0.4 m wide and 0.3 m deep, with a light greyish brown fill.

Pits near Structure 1
Two very similar pits lay to the east of Structure 1. Pit 1078 was 1.4 m in diameter and 0.4 m deep with steep sides and an uneven, flattish base with a single light brown stony silt fill. It was cut by the first phase eastern side of ring ditch 1082 and was therefore relatively early (Fig 2.19, Section 39). Just 1 m to the east was pit 1074 measuring 1.3 m in diameter and 0.4 m deep with sloping sides and a flat base with a dark greyish brown silt fill with moderate amounts of limestone fragments and a small amount of pot and animal bone.

Feature 1065 was a shallow depression cutting the northern ditch terminal 1063. It was 0.7 m in diameter and 0.15 m deep. Its dark greyish brown fill was without finds.

Other pits near southern boundary
A scatter of pits (1044, 1016, 1039 & 1052) near the southern edge of the site were not part of the line of pits (Fig 2.15).

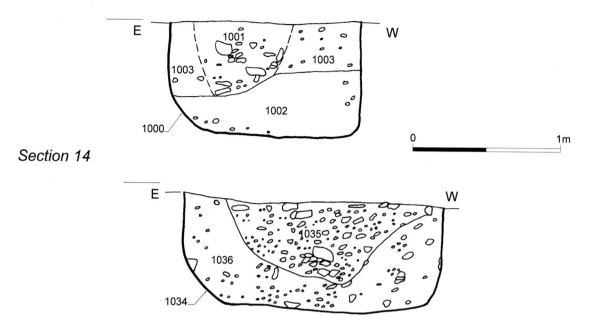

Fig. 2.16: Silverstone 2, pit sections 10 and 14.

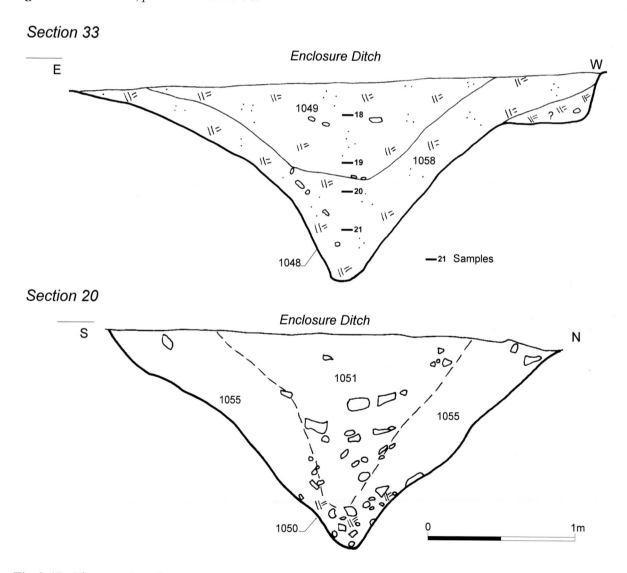

Fig. 2.17: Silverstone 2, enclosure ditch, sections 33 and 20.

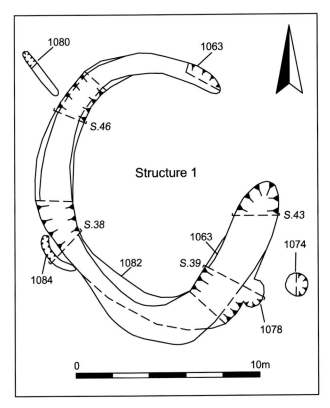

Fig. 2.18: Silverstone 2, Structure 1, detail of ring ditches 1082 and 1063.

Pit 1044 was similar to the larger pits but was offset to the north. It was 1.8 m in diameter and 1.1 m deep. Above a thin light brown primary fill the pit was largely filled with a dark brown stony fill. It was cut by gully 1014.

Pit 1016, south of the southern boundary, was 1.0 m in diameter and 0.5 m deep with steep sides and a rounded base. It had a light brown primary fill with few stones and a darker stonier upper fill. It was cut by ditch 1006, and was therefore a relatively early feature.

Pit 1039, adjacent to the southern boundary, was 0.7 m in diameter and 0.4 m deep with vertical sides and a flat base and may have been a large posthole. The fill was a dark grey-brown silt with moderately frequent limestone. It was cut by Pit 1086 and was therefore relatively early and was not contemporary with ditch 1023 and could not have been part of a gateway associated with this entrance.

Pit 1052, adjacent to the southern boundary, was 1.0 m in diameter and 0.25 m deep with moderately sloping sides and a flat base with a single dark brown, relatively stone-free fill. It was shallower than the other pits in this part of the site.

Postholes near southern boundary

A group of four postholes, 1025, 1008, 1010 and 1012, were similar in form, being 0.4-0.5 m in diameter and 0.2-0.3 m deep with vertical sides and flat bases (Fig 2.15). Posthole 1008 contained charred cereal remains and weeds.

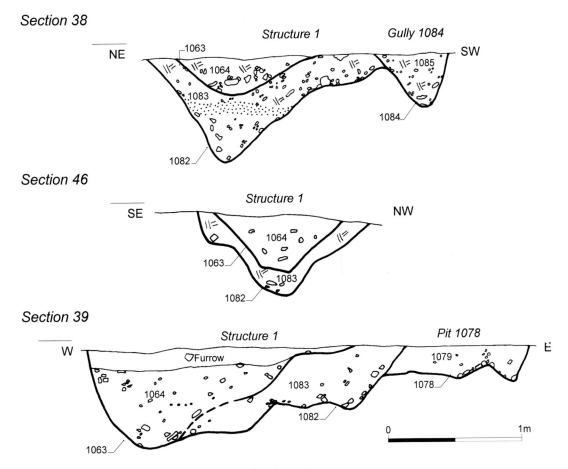

Fig. 2.19: Silverstone 2, Structure 1, sections 38, 46 and 39.

Plate 3: Silverstone 2. Northern arm of enclosure, ditch 1050, looking east.

Gully 1014 near southern boundary

Gully 1014 was 0.6 m wide and 0.3 m deep with sloping sides and a flat base (Fig 2.15). It ran east-west for more than 18 m, at about 7 m away from the southern boundary. The western end turned abruptly northward and terminated. Its light brown fill was without finds. It cut pit 1044.

Pits in north-east corner of enclosure

Two very similar pits, 1059 and 1069, lay in the north-east corner of the enclosure (Fig 2.14). Pit 1059 was 2 m in diameter and 0.8 m deep with moderately steep, uneven sides and a flattish base. The primary fill was a dark brown clay-silt with few small limestone inclusions. This was overlain by the main fill, a lighter brown clayey silt, with a very dark brown silt filling the upper 0.2 m. A small quantity of pot and animal bone came from the upper fill. The pit appeared to cut the enclosure ditch.

Pit 1069 was 1.3 m in diameter and 0.7 m deep with steep, uneven sides and a flattish base. The lower, main fill was a clean light brown silt-clay. This was overlain by a darker silt-clay with occasional limestone inclusions. There were no finds.

SILVERSTONE FIELDS FARM: IRON AGE SETTLTMENT

General description

The settlement consisted of a group of roundhouse gullies and pit groups, more or less confined within a shallow-ditched, trapezoidal enclosure (Fig 2.20). In the north-west corner there was the smaller enclosure, defined by a deeper ditch of two phases, with an east-facing entrance. There were about eighty pits, mostly grouped by the northern and eastern boundary ditches, of which thirty-three were examined. There were also irregular quarry pits on the northern and southern edges of Enclosure 2, which were also examined. The site yielded the largest assemblage of Iron Age pottery from among the sites on the project, along with a few Roman types from the later phases of the site.

Enclosure 1

Phase 1
The enclosure was sub-rectangular in shape, measuring 20 m north-south by 15 m east-west, with a 2 m wide entrance facing east (Fig 2.21).

The northern terminal, 117, was only 0.45 m deep with a single fill (118), which contained pottery, while the southern terminal, 121, was 0.7 m deep. Both had U-shaped profiles (Fig 2.23, S 19 & 22). Elsewhere the ditch was approximately 1.6-1.8 m wide with a rounded V-shaped profile, reaching a maximum depth of 0.9 m on the southern side (Fig 2.23, S.2). This ditch, 44, had a primary fill of light brown clayey silt loam (93), overlain by a stonier yellow-brown silt loam (48) and a greyish brown silt loam (47), both containing pottery. Elsewhere only the lowest fills survived. These tended to be yellowish brown clayey loams with moderate to frequent quantities of weathered limestone although the primary fill (125) at the southern terminal (Fig 2.23 S.22) was dark brown. The secondary fills also tended to be yellowish brown silty clay loams with limestone.

Adjacent to the southern terminal was a large pit, 142, measuring 2.0-3.0 m in diameter and 0.80 m deep with moderately sloping or stepped sides and a flat base (Fig 2.23, S. 22). There was a thin primary silt (145) of weathered limestone.

Phase 2
The second phase replicated the first almost precisely (Fig 2.2, Plate 4). It also cut gully 196 and pit 142 by the southern terminal.

The ditch was generally a broad V- shape, 2.0-2.5 m, wide, with moderately sloping sides, and a little under 1 m deep to the north and west (Fig 2.24, S. 7 and 10), but shallower, with a U-shaped profile up to 0.5 m deep, on the southern side (Fig 2.23, S. 1 and 2). The northern terminal 100 was 3.5m wide and 1.50m deep, with the upper fill containing, 9.7 kg of pottery, one third of all the pottery, and all six iron objects from the site, including a socketed spearhead (Fig 4.10, [catalogue number] 65). The southern terminal was wide and shallow, being 2.5 m wide and only 0.50 m deep, and contained an infant burial (Fig 2.23, S. 19 and 22).

The ditch on the southern side had a dark greyish brown clayey silt loam fill containing much animal bone and moderate quantities of pottery. Elsewhere, the primary fill was generally a mid or yellowish brown clayey silt with moderate quantities of degraded limestone. This was overlain by greyish brown stonier silty clay loams containing more deposits, and probably equivalent to the fill on the southern side. The upper fill was a dark or very dark grey-brown silty clay loam with frequent limestone

lumps and notably more charcoal, sometimes appearing as distinct bands (Fig 2.24, S.7 and 10).

Five infant burials were found, two of them being practically complete and the others partial. Burial 3 was in the southern terminal, burial 5 in the south-west corner of the ditch, while burials 1a and 1b were in the north-west corner. Burial 2 had been placed in the northern arm of the ditch (Plate 5). Part of an articulated cattle skeleton (burial 4) lay just above burial 5 (Plate 6).

Internal features
There was no evidence of structures within the enclosure, but there were a few pits, 113, 115, 133 and 135, mainly lying close to the ditch. Three of these were oval in shape, between 0.65-1.10 m long and 0.45-0.70 m wide, while pit 113 was sub circular c 1.5 m in diameter, but they were all shallow only 0.12-0.27 m deep. They were bowl shaped with gently sloping sides and fills of brown clay loam. Pits 115 and 133 contained pottery, and the latter also some charcoal. Pit 133 was cut by 135.

Enclosure 2

Enclosure 2 measured 80 m north-south by up to 40 m east-west (Fig 2.20). The ditch was 0.5-0.7 m wide and 0.3-0.4 m deep with a steep-sided V-shaped profile. It was cut by Phase 2 of Enclosure 1, suggesting that it was contemporary with Phase 1 of the smaller enclosure. It was also cut by Structure 3 and the quarry pits.

The ditch did not appear to be continuous on the eastern side, but both ditches became shallower and could not be traced to terminals. However, as the two arms did not align it is possible that there was a staggered entranceway.

The ditch was filled with a mid brown clay loam containing frequent limestone inclusions and an upper greyish fill. Small quantities of pottery and animal bone were recovered.

Structure 1
This roundhouse gully formed a slightly flattened circle about 11 m in diameter, with a 3 m wide entrance facing north-east (Fig 2.22).

The gully was 0.4-0.6 m wide and 0.12-0.3 m deep, being larger on the southern side. It had a V-shaped profile with a sharp or rounded base. There was no evidence that it had held stakes or timbers and it was probably an eaves drainage gully for a roundhouse.

It was filled with a brown clay loam with moderately frequent limestone and pebble inclusions which contained small quantities of pottery and bone.

There were three internal pits. Two were 1.05-1.20 m in diameter and 0.40 m deep with near vertical sided U-shaped profiles. The fill of pit 59 was a stony brown clay loam containing some pot and bone. The primary fill of pit 183 was a very dark brown loam which contained a worked bone object (Fig 4.19, 93) – possibly a pin beater used in weaving - and some pot and bone. Sub-circular pit/posthole 194 was 0.42-0.58 m by 0.15 m deep. It was

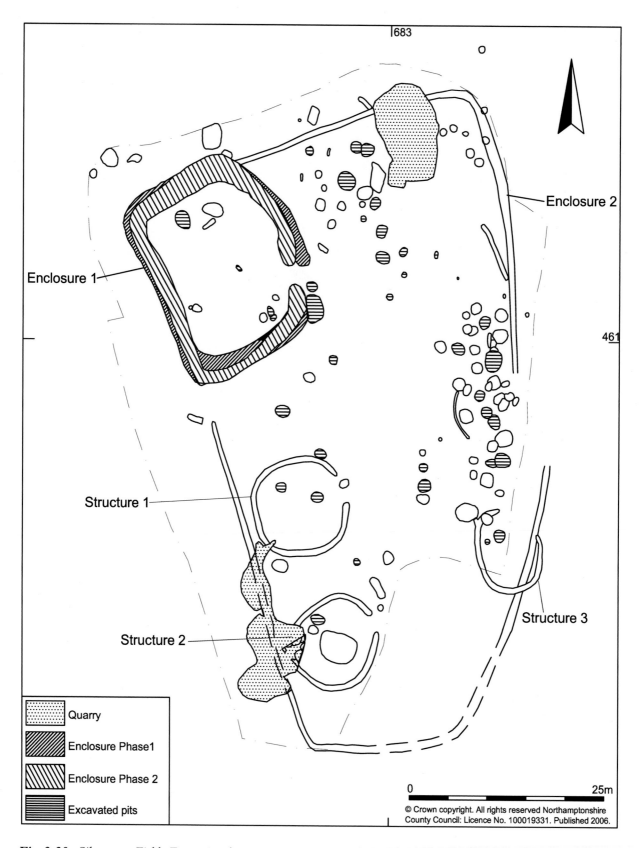

683

461

Enclosure 2

Enclosure 1

Structure 1

Structure 3

Structure 2

Quarry

Enclosure Phase1

Enclosure Phase 2

Excavated pits

0   25m

© Crown copyright. All rights reserved Northamptonshire
County Council: Licence No. 100019331. Published 2006.

Fig. 2.20: *Silverstone Fields Farm, site plan.*

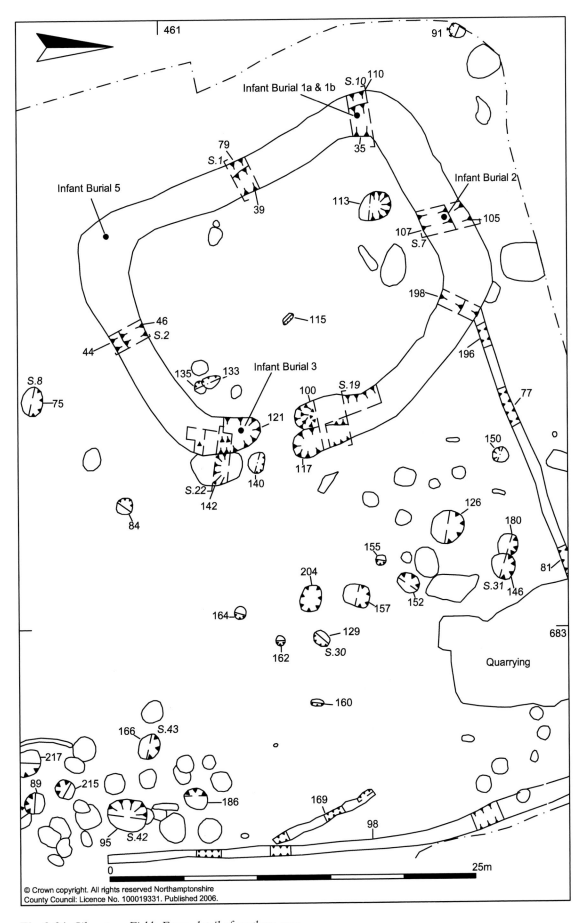

461

91

Infant Burial 1a & 1b   S.10   110

35

79

S.1

Infant Burial 5

Infant Burial 2

39

113

S.7   105

107

Infant Burial 5

198

196

46

S.2   77

44

S.8   135   133   Infant Burial 3   S.19

75   100

121   150

117

S.22   140   126   180

142   84   S.31   146

155   81

204   152   157

164   683

129   Quarrying

S.30

162

160

166   S.43

217

89   215

186   169

95   S.42   98

0   25m

Fig. 2.21: *Silverstone Fields Farm, detail of northern area.*

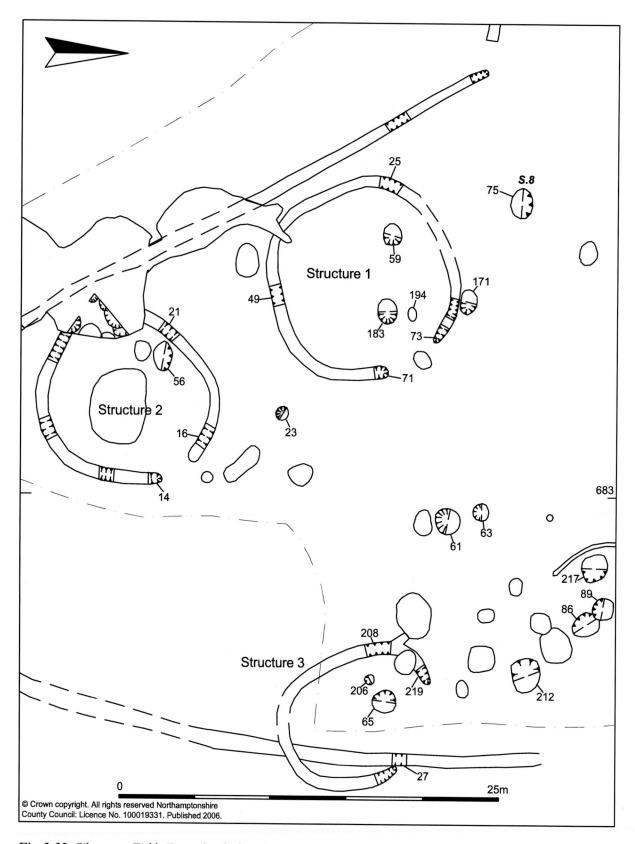

Structure 1

Structure 2

Structure 3

S.8

Fig. 2.22: *Silverstone Fields Farm, detail of southern area.*

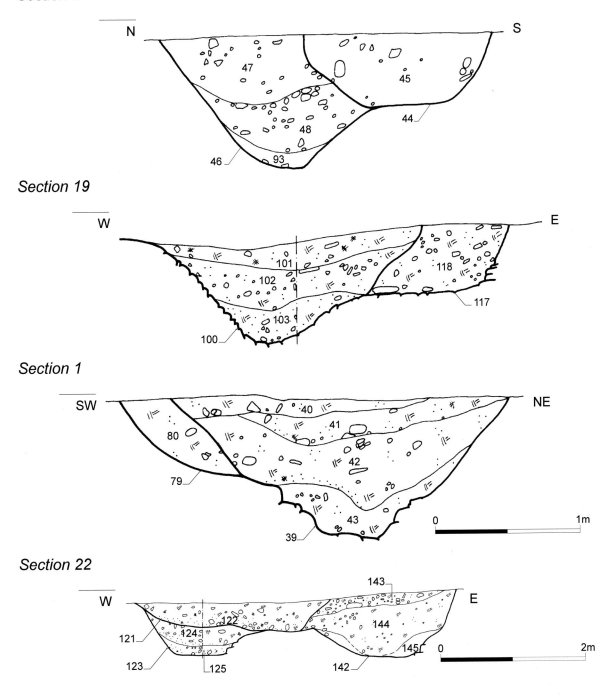

Fig. 2.23: *Silverstone Fields Farm, Enclosure 1 sections 22, 19, 1 and 2.*

located just inside the northern gully terminal, there were no finds.

Adjacent to the northern terminal, pit 171 was 1.2 m in diameter, but fairly shallow 0.36 m deep, and contained a small quantity of pottery.

Structure 2

This roundhouse gully had flattened sides to the north and west, and on the southern arm to its eastern terminal. It was about 10 m in diameter with a 2 m wide north-east-facing entrance (Fig 2.22). The gully was 0.55-0.70 m wide and 0.25-0.58 m deep, wider and deeper at the northern

terminal and less substantial around the southern side. The northern side also showed a sharper profile.

The gully was filled with a brown clay loam with a darker upper fill at the northern terminal. This contained relatively large amounts of pottery and some animal bones.

The gully was cut away in the western side by a 'quarry pit'. A large, possible quarry pit, also occupied part of the interior. There were two other interior pits, one of which, 56, was excavated. It was roughly circular, 1.3-1.45 m in diameter and 0.56 m deep, with nearly vertical sides and a flat base. The primary fill was a stony brown clay

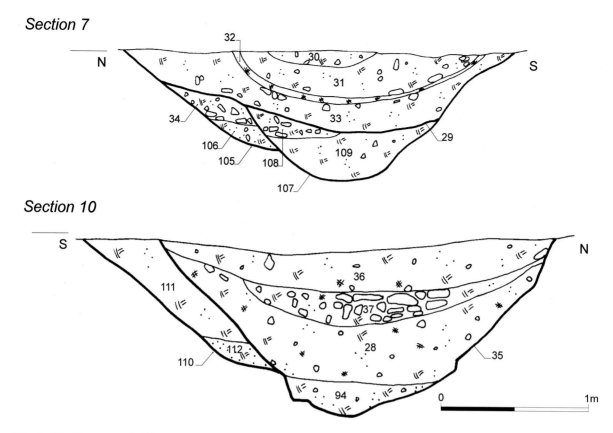

Fig. 2.24: Silverstone Fields Farm, Enclosure 1 sections 7 and 10.

Plate 4: *Silverstone Fields Farm. Enclosure 1, entrance between ditch terminals.*

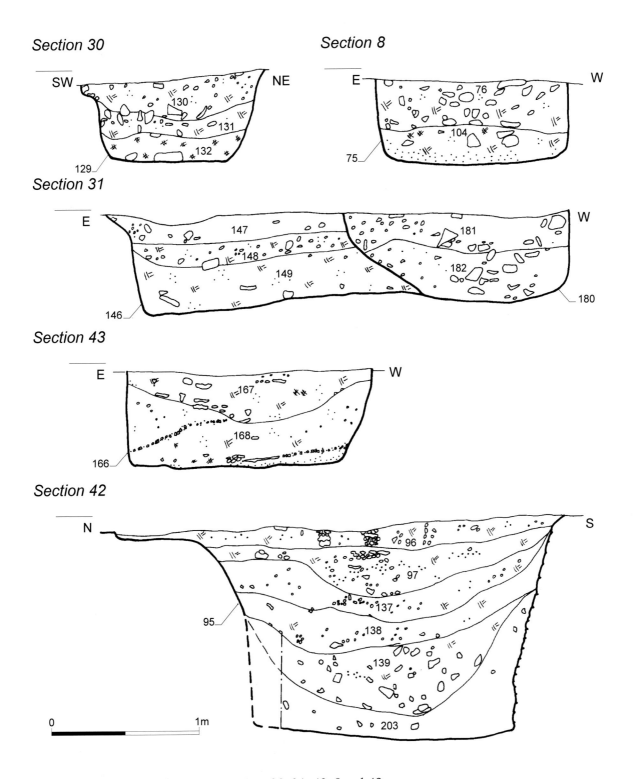

Section 30

Section 8

Section 31

Section 43

Section 42

0   1m

Fig. 2.25: *Silverstone Fields Farm, pit sections 30, 31, 43, 8 and 42.*

loam without finds. The upper fill was a greyer clay loam with fewer stones and a few fragments of potentially early pottery.

Structure 3

This gully formed a partial oval enclosure, about 9 m north-south by 6 m east west, with a 5 m wide entrance on the northern side (Fig 2.22). It cut the boundary ditch. The gully was 0.6 m wide and 0.22 m deep with steep

sides and a U-shaped profile. The fill was a brown clay loam containing a small quantity of pot and bone.

Gully 169

This was a short length of gully, 7.5 m long, 0.75 m wide and 0.38 m deep in the north-eastern part of the enclosure stopping short of the boundary ditch (Fig 2.21). It had very steep sides and a flattish base. It contained a lower grey brown clay loam overlain by a darker fill with large

Plate 5: *Silverstone Fields Farm. Infant burial 2 within the ditch of Enclosure 1.*

Plate 6: *Silverstone Fields Farm. Burial of partial cattle carcass within the ditch of Enclosure 1.*

lumps of limestone and pebbles. Both contained relatively large amounts of pottery and animal bone.

Pits

There were two groups of pits. The northern group lay just beyond the entrance to Enclosure 1, while the eastern group lay alongside the eastern arm of Enclosure 2 (Figs 2.21 and 2.22). A sample of 33 pits was excavated and another three were examined in the course of excavating other features. Most were circular in plan, but they ranged from a little over 1 m in diameter and about 0.5 m deep to 2.3 m in diameter and 1.45 m deep (pit 95). Most were steep or vertically sided and flat based. Pottery was recovered from a large proportion of them but there were few other finds. Soil samples were taken from seven pits which appeared to contain the potential for charred plant remains. A small number of the pits were intercutting, but it has not been possible on stratigraphic or ceramic grounds to suggest a phasing sequence.

The pits were filled with deposits of mid to dark brown silt loam containing moderate quantities of limestone. There were occasional darker deposits with charcoal but generally the fills were unremarkable. Burnt stones were found in some of them but in no particular concentrations. Scatters of burnt stone were characteristic of the site in general. Most were quartzite cobbles which would have been from local drift deposits collected from streams (identification by Dr D Sutherland). None of the pits was burnt, and there were no clay-lined or stone-filled pits, such as occur on some sites of this period. There was little sign of eroded pit-edge deposits, and it appears that generally they were not left open to weather.

Fifteen of the pits can be described as potential storage pits, typically around, or over, 0.5 m deep with near-vertical sides and flat bases (Fig 2.25).

Northern group
Of the potential storage pits, pit 129 (Fig 2.35, S.30) yielded moderate quantities of charred cereals and weeds from the lowest fill (132). The dark primary fill of pit 146 (Fig 2.25, S.31) contained small quantities of charred plants. Two bone objects (92 and 94) came from the upper fills. This pit was cut by pit 180, a moderately sized pit similar to 152 (Figs 2.21 & 2.22). Pit 126 had sterile fills.

There were also four shallower pits, only 0.4 m deep or less. Pits 157, 164 and 204 contained small quantities of pottery, while 204 also had a glass bead or ring (Fig 4.21, 91) within the fill. Pit 150 contained no finds.

Pits 155, 160 and 162 were all small, 0.45-0.68 m in diameter and 0.15-0.23 m deep with concave or irregular bases. They probably had a different, albeit unknown, function to the larger pits.

Eastern group
Within the eastern group, pit 95 was exceptionally large (Fig 2.25, S.42), but the fills were relatively sterile. Pits 215, 166 (Plate 7) and 186 were moderately sized pits 1.2-1.3 m across and 0.45-0.60 m deep. A soil sample from near the base of Pit 166 yielded a moderate quantity of charred cereal and weed seeds. Pit 217 was the second deepest pit excavated at 0.95 m deep. A soil sample from the lower fill yielded occasional cereal remains.

Of the shallower pits, 0.10-0.36 m deep, pits 63, 65, 89, 140 and 206 yielded small quantities of pottery, while Pit 61 contained moderate quantities of charred cereals and weeds.

Other pits
Pit 75, lying south of Enclosure 1, was of average size, 1.2 m in diameter and 0.52 m deep (Fig 2.25, S.8). It contained a large quantity of pottery and the dark lower fill yielded exceptional quantities of cereals and other plants, particularly chess (sample 11). Neighbouring pit 84, while over 1 m in diameter, was very shallow with a small quantity of pottery. Pit 23, lying between Structures 1 and 2, was 0.75 m in diameter and only 0.07 m deep. It yielded some pottery of possibly earlier Iron Age date.

Pit 91 lay outside the enclosures, in the north-west corner of the site (Fig 2.22). It was 1.1 m in diameter and 0.55 m deep, but unlike the potential storage pits it had a somewhat concave profile. It was without finds.

Quarries

The quarry pits were examined to a limited extent. They consisted of densely intercutting pits, which reached a maximum depth of 0.85 m in the areas examined. In contrast to the potential storage pits, a number of the pits had shallow sides and concave or irregular bases, but it was possible that the group included some truncated storage pits. Few finds were retrieved. The quarry edges were seen to cut the boundary ditch and the ring ditch gullies, although it is possible that the quarried areas included pits that were contemporary with these features.

SILVERSTONE 1: ROMAN ROAD

A possible roadside ditch or hollow-way had been identified in one of the trial trenches targeted on the projected course of the Roman road from Towcester to (Fig 2.26, SL1). For the main phase of mitigation, an area was opened around the evaluation trench (Fig 2.27). This revealed the trace of a cobble layer higher up the slope, to the west of the evaluation trench, as well as the expected hollow-way. A strip was cleaned by hand and excavated to examine both the cobbles (18) and hollow-way (14).

Phase 1

Cobble layer 18
A thin layer of stones, comprising small and medium river pebbles as well as worn limestone fragments, formed a roughly linear spread running NNE-SSW. The layer was heavily plough-damaged and uphill, to the south, barely survived as a definable feature. The cleaned area was 5-6 m wide, but with ill-defined edges to the cobbles, which were only 1-2 courses deep. It overlay the limestone bedrock and a pocket of natural sterile silt.

Plate 7: *Silverstone Fields Farm. Pit 166, a possible grain storage pit.*

The feature was interpreted as the eroded remnants of the Roman road from Towcester and it aligned correctly with the known section of road in the field to the north. There was no supporting dating evidence from within or under it. Some post-medieval pottery, tobacco pipe, and brick and tile were retrieved from its surface during cleaning.

It can be assumed to be in a better state of preservation further downhill to the north. A similar linear spread of pebbles was identified on this alignment in the field to the south, 5-10 m away, during the watching brief.

Possible quarry pit 19

A large pit, at least 3.5 m wide and 0.4 m deep with almost vertical sides and a flat base, lay to the south-east of the Roman road. Its fill was a light to mid brown silt without finds. The pit was stratigraphically earlier than the hollow-way (14).

Possible quarry pit 12

A pit, 1.8 m across and 0.25 to 0.35 m deep, with vertical sides and a flat base, lay north-west of the Roman road. Its fill was light brown silt, without finds. Like pit 19 this may have been a quarry pit flanking the Roman road, although there was no overlying stratigraphy in this case.

Phase 2

Colluvial layer

A thin light to mid brown rubbly silt sealed the filled pits and part of the road surface. This presumably represented soil accumulation during and after the use of the road surface. Some possible medieval pottery, a nail and fragments of brick or tile were recovered.

Phase 3

Hollow-way

Recorded as cutting the colluvial layer, but probably partly contemporary with this. The hollow-way was a linear feature running parallel to the Roman road. It was 4-5 m wide at the top and 0.5 m deep with an asymmetrical profile – the western edge being very gradual and the eastern edge steep.

On the base, which was flat and about 2-3 m wide, was a layer of pebbles. A deposit of limestone rubble on the eastern side may represent deliberate consolidation of the steeper edge, or a fortuitous collection of eroded debris.

The hollow was mainly filled with orange-brown colluvial silt, cut by a small feature of uncertain interpretation. There were no finds from this feature.

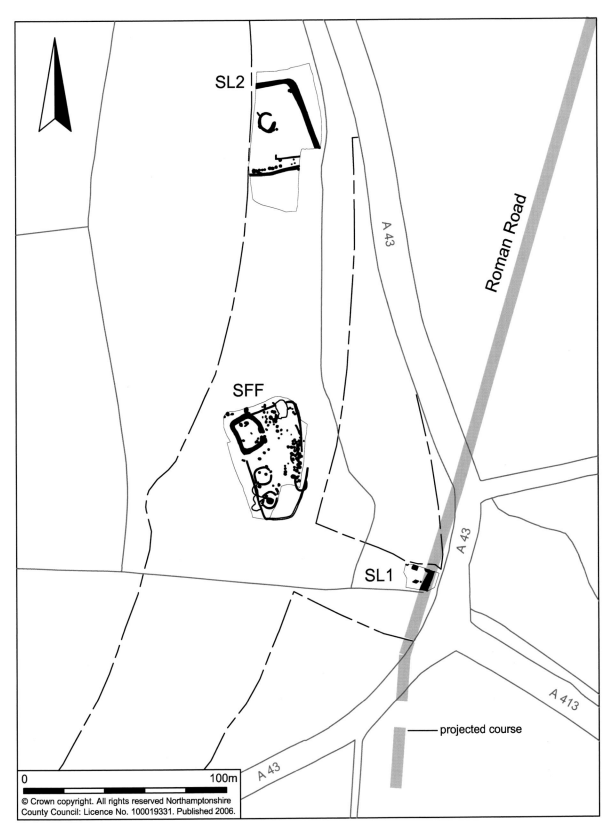

Fig. 2.26: *Location of site Silverstone 1 (SL1) in relation to Silverstone 2, Silverstone Fields Farm and the Roman road from Towcester to Alchester. The road's projected course southward was not confirmed.*

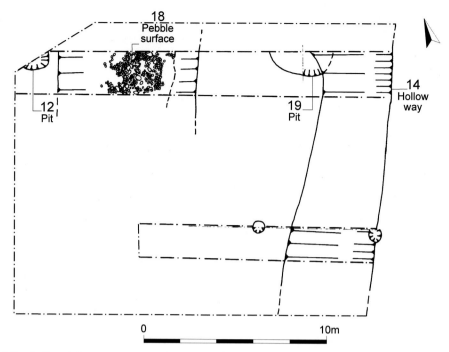

Fig. 2.27: *Silverstone 1, site plan. The cobbles of the remnant Roman road (18) lay upslope of a later hollow-way (14).*

The hollow-way was relatively narrow and without wheel-ruts in the base. It appears likely, however, to have replaced the Roman road, taking traffic along a gentler incline further down the hill slope. The basal pebble layer was probably derived, deliberately or otherwise, from the Roman road, and would have provided a better surface than the bare limestone bedrock. It need not have been the only road in this direction in the post-Roman period. The Whittlewood Forest map (c 1608, NRO Map 4210) shows the road running higher up the hill to the west (Frontispiece), and the hollow-way may have been an alternative, minor, route in the medieval and post-medieval periods.

SHACKS BARN FARM: IRON AGE AND ROMAN OCCUPATION

Introduction

An area of 33 ha at Shacks Barn Farm was used by Walters UK Ltd for the construction of a site compound and for the disposal of surplus soil (Fig 2.28). The underlying geology comprised Boulder Clay with an outcrop of glacial gravel on the higher ground. The scheme of mitigation for this area comprised a desk-based assessment, a geophysical survey covering 10% of the site, and a trial trench evaluation (NA 2001a and c). These assessed the impact of the works proposals, and suitable protective measures were undertaken to preserve, under the re-instated ground, any archaeological features discovered.

Early maps indicated that the only feature of archaeological significance still visibly surviving in the landscape is the parish boundary between Silverstone and Whitfield. This is shown on the 1608 map of the Whittlewood Forest (Frontispiece). The line of this boundary was followed by a recent hedgerow, running in a continuous albeit irregular alignment across the site. The hedgerow has been replanted as part of the re-instatement strategy. Other boundaries and divisions within the study area largely date to the time of enclosure in the early nineteenth century, with further modifications being made in the early twentieth century, when Shacks Barn Farm was built.

In the field immediately to the south of the evaluation area, an area of former closes and a hollow-way indicate the site of the deserted medieval settlement of Netherends. This was formerly connected to the Towcester Road (the A43) by a trackway running across the evaluation area. This feature is no longer evident, although its course can be postulated.

The Northamptonshire Sites and Monuments Record also shows the projected (though not demonstrated) line of the Roman road between Towcester and Alchester, running north to south across the eastern half of the site. The exact course of this road is not known and there is no evidence for it on the ground.

A reconnaissance geophysical survey was carried out over the entire site. This identified several anomalies which were targeted, together with some of the blank areas, in the detailed sample. The detailed survey was conducted in 'meshes', each comprising four 20 m by 20 m grids. Features of archaeological potential were noted, particularly in the western part of the site. These were later targeted by trial trenching. A number of the anomalies recorded in the reconnaissance scan were shown to be probable quarry pits immediately east of Shacks Barn Farm.

The trial excavations comprised forty-three trenches (1425 m in total length). The only trenches to produce evidence for prehistoric and Roman activity in the area were trenches 27, 31, 32, 35, 36, and 39 (Fig 2.28). Of the remainder, evidence for human activity was limited to medieval ridge and furrow (trenches 6, 9, 10, 21, 26, and 28), and post-medieval to modern activity (trenches 2, 7, 10, 14, 23 and 25). Trenches 5, 13, 15, and 17 revealed undated features that may be of minor archaeological interest. Twenty-three trenches produced no features whatsoever. Seven had been positioned to investigate geophysical anomalies (trenches 1, 3, 4, 18, 22, 29, 33). Excavation showed these anomalies to be natural formations.

Trench descriptions

Trench 27: Iron Age enclosure

This trench was positioned to cut across the eastern corner of an enclosure (Fig 2.29). The northern ditch (2774) measured c 1.2 m wide and 0.45 m deep, and contained small quantities of animal bones and pottery, the latter of middle Iron Age date. A possible former cut of the ditch (2777) suggests some reworking of the enclosure on this side. The southern ditch (2775) was more substantial, being up to c 2.5 m wide and 1.15 m deep. A small pit (2776), measuring 1.4 by 1.1 by 0.25 m, was cut into its external edge and contained pottery of similar date to that found in ditch 2774 (Fig 4.4, 59). A single sherd of early Roman pottery was also recovered, though this may be intrusive.

Trenches 31 and 32: Roman ditches

These trenches were positioned in a T-shape to pick up two linear geophysical anomalies, which ran at right angles to each other, probably forming the corner of a field or enclosure (Fig 2.30). In trench 31 a linear ditch (3186), measuring 1.21 m wide and 0.33 m deep, contained sherds of late first/early second-century Roman pottery. It also produced a fragment of possibly worked bone (97). Unfortunately, due to a slight misalignment of the trench, the corresponding ditch in trench 32 was not found. However, a small quantity of Roman pottery, dating to the second century AD, came from a possible pit (3289) that had been heavily disturbed by animal activity. This suggests Romano-British occupation in the vicinity.

Trenches 35 and 36: Roman occupation

These two trenches provided the clearest evidence for Romano-British occupation within the area (Fig 2.31). In trench 36 there was a complex cluster of gullies and small ditches cut by a large posthole (36102) at the east end of the trench. There was also a linear ditch (36103) containing a twisted copper earring (44) and sherds of a third century or later mortarium. A buried soil horizon yielded sherds of first-century Roman pottery.

Trench 35 provided a profile through a natural linear depression (3596) that ran down the centre of the field. Although no dating evidence was recovered, the very pale grey colour of the lower fill suggested a possible anthropogenic input into its formation.

Trench 39: Roman ditches

One of the tree ditches (39117) yielded a number of pottery sherds of the first/early second century AD (Fig 2.32). Ditch 39117 ran at right angles to ditch 39119, and they may possibly have formed the corner of an enclosure. Feature 39120 appeared to be a ditch terminal, which had been recut at least twice. This field was later taken out of the scheme for soil disposal.

Other features

A shallow concave cut was visible in section below the subsoil in trench 5. The fill contained quantities of charcoal and the surrounding natural was scorched red, indicating burning in situ. This feature was interpreted as a clamp or external hearth of unknown date.

A poorly defined ditch in trench 13, up to 4 m wide and 0.6 m deep, crossed the centre of the trench on a north-west to south-east alignment, following the lowest contours of the field. Given its location in an area of poor drainage, its primary purpose is likely to have been to drain water into the watercourse which runs west into Bandbrook. The ditch fill, which was very similar to the subsoil and was probably colluvial, produced no dating evidence.

A linear gully, of unknown date, crossed the centre of trench 15 on a roughly east-west alignment. This corner of the field appears to have been heavily disturbed in recent times, perhaps as a result of land improvement schemes during the mid twentieth century.

Two pits and a possible ditch were found in trench 17. No dating evidence was found, though the smaller of the two pits produced a small rectangular piece of shale (96), which may have been worked.

Trench 38 produced no archaeological remains, although a fragment of a Millstone Grit quern (98), a material commonly used in the Iron Age, Roman and medieval periods, was found in the topsoil adjacent to the trench.

Discussion

The evaluation identified sparse but distinct areas of activity, dating to the mid to late Iron Age and the early Roman period. Iron Age activity was focused on the enclosure detected by the geophysical survey (trench 27). The enclosure ditch produced pottery dating to the middle Iron Age, although the assemblage is small and not closely datable. The size of the enclosure is not known, but the absence of features in adjacent trenches indicates that it was quite discrete.

Roman activity, largely dating to the first and second centuries AD, was located in three areas. The main concentration was in trenches 35 and 36, and the others areas were trenches 31 and 32 and on the western side of Bandbrook, trench 39. The nature of the activity in trenches 35 and 36 cannot be determined, though a small agricultural settlement, perhaps located on the shallow

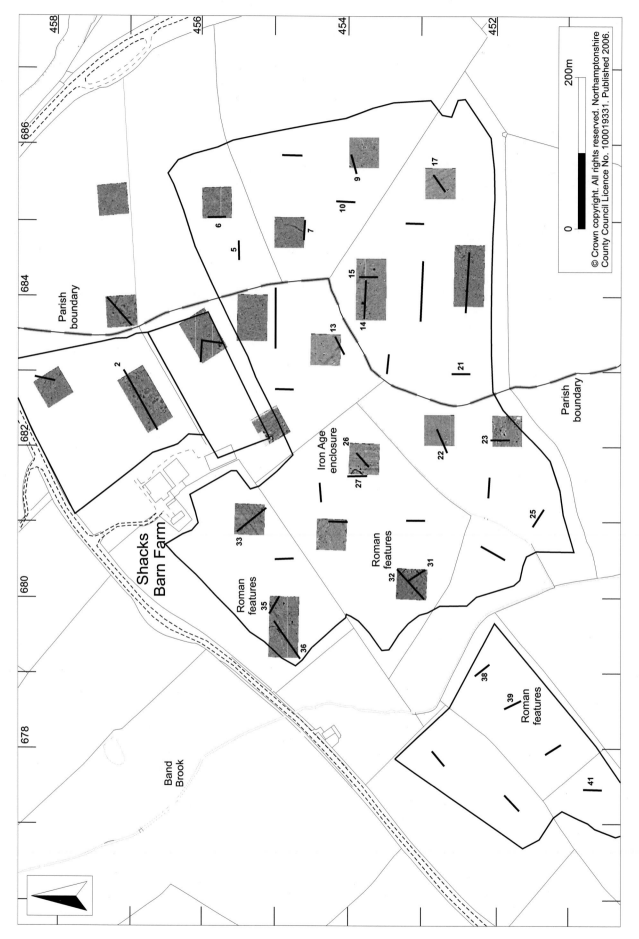

Fig. 2.28: *Shacks Barn Farm soil disposal area. Geophysical meshes and trial trench locations.*

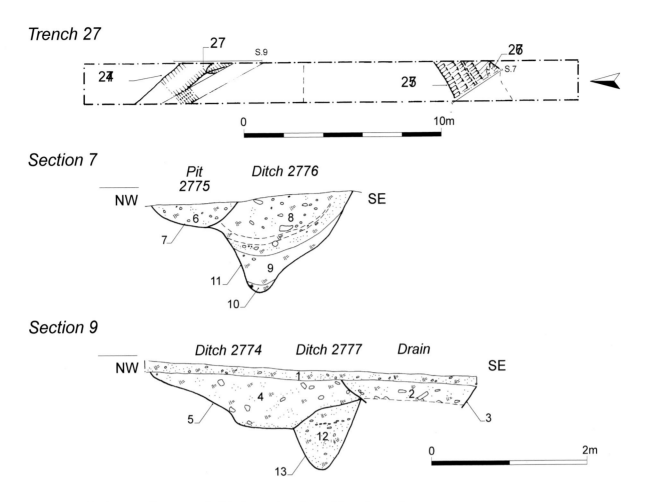

Fig. 2.29: *Shacks Barn Farm, trench 27 plan and sections of Iron Age enclosure.*

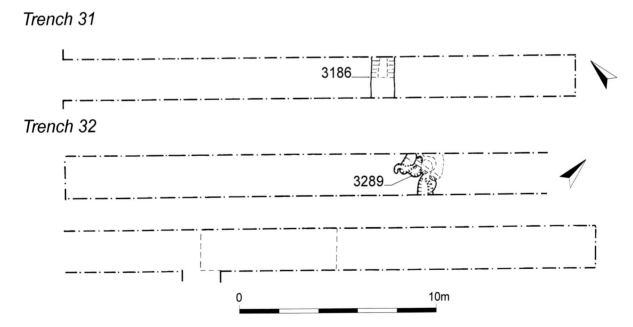

Fig. 2.30: *Shacks Barn Farm, trenches 31 and 32 plans.*

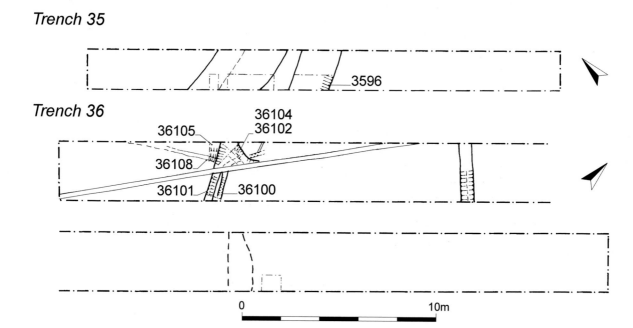

Fig. 2.31: *Shacks Barn Farm, trenches 35 and 36 plans.*

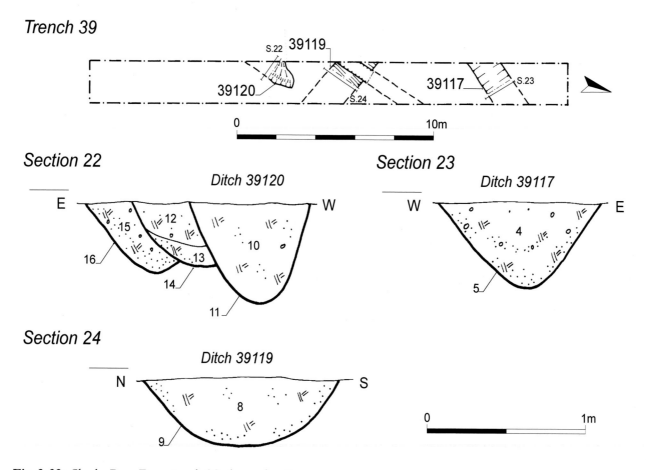

Fig. 2.32: *Shacks Barn Farm, trench 39 plan and sections.*

sloping terrace on the north side of the field, is a possibility. Based on the evidence from trench 36, there appears to have been an extended period of occupation in this area, beginning in the second half of the first century AD and possibly lasting into the third century AD, although it is not clear that this was continuous. In trenches 31, 32 and 39 the archaeological remains may be associated with outlying field systems and a possible rubbish pit, though more intensive occupation cannot be ruled out on current evidence.

Some of the undated ditches and gullies in the eastern area of the evaluation may be related to Roman fields, although they could be of later origin.

Ridge and furrow was observed in many of the trenches, and is consistent with the evidence for the use of this area for arable agriculture throughout the medieval period and into modern times. No evidence was found for the projected line of the Roman road between Towcester and Alchester. There was a small quarry in trench 2, though there was no evidence to link this with the construction of the Roman road. Much of the area covered by the evaluation produced no archaeological remains of any kind.

SILVERSTONE 4: IRON AGE AND ROMAN FEATURES

Description

The site lay on a north-facing outcrop of limestone south of Bandbrook (Fig 2.33). Its presence was suspected when fieldwalking produced a concentration of Roman pottery and a probable late Roman coin. Subsequent trial trenching failed to identify any subsurface features, but during the Watching Brief a group of pits was discovered towards the edge of the road corridor, and perhaps at the margin of a Roman settlement lying further to the west (Fig 2.33). There are recorded Roman funerary remains lying about 300 m to the north which may be associated (Northamptonshire SMR No. 721).

Pits 3 and 5 contained three sherds of Iron Age pottery. Two more pits (7 and 9) were more or less rectangular in shape, 0.35 m and 0.4 m deep respectively, with vertical sides and flat bases. They were packed with stone suggesting that they may have been structural foundations. They yielded eight sherds of second to third -century Roman pottery.

GREAT OUSE CULVERT: ROMAN MIDDEN

Description

The site was located on the south-east facing slope of the valley of the River Great Ouse, c 1 km to the south-east of Syresham (Fig 2.34). It lies at approximately 126 m OD on Boulder Clay, which includes outcrops of fluvio-glacial sands and gravel.

The site was discovered during the Watching Brief when a buried soil horizon, containing significant quantities of Roman pottery (Timby, Chapter 4), was uncovered beneath the subsoil deposit. This deposit appeared to extend the full width of the road corridor, filling a natural linear depression, c 80 m wide, which ran downslope across the line of the road corridor and opened out to the south-east. A spring was situated in the base of the depression, c 30 m south-east of the road corridor.

The topsoil, 0.3 m thick, overlay mid brown subsoil, which was approximately 0.25 m thick. Both layers had been removed by machining prior to the commencement of the archaeological excavation. The underlying buried soil was a dark greyish brown, in places black, clay-silt, which contained charcoal flecks, occasional limestone cobbles (some partly burnt), numerous sherds of Roman pottery, and metal objects. It had a maximum thickness at its centre of c 0.25 m, becoming progressively thinner towards the edges. Due to the need to maintain access the site was examined in two parts - Area A to the north of the haulage track and Area B to the south.

In Area A the undisturbed remnants of the buried soil survived in the base of the depression. The deposit was removed by machine under archaeological supervision after scanning with a metal detector. A cluster of coins, mostly dating to the first half of the fourth century, came from the western part of the area, and a large number of iron nails and other objects were also found. The spoil heaps yielded further metal objects. A soil sample yielded nothing more than a wheat chaff fragment and a possible pea.

The only potential archaeological features discovered in Area A were two small oval pits, 5 and 14, but both had been heavily truncated by machining. Pit 14 only survived to a depth of only 10-30mm, while pit 5 was 0.27 m deep. These features were filled with a bluish grey silt-clay, which suggested that they were sealed by the buried soil, although this relationship had not been observed. The date and purpose of these features is unknown and it is not clear that they were man-made. A nearby linear gully (6) contained several small pellets of lead shot of post-medieval date (53). There were a number of other irregular, probably natural features, both here and in Area B.

In Area B the buried soil horizon had largely been removed by machining although remnants were found to survive in isolated irregular hollows (possibly tree root holes). The remnants of buried soil had a spongy, almost peaty, consistency. The south-western and central areas were also disturbed by activities related to drainage improvements over the last century. Small quantities of Roman pottery were recovered from this area.

Discussion

The considerable amount of Roman material from this site indicates occupation nearby, presumably on the higher ground to the north. This is dated almost exclusively to the later Roman period, a disc brooch being the only diagnostically early piece (46). The natural depression here was probably a convenient spot to dispose of rubbish which would have accumulated as a midden. Notwithstanding the presence of a spring a short distance to the south-

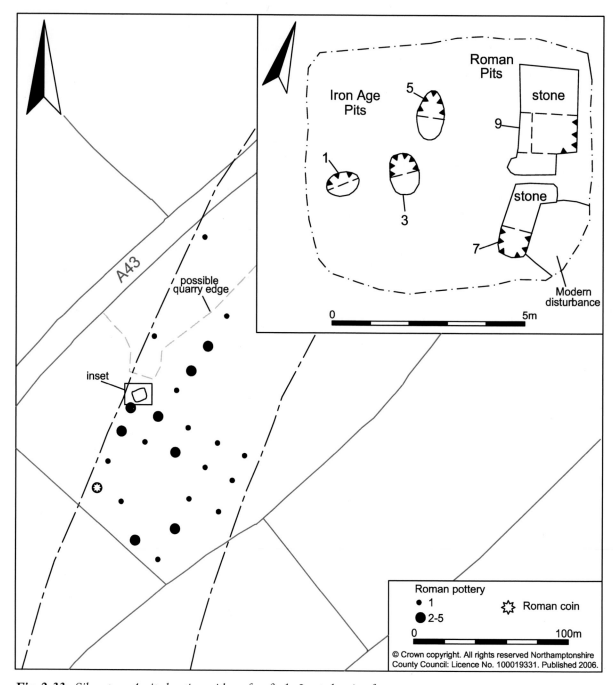

Fig. 2.33: *Silverstone 4, site location with surface finds. Inset showing features.*

east, and the peaty character of some of the lower midden deposits, there is nothing in the character of the cultural material to suggest votive or ritual deposition. In addition to twelve coins, the material includes numerous hobnails and carpentry nails, a possible iron tile clamp, and fragments of roof and box-flue tile.

BIDDLESDEN ROAD BRIDGE: IRON AGE IRON SMELTING SITE

General Description

The site comprised a linear boundary ditch to the west and a number of ring ditches and other curvilinear ditches, linear ditches, pits, postholes and three iron smelting

furnaces (Figs 2.35 and 2.36). A relatively small quantity of highly fragmented pottery was recovered, dating largely to the middle and late Iron Age. The arrangement of features appears to have been fairly static, with these often re-cut one or more times, and the site is described by feature group, rather than by phase.

Western boundary: Ditch 1

This ditch formed the western boundary to the settlement, and roughly defined the boundary between the yellow clay geology to the west (up slope) and the gravelly deposits to the east (Fig 2.36). The ditch might also have served to divert water running off the impermeable clay away from the settlement, and runoff from the north-west

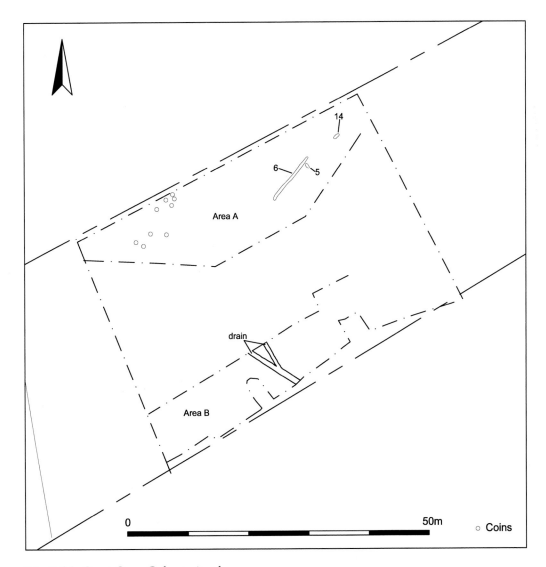

Fig. 2.34: *Great Ouse Culvert, site plan.*

corner of the field caused considerable flooding during the excavation.

The ditch varied considerably in width, from 1.7 m to 2.8 m, and from 0.40 m to 0.76 m deep. Its profile was generally U-shaped, with moderately steep sides and a concave base. In one section an earlier phase of the ditch, 0.76 m deep and U-shaped, survived beneath one of the shallower later cuts.

Features west of the Ditch 1

Gully 3
This curvilinear gully lay to the west of ditch 1 (Fig 2.36). It was 0.5 m wide, 0.2 m deep, and 12 m long, but the western end had been removed by a possible root-hole. It may be the truncated remains of an early ring ditch, although its arc had a diameter of about 14 m, which is large for a roundhouse.

Ditch 2
This curving ditch ran was 18m long running from ditch 1 to an eastern terminal. It was 1.2 m wide and generally about 0.40 m deep, with a U-shaped profile (Fig 2.36).

It cut a small pit or posthole with a charcoal-rich fill. Its purpose is unclear as it curved insufficiently to have been a roundhouse ring ditch.

Structure 1

Structure 1 was the most substantial of the ring ditches, and could have accommodated a roundhouse about 10 m in diameter (Fig 2.37). The ditch was dug in two phases, each phase showing one or more recuts. Due to the fairly complex sequence, particularly along the northern side, it was not possible to co-relate the sub-phases identified in the individual sections.

The ring ditch was also bisected by a modern pipe trench, which cut a 5 m wide swathe through the centre of the interior and removed the southern terminal. There were no observed internal features other than a hearth, 1127, which cut the latest phase of the ring ditch.

Phase 1
Initially the ring ditch was C-shaped, with a diameter of 12.5 m and an open side to the east, with distinctively

squared terminals 18 m apart. The ditch was about 2 m wide and up to 0.90 m deep. The western and south-western sides were heavily truncated, only the base surviving below the later cut.

The southern terminal, 1330, was 2 m wide and 0.88 m deep, with a broad V-shaped profile (Fig 2.38, S.134). The fill (1329) was a mid brown sandy silt with gravel, in places weakly cemented into concreted lumps. The northern terminal, 1345, had a similar profile, with a notably greyer upper fill. In plan it was angular with rounded corners, the point of the terminal being on the internal edge of the ditch.

On the northern side the ditch showed a sequence of two cuts in the first phase (Fig 2.38, S.71). The earliest cut, 1140, would have been 0.8 m deep. Further west the ditch was 1.2 m deep and had steeply sloping sides and a broad, flat base 0.9 m wide.

The recut, 1138, was 2.0 m wide and 0.92 m deep, with a steep southern slope and a flat base. The primary fill (1137) probably resulted largely from edge silting, and above this were greyer fills (1136 and 1135) and an upper dark brown sandy silt (1134). Further west the ditch was slightly smaller.

On the southern side of the enclosure the ditch (1196) showed just one recut. It survived as a moderately steep sided, concave cut to a depth of 1.1 m.

Phase 2

The ring ditch was recut and extended to leave a narrower entrance. The southern terminal had been removed by a modern water pipe, but the entrance would have been between c 3.0 m and 6.5 m wide. It is unclear whether the curving feature, ditch 8, was associated with the entrance or was a separate feature.

This ditch was generally more substantial, characteristically approaching 3 m in width. On the southern side it was also broader, although cut to the same depth (Fig 2.38, S.134). The primary fill, 1326, was pebbly sandy silt, overlain on the southern (external) slope by a relatively stony deposit (1327). The line of these pebbles, which extended for c 7 m, clearly defined the interface between the Phase 1 and Phase 2 ditches on the surface. The upper fill (1323) contained some animal bone fragments and pottery sherds.

Towards the southern terminal, the earlier cut survived as a steep-sided, concave cut in the base of the ditch section. The later cut, 1304, was c 2.7 m wide, 0.68 m deep, and

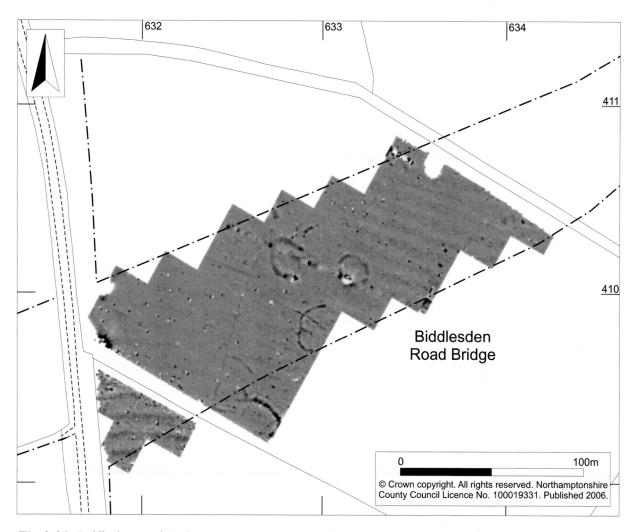

Fig. 2.35: Biddlesden Road Bridge, magnetometer survey results.

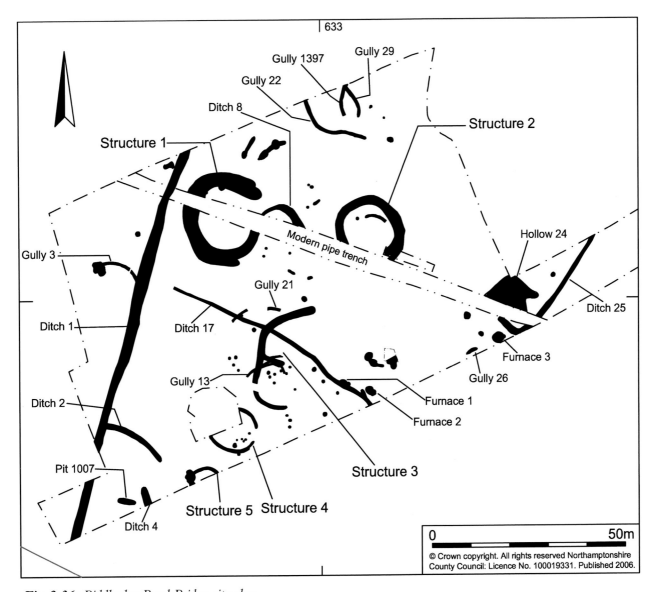

Fig. 2.36: Biddlesden Road Bridge, site plan.

had fairly shallow sloping sides becoming steeper nearer the base. Both fills of this cut appeared to be the result of natural silting, combined with the disposal of some domestic waste.

A circular pit or hearth, 1325, cutting the ring ditch, had a diameter of 0.8 m and was of 0.3 m deep. The edges were scorched red, indicating burning in situ. The fill (1324) consisted almost entirely of charcoal.

To the west the ditch showed three cuts. The two earliest survived to 0.9 m deep, while the latest cut, 1314, had a broad shallow U-shaped profile, 3.3 m wide, with an off-centre V-shaped dip in the base on its northern side, giving it a depth of 0.8 m. The primary fill was an orangey brown silt, and was overlain by a secondary fill (1312) that was darker and contained fragments of animal bone and sherds of pottery.

On the northern side at least two ditch cuts were evident (Fig 2.38, S.71). The first of these, 1133, was only fragmentary, 0.71 m deep, surviving near the base of the recut on its southern (internal) edge. The recut, 1131, was

2.0 m wide, 0.91 m deep and had a roughly V-shaped profile and three progressively darker fills (1130, 1129 and 1128). A shallow hollow, 1150, stratigraphically between the two ditch phases had a fill (1149) almost entirely composed of charcoal, and it also contained several sherds of pottery. On the inner edge of ditch 1314 there was a small oval pit, 1322.

A large circular hearth, 1127, cut the upper ditch fill (Fig 2.38, S. 71). The sides and base were scorched red, indicating burning in situ. The lower fill (1125) was a grey silt which was overlain by a black silt (1124) which had a very high charcoal content.

The northern ditch terminal had a single cut, 1113. It was 3.1 m wide and 0.65 m deep with a broad U-shaped profile. The fills were progressively darker from base to top.

Ditch 8

This curvilinear ditch had been truncated by a modern pipe trench, which had removed both terminals, and left

51

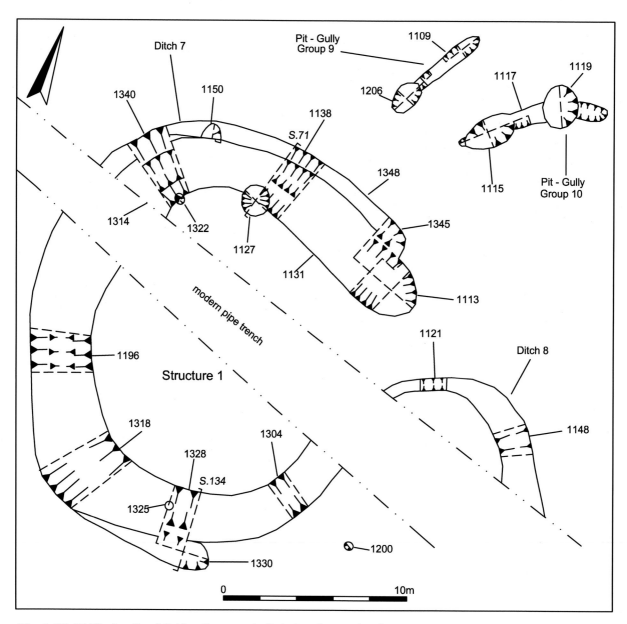

Fig. 2.37: *Biddlesden Road Bridge, Structure 1, ditch 8 and pit and gully groups 9 and 10.*

its relationship to Structure 1 undefined. It could have accommodated a roundhouse up to 7 m in diameter. At its westernmost end, 1121, the ditch was 1.1 m wide, and 0.25 m deep with a broad U-shaped profile. To the southeast, 1148, it became progressively wider and deeper with a V-shaped profile, 1.8 m wide and 0.59 m deep.

Pit and gully groups 9 and 10

North of Structure 1, there was a shallow oval pit, 1206, cutting the southern end of a shallow linear gully, 1109 (Fig 2.37). The pit was 1.8 m long, 1.4 m wide and 0.16 m deep, with a gently concave profile. It was filled with a dark silt, containing burnt cobbles, charcoal flecks and fragments of burnt clay and slag (1205). The gully was 4.20 m long, 0.80–0.90 m wide and 0.15 m deep, with a cross-profile and a fill similar to that of the pit.

There was no sign of in situ burning and the purpose of the feature is unknown. It was very similar in character

to Pit and Gully Group 10, to its immediate south, and to Pit and Gully group 18 associated with the iron smelting furnaces, see below. Groups 9 and 10 probably had some function relating to the conversion and processing of iron ore, but their distance from the furnaces and other industrial features may suggest that they were connected with a process distinct from smelting.

Group 10 comprised a curvilinear gully, 1117, cut by an oval pit, 1115, and a circular pit, 1119 (Fig 2.37). The gully was 9.0 m long, 0.9 m wide and up to 0.38 m deep, with moderately steep sides and a concave base. The fill was orange-brown sandy silt. Pit 115 was 2.0 m long, 1.40 m wide and 0.50 m deep with a flat base, and was cut close to the southern terminal of the gully. Pit 119 had a diameter of 1.65 m and was 0.47 m deep, with moderately steep sides and a concave base. The fills of the two pits were very similar greyish silts with occasional burnt cobbles and fragments of slag.

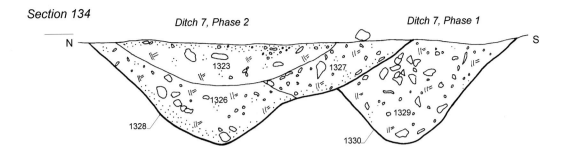

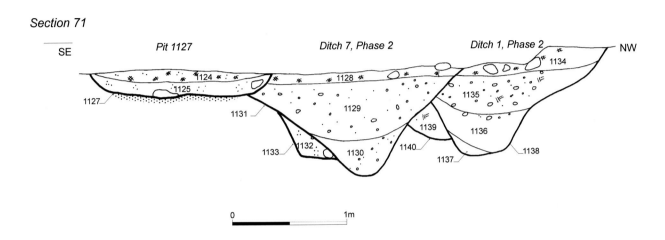

Fig. 2.38: Biddlesden Road Bridge, Structure 1 sections 134 and 71.

Structure 2

Structure 2 lay 20 m to the east of Structure 1. This ring ditch had a sub square plan, with a diameter of 10.5 m (Fig 2.39). The entrance faced south or south-west, but all but one of the terminals had been removed by the modern pipe trench. Two phases of ditch were traceable on the stripped surface, with several re-cuts in each phase. The only surviving internal feature was a curvilinear gully.

Phase 1

The eastern ditch terminal showed three cuts (Fig 2.40, S.151). The first two, 1389 and 1387, were very similar with steep-sided, U-shaped profiles, up to 0.90 m deep. The third cut, 1385, was broad and shallow with a much darker fill (1384).

Further north, the ditch was broad and shallow, but gradually deepened further round the circuit (Fig 2.40, S.135, 1362; S.108, 1285), but to the west all trace of the earlier ditch had been removed by the later cut, 1275.

Phase 2

The re-cut ditch was also relatively shallow on the eastern side (Fig 2.40, S.151, 1395). Above the primary fill (1394), was a dark, stony silt (1393), while the upper fill (1392) was relatively stone-free. A thin brown silt (1390) covered the ditches in this area which lay in a slight hollow.

Further round the circuit the ditch became deeper, but was fairly narrow (Fig 2.40, S.135, 1359; S.108, 1282). On the western side (1279) it became more substantial, 1.9 m wide by 0.85 m deep, with steeply sloping sides and a flat base, 0.7 m wide. The fills showed progressively darker deposits. An iron bar (71) was recovered from the upper fill. To the south-west the ditch 1275, was of a similar size and form. Above a primary fill of edge silting were a series of brown and greyish tip fills against the eastern (interior) side of the ditch. These were overlain by a grey-brown silt.

Gully 20

Gully 20 was 5.5 m long with a rounded terminal to the west, but its south-eastern end had been ploughed away (Fig 2.39). It was 0.39 m wide and 0.22 m deep, with a U-shaped profile. It may be a drip gully or the wall line of a roundhouse. Its projected curve would have been 9 m in diameter. With the exception of a single posthole, 1214, there were no other features in the interior.

Northern gullies

A group of shallow curvilinear gullies to the north of Structures 1 and 2 are difficult to interpret, but may have been be associated with occupation further to the north. A small pit and three postholes lay to the east near the gully terminals (Fig 2.36).

Gully 22 was no more than 0.20 m deep, and its fill contained a few fragments of slag. Gullies 29 and 1397 joined to the north, but it was not possible to determine their relationship. Both features were very shallow.

Structure 3

A complex of ditches, gullies and small clusters of postholes, lying south of Structures 1 and 2, may indicate the presence of a roundhouse and an adjacent annexe (Fig 2.41).

Curvilinear gullies 14 and 1266

Curvilinear gully, 14, which was cut into separate lengths by ditch 12, belonged to the earliest phase of features, and was 7m long, 0.40 m wide and 0.16 m deep. It could have been the northern side of a roundhouse ring gully that was largely replaced by later ditches to the west and south. Gully 1266, to the north, was of similar size.

C-shaped enclosure, ditches 11 and 12

This was a roughly C-shaped enclosure, which was open to the east and measured 22 m north-south by 10 m east-west (Fig 2.41). The ditch varied between a little over 1m and about 2 m wide, and was 0.30 m to 0.76 m deep, becoming progressively smaller from north to south. The ditch profile generally was U-shaped and moderately steep-sided. In the base of the northern terminal a cow skull had been placed with its horns pointing to the east.

Just south of centre the enclosed space was divided by ditch 12, which projected eastward, and was about 1.0 m wide and 0.5 m deep, with a steep-sided, U-shaped profile. It may have replaced gully 14, perhaps still bounding a roundhouse lying to the south. A roundhouse up to 9m in diameter, with an eastern entrance, could have been contained between ditch 12 and the arc of the southern ditch.

A number of small pits and postholes in the southern area formed no clear pattern. Beyond the southern terminal were three small pits, 1011, 1009 and 1019. Pit 1011, measuring 0.30-0.40 m in diameter, and 40 mm deep, yielded several sherds of a carinated cup (Fig 4.3, 55). Pit 1019, measuring 0.6 m in diameter and 0.18 m deep contained stone packing and may have been a posthole, while pit 1009 was of a similar size. A medieval furrow may have removed other small features.

Curvilinear gully 13

Gully 13 was a shallow curvilinear gully, 10 m long. It may have been an eaves gully replacing both gully 14 and ditch 12, and suggests that a roundhouse still stood in the southern part of the C-shaped enclosure.

Structure 4

This ring ditch was c 11 m in diameter, with a 3.2 m-wide opening to the south-east (Fig 2.41). The ditch was 0.43 to 0.80 m wide and 0.10 to 0.26 m deep, with a flattish base. At least the southern side had been re-cut. The north-west quadrant was not excavated due to the presence of a high voltage electricity pylon.

A number of shallow postholes survived within the southern part, probably due to the thicker subsoil in the southern fringe of the site. There were two possibly associated external postholes, 1004 and 1060, on the southern perimeter of the gully.

Structure 5

A curving gully continued beyond the excavated area, but the geophysical survey suggests that it was a ring ditch, approximately 8 m in diameter, with an opening to the south-east (Figs 2.35 & 2.36). There were no associated features. The ditch was 0.4 m wide and 0.2 m deep, with its western end disturbed by a probable root hole.

Curvilinear gully 21

Two separate lengths of curving gully, probably part of a single feature in an area heavily scoured by ploughing, lay immediately north-west of the C-shaped enclosure (Fig 2.36). The gully was about 0.30 m wide and 0.08 m deep. There were no associated features, with the possible exception of a posthole. It was cut by ditch 17.

Ditch 4 and pit 1007

The geophysical survey indicates that Ditch 4 (Fig 2.36) formed the terminal of a short spur extending from a substantial curving ditch that formed a C-shaped enclosure open to the south and west (Fig 2.35). The ditch terminal was 1.5 m wide by 0.5 m deep.

Immediately to the west was a linear pit (1007), 5.0 m long, 1.1 m wide and 0.55 m deep, with a steep sided V-shaped profile. The feature contained a primary fill and a darker upper fill.

Ditch 17

Ditch 17 followed a slightly sinuous course across the centre of the site (Fig 2.36). At its south-eastern end it was about 1.0 m wide and 0.38 m deep, but it became progressively shallower to the north-west. It cut all features with which it had a relationship, suggesting that it formed a partition introduced late in the life of the settlement.

To the south-east it cut Furnace 1 and there was slag in the ditch fills in this area (Figs 2.42 & 2.44, S. 23 and 24, 1074). It also cut feature 1054, a length of ditch or an elongated pit, which was 0.21 m deep and contained large quantities of slag and burnt clay, possibly furnace lining.

The iron smelting furnaces

In the eastern part of settlement, along the south-eastern limit of excavation, there were three iron smelting furnaces and a number of associated pits and gullies that contained related debris (Fig 2.36).

Furnace 1

This furnace comprised a small circular pit, 1071, in which the furnace body itself had been constructed, and a larger

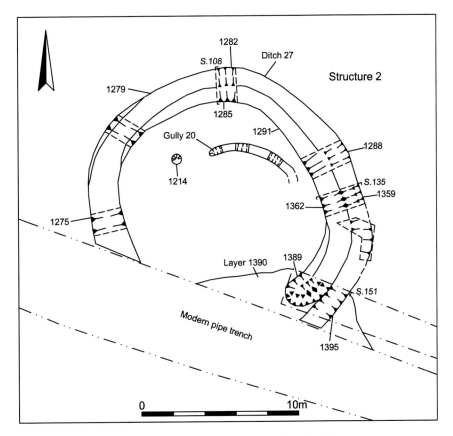

Fig. 2.39: *Biddlesden Road Bridge, Structure 2 and gully 20.*

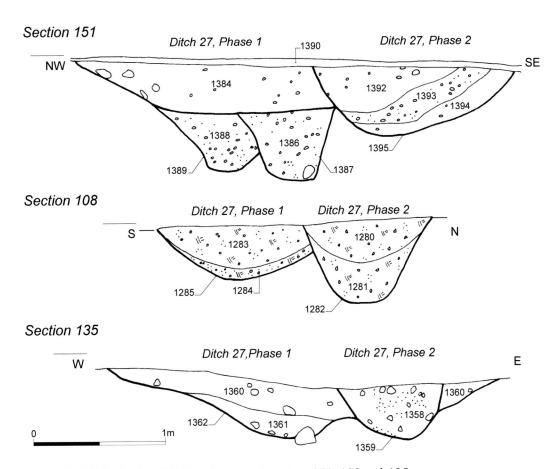

Fig. 2.40: *Biddlesden Road Bridge, Structure 2 sections 151, 108 and 135.*

oval raking pit, 1073, on the north-western side (Fig 2.42). The furnace had been cut by ditch 17 (Plate 8).

The furnace pit had an estimated diameter of 1.10 m and a surviving depth of 0.33 m with almost vertical sides and a flat base (Fig 2.43, S.22-24). The packing of the pit (1070) was with mid brown silty clay, with a gradation of red scorching radiating out from the central furnace body. The furnace body (1081) was lined with clay 20-40 mm thick, which was cracked, spalled and burnt red, and formed a hollow cylinder with a diameter of 0.45 m, tapering slightly towards the base. The north-west side of the lining had been broken down into the raking pit.

The fill of the furnace chamber (1068) was a pinkish brown silty clay with unsorted pebbles, charcoal flecks, fragments of kiln lining and pieces of slag. The base of the fill contained one large piece of slag, measuring 250 by 250 by 90 mm.

The oval raking pit was 1.8 m long and 0.34 m deep, but its original width could not be determined. It had been cut into the upper part of the furnace body, presumably to extract the iron bloom. Over a thin primary fill (1069), there was a dark greyish fill with slag, pottery and a huge quantity of charcoal (484 g) consisting entirely of oak (1072).

Furnace 2

Furnace 2 was located a few metres away from Furnace 1, and was of a similar form (Fig 2.42, Plate 9). The furnace pit (1087) had a diameter of 1.26 m and a surviving depth of 0.37 m (Fig 2.44, S. 25-27). The flat base of the pit was scorched red. The furnace pit and body (1088) were similar to those of Furnace 1, and the clay lining was likewise scorched red and cracked. The fill of the chamber (1089) contained fragments of kiln lining and pieces of slag, with several larger lumps of slag towards the base.

The north-west side of the lining had been broken down into the raking pit (1023) which was 1.8 m long, 1.50 m wide, and 0.45 m deep. The primary fill (1100) was a mid yellow-brown silty clay, deposited against the

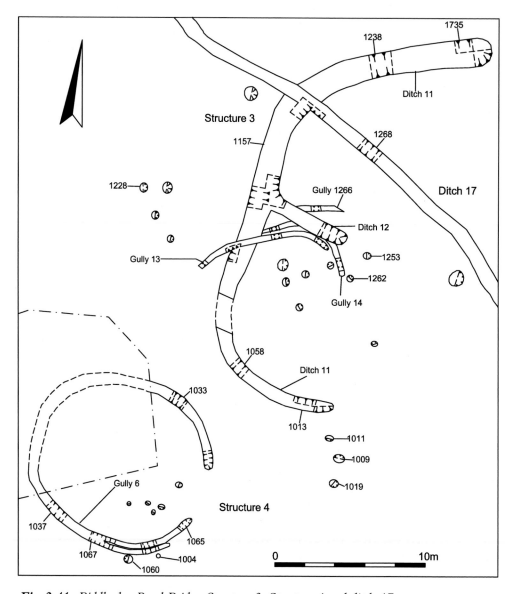

Fig. 2.41: *Biddlesden Road Bridge, Structure 3, Structure 4 and ditch 17.*

Plate 8: *Biddlesden Road Bridge. Iron smelting Furnace 1. The partly exposed firing chamber lies within the pit to the fore. The rake-out pit is cut by ditch 17 on the left.*

Plate 9: *Biddlesden Road Bridge. Iron smelting Furnace 2 under excavation.*

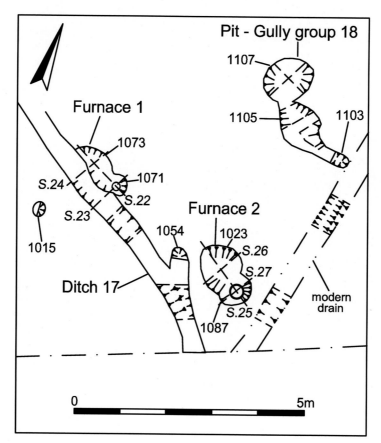

Fig. 2.42: *Biddlesden Road Bridge, Furnaces 1 and 2, and pit and gully group 18.*

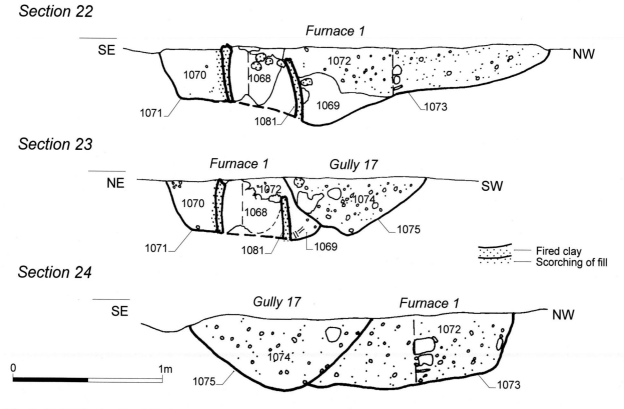

Fig. 2.43: *Biddlesden Road Bridge, Furnace 1 sections 22, 23 and 24.*

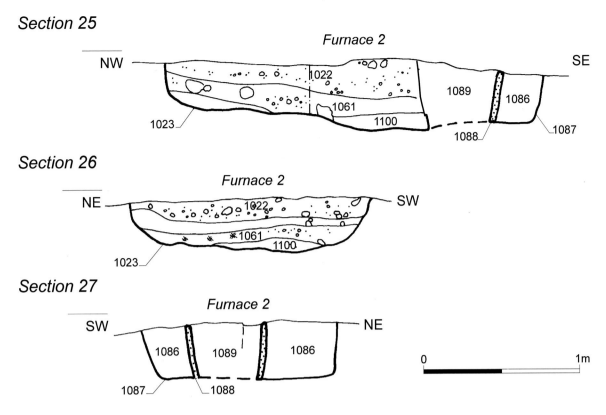

Fig. 2.44: *Biddlesden Road Bridge, Furnace 2 sections 25, 26 and 27.*

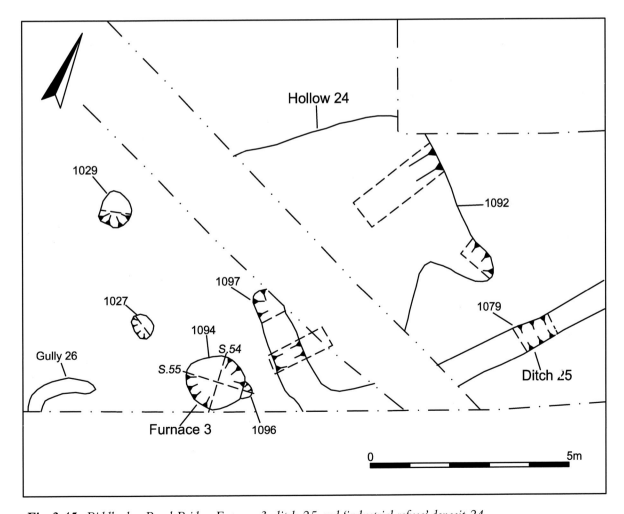

Fig. 2.45: *Biddlesden Road Bridge, Furnace 3, ditch 25 and 'industrial refuse' deposit 24.*

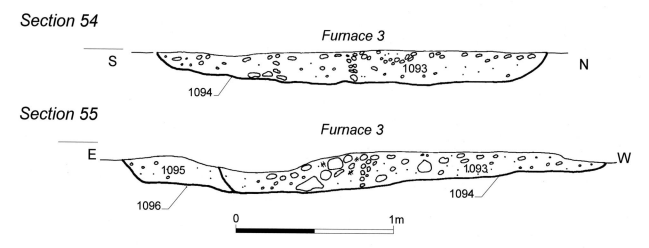

Fig. 2.46: *Biddlesden Road Bridge, Furnace 3 sections 54 and 55.*

broken side of the kiln body. The secondary fill (1061) was a dark greyish brown silty clay, with lenses of black slag and with oak being the dominant charcoal. This was overlain by a greyish brown soil (1022).

Pits and gully group 18

Close to Furnaces 1 and 2 there were two oval pits, 1105 and 1107, and a curvilinear gully, 1103 (Fig 2.42). The exact shape of the individual components and the relationship between them was unclear as the dark grey/black silts fills were identical in all three. The pits were similar in size, both c 2.0 m long, 1.5 m wide and 0.30 m deep with concave sides and bases. Their long axes may have been oriented at right-angles.

Gully 1103 ran south from the edge of pit 1105, and was only 0.13 m deep. It may have run northwards between the pits as a flat-based and vertically sided slot, 0.50 m wide, cut to the same depth as the pits. The purpose of this group of features is unknown but they were probably associated with iron smelting or secondary working. Two similar features, Groups 9 and 10, lay to the north-west, close to Structure 1, see above.

Furnace 3

This furnace lay further east (Fig 2.36). It had been heavily truncated by ploughing and only the base of the raking pit and the basal packing of the furnace survived (Fig 2.45).

The furnace pit, 1096, had a diameter of 1.05 m and a surviving depth of 0.18 m (Fig 2.46, S.54 and 55). The form of the original cut could not be accurately determined, but it had a flat base and the sides appear to have been steeply sloping. The packing material (1095) was a yellowish brown silty clay with a C-shaped scorched patch near the centre, evidence for the likely presence of the kiln body above. This material was similar to that used in the construction of the other two furnaces.

The furnace pit was cut on its western side by the raking pit 1094. This was an oval cut surviving to a depth of 0.21 m. The fill (1093) was dark greyish brown silt with large quantities of slag, including a piece that may have come from the base of the kiln.

Industrial refuse; hollow 24

To the north of Furnace 3 there was an irregular hollow, with an ill-defined, shallow slope and an irregular base, measuring 12 m by 7 m and 0.4 m deep (Fig 2.45, 1092). It was filled with dark grey/black silty clay containing slag, charcoal flecks, and burnt cobbles (1091), indicating that it had been used for dumping smelting refuse. Due to persistent flooding, the sections were not fully excavated or drawn.

Curvilinear gully 26

Near Furnace 3 there was a 2.5 m length of curvilinear gully with a rounded eastern terminal (Fig 2.45, 1099). It was up to 0.71 m wide and 0.15 m deep. Its dark fill (1098) contained some slag.

Pit group 28

Three pits were situated close to Furnace 3 (Fig 2.45; 1027, 1029, 1085). It is possible they were associated in some way with the process of converting iron ore. All were circular, and not very deep.

Pit 1027, the smallest of the group, was 1.20 m in diameter by 0.21 m deep, with variable sides sloping to a flat base. The fill (1026) was dark containing many burnt pebbles and a moderate quantity of mostly small lumps of iron slag. There was no evidence for in situ burning. Pit 1029 was the largest, at 1.40 m in diameter by 0.32 m deep. The sides were steep coming down onto a gently concave base. The northern edge of the pit was scorched red. The fill (1028) was dark, and contained burnt pebbles, charcoal and moderate quantities of slag. The in situ burning suggests that it had an industrial use, although it is possible that the disposal of hot waste material could have scorched the sides. Another pit further to the east, pit 1085, was similar to pit 1027, and had a fill (1084) with a high charcoal content and containing burnt pebbles and slag fragments. There was no evidence for in situ burning.

Ditch 25

A ditch on the eastern side of the site may have been a settlement boundary, but beyond the excavated area to the east it was not observed in the watching brief and did not appear in the geophysical survey (Fig 2.36). It was generally 0.20 m deep with a broad U-shaped profile, and to the south-west it terminated after an abrupt right-angled turn (Fig 2.45). The terminal was 0.26 m deep and the south-western edge of the ditch was scorched red (Fig 2.43, 1097). The fill near the terminal was dark with inclusions of slag, burnt clay and pebbles and charcoal. Further east the fill faded to a greyish brown.

AREA G SYRESHAM (PIMLICO): IRON AGE AND ROMAN OCCUPATION

Introduction

Geophysical survey and trial trenching were carried out in an area of 15.5 ha lying between Biddlesden Road, Syresham and Whitfield, which was to be used for permanent soil disposal: Area G in the mitigation strategy (Fig 1.3). It comprised two parts: Field A to the south of a stream known as The Brook, which is a tributary of the River Great Ouse (Fig 2.47), and Fields B, C, D and E to the north of the stream (Fig 2.48). The results of the archaeological work were used to inform suitable measures to preserve the archaeological remains under the re-instated ground.

The underlying geology here is shown as Blisworth Limestone, with Upper Estuarine Series sands, silts and clays on the lower ground. Fieldwork showed the limestone to be covered in a thin clay deposit in most places. The ground generally sloped down towards The Brook in each area. The only surface feature of archaeological interest was a small area (0.3 ha) of medieval ridge-and-furrow, which survived as earthworks in the south-eastern corner of Field B. The earthworks had suffered some erosion from The Brook as well as by more recent agricultural activity. Immediately to the north, light scatters of flints, medieval, Roman and unidentifiable pottery were recovered during surface collecting as part of fieldwork in advance of road construction (Audouy and Sharman 1993, Fields 3, 5, & 6).

The archaeological programme comprised a geophysical survey covering a 10% sample of the site (NA 2001b), followed by trial trenching covering about 1% of the area. In the event, this sample proved inadequate to define the areas of archaeological significance, and an additional 6 ha of geophysical survey was subsequently undertaken to identify the extent of the remains found (Fig 2.51).

The initial geophysical survey sample produced useful, but on the whole inconclusive results. Most of the sample meshes were subsumed into the wider survey which provides a far more comprehensive view of the archaeological remains, and for this reason the results of the initial survey are not included in this report.

Trial Excavation

A total of thirty-two trenches were positioned to investigate the potential archaeological features found in the geophysical survey, and also to investigate blank areas (Figs 2.47 & 2.48). Ten trenches produced evidence for prehistoric and Roman activity (Trenches 4-6, 9-11, 22, 23, 29 and 31). A further seven revealed traces of ridge-and-furrow cultivation.

Trenches 4 – 6: Iron Age Enclosure

The trenches in Field A (Figs 2.47 and 2.49) were positioned to investigate a rectangular feature revealed by the geophysical survey, tentatively interpreted at the time as the foundations of a building. Excavation revealed that much of the signal was caused by geological variation, which comprised outcrops of limestone and reddish clay. However, part of the geophysical anomaly proved to be a small Iron Age enclosure, probably of sub-rectangular form, approximately 10-15 m across with a south-facing entrance.

The rounded terminal on the eastern side of the entrance was 1.2 m wide and 1.0 m deep (Fig 2.49; 412, S.22). It had a steeply sloping, U-shaped profile that was slightly stepped up at the terminal. The terminal cut a small, undated oval pit, 413. Part of the northern circuit of the enclosure was 1.0 m wide by 1.0 m deep, with a steeply sloping, almost vertical sided, rounded V-shaped profile (Fig 2.49; 516, S 20 and 21). The fills of both excavated ditch lengths contained Iron Age pottery, animal bone fragments and burnt rounded cobbles. The evaluation did not reveal any internal features.

Trench 6 contained a circular posthole, 621, 0.24 m deep with a diameter of 0.40 m, and a shallow linear gully, 620. The gully was 0.6 m wide and 0.17 m deep, and contained Iron Age pottery. Both features were cut into a buried soil horizon (619) that extended across the entire trench and was at least 0.21 m thick. The base of a truncated jar was found embedded in this deposit. There appeared to be no physical association between these features and the small enclosure.

Trenches 9, 29 and 31: Buried soils

Trench 9 was situated in an area of level ground at the base of the south-facing slope in Field B (Fig 2.48), immediately south of the ridge-and-furrow earthworks. A buried soil horizon, up to 0.62 m thick at the eastern end of the trench, and petering out 18.0 m further west, lay under 0.70 m of colluvium. The deposit contained charcoal flecks and a single grog-tempered sherd of Roman pottery.

Buried soils of a greyish cast and lying beneath up to 1.4 m of colluvium were also found in trenches 29 and 31 (Field E). The trenches here were cut into a natural depression running towards The Brook. No dating evidence was retrieved from this horizon, although a sherd of Roman pottery came from the upper colluvium in trench 31.

Trench 10: Roman gullies

The most substantial feature in trench 10, field C, was a ditch crossing the trench at its northern end (Figs 2.48 & 2.50, 1029). The ditch was 1.3 m wide and 0.45 m deep. A darker layer within its fill contained fragments of bone and Roman pottery dating to the later second to third centuries AD.

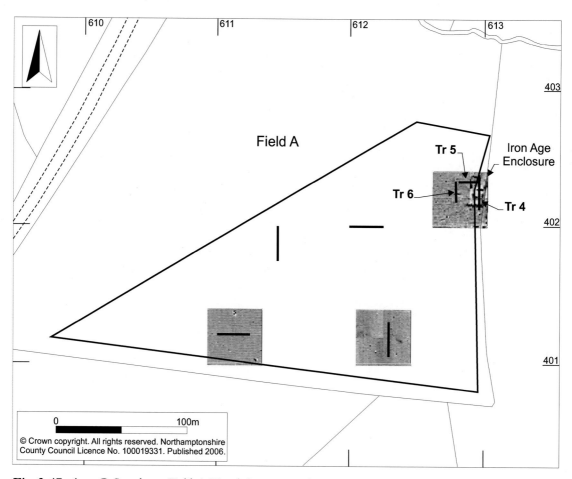

Fig. 2.47: Area G Syresham, Field A. Trench locations and magnetometer survey.

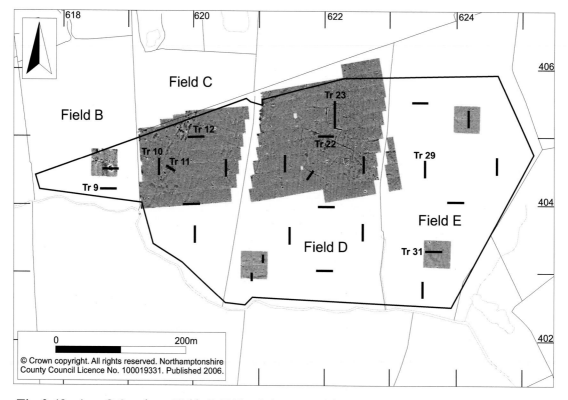

Fig. 2.48: Area G Syresham, Fields B-E. Trench locations and magnetometer survey.

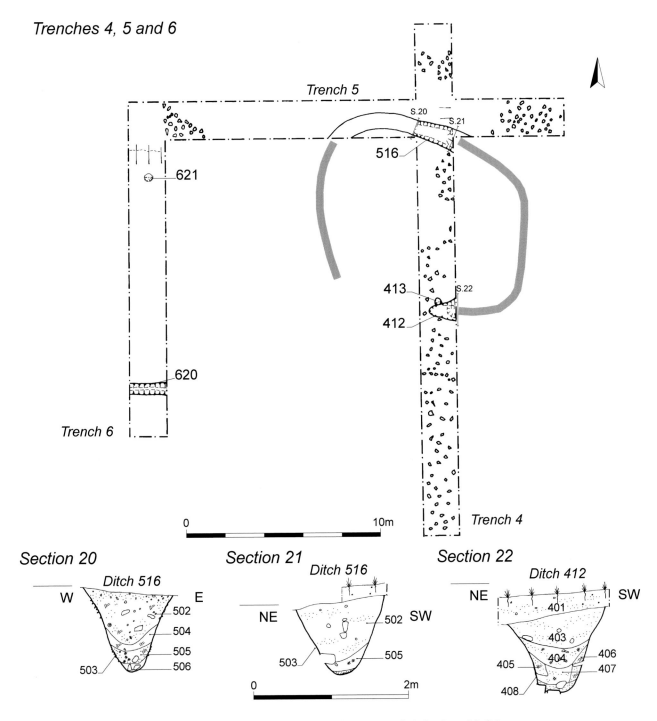

Fig. 2.49: *Area G Syresham, Field A. Iron Age enclosure, trenches 4, 5 and 6. Sections 20-24.*

In the central area of the trench there was a complex sequence of shallow gullies, many of which contained quantities of Roman pottery dating to around the second century (Fig 2.50, 1036-1039). The earliest of these, 1038, was aligned north-south, and was 7.8 m long and 0.7 m wide with a shallow concave profile. As well as pottery, there was a bone pin (102) and an iron band (Fig 4.11, 73) in the fill. This feature was re-cut by an almost identical gully, 1037, which contained a number of iron objects (74, 75, 77 & 80), a bone pin (103) and an intaglio (Fig 4.21, 101). The later features were successive curvilinear gullies, 1036 and 1039, which were 0.20 m deep, and contained large quantities of Roman pottery.

Partly overlying the earliest gully and extending beyond the eastern trench edge, was a thin layer of mid brown soil containing Roman pottery and bone. This may have been a rudimentary surface.

Trench 11: Roman ditch

This trench, just east of trench 10, investigated a linear anomaly, running on a north-east to south-west alignment, detected by the geophysical survey (Figs 2.48 & 2.51). Excavation revealed a ditch 1.25 m wide and 0.58 m deep. On either side there were shallow remnant cuts suggesting an earlier phase (or phases) of the ditch. Two sherds of probable first century pottery and a piece of vessel glass

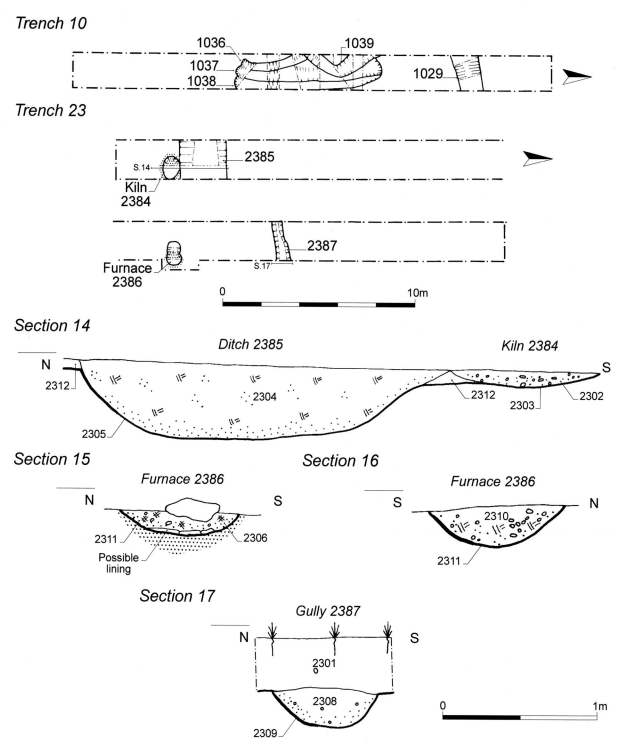

Fig. 2.50: *Area G Syresham, Field C. Roman occupation, trench 10; Roman pottery kiln and iron smelting furnace, trench 23. Sections 14-17.*

came from one ditch, pottery of second century date came from the other.

Trench 22: Roman gully

The only archaeological feature in this trench, in the middle of field D, was the terminal of a linear gully, 0.50 m wide and 0.19 m deep, aligned north-west to south-east (Fig 2.48). The gully yielded animal bone and slag fragments, and pottery sherds of Roman date.

Trench 23: Roman ditches, pottery kiln and iron smelting furnace

This trench was positioned to investigate two linear features, running east-west, and a group of discrete anomalies, all found in the geophysical survey (Fig 2.50). In the north of the trench there was a shallow gully, about 0.5 m wide and 0.23 m deep, which contained 12 sherds of second century Roman pottery (Fig 2.50, 2387). To the south was a more substantial ditch, 2385, 2.4 m wide and 0.49

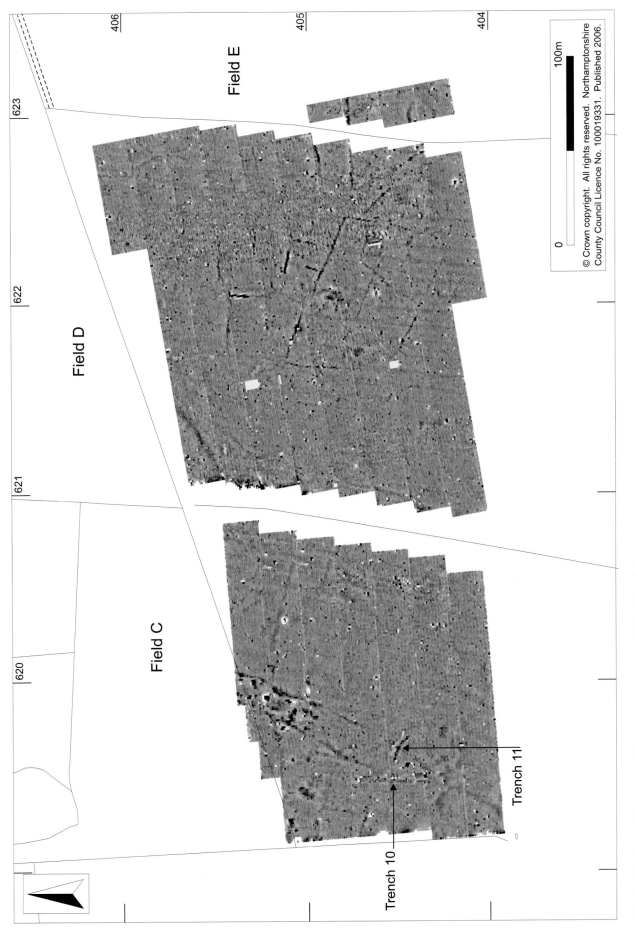

Fig. 2.51: Area G Syresham, Magnetometer survey, Fields C and D.

m deep, containing sherds of first century Roman pottery and bone (Fig 2.50, S.14). All the features were cut into a buried soil horizon, which extended across the entire trench and was at least 0.1 m thick.

On the southern edge of ditch 2385 there were the remains of a heavily truncated pottery kiln, 2384). This comprised a shallow circular cut, 0.8 m in diameter, filled with a deposit of charcoal, Roman pottery sherds and the fragments of several kiln bars. The surrounding natural substrate into which the kiln was cut was scorched red.

An iron smelting furnace, 2386, was also found, corresponding to one of the discrete geophysical anomalies (Fig 2.50, S.15 and 16). This consisted of a circular pit with a diameter of 0.8 m and surviving depth of 0.12 m, containing a black fill with charcoal and two large fragments of slag. This was cut by a roughly circular raking pit, 0.6 m in diameter and 0.17 m deep, which also contained charcoal, burnt clay and slag.

Extended geophysical survey

The extended geophysical survey was undertaken in Fields C, D and E where the extent of Roman activity had proved difficult to define from the earlier work (Fig 2.51).

Field C
Archaeological features are largely limited to the western side of the field where there is a pair of parallel ditches and groups of chaotic readings to the north and south. There is also a fainter linear anomaly running at right-angles in the northern part of the field. The eastern linear ditch was sectioned in trench 11, above, and is probably of first to second century date. The western ditch, 15-20 m away, joins a rectangular enclosure which extends westward beyond the field. The enclosure ditch was examined in trench 10 (Ditch 1029) and yielded later second/third century pottery. South of the enclosure ditch were recorded a number of re-cut gullies yielding pottery of mainly second century date, and other finds. These may have been house gullies, but there is no pattern of features visible on the geophysical survey plot. A group of chaotic readings to the south may indicate associated activity of some sort, and it may be significant that a lump of tap slag came from one of the gullies in trench 10. The anomalies could therefore represent industrial activity in the form of pits or even small furnaces.

The northern area of chaotic readings seems likely to represent a zone of archaeological features of an industrial nature. Furnaces characteristically show up as anomalies with both high positive and negative values in a concentric pattern.

Fields D and E
This area shows a clear sub-rectangular enclosure and various linear features to the north and east which may represent other enclosures or fields. The sub-rectangular enclosure measures about 80 m by 60 m. It appears incomplete on the western side, although the ground here might simply have been unresponsive. There appears to be an entrance on the eastern side marked by short

out-flaring ditch terminals and some disturbance, perhaps activity immediately inside the entrance. The enclosure is sub-divided by ditches. Further activity within the enclosure is represented by pit-like anomalies.

Running east is another linear feature perhaps the north-west corner of another enclosure, but this interpretation is tentative. There are other ditches in this area and beyond the modern field boundary (in Field E) would appear to be a small circular enclosure with a diameter of 10-15 m and an entrance facing east.

To the north of the large enclosure there would appear to be the indistinct remains of a pattern of enclosure ditches. Trench 23 identified probable first and second century gullies here, the northern of which is more distinct on the survey plot. A pottery kiln and an iron-smelting furnace were discovered in this trench, but they are not readily identifiable on the survey. It appears likely that the clearly defined sections of ditches in this area contain dumps of industrial debris which show up well on geophysical survey while other remains are too subtle to be clear.

Lengths of ditch on the western side of the mesh are not associated with the enclosures in the central area and are of uncertain date. The trace of a ditch along the field margin may relate to the land divisions in Field D, to which it is orientated. The ditch in the north-west corner may be unrelated to the Roman occupation.

BRACKLEY HATCH 4: ROMAN POTTERY PRODUCING SITE

Introduction

The site lay at the southern end of the Syresham bypass section of the route on Boulder Clay substrata (Fig 1.3). It comprised a generally sparse scatter of ditches and pits, some minor features and two pottery kilns (Fig 2.52). The extended geophysical survey shows the site to have been extensive, with the excavated area probably towards the margin of the settlement (Fig 2.53). The overall pattern of features is unclear, but the site probably included buildings, virtually all trace of which has been lost. On the basis of statigraphy and pottery, three phases are shown for the excavated area (Figs 2.54-2.56).

A large assemblage of pottery was recovered, for the most part dating to the second and third centuries AD. These included jars and bowls in sandy grog-tempered fabric which appear to have been made on the site.

Phase 1 (second century AD): south-western enclosure

The earliest feature, gully 39, was a small, flat-based, curving feature on the southern edge of the site (Fig 2.54). It contained a few sherds of second century pottery. This was cut by gully 41, a feature of similar character and date, which was cut by ditch 48.

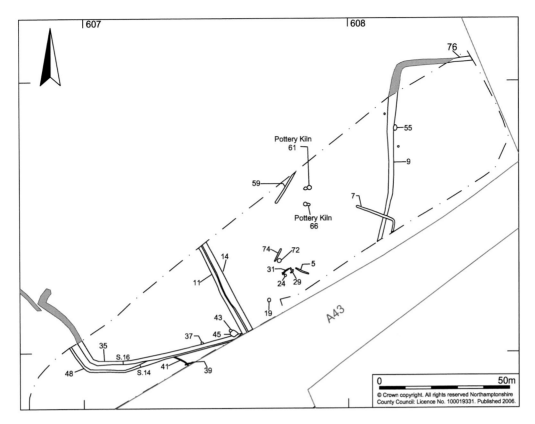

Figs. 2.52: *Brackley Hatch 4, site plan.*

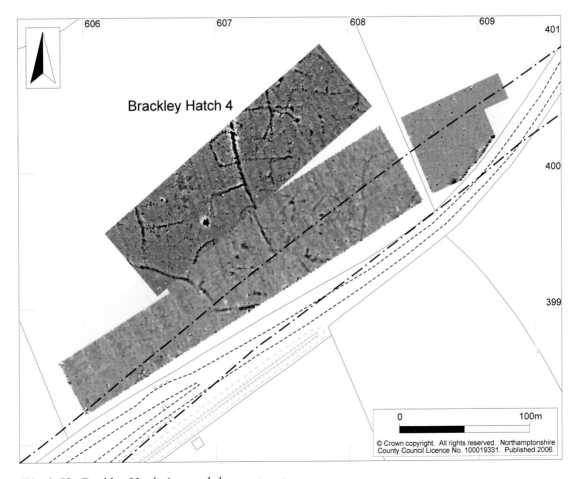

Fig. 2.53: *Brackley Hatch 4, extended magnetometer survey.*

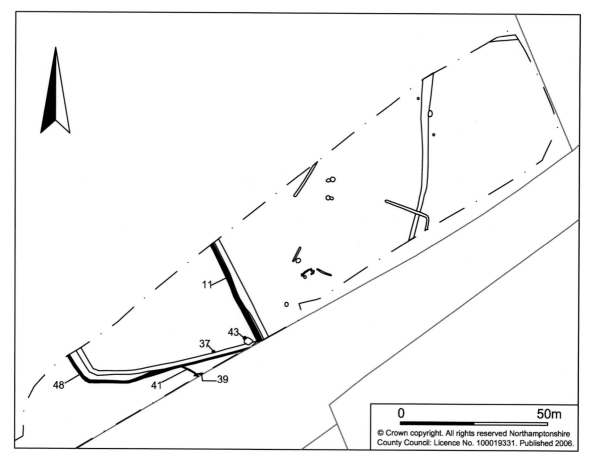

Fig. 2.54: Brackley Hatch 4, Phase 1 (early to mid second century AD).

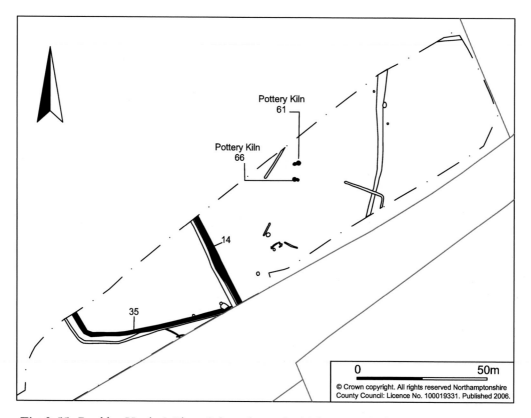

Fig. 2.55: Brackley Hatch 4, Phase 2 (second to early third century AD).

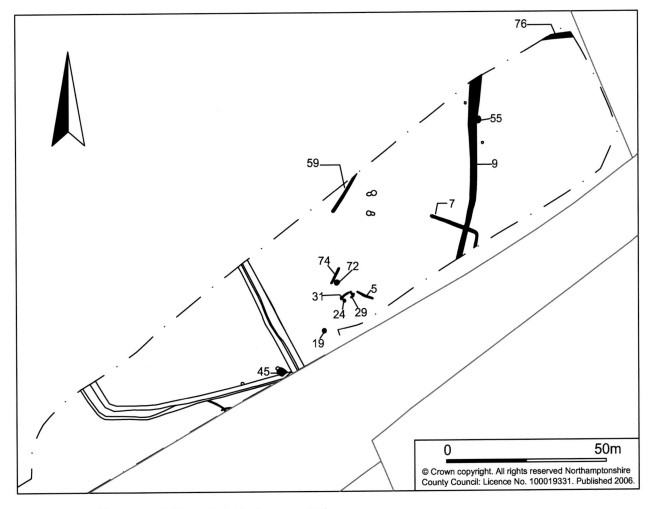

Fig. 2.56: *Brackley Hatch 4, Phases 2-3 (third century AD).*

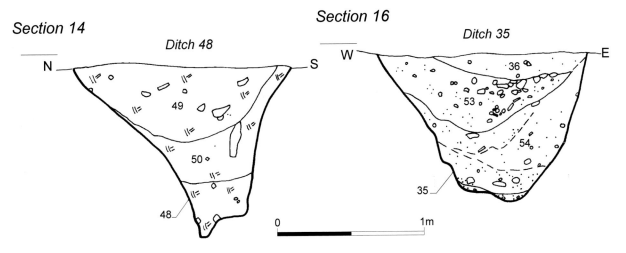

Fig. 2.57: *Brackley Hatch 4, Ditch 48 and Ditch 35, sections.*

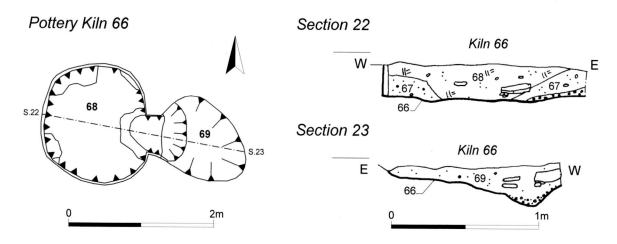

Fig. 2.58: Brackley Hatch 4, Pottery Kiln 66, plan and sections.

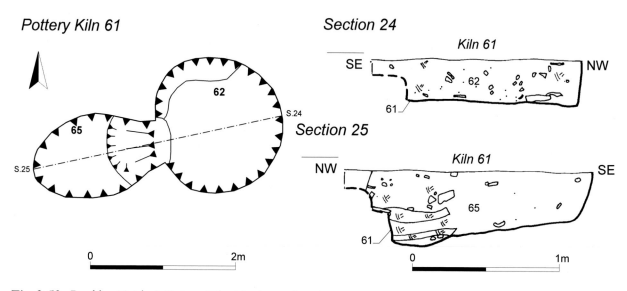

Fig. 2.59: Brackley Hatch 4, Pottery Kiln 61, plan and sections.

Ditch 48 ran east to west across the site for about 70 m before turning northward. It probably formed the southern and western boundaries of a polygonal enclosure, measuring c 60m east to west. Ditch 48 had a relatively narrow and deep, almost vertically-sided, V-shaped profile, measuring 1.3 m wide by 0.75-0.9 m deep (Fig 2.57, S.14). The lower fill (50) was a light brown silt-clay containing large quantities of pottery and animal bone. This was overlain by a darker, grey-brown silt-clay (49), also containing large quantities of domestic refuse. The total quantity of pottery from the excavated sections was about 4 kg, all of second century date.

Ditch 11, to the south-east, probably formed the eastern side of the enclosure. It was less substantial than ditch 48, measuring 1.3 m wide and 0.46 m deep, with a U-shaped profile. The lower fill was a light brown silt-clay without finds. The upper fill was a stonier, dark greyish brown silt-clay containing some pottery dated to the second century, kiln lining and animal bone.

There were two associated pits. pit 37, close to ditch 48, was 1.2 m in diameter and 0.5 m deep with nearly vertical

sides and a flat base. It was filled with a light brown silt-clay, which contained a sherd of pottery and some animal bone. Pit 43 was very close to the corner of ditches 48 and 11, and was 0.9 m in diameter and 0.46 m deep with sloping sides and a rounded base. It was filled with a light brown, relatively stony silt-clay containing some pottery.

Phase 2 (second to early third century AD): south-western enclosure and pottery kilns

The enclosure ditches were re-cut (Fig 2.55). Ditch 35, to the west, was 1.5-1.7 m wide and 0.9-1.0 m deep with steep sides and a rounded base (Fig 2.57, S.16). It yielded the largest quantity of pottery of any feature on the site, a total of 8.1 kg. Two samples taken during the evaluation (ev 1 and ev 2) contained primarily charred grain, probably being processed grain discarded amongst household waste, since pottery was abundant in this feature The primary fill was a light brown silt-clay (54) and was overlain by a dark grey fill (53) with abundant charcoal and domestic debris. Near the southern edge of the site there was a horse burial

(70 and 71). The upper fill (36) was a lighter clayey silt. Near the south-east edge of the site the ditch was cut by a large possible quarry pit (45).

Ditch 14, to the east, was a substantial ditch, 2.9 m wide and 0.8 m deep. The lower part of the cut was narrow, as a result of cutting through a limestone outcrop, and the fill within this deeper section was without finds. Above this the cut was broader, with a flat ledge onto the limestone. Above this, the main fill was a light brown silt-clay which contained some pot and animal bones. The final fill was darker, also with pottery and bone. All the pottery is dated to the second and early third centuries.

Kiln 66

This comprised a circular firing-chamber, 68, 1.3 m in diameter, with a flue to the south-east leading to an irregular bowl-shaped rake-out pit, 69 (Figs 2.55 & 2.58). The feature survived only to a depth of 0.25 m. The walls of the firing-chamber and flue were partly lined with thin limestone slabs. The natural clay floor and walls were scorched red.

A thin layer of ash and charcoal (67) lay on the floor of the firing-chamber, and was overlain by the main fill (68) of light brown clay mixed with abundant pottery and kiln debris, probably representing a mixture of collapsed kiln structure and a dump of refuse after the kiln had gone out of use. The rake-out pit contained a dark, charcoal-rich fill (69) with a similar range of material present.

Kiln 61

This was of a similar form to Kiln 66, but slightly larger, 1.5 m in diameter, and with an elongated rake-out pit on the western side (Fig 2.59). The firing-chamber was filled with light brown silt-clay (62) containing abundant pottery and kiln debris. The fill of the rake-out pit (65) was a dark grey silt-clay, with a similar range and quantity of material.

The pot kiln firing chamber and rake-out pits did not produce particularly rich samples, but the overall ratio of grain to chaff to weed seeds (3 : 1 : 5), suggests that crop processing waste had probably been used as kindling.

Gullies and pits north-east of the enclosure: Phase 2-3 (second/third centuries AD):

A cluster of gullies and pits lay to the north-east of the ditched enclosure. The gullies were generally about 0.3 m wide, less than 0.1 m deep, with vertical sides and flat bases (Fig 2.56; 5, 29, 31 and 74). It is possible that they were beam slots. The pits varied in size between around 1.0 m in diameter and 0.6 m deep (19 and 72). The postholes were about 0.3 m in diameter and 0.14-0.24 m deep (27).

The small and shallow features here may represent the remains of structures which have been largely lost to the plough. An evaluation trench in this area also identified a shallow gully and a possible posthole with some spreads of rubble, interpreted as remnant structures. Small quantities of pottery, dating to the second and third centuries, were recovered from a number of the features. Several phases

of activity may be represented, but the features are too fragmentary to interpret.

Phase 3 (third century AD): ditches and gullies in north-eastern area and Pit 45 in south-western area

Ditches 9 and 76 were parts of a single ditch system that ran north and then turned abruptly to the east (Figs 2.52 and 2.56). Ditch 9, between 2.0 and 1.3 m wide, and 0.55 to 0.7 m deep, was widest to the north. It generally had moderately sloping sides and a flat base. A slot in the base of the ditch was found in the north and south, but not in the middle. Ditch 76 was 2.5 m wide and 0.65 m deep. They each had a mid to dark grey brown clay-silt fill which yielded some pottery of third century date and animal bone. Kiln lining also came from Ditch 9.

Gully 7 ran from a western terminal for 15 m, cutting ditch 9, and then turned a right angle south, and continued beyond the limit of excavation. It was 0.5 m wide and just 0.12 m deep with a fill containing some pottery dated to the third century.

Ditch 59 was a linear feature running north-east to south-west about 40 m west of ditch 9, to a terminal. It was 1.0 m wide and 0.3 m deep with sharp sides and a flat base. Its fill was a light brown silt-clay containing some pottery.

Pit 55 was 1.5 m in diameter and 0.3 m deep with sloping sides and a flat base. t was filled with a light grey silt-clay containing pottery and animal bone. It cut Ditch 9. Two possible postholes lay nearby.

A large sub-circular pit 45 was 1.8 m in diameter and 0.95 m deep with rather irregular sides and base. The primary fill was a dark grey-brown silt-clay. This was overlain by a dark brown silt-clay containing some pottery, generally of second century date, kiln lining and bone. The pit cut the partly filled ditch 35 and pit 43, and was therefore the latest feature in the south-western part of the site.

The overlying hillwash/ploughsoil had partly filled the top of this pit and the adjacent ditch. Elsewhere it was generally around 0.10 m deep, deepening towards the southern edge of the site. It contained one of the largest assemblages of pottery from the site (3.5 kg) with a date range from the third to fourth centuries, together with four post-medieval sherds.

COTTISFORD TURN, TUSMORE: IRON AGE PIT ALIGNMENT

Introduction

The site lay on the limestone upland opposite the junction of the Cottisford road with the A43 (see Fig 1.3). It comprised a linear alignment of pits and segments of ditch running approximately north to south, which were traced for a distance of nearly 50 m within the land-take of the road corridor (Fig 2.60 & Plate 10). The pits were not traced north or south of the road corridor during the Watching Brief and the true length of this feature is

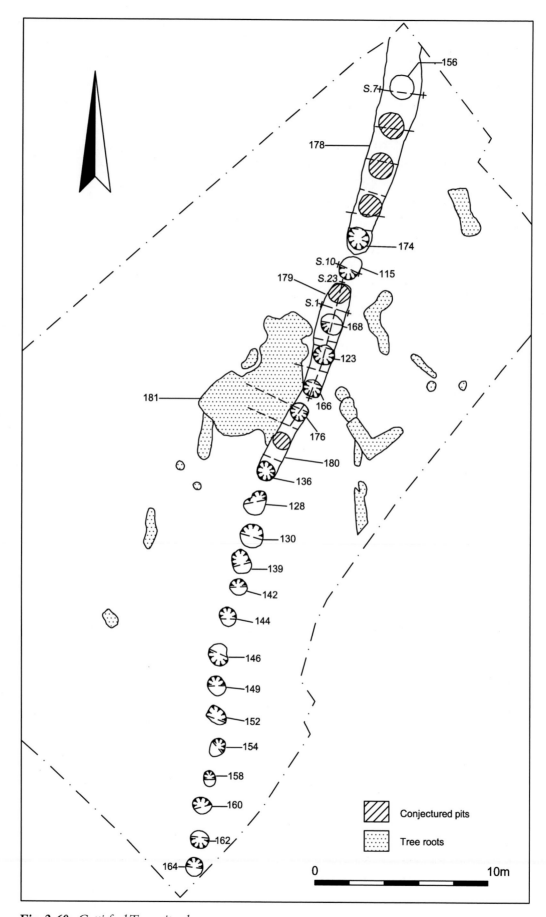

Fig. 2.60: *Cottisford Turn, site plan.*

Plate 10: *Cottisford Turn. Ditch and pit alignment, looking south from ditch 178.*

Plate 11: *Cottisford Turn. Pit 139.*

Plate 12: *Cottisford Turn. Terminal of ditch 180 and underlying pit 136.*

therefore unknown. That it was not found to the south, under the former road, is unsurprising, but the lack of evidence for a continuation to the north in the balancing pond area is, and may suggest that the alignment never continued this far north, perhaps either terminating at, or short of, the former stream here (Ockley Brook), or turning eastward onto a new alignment.

Excavation showed that where the ditch segments were present they cut earlier pits, and therefore two phases of activity are represented. There were no other features on the site other than several tree-root holes. Several of these were shown to pre-date the ditch/pit alignment. An area of root disturbance obscured part of the ditches in the central part of the site. The soil in both features was very similar, perhaps indicating that they may have been filled at the same time. It is possible that the tree here was integrated into the original alignment of the pits, perhaps serving as a marker.

Pits

The alignment was not quite straight, following a slightly sinuous course (Fig 2.60). One possibility is that to the south it comprised groups of three or four pits each slightly offset and on a slightly different alignment to its neighbouring group. In particular, there appears to have been a more abrupt shift in direction between Pits 136 and Pit 176, perhaps to accommodate a tree that had stood in feature 181.

The pits were quite regularly and closely spaced at distances of between 1.5 m and 2.0 m centre to centre. In the section re-cut as by ditch lengths, there were gaps of

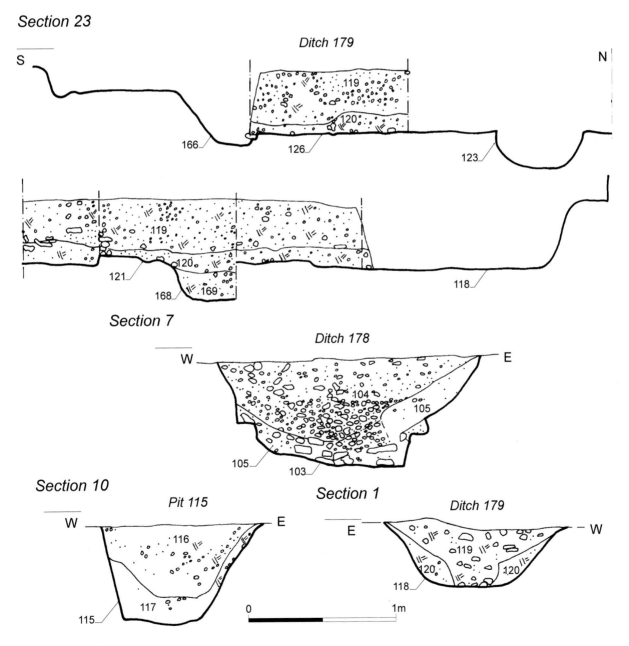

Fig. 2.61: *Cottisford Turn, sections 1, 10, 7 and 63.*

4.0 m, 3.4 m and 9.0 m between the visible remains of the pits, suggesting that the alignment was originally complete and regular, and that six pits had been completely removed by the ditches.

Twenty-one pits were examined. Eight of these were truncated by later ditches and their overall dimensions were not recoverable, although they would appear to have been similar to the undisturbed examples, which were roughly circular, between 0.7 m and 1.3 m in diameter (average 1.0 m). One pit to the south, 160, was exceptionally shallow at 0.26 m deep, but the rest were generally 0.50-0.60 m deep. The northernmost pit (156), whose base survived beneath ditch 178, would have been about 0.80 m deep, the deepest pit on the site.

The pits were all filled with compact and moderately stony light brown silt loam. The lower quarter to third of each fill tended to be a lighter colour with a more clayey consistency, as a primary filling by natural weathering and erosion. The upper fill was generally stonier (Fig 2.61, S.10; Plate 11). The sequence of increasing shell concentration in samples 14 to 16from pit 115 showed that the pit filled slowly and developed its own fauna of snails (Robinson, Chapter 6).

Finds were very sparse. Small sherds of pottery were retrieved from the upper fills of pits 130 and 162, and fragments of bone from pits 160, 156 and 144. A flint scraper and a flint flake also came from pit 144. The pottery is not chronologically diagnostic but is early Iron Age in character.

Sediment samples for luminescence dating were taken from pits 158 and 164. The sample from pit 164 was analysed but the results proved to be unreliable (Appendix 1). A fragment of cattle bone from pit 160 was submitted for radiocarbon dating. The result was 386-200 cal BC (95% confidence, 2232 +/- 24 BP, NZA 16362) placing the silting of the pit within the middle Iron Age (Appendix 1).

Ditches

The three ditch segments, 178, 179 and 180, were restricted to the northern end of the alignment. Ditch 178, to the north, was the longest and deepest (Fig 2.61, S. 7). It was in excess of 13 m long, 1.2 -1.7 m wide and 0.55-0.70 m deep, widening and deepened towards the north. The bases of two pits, 156 and 174, were recorded in the base of the ditch.

Ditch 179 was 6.5 m long, 1.1-1.2 m wide and 0.40-0.45 m deep (Fig 2.61. S.1 and 23), and cut pits 166, 123 and 168. Ditch 180, to the south, was 5 m long, 0.95-1.2 m wide and 0.45-0.56 m deep, cutting pits 136 and 176 (Plate 12). All the ditches were of a similar form with steep sides and flat bases. The well-defined terminals were evidently deliberately positioned directly over pits.

Above a thin primary fill of clayey silt, all the ditches were filled with a very stony silt loam, which may suggest that they were rapidly backfilled, either through the deliberate levelling of an adjacent bank or by deep ploughing. There is a suggestion from the northernmost section (Fig 2.61,

S.7) of a relatively stone-free final fill, perhaps representing a more stable period of natural silting.

There are indications therefore that the ditches had a relatively short existence. However, it is possible that the absence of deep primary silting was the result of periodic cleaning out. Several of the sections show more substantial primary silts on the edges of the ditches, a situation which could have arisen through cleaning out the central portion of the ditch.

The only finds from any of the ditch segments were a few fragments of pot and bone from the main fill (104) of ditch 178.

TUSMORE DRAIN OUTFALL AND PARK:
IRON AGE AND ROMAN OCCUPATION

Introduction

The circumstances of the archaeological work at this site were related to the reconfiguration and re-cutting of an existing drainage ditch along the edge of the Scheduled Ancient Monument of Tusmore Park Deserted Medieval Village (Oxfordshire No. 103, National Monument No. 28141), for which consent was granted subject to conditions of archaeological monitoring and investigation (NA 2001d) (see Fig 1.3). The scheduled area includes the earthworks of the former settlement, although they lie at some distance from the new drain. The extension beyond the southern end of the new drain entailed regrading the existing drain on the southern field boundary to a depth of 0.3 m. While this extended into the area of earthworks, this aspect of the work had no effect on archaeological deposits and will not be discussed further.

The drainage works involved the excavation of 230 m of new pipe trench from the A43, 100 m of which was within the boundary of the scheduled monument (Fig 2.62). The trench itself was 0.6 m wide and 2.0 m deep, although the work took place within a 6 m-wide easement which was the object of archaeological attention. An initial field inspection was undertaken to identify any archaeological remains or earthworks, followed by the topsoil stripping under archaeological control of the pipe-easement.

Iron Age ditch

The evidence for Iron Age occupation came from a single ditch running approximately east to west. It was 1.7 m wide and 0.3 m deep. The 4 m of excavated section contained 47 sherds of pottery of probable early Iron Age date, together with a small quantity of animal bone and slag. A collection of Roman pottery of second to third century date came from the topsoil, and a single sherd from a possible posthole at the southern end of the trench in an area of tree-root disturbances. The results indicated both Iron Age and Roman occupation of undefined character in the vicinity.

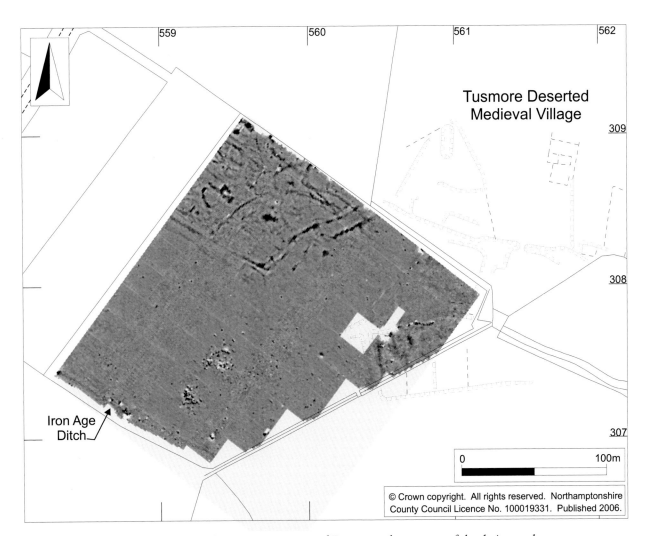

Fig. 2.62: Tusmore Drain Outfall, magnetometer survey of Roman settlement east of the drain trench.

Extended geophysical survey: enclosed Roman settlement

In view of the archaeological interest in the field, an extended geophysical survey was undertaken in June 2002 (Fig 2.62). The survey was funded through an English Heritage grant. It had the objective of discovering the extent and pattern of Iron Age and Roman features to enable the earlier findings to be put in context.

The survey was carried out using a magnetometer and magnetic susceptibility techniques over the whole field within the boundary of the Scheduled Ancient Monument. The area of investigation lay to the west of the main group of earthworks of the deserted medieval village. The land is flat except where earthwork remains occur in the north-east corner of the survey area. A hollow-way here is clearly evident and shows a pronounced local dip (possibly a quarry) which was the only part of the field which could not be surveyed. It can be noted that, while the DMV lies on the North Oxfordshire Jurassic Ridge at about 120 m OD where the geology is predominantly Oolitic Limestone, the site itself lies on a local outcrop of gravel.

The main area of activity was detected in the north-western corner of the field, with magnetic responses also

evident in the area of the DMV earthworks to the east. It is clear that the survey shows only part of both sites which extend beyond the northern and eastern limits of the survey area.

Two curvilinear ditches, approximately 8 m apart, appear to form the southern and eastern boundaries of a settlement. The outer ditch shows a possible southern entrance. The enclosure contains a dense pattern of features, evidently of several phases. It appears to be sub-divided by a curving ditch with slightly different signatures of features inside compared with outside. The eastern part of this ditch may have formed one side of a droveway which runs for about 50 m before opening out into a small enclosure. This is one of a number of curvilinear features in the northern and western part of the principal enclosure which appear to form sub-circular enclosures as well as fragmented ditch lengths. In the southern corner several short rectilinear anomalies are visible, perhaps denoting ditches and outlines of buildings. Similar features are also present in the northern area but the patterns are less clear. Individual anomalies scattered within the enclosed areas represent pits of varying shapes and sizes or may even indicate hearths. An approximately rectangular anomaly with a low core reading and a high outer reading may denote the remains of a kiln.

77

The pipe trench on the southern side of the survey area has been detected as a linear positive anomaly. The Iron Age ditch uncovered in the trench was also detected and extends north-eastwards for a distance of c 50 m from the trench as a weak magnetic anomaly.

Two discrete sub-circular areas of strong bipolar response of the anomalies are due to the scatter of slag observed during the survey. There is no way of dating the slag and it may be modern.

A series of weakly magnetic linear, curvilinear and rectilinear anomalies can be seen to the south of the main enclosure. These may represent further ditches and possible outlines of buildings associated with Iron Age and Roman settlement. Given the known presence of an Iron Age gully on the southern edge of the field, it is quite possible that the site is extensive but that features are magnetically too weak to be depicted with any clarity.

In the eastern corner of the field, the earthwork remains of the DMV are represented by a broad and slightly sinuous hollow-way. A plot boundary with possible sub-divisions are indicated as positive magnetic rectilinear anomalies on the south-eastern side.

CHAPTER THREE
MEDIEVAL AND LATER PERIODS

Introduction

Evidence for medieval and later activity was very limited. While the initial project design anticipated some evidence for woodland activities in the medieval period, in the event this potential was not realised. The investigation of the medieval and later archaeology fell into five main categories:

- Survey and trenching of relict boundaries on the edge of Hazelborough Wood.

- Trial trenching of other boundary features on the Silverstone bypass section of the route.

- Recording medieval/post-medieval trackway and hollow ways at Silverstone 3 and Silverstone 1, with a possibly associated post-medieval structure at Silverstone 3.

- The assemblage of post-medieval finds from Wood Burcote Bridge.

- Recording ridge and furrow on excavated sites.

Brief reports on the above are included in this chapter and illustrated by Figures 3.1 and 3.2. The distribution of medieval pottery from the fieldwalking phases of mitigation is also included since the presentation of these data has some value as an indication of the extent of manuring, and therefore arable cultivation, in the medieval period.

HAZELBOROUGH WOOD SURVEY AND TRENCH EXCAVATIONS

Earthwork survey

A survey was undertaken of the surviving earthworks on the north side of the A43 in Hazelborough Wood in March 2000 after the trees and a certain amount of the undergrowth within the road corridor had been cleared (Fig. 3.3). Earthworks on the southern side of the road were not able to be surveyed due to the presence of dense woodland. The underlying geology is Boulder Clay.

The survey was undertaken using a Total Station. Although only the earthworks within the road corridor were required to be surveyed, it proved possible to extend the survey into the partly cleared zone of replanting outside the CPO boundary, and to a more limited extent into undisturbed woodland. This enabled more sense to be made of the overall pattern of earthworks, although the pattern outside the road corridor is by no means complete.

A sinuous ditch was the most prominent feature on the ground, traced for much of the length of the road corridor and between about 8 m to 26 m distant from the former road edge. A bank was present in places on the north-west side of the ditch. It was probably originally continuous with the ditch but only survived as a prominent feature in the areas furthest away from the road.

The bank and ditch appeared to be a woodland boundary although its date could not be determined from the survey itself, and there were suggestions that it had been modified relatively recently for drainage purposes. It clearly respected the present trackways from the road, but it is not known whether this meant that it post-dated the trackways or the boundary had been modified to accommodate the insertion of the trackways at these points.

Trench HAZ1

This trench was positioned across the bank and ditch in the only suitable location within the designated CPO boundary. The ditch was found to be a little over 2 m wide and about 1.2 m deep, with a low bank on its north-western side. The feature possibly represented a woodland boundary, but no evidence of its date of construction was found. The ditch held water at the time of the excavation and still functioned as a drain, so it can be assumed that it had been cleaned out at intervals in the recent past.

The bank survived as a low feature, but had been relatively severely denuded in this zone, possibly from the construction and maintenance of the original single carriageway A43 and management of the woodland here.

Trench HAZ2

The excavation of a second trench, about 10 m in length, was undertaken in response to a change in the planned

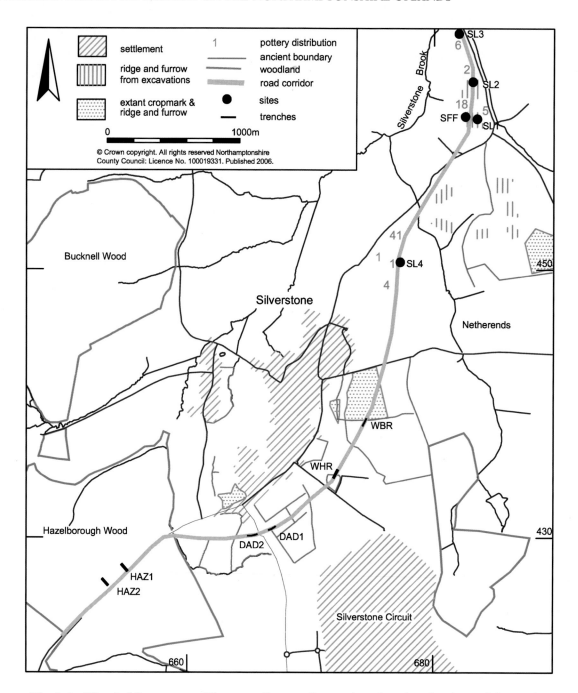

Fig. 3.1: *Historical features near Silverstone. Sources: Cropmark and earthwork ridge and furrow from NCCHET Historic Landscape Characterisation; Ancient boundaries from NRO Map 4210 (c 1608) and Silverstone Inclosure Map (c 1825); other ridge and furrow and surface distribution of medieval pottery from present project. (Ridge and furrow not oriented). For detail of Hazelborough Wood trenches see Figure 3.3.*

road alignment whereby the area of land-take was to be widened to include more of the earthwork remains. The trench was positioned at the extreme margin of the road corridor where the earthwork was reasonably well preserved. A complete profile of the bank was, however, not obtainable.

The ditch and bank were partially visible before excavation, the ditch surviving as a slight hollow and the bank heavily degraded. The extant ditch proved to be a recent recut which was filled with a humic soil similar to the topsoil. It cut a subsoil, which was orange clayey silt, 0.4 m deep, disturbed by root activity.

There was also an earlier, deeper, ditch reaching a depth of 1.0 m below the modern ground surface. It was about the same width as the recut. Above a fairly clean primary silt, it appeared that the bank had eroded and partly filled the remaining hollow. The bank was composed of a homogeneous orange silty clay. It survived to a height of 0.5 m above a possible buried soil layer or perhaps the upcast topsoil from the original ditch.

No archaeological material was found in any of the deposits. While the earthwork was better preserved in this trench, there was no evidence for its date of construction. As with HA1 the later ditch was recent. While an earlier

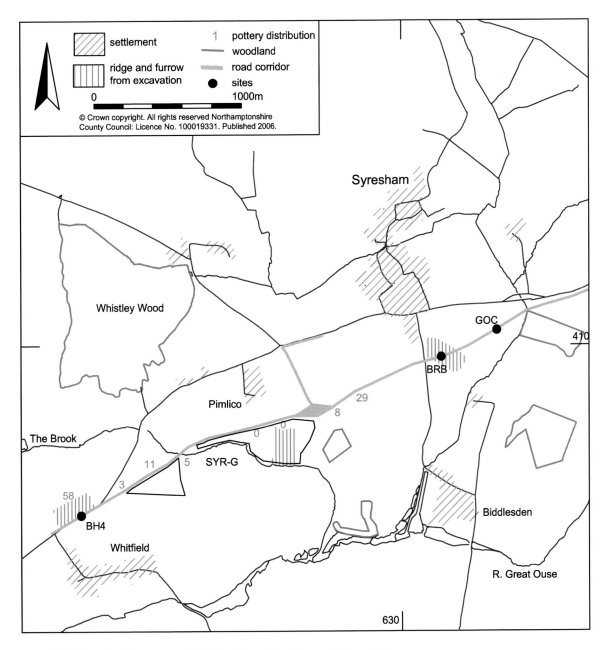

Fig. 3.2: *Historical features south of Syresham. (For key, see Figure 3.1).*

ditch cut was found in this trench, it remains unclear whether this was the original ditch or a cut related to later maintenance.

FOUR FIELD BOUNDARIES EAST OF SILVERSTONE

Four trenches were excavated to examine field boundaries of historical interest (Fig. 3.1). Two were located on either side of Dadford Road (DAD1 and DAD2), one was located just north of Winterhills Road (WHR1) and the fourth further north, east of Catch Yard Farm (WBR).

The map of Whittlewood Forest shows villages, closes, lodges, woodland and coppices in the early 17th century (NRO Map 4210, Frontispiece). Hazelborough Wood is

depicted as woodland. From Hazelborough Wood to the Dadford Road and from the Dadford Road up to, but not including, the fields adjacent to Winterhills Road, the road corridor crosses fields shown as comprising several "Sarts", or assarts. This indicates their origin as woodland clearances. They may include some of the assarts mentioned as being in Silverstone in 1273 (RCHM 1982, 134). Winterhills Road is not depicted; the fields immediately west and east of this road all comprised part of Winterhills, shown as woodland, which had recently been common land, ("comon of late"). The fields to the immediate south of the Whittlebury Road are shown as further woodland, "Barneyard coppice". The map therefore indicates that the entire area to the south and east of Silverstone, from Hazelborough Wood to the Whittlebury Road, was probably wooded in the medieval

81

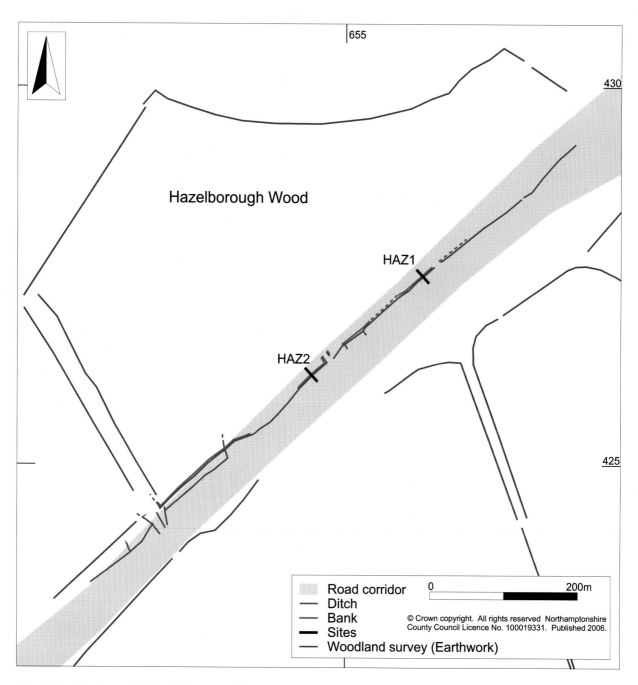

Fig. 3.3: *Hazelborough Wood, locations of woodland boundary and trenches HA1 and HA2. Features outside road corridor from Hall (2000, figure 13).*

period, with some areas of woodland clearance probably appearing before the later thirteenth century.

Trench DAD2

A 30 m trench was positioned across a former field boundary which showed as a slight hollow in the field. The natural clay substrate was encountered directly under the modern topsoil. It was cut by a shallow ditch containing exclusively modern fill. It is apparent that, whatever the origin of this boundary, the ditch had been cleaned out relatively recently.

Trench DAD1

This trench was positioned across the line of the current field boundary. On the Whittlewood Forest Map the boundary of a riding is shown running from the edge of Silverstone village almost as far as Luffield Priory approximately along this line with assarts on either side. This riding later became part of the Stowe estate. Two lodges (now listed buildings) were built in the eighteenth century flanking an entranceway to an avenue which led to the Georgian mansion at Stowe.

The length of trench, at 40 m, allowed for a certain margin for imprecision in the cartographic evidence. It revealed a ditch on the north-eastern side of the modern hedgerow. This had been cut from the topsoil to a depth of 0.8 m and was undoubtedly completely modern. There were no other features in the length of the trench. It appears that evidence of the riding boundary has not survived. It is possible that the riding boundary and the modern field boundary coincided and that the modern ditch had completely obliterated earlier ditches, or that the riding boundary lay to the north-east and has been lost.

Trench WHR

The trench was positioned across the modern field boundary. This boundary forms the northern side of a small enclosure shown on the on the Silverstone Inclosure Map (c 1825, NRO Map No. 2948) and containing buildings labelled Winterhills on later maps. At the time of fieldwork, the boundary was defined by a dense hedgerow which, within the CPO boundary, had been grubbed out. The 20-m trench revealed a ditch on the northern side of the hedgerow. This was over 2 m wide and about 0.8 m deep and cut through the modern topsoil. The ditch did not contain any finds, but it was undoubtedly recent. There was the trace of a possible bank on the southern side of the hedgerow where the ground rose, but there was no indication that this had been man-made, and it may have derived from soil-creep building up against the hedge.

Trench WBR

The trench, which was 20 m long, was cut through a field boundary which survived as a prominent earthen bank and ditch. This earthwork ran east-west along the crest of the south-west facing slope. The bank was about 4 m wide at its base and stood about 0.5 m above ground level. It was crowned by the stumps of two recently felled mature oaks. The bank was visible as a feature extending in a westerly direction as far as Catch Yard Farm. A boundary is shown here on the Whittlewood Forest Map, forming the southern limit of an enclosure called The Ridge Way covering nearly 19 ha, with a riding to the south.

The trench revealed that the ditch was 2.6 m wide and 1.2 m deep with a broad V-shaped profile. It lay predominantly on the southern side of the bank, but also partly under it. A modern water-pipe trench cut through the centre line of the ditch. On the southern side of this trench the base of the ditch contained a drain constructed of limestone blocks. On the northern side the yellowish brown clayey fill appeared to represent bank slumping. The bank was constructed of a similar material, heavily root-disturbed. There was no sign of a buried soil and no finds were retrieved from the ditch or the bank.

Conclusions

The trenches yielded little evidence as to the nature of the historical boundaries in these areas. The only features of possible archaeological interest were the bank and ditch in trench WBR. The stone drain within the ditch suggests that the ditch was dug or re-dug in the post-medieval period, while the insertion of the modern water-pipe into the southern side of the bank shows that the bank has been at least partly remade without any immediately obvious signs. It is likely, therefore, that the bank and ditch are not the original boundary features depicted on the Whittlewood Forest map but were later redefinitions. The absence of visible remains of any of the other early boundaries in this area indicates that these features have not normally survived into the present landscape. There would therefore have to be special circumstances for the continued persistence of this feature, if it is indeed of such an early date.

The ditch in trench DAD2 contained modern finds. The ditches found in trenches DAD1 and WHR appear to be modern on the basis of stratigraphy and the character of their fills. There is no reason to suspect a particular antiquity for any of them. The boundary cut by trench DAD2 is not depicted on the Whittlewood Forest map or the 1825 Inclosure map and is likely to a mid-nineteenth century sub-division of the field. The ditch in trench WHR relates to an enclosure around the house at Winterhills. The enclosure has an early origin, but it is not depicted on the Whittlewood Forest map, and is likely to be of seventeenth or eighteenth century date. It is possible that an early ditch has been completely removed by the present one, or simply that the original enclosure was not ditched. There was no sign of an early boundary feature in trench DAD1. The boundary shown on the Whittlewood Forest map can be estimated to have lain close to, or to the north-east of the present field boundary, but there was no trace of it in the length of trench. Any bank or ditch may have been completely ploughed out.

POST-MEDIEVAL FEATURES AT SILVERSTONE 3 AND WOOD BURCOTE BRIDGE

The post-medieval features found at Silverstone 3 comprised a trackway, a posthole structure of uncertain function, a drainage ditch, and two oval pits. At Wood Burcote Bridge, where the new road crossed Silverstone Brook, a number of finds of post-medieval date were recovered during the Watching Brief.

Trackway at Silverstone 3

The evidence for the trackway (2115) consisted of a heavily rutted zone running north-south along the length of the site cutting all the Iron Age features (Fig. 2.2). This was not examined extensively, but the ruts were 0.30 m deep and filled with soil similar to the subsoil. The Whittlewood Forest map (dated c 1608) indicates that the road between Silverstone and Towcester ran in a more direct line over the higher ground at this time and close to the line of the recorded trackway here (Frontispiece). The trackway is almost certainly either the road itself, or a result of general traffic within a route corridor. This presumably had its origin in the medieval period. The Inclosure map (c 1825) shows that this route had been superseded by the early nineteenth century in favour of a road along the lower ground to the east, and no trace of the former road remained.

At Silverstone 1, a hollow-way, possibly of medieval or later date, was encountered just east of the Roman road and has been described (Chapter 2). This is likely to have been a minor routeway, perhaps an alternative to the road over the higher ground to the west.

Posthole structure at Silverstone 3

This post-medieval structure, or perhaps more likely a group of several structures, was situated east of the trackway and overlay the entrance to the large Iron Age enclosure (Figs 2.2 & 2.5). The structures comprised a number of postholes forming roughly rectangular building plans. The majority of the postholes were square in plan although a series of rectangular postholes lay to the east. The square cut postholes were generally 0.4m-0.5m wide and 0.4m-0.5m deep. The rectangular features were 0.45m-0.55m wide, 1m long and 0.55m-0.75m deep. Light brown clayey silt deposits were found within these features. No pottery was recovered from any of these post-holes although a Rose Farthing coin of Charles I (40) came from one of them. The structures appear to have been aligned with the trackway and are likely to have been contemporary with it. They were perhaps small agricultural buildings taking advantage of access to the road.

Other features at Silverstone 3

A drainage ditch and two oval pits (2116 and 2117), also post-medieval in date, were found in the central and northern part of the site (Figs 2.3 & 2.4). The purpose of the pits is unknown.

Finds from Wood Burcote Bridge

A concentration of pottery, mainly dating to the seventeenth and eighteenth centuries, horseshoes and other metal finds, came from the subsoil overlying a narrow gravel terrace on the western side of the former bridge and south of the brook (Fig. 1.3). They were retrieved during earthmoving for bridge construction, with the aid of a metal detector. All the finds were unstratified and not necessarily contextually related. Much of the pottery came from a discrete area and may have come from a dump. The concentration of material, which included 12 complete horseshoes, was considered to be unusual, but the absence of any subsurface features casts doubt on the likelihood that there was occupation - such as a wayside smithy - here. There is, furthermore, no cartographic record

of a structure here. It is perhaps more likely that this was a convenient spot for dumping rubbish. The horseshoes may have derived principally from losses sustained while fording the stream.

MEDIEVAL CULTIVATION

Introduction

The evidence for medieval cultivation comes in two forms: the direct traces of furrows encountered during the excavations, and the distribution of pottery in the modern ploughsoil collected as part of the fieldwalking surveys. The latter is commonly thought to represent manuring scatters and hence evidence of land under cultivation. Both types of evidence are fragmentary and yield data of an uneven nature. Two drawbacks to the data can be noted which limit their value as research tools for the investigation of medieval land use in the project area. One is the fact that it was limited to the road corridor, so that even the fieldwalking was confined to narrow groups of transects rather than whole fields. The other is that post-Roman cultivation features were discriminated against in excavation. This evidence is therefore largely a by-product of other enquiries directed towards defining occupation sites and associated features. Nevertheless, it is thought useful to present the results here in summary form, particularly as similar kinds of data have been collected, albeit with different methodologies, in nearby parishes as part of the Whittlewood Project of the Medieval Settlement Research Group (Jones 2003).

In the following it has been assumed that the furrows broadly date to the medieval period although there was no strict confirmation of this from the excavations. The limited finds, where they could be dated, provided only a terminus post quem. It is quite likely that a similar ploughing regime continued into at least the early post-medieval period and possibly until enclosure. It is indeed possible that some of the ploughing had a post-medieval origin, although the retraction of arable farming in the later medieval and post-medieval period is well documented generally (Lewis et al 1997, 194-6), and a broad designation of medieval is here employed as a useful shorthand. The distributions of recorded furrows and medieval pottery are shown in Figs 3.1 and 3.2, to which the distribution of standing or recent ridge and furrow in adjacent fields has been added (from Northamptonshire County Council's Historic Landscape Characterisation database).

Evidence of Ridge and Furrow

Furrows were recorded on all the sites of excavation and evaluation except Silverstone 3, Great Ouse Culvert and Cottisford Turn. Their absence at these sites may be genuine, due to the presence of a trackway crossing the former and the marginality of the latter. Furrows were not consistently recorded during the Watching Brief, so this record has been disregarded.

Between Barley Mow roundabout and the M40 the route passes through land which appears to have belonged to small, poor parishes (Cottisford, Tusmore, Hardwick, Ardley) in the medieval period. Much of the land within the study corridor remained as heath and common pastureland outside the enclosed fields of the surrounding villages until the late 18th/early 19th century. Much marginal land was brought under the plough as a result of the Napoleonic wars and the need to increase agricultural production (WA 1993, 4-6).

Silverstone 2 excavation

Traces of four furrows were recorded running east-west across part of the site. These were spaced at 6.0 m, 6.5 m, 7.0 m and 6.0 m. This is undoubtedly part of what was a wider pattern of medieval ploughing across this field, evidence of which has been lost to later cultivation.

Silverstone Fields Farm excavation

Four furrow bases were recorded running east-west and spaced 8-9 m and 15 m apart. As at Silverstone 2, this is the surviving traces of widespread cultivation in this field.

Shacks Barn Farm evaluation

Three furrows were recorded in each of trenches 6, 9 and 21. These were all relatively close together at 5.5 m apart in trenches 6 and 9, and 4.0 m and 6.0 m apart in trench 21. A pair of possible furrows was also recorded in trench 10, but these were only 2.5 m apart and may have been shallow drainage gullies. Other possible plough furrows can be interpreted from the geophysical survey in the grids adjacent to trenches 17, 31 and 33. The recorded remains across this area are therefore fragmentary. The draft Inclosure Map for Silverstone (c 1825; NRO Map No. 2948) shows much of this part of the parish to have been open fields, and at least part of the furlong layout indicated correlates with the orientation of furrows near trenches 31 and 33. The Inclosure map for Whittlebury (1800; NRO Map No. 6100) is less informative. The land in this parish was called 'Lords Leze Field' in 1608 (NRO Map No. 4210).

Biddlesden Road Bridge excavation

Furrow bases were recorded across the entire excavation area. They ran downslope in a roughly north-west to south-east direction, between 9 m and 11 m apart. This is a similar pattern to that surviving as ridge and furrow earthworks in the field to the south. To the north, the field called 'Water Furrows' has ridge and furrow running on a more east-west alignment.

There is no means of dating the origin of these furlongs. The furrows themselves were excavated only in cases where they obscured underlying features, although metal-detecting recovered a small number of objects from the furrow bases. The more diagnostic items comprised a bronze crotal bell fragment (54) and an aulnager's wool or cloth seal, made of lead (57). These are likely to be late medieval.

Area G Syresham evaluation

Furrows were recorded in various trenches spread across Fields B, C, D and E. In all cases the furrows were aligned north-south and ran downslope. Where there was more than one furrow in a trench, they were spaced between 7 m and 10 m apart. Traces of surviving earthwork ridge and furrow was also evident in Field B and recorded in section in trench 8 (archive). No finds, other than a few scraps of iron slag, came from any of the furrows.

Brackley Hatch 4 excavation

A large number of furrows, running north-west to south-east, were recorded at intervals ranging from 5.5 m to 29.0 m. There may have been evidence of two ploughing regimes here, a 'narrow-rig' system with furrows at 5-6 m intervals, and a 'broad-rig' with furrows at 8.5-10.0 m intervals. Alternatively there may have been just one, rather irregular, narrow system with some of the furrows having been lost to later cultivation.

Medieval pottery from fieldwalking

Among the pottery collected during the early fieldwalking stages were 177 medieval sherds. Since no medieval occupation sites were identified, it is probable that all represent manuring scatters. Their distribution broadly reflects what is known of the extent of medieval arable farming and is shown in Figures 3.1 and 3.2. The quantities of pottery varied greatly between fields. In the Silverstone bypass section 47 of the 75 sherds retrieved came from four fields south of Bandbrook, while in the Syresham bypass section 58 of the 100 sherds came from the single field opposite Whitfield Turn (Site Brackley Hatch 4). These probably reflect variations in the intensity and longevity of arable farming during the medieval period. In contrast, the 12 fields surveyed in the section between the Barley Mow roundabout and the M40 yielded only two medieval sherds (WA 1993). There are clearly difficulties with making quantitative comparisons in view of the variations in field conditions. The methods involved walking transects 20 m apart in the Silverstone bypass and M40 sections, and 30 m apart in the Syresham section.

Discussion

There was no evidence of medieval cultivation immediately south of Wood Burcote Bridge. The Whittlewood Forest Map shows enclosures here, including one called J Wines Close, on either side of the road from Towcester to Silverstone. The wheel ruts crossing Silverstone 3 almost certainly relate, if not to the road itself, to a general corridor of traffic in the medieval/early post-medieval period which took a more direct line over the ridge than the later road. The indication that these lands were not ploughed would seem to gain some support from the paucity of medieval pottery and the lack of plough furrows at Silverstone 3.

Further up the slope lay 'Whittlebery Field' shown on the Whittlewood Forest Map extending as far as Bandbrook. Both Silverstone 2 and Silverstone Fields Farm showed plough furrows on an east-west alignment and there was more fieldwalking pottery from this field, both lines of evidence suggesting cultivation in the medieval period.

From Bandbrook as far as Whittlebury Road in Silverstone was 'Silson Common'. All this land was probably under the medieval plough although there was no direct evidence for this from fieldwork. Pottery was collected from the northern part of this section in areas of modern arable. To the south of Whittlebury Road is a block of extant ridge and furrow occupying a plot which is called 'The Ridge way' on the Whittlewood Forest Map. From here southward to Syresham evidence of medieval cultivation is entirely lacking and this is almost certainly due to the predominance of woodland in the medieval period.

There is extensive evidence for medieval ploughing around Syresham and north of Whitfield, and it appears that most of the fields from Biddlesden Road Bridge to Brackley Hatch 4 were given over to arable at this time. In contrast, there was no evidence of medieval cultivation in the Oxfordshire section of the route where the land may all have been pastureland and heath in the medieval period.

CHAPTER FOUR
THE FINDS

THE FLINT
A Thorne

Introduction

A small collection, comprising a total of 72 worked flints, was recovered from the excavated sites. The majority of these (56) were from Silverstone 3 (SL3). Others were from Silverstone Fields Farm (SFF), Biddlesden Road Bridge (BRB), Area G Syresham (SYR), Brackley Hatch 4 (BH4), Juniper Hill (JH) and Cottisford Turn (TCT) (Table 4.1). All flints were from residual contexts. The presence of the flints shows that there was prehistoric activity in the area and the varying concentrations demonstrate that this varied in density between the different sites.

The activity at Silverstone 3 was on the mixed clays of the Upper Estuarine Series, on the edge of the Blisworth Limestone upland and sited close to a spring. Silverstone 2 and Silverstone Fields Farm were higher up on the limestone geology, as were Cottisford Turn and Juniper Hill at the southern end of the route. The other sites were in Boulder Clay areas, although Biddlesden Road Bridge was actually sited on an outcrop of glacial gravel.

Raw material

The majority of the grey-brown flint utilised was of good quality, although the nodules used were generally very small. There are six different types of raw material identifiable, some of which were present within the Boulder Clay, others brought in from other sources:

- Small and one larger nodule of flint with a thick cream (and smooth) or brown stained (and rough) cortex, or with a white patinated surface where this is absent. This is a type of flint that occurs as fresh nodules within chalk, or weathered on the

Category	SL3	SFF	TCT	SYR	BRB	BH4	JH
TOOLS							
Scrapers	1	1	1				
Thumbnail scrapers	1						
Notches pieces	3				1		
Utilised blades/flakes	6			1		2	1
Misc. retouched pieces	2						
Knives	3						
Denticulated pieces	1						
Fabricators				1			
Axe fragment	1						
Microliths	2	1					
DEBRIS							
Waste flakes	28	2	1	1			
Cores	4				2		
Shattered pieces and other debitage	1	2					
Burnt flint fragments	2						
TOTALS	56	6	1	1	3	3	2

Table 4.1: Worked flint by category and site.

surface on chalklands. This may have been brought in from a chalkland source elsewhere or occurred as erratics in the local Boulder Clay.

- Small pebbles with thin ochreous brown cortex, presumably derived from the Boulder Clay.

- Small pebbles with a white patina/cortex, ochreous or stained brown. Probably local in origin from the Boulder Clay.

- Occasional small gravel or river pebbles with thin smooth grey, cream or brown cortex. One piece exhibits surface percussing from abrasion. May not be immediately local, but could be from a nearby stream.

- Occasional flint that is a milky grey-brown, and one piece that is very cherty. May not be local.

General Discussion

The assemblage contained diagnostic pieces of flint from a number of different periods. The earliest dateable item was a single flake from Silverstone 3 which was very abraded and a dark ochreous brown. It is likely to have been worked in the Palaeolithic period, but is not indicative of a primary context site, for this has been heavily rolled and redeposited. This piece had later been used as a core.

Three microliths were found, one from Silverstone Fields Farm and two from Silverstone 3. All were long thin prepared bladelets, two showing small areas of retouch along one edge, and the other slightly denticulated. These can be dated to the Mesolithic period. It is not clear whether these are of the earlier or later period. Mesolithic settlement patterns within Northamptonshire and the Midlands have not usually included clay areas for habitation, but for hunting, with dwelling areas targeting well-drained soils, proximity to water and areas of topographic prominence (Phillips 1999, 4 – 5). Both these sites would be typical in some of these respects.

Apart from Silverstone 3, the flints were limited, and, although containing several diagnostic pieces, do not suggest any sustained occupation nor a specific date range for this activity. Silverstone Fields Farm yielded a crude end scraper on a large hammer struck flint which was probably of later Neolithic/early Bronze Age manufacture, as well as the Mesolithic artefact. Another end scraper was recovered from Cottisford Turn, but is not closely dateable. A fabricator found in Field A, Area G Syresham, is a typical later Neolithic/early Bronze Age tool.

Silverstone 3

The 56 flints from Silverstone 3, on the other hand, are numerous enough to enable a characterisation of the assemblage. The activity probably dates to the earlier Neolithic, although it may also have continued into the later Neolithic/early Bronze Age period, suggested by

several cruder flakes used as tools, with little preparation, and a poor quality thumbnail scraper. This site is typical of earlier prehistoric sites in the region in the paucity of features associated with the flint scatters (Chapman 1999, 6). In this case all the flints came from features of the Iron Age settlement.

There were 16 pieces classified as tools, including utilised but unretouched blades. Tools diagnostic of the period are represented by knives, three retouched and backed for prolonged use, a further seven utilised blades and flakes, and three notched pieces which were used for shaving wood. A fragment of a flint axe was also found and there were several denticulated blades. A single end scraper was not dateable. The character of the flintworking technology also points to the assemblage being of a consistent date. Eleven flakes were soft hammer struck, and seventeen with a hard hammer, mostly primary cortex removal flakes. Despite the small size of the raw material, the flint appears to have been prepared for cores, although there are few of these present, in order to manufacture blades for use as tools.

The presence of both waste debitage and the various knives and other tools suggest that both flintworking and subsistence activities were taking place on site. It is, however, unusual that there was only one scraper, perhaps suggesting that skinning of animals was taking place off site.

A complete catalogue is retained in archive.

THE IRON AGE AND ROMAN POTTERY
J Timby

Introduction

The following report describes the later prehistoric and Romano-British pottery from thirteen sites investigated. In total some 8381 Iron Age and Romano-British sherds were recorded, weighing 121.2 kg. As far as is feasible, a single fabric series has been developed for all the pottery.

Many of the groups were very small, making positive identification and dating slightly tenuous. Whilst some broad concordance was observable between sites in terms of fabrics, there were also some variations which could be due to minor chronological differences or geography (ie. the exploitation of different sources of raw materials). Many of the sites show occupation spanning the Iron Age and/or early Roman periods, the second half of the first century AD. Many of the Iron Age potting traditions continue with no apparent change well into the later first century AD before there is any appreciable change in vessel form which might be regarded as reflective of the process of Romanisation. In the Roman period there is still a considerable emphasis on material of local origin with imported continental or regional vessels forming a very minor component overall. This has had some impact on the ability to closely date some groups. There were also considerable differences in sherd preservation both in terms of fragmentation and the effect of adverse ground conditions leaching calcareous fabrics at some sites.

Six sites produced moderately good-sized assemblages and these are discussed in detail below: Silverstone Fields Farm, Silverstone 2, Silverstone 3, Biddlesden Road Bridge, Syresham (Area G) and Brackley Hatch 4. The small assemblages recovered from the remaining seven sites are summarised at the end.

Methodology

The sherds were sorted into fabrics on the basis of the type and character of the inclusions in the pastes, following the guidelines set out in the Prehistoric Ceramics Research Group guidelines (PCRG 1997) for the later prehistoric period and with reference, where relevant, to the National Roman reference series (Tomber and Dore 1998) for the traded Roman wares. The sorted fabrics were quantified by sherd count, weight and estimated vessel equivalent (rim) (EVE) for each recorded context (cf. Orton et al. for methodology). In addition to the quantification, broad details of form, the presence of decoration and other features, such as evidence of use in terms of sooting, residues etc, were noted. A selection of material from key contexts or of a diagnostic nature is illustrated. The incidence of featured diagnostic sherds was overall quite low and in statistical terms no one site produced sufficient numbers of large enough sherds to allow comparison of specific forms within or between assemblages a valid exercise. Moreover, many of the more diagnostic forms were one-off occurrences, with the bulk of the sherds falling into the category of ovoid jar. The view was also taken that the fragmentation of sherds, as demonstrated by the low estimated vessel equivalents counts shown in the tables, made detailed vessel size analysis on the basis of rim diameters, again, statistically uninformative and that such approaches are better undertaken on larger assemblages when available.

Form Classification

Five classes of vessel have been distinguished for the Iron Age material on the basis of variations in their profile and a further ten classes for the later Iron Age-early Roman wares. The Iron Age classification broadly follows that established by Knight (1984; 1993). In addition, twelve rim forms have been defined (see below).

Iron Age

A   Carinated vessels (cf. Fig 4.3, 55). Only one vessel was positively identified with a carination. It came from Biddlesden Road Bridge. To a certain extent this is a reflection of the date range of the material as such vessels tend to be more typical of the earlier Iron Age.

B   Round shouldered vessels. This form is one of the commoner types recognisable in the assemblage and vessels tend to show simple undifferentiated rims.

C   Ovoid or barrel-shaped vessels with either no neck or with an upright, concave or everted rim.

D   Open vessels.

E   Vertical-sided vessels.

Late Iron Age - early Roman

F   Necked bowls.

G   Necked bowls with body bulge(s).

H   Miscellaneous bowls.

I   Necked jars.

J   Necked cordoned jars.

K   Miscellaneous neckless jars.

L   Carinated bowls.

M   Dishes.

N   Large storage vessels.

O   Flagon.

Rim forms:

1   Rounded, undifferentiated.

2   Flattened or squared top, undifferentiated.

3   Internally bevelled.

4   Rounded expanded rim a) externally; b) internally.

5   Finger-tipped.

6   Flat, squared or rounded rim.

7   Grooved or channelled rim.

8   Everted rim.

9   Beaded rim.

10   Moulded or shaped rim.

11   Reeded rim.

12   Slashed or notched rim.

Fabrics and associated forms

In total 28 Iron Age fabrics and 30 Roman fabrics have been defined. The codes used to distinguish the wares are alpha-numeric for the later prehistoric and early Roman wares where the principal inclusion(s) type is taken as the identifier of the fabric: GR = grog; SH = shell; SA = sand. The distinction between Roman and Iron Age is difficult to sustain with wares that could be regarded as native in tradition in terms of the potting clays and tempering materials used. In particular, this encapsulates many of the shelly wares and grog-tempered wares which span the Iron Age and Roman periods, some of which transform themselves into Roman types using wheel technology and adopting Roman forms. The term Roman is used here specifically for wares which are wheelmade, well-fired, standardised products which are culturally distinctive from the pre-existing native traditions. For the Roman wares where no national code exists, the sandy wares are largely divided on the basis of firing colour (reduced (GREY), oxidised (OXID or WW) or surface finish (mica-slipped, colour-coated). These are then further subdivided on the basis of texture (size and frequency of inclusions). The fabrics are described below, followed by a summary of the main forms and a list of the sites on which they occur. ,Sherds of less than 10 mm or with no surviving surfaces were classified as crumbs (OO).

Iron Age

Shelly wares

Six shelly fabrics have been defined on the basis of the quantity of shell and texture of the fabrics. The shell is typical of that found in local Jurassic beds and it is unclear whether it should be seen as a naturally occurring constituent of the clay or as an added temper. Shelly wares dominate the Iron Age assemblages and of the six fabrics SH6, the coarsest, is probably one of the earliest chronologically. Fabric SH1encapsulates material of Iron Age and Roman date, whereas SH2–SH5 seem to appear from the middle Iron Age, probably continuing into the later Iron Age phase.

The use of such clays was a native tradition and one of the most frequently found forms in this fabric, the channel-rimmed or lid-seated jar, is a late Iron Age form perpetuated into the Roman period. Roman kilns known to have been producing such wares include Harrold, Bedfordshire and Emberton, Buckinghamshire.

SH1: Standard mid-late Iron Age- early Roman dense shelly ware with a smooth, soapy feel. The matrix contains a common frequency of fossil shell fragments and occasional iron pellets. An absence of sand or other coarse inclusions gives the smooth feel. Usually brown or black in colour. The chronology of the fabric is difficult to distinguish without featured sherds or other associated material.

Forms: Channel rim jars, everted rim necked jars. Decoration includes slashing of the rim edge and incised lattice. Amongst the earlier forms are ovoid jars with expanded rims (C4a/b) (Fig 4.3, 57), shouldered jars (B7) (Fig 4.2, 39) and slightly carinated bowls (A1) (Fig 4.2, 34). Other forms include ovoid vessels with shaped rims (C7/10) (Fig 4.6, 96) or bevelled rims (Fig 4.2, 50), miscellaneous neckless jars (K7) (Fig 4.1, 13 and 16); beaded rim jars (K9) (Fig 4.1, 22); necked jars with expanded rims (I4) (Fig 4.2, 41); dishes with moulded rims (M10) Fig 4.2, 46), necked bowls with rolled/ expanded rims (F4a) (Fig 4.6, 99) and miscellaneous bowls (H10) (Fig 4.6, 94).

Sites: Brackley Hatch 4, Syresham, Biddlesden Road Bridge, Silverstone 2, Silverstone 3, Silverstone Fields Farm, Great Ouse culvert, Shacks Barn Farm, Juniper Hill, Tusmore Cottisford Turn.

SH2: A slightly sandy textured ware containing a sparse scatter of fossil shell.

Forms: Channel rim jars, necked everted rim jars, sharply everted rim jars. One vessel from Biddlesden Road Bridge has a handle springing. Earlier vessels include simple rim ovoid vessels (C1) (Figs 4.2, 32; 4.3, 54; 4.4, 63); (C2) (Fig 4.1,

6); ovoid vessels with defined rims (C4a) (Figs 4.2, 23; 4.3, 51); (C7) (Fig 4.6, 97); (C9) (Fig 4.2, 24). One jar from Silverstone 3 has a finger-tipped rim. Also early are the round-shouldered jars (B1) (Fig 4.1, 9); (B4a) (Fig 4.2, 36); (B5) (Fig 4.2, 43) and carinated vessels (A4a) (Fig 4.3, 55). Other open vessels include D1 (Figs 4.1, 8; 4.2, 28, 33, 37) and neckless jars with everted rims (K13) (Fig 4.1,21).

Sites: Brackley Hatch 4, Syresham, Biddlesden Road Bridge, Silverstone 2, Silverstone 3, Silverstone Fields Farm, Shacks Barn Farm, Juniper Hill.

SH3: A sandy textured paste containing a moderate to common frequency of fossil shell. Slightly rough texture. Handmade. Spans the Iron Age into the first century AD.

Forms: Jars, including middle Iron Age handled forms and later channel rimmed jars. Finishes include vertical scoring. One ovoid vessel with a bevelled rim (C3) from Silverstone Fields Farm shows paddle marks where the vessel walls have been consolidated during manufacture (Fig 4.1, 4). Amongst the earlier forms is a round shouldered jar with a finger-tipped rim (B1/5) (Fig 4.1,3).

Sites: Brackley Hatch 4, Syresham, Biddlesden Road Bridge, Silverstone 3, Silverstone Fields Farm.

SH4: A handmade, generally thick-walled ware containing a sparse frequency of fine shell and limestone with rare fragments up to 3 mm in size. Rare, fine sub-angular grog is also present.

Forms: Closed forms with a burnished finish. Featured sherds are sparse but include a vertically sided vessel with a notched rim (Fig 4.1, 1).

Sites: Syresham, Silverstone Fields Farm, Silverstone 2, Silverstone 3.

SH5: A reddish-brown ware with a black core. The paste contains a moderate frequency of fairly fine limestone and fossil shell, with occasional larger grains up to 3 mm mixed in with rare flint (or chert) and calcite. A variant noted at Silverstone 3 had a number of ferruginous grains present.

Forms: Handmade closed forms. Featured sherds include round shouldered jars with simple rims (B1) (Fig 4.2, 26) and open vessels (D1) (Fig 4.2, 25).

Sites: Silverstone Fields Farm, Silverstone 2, Silverstone 3, Shacks Barn Farm, Tusmore Cottisford Turn, Tusmore Drain Outfall.

SH6: A brown ware with a black core and a soapy feel. The paste contains very coarse sparse fossil shell fragments (up to 10 mm) and occasional limestone.

Forms: Jars including a small ovoid one (form C1) with a complete profile from Silverstone 3 (Fig 4.2, 31). Other ovoid jars also feature in this fabric including examples with bevelled rims (C3) (Fig 4.4, 59). Also in this fabric are necked bowls (G1) (Fig 4.3, 52).

Sites: Biddlesden Road Bridge, Silverstone 2, Silverstone 3, Shacks Barn Farm, Silverstone 4, Tusmore Cottisford Turn.

SH7: **sandy with limestone**

A moderately hard ware with a sandy texture containing a common to dense frequency of fine limestone with a scatter of coarser fossil shell, 6-7 mm in size. Fine speckled appearance to matrix.

Forms: No featured sherds.
Site: Silverstone 2.

LI - *Limestone-tempered*

Fairly soft fine textured paste with a sparse to moderate frequency of ill-sorted rounded greyish-white grains of limestone up to 4 mm in size. No other macroscopically visible inclusions.

Forms: Handmade ovoid jar with a simple inturned rim (C1).
Sites: Silverstone 3

GROG - *grog-tempered*

A great variety of grog-tempered fabrics exist and while some seem quite clearcut in nature, others appear to fall into a continuum where it is difficult to decide to which group it should belong. The tradition appears in the mid-later Iron Age period and continues to manifest itself into the Roman period, generally in sandier versions. The grog and shell ware (GR3) may go back earlier into the early-middle Iron Age. The term grog is adhered to although in some cases it is difficult to determine whether it is grog or clay pellets. Grog-tempered ware (GR8) is associated with the kilns at Brackley Hatch and Syresham, indicating local manufacture. In the mid to later Roman period the grog-tempered tradition manifests itself as fabric PNK GT, mainly found as large storage jars. From the second century AD grog-tempered wares replace the shelly wares and become one of the commonest fabrics found across the region alongside sandy wares.

GR1: Grog-tempered ware. Smooth soapy feel. Mainly reduced fabrics, black or dark brown/ grey in colour, occasionally brown with a dark grey or black core. Handmade and wheel-turned. Typical later Iron Age - early Roman 'Belgic' type ware.
Forms: Earlier types include ovoid jars with simple rims (C1) (Figs 4.3, 58; 4.4, 62) or rounded rims (C4a) (Fig 4.1, 11), flat or thickened rim bowls (D6) (Fig 4.4, 61); carinated bowls (L1) (Fig 4.5, 79) and open vessels with simple undifferentiated rims (D1) (Fig 4.2, 30). Later types include wheelmade everted rim jars, jars/bowls (G4a) (Fig 4.3, 53) with a defined shoulder bulge, cordoned necked jars/ bowls (F/J4) (Fig 4.1, 18), large storage jars (N13) (Fig 4.1,10) and channel rim jars (K7). Some vessels have a burnished finish. Decoration includes incised wavy lines, burnished line chevrons, impressed shapes and vertical scoring.
Sites: Brackley Hatch 4, Syresham, Biddlesden Road Bridge, Silverstone 2, Silverstone 3, Silverstone Fields Farm, Shacks Barn Farm, Juniper Hill, Tusmore Drain Outfall.

GR2: A moderately soft ware with a sandy texture and a sparse to moderate frequency of sub-angular grog/ clay pellets. Occasional grains of limestone are sometimes present.
Forms: Handmade vessels, usually closed forms.
Sites: Brackley Hatch 4, Biddlesden Road Bridge, Silverstone 2, Silverstone 3, Silverstone Fields Farm, Silverstone 4.

GR3: A soapy grog-tempered ware with sparse fossil shell. Both oxidised and reduced examples.
Forms: Wheelmade and handmade forms including vertically-sided vessels (E1) (Fig 4.1, 2); round shouldered vessels with defined rims (B4b) (Fig 4.2, 29) (B3/4 a/b) (Fig 4.4, 60), round shouldered or neckless jars with grooved, channelled or moulded rims (B7/ K7/10) (Figs 4.1, 15; 4.2, 42; 4.5, 75); ovoid jars with simple rims (C1) (Figs 4.1, 5, 12; 4.2, 35; 4.6, 88) or expanded rims (C4a) (Fig 4.3, 56); carinated bowls or tankards (L4a) (Fig 4.6, 86), and open forms (D1) (Fig 4.2, 27). Non-illustrated material includes lid-seated jars, bevelled rim jars (I3), everted, thickened rim jars (I/N13/4), beaded rim jars (I9), ovoid jars with loop handles, necked cordoned bowls (F/J) and carinated bowls (L). Some sherds have a burnished finish.
Sites: Brackley Hatch 4, Syresham, Biddlesden Road Bridge, Silverstone 2, Silverstone 3, Silverstone Fields Farm, Great Ouse culvert, Shacks Barn Farm, Tusmore Drain Outfall.

GR4: A sandy textured, grog-tempered ware with rarer flint and sparse shell. Mainly reduced.
Forms: Handmade and wheel-turned vessels. Handled jars, ovoid jars with simple in-turned rims (C1) (Fig 4.1, 7) and cordoned bowls.
Sites: Brackley Hatch 4, Syresham, Biddlesden Road Bridge, Silverstone 2, Silverstone 3, Silverstone Fields Farm.

GR5: A handmade or wheelmade ware distinguished by distinctive red-orange surfaces and a dark grey core. The vessel surfaces are usually evenly coloured. Smooth, soapy feel. The ware is probably related to one recognised over quite a large territory covering the Hertfordshire, Buckinghamshire and Bedfordshire region from the first century AD (Thompson 1982).
Forms: Simple everted rim and thickened rim jars (I4/13) (Fig 4.2, 44), cordoned bowls/ jars (F/J4) (Fig 4.6, 100), jars/ bowls with a shoulder bulge (G) and carinated bowls/ tankards (L4) (Fig 4.1, 19). Two flagons featured in this fabric, both from Silverstone Fields Farm (Fig 4.1, 14 and 17). A sherd from Silverstone 3 had been turned into a counter.
Sites: Brackley Hatch 4, Syresham, Biddlesden Road Bridge, Silverstone 2, Silverstone 3, Silverstone Fields Farm.

GR6: A very sandy ware with sparse grog / clay pellets.
Forms: Channel rim jars, everted rim jars, beaded rim jars, necked cordoned bowls/ jars and colander.
Sites: Brackley Hatch 4, Syresham, Silverstone 2, Silverstone 3, Shacks Barn Farm.

Sandy wares

SA1: An oxidised or brown ware with a grey core. The paste contains a common frequency of moderately well-sorted quartz sand, some iron stained and some fine mica. Most of the quartz is 0.5 mm and less in size but there are occasional large rounded grains up to 1 mm in size.
Forms: Handmade jars and bowls.

Sites: Biddlesden Road Bridge, Silverstone 2, Silverstone 3, Silverstone Fields Farm.

SA2: A fine sandy ware with a smooth feel and dark brown surfaces and a black core. The paste contains a moderate to common frequency of very fine quartz and rare calcareous grains (up to 1mm).
Forms: Thick-walled handmade vessels.
Sites: Syresham, Biddlesden Road Bridge, Silverstone Fields Farm, Silverstone 2, Silverstone 3.
SA3: A handmade black ware. At x20 magnification the fabric contains a moderate scatter of well sorted, rounded, quartz sand, a sparse to moderate frequency of fine calcareous inclusions (limestone maybe and fossil shell) and rare flint.
Forms: Handmade jars.
Site: Silverstone Fields Farm.

SA4: A black hard ware, with some fine mica. The paste contains a common frequency of moderately well-sorted, rounded, polished grains of quartz some with iron staining. Occasional grains up to 4 mm are visible.
Forms: No featured sherds.
Site: Silverstone Fields Farm.

Other wares
SACA: *Sandy with calcareous inclusions*
Moderately hard, sandy textured ware as SA2 but with less frequent fine shell and limestone.
Forms: Handmade vessels.
Site: Silverstone 3.

SST: Sandstone-tempered ware
Forms: No featured sherds.
Site: Silverstone 2.

SST2: *Sandstone-tempered ware*
An orange-brown ware with a black core. The fabric has a hard, dense sandy texture with some mica. The paste contains a sparse to moderate well-sorted frequency of sub-angular quartz sand, rare organic inclusions and sparse quartz sandstone and calcareous grains.
Forms: Jar.
Site: Biddlesden Road Bridge.

ORCA: *organic and calcareous-tempered*
A smooth fabric containing sparse organic inclusions, and a sparse to moderate frequency of rounded grey limestone (2 - 3 mm in size) and rare fossil shell.
Forms: Handmade closed forms.
Sites: Biddlesden Road Bridge, Silverstone 2, Silverstone 3, Silverstone Fields Farm.

ORGR: *organic and grog-tempered*
Forms: Handmade closed forms. Featured sherds are sparse but include at least one ovoid jar (C1) (Fig 4.2, 38).
Sites: Silverstone Fields Farm, Tusmore Drain Outfall.

ORG 1: *organic-tempered*
A dark brown, handmade ware with a black core. The paste contains a moderate frequency of organic matter largely visible as linear blackened voids. At x20

magnification the paste contains a scatter of fine quartz sand and rare calcareous inclusions 1 mm or less in size.
Forms: Handmade closed forms.
Sites: Silverstone Fields Farm, Silverstone 3.

FE1: *Sandy with iron inclusions*
A hard ware with a rough, sandy feel containing a moderate frequency of red-brown iron, 2-3 mm across and some fine mica. At x20 grains of fine quartz sand are visible.
Forms: Handmade vessels with vertical scoring.
Site: Silverstone Fields Farm.
FE2: *Iron-rich fabric*
A smooth, soapy ware with red-brown surfaces and a black core. The only visible inclusions are red-brown ferruginous grains up to 2-3 mm in size occurring in moderate frequency.
Forms: Handmade jars.
Site: Silverstone Fields Farm.

FECA: *Iron rich with calcareous inclusions*
Forms: No featured sherds.
Site: Silverstone 2.

FEGROR: *Iron rich with grog and organic inclusions*
A red-brown ware with a black interior and dark brown core. The finely micaceous paste contains sparse, sub-rounded grog/ clay pellets, a fine scatter of red-brown, rounded iron and a moderate frequency of coarse organic matter visible as linear voids.
Forms: Handmade closed forms.
Site: Tusmore Drain Outfall.

BO1: *Bone-tempered*
Orange-brown ware with a darker brown core and interior. Slightly sandy textured ware with a moderate frequency of white specks up to 1 mm in size. At x20 magnification these can be seen to be calcined bone accompanied by occasional fine quartz sand and occasional iron.
Forms: Handmade closed forms.
Site: Tusmore Drain Outfall.

GRBO: *Bone and grog-tempered*
As above but with a soapy texture. The paste contains fine iron, some fine irregular-shaped voids and a sparse scatter of fine (less than 0.5 mm) of calcined bone along with sparse sub-rounded black grog/ clay pellets.
Forms: Handmade closed forms.
Site: Tusmore Drain Outfall

CA1: *Calcite-tempered*
Handmade reduced ware with a moderate frequency of moderately fine (up to 1 mm) calcite crystals.
Forms: Handmade closed forms.
Sites: Silverstone Fields Farm

Roman wares

Grog-tempered
GR7: A grog-tempered white ware, often with a blackened exterior. The grog is generally a distinctive dark red or orange in colour and quite fine (1-2 mm).
Forms: Vessels include channel rim jars (K7), everted simple and thickened rim jars (I4a) (Figs 4.5, 76; 4.6, 95), jars with

a double-grooved rim, storage jars and open bowls with moulded rims (H10) (Fig 4.6, 101).

Sites: Brackley Hatch 4, Syresham, Great Ouse Culvert.

GR8: Sandy textured, grog (clay-pellet) tempered ware. The quartz is not particularly visible macroscopically and the grog/ clay pellets only feature in moderate frequency. Includes most of the material from the kiln pits at Brackley Hatch and Syresham. Mainly oxidised, orange or pink in colour, but occasionally reduced. Slightly lumpy appearance. May broadly equate with Milton Keynes fabric 2b (Marney 1989, 175).

Forms: Ovoid jars with expanded rims (C4a) (Fig 4.6, 93); open bowls with reeded rims (D10/7) (Fig 4.4, 64-5), dishes (M1) (Fig 4.5, 80-1), channel rim jars, everted thickened rim jars, cordoned necked jars/ bowls (K) (Fig 4.5, 74 and 76), large storage-type jars (N/I4) (Figs 4.5, 73 and 85; 4.6, 89), carinated (L4) and other bowls (H4) , in particular some distinctive examples with moulded rims (H10) (Figs 4.5, 71-2, 77-8; 4.6, 87, 90 and 98).

Sites: Brackley Hatch 4, Syresham.

PNKGT: (Tomber and Dore 1998, 210). Standard Midlands pink or orange grog-tempered ware (cf. also Marney 1989, 64). Very similar to fabric G2. Handmade and wheelmade vessels.

Forms: Mainly used for very large storage jars/dolia (Fig 4.6, 103) and smaller everted rim jars and less commonly channel rim jars.

Sites: Brackley Hatch 4, Syresham, Biddlesden Road Bridge, Silverstone 2, Silverstone 3, Silverstone Fields Farm, Shacks Barn Farm, Great Ouse Culvert, Silverstone 4, Tusmore Drain Outfall.

GRL: A hard, grey medium to fine sandy ware. Well-fired. The paste contains very fine grog/clay pellets or fine limestone giving a dark grey speckled effect.

Forms: Wheelmade everted rim jars and necked cordoned jars/ bowls.

Sites: Brackley Hatch 4.

Sandy wares – reduced

GREY 1: A fine grey ware with a slightly sandy texture. The paste contains a scatter of dark grey iron or iron compounds, and very fine mica is visible at x20 magnification.

Forms: Sharply everted rim beakers, everted rim jars, dishes and bowls.

Sites: Brackley Hatch 4, Syresham, Silverstone 3, Silverstone Fields Farm, Great Ouse Culvert, Silverstone 4, Tusmore Drain Outfall.

GREY 2: A slightly coarser, very finely micaceous ware without any obvious clay pellets. Usually grey with an orange-brown core. Very fine quartz sand is just visible at x20 magnification.

Forms: Everted rim jars, flat rim bowls, lids and plain rimmed dishes.

Sites: Silverstone 2, Brackley Hatch 4, Syresham, Shacks Barn Farm.

GREY 3: A fine grey ware usually with a red-brown inner core. Very fine textured with occasional dark brown, rounded, iron pellets and very sparse, fine quartz.

Forms: Everted rim jars, flat rimmed bowls, plain rimmed dishes and thickened rim dishes similar to Camulodunum type 37 (Symonds and Wade 1999).

Site: Brackley Hatch 4, Syresham.

GREY 4: A black ware with a buff core with brown margins. Very sandy texture. At x20 a scatter of dark brown iron and a few grains of quartz are visible.

Forms: Everted rim necked jars and dishes.

Sites: Silverstone 2, Brackley Hatch 4, Syresham, Great Ouse Culvert, Tusmore Drain Outfall.

GREY 5: A very well fired fine dark grey ware with a slightly speckled appearance and with a white core. The paste contains a moderate frequency of fine, well-sorted quartz, rare black iron ands rare larger white inclusions 2-3 mm across.

Forms: Grooved rim bowl.

Sites: Brackley Hatch 4, Great Ouse Culvert.

GREY 6: A very fine grey ware with a silky texture and a surface sheen.

Forms: Everted rim beaker.

Site: Silverstone 2, Brackley Hatch 4.

GREY 7: A black sandy wheelmade ware contains a well-sorted, moderate frequency of fine, sub-angular quartz sand less than 0.25 mm.

Forms: Necked everted rim jars and bowls.

Sites: Brackley Hatch 4, Syresham, Great Ouse Culvert.

GREY 8: A light or dark grey, well-fired sandy ware with a medium grade sand temper. One distinctive variant has a blue-grey surfaces and a dark red-brown core.

Forms: Sharply everted rim beaker, everted rim necked jars and necked cordoned jars.

Sites: Silverstone 2, Brackley Hatch 4, Syresham, Great Ouse Culvert.

GREY 9: Nene Valley grey wares. Generally dark grey ware with a lighter core. The paste contains a moderate to common frequency of fine white and clear quartz. The fabric is very similar to GREY5 indicating similar sources. A large number of kilns are known in the Upper Nene Valley using similar clays making discriminating material from different kilns almost impossible.

Forms: Everted rim jars and bowls.

Sites: Brackley Hatch 4, Syresham, Shacks Barn Farm, Great Ouse Culvert, Tusmore Drain Outfall.

Sandy wares – oxidised

OXID1: Very fine, orange ware with no visible inclusions apart from occasional iron. Usually in a soft, slightly powdery state.

Forms: Cornice rim beakers, reeded rim bowl and flat rim dishes.

Sites: Silverstone 2, Brackley Hatch 4, Syresham, Biddlesden Road Bridge, Shacks Barn Farm.

OXID2: A broad group for any fine to medium orange wares with no other distinguishing features.

Forms: Cornice rim beakers, bowls, everted rim necked jars, lids, flat rim bowls and dishes.

Sites: Brackley Hatch 4, Syresham, Silverstone 3, Silverstone Fields Farm, Great Ouse Culvert, Shacks Barn Farm, Tusmore Drain Outfall.

WW1: A fine to medium white sandy ware, very similar to the Oxfordshire white ware but a less pure white and probably of a more local source. Some sherds show traces of a colour coat.

Forms: Everted rim necked jar, necked cordoned jar and sharply everted neckless jar, segmented bowl (as Young 1977, type W49), reeded rim bowls and necked cordon bowls.

Sites: Silverstone 2, Syresham, Great Ouse Culvert.

WW2: A fine white ware with no visible inclusions apart from occasional red iron smears. Source unknown.

Forms: Camulodunum type 113, butt beaker with rouletted decoration.

Sites: Brackley Hatch 4, Silverstone Fields Farm.

Other traded wares

SGSAM: South Gaulish samian
Forms: Dragendorff type 18.
Sites: Brackley Hatch 4, Silverstone Fields Farm.

CGSAM: Central Gaulish samian

Forms: Dragendorff types 33, 31.
Sites: Brackley Hatch 4, Syresham, Silverstone 2, Silverstone 3, Shacks Barn Farm, Great Ouse Culvert, Tusmore Drain Outfall.

DOR BB1: Dorset black burnished ware (Tomber and Dore 1998, 127).
Forms: plain sided dishes and grooved rim bowls.
Sites: Brackley Hatch 4, Syresham, Silverstone 4.

LNV CC: Lower Nene Valley colour-coated ware (Tomber and Dore 1998, 118)
Forms: Indented beaker.
Sites: Brackley Hatch 4, Syresham, Shacks Barn Farm, Great Ouse Culvert, Silverstone 4.

OXF BW: Oxfordshire burnt white ware (Young 1977; 2000)
Form: Jar.
Site: Great Ouse Culvert.

OXF RS: Oxfordshire colour-coated ware (Tomber and Dore 1998, 176; Young 1977; 2000).
Forms: Young 1977 types C48, C51, C71 and C75.
Sites: Brackley Hatch 4, Great Ouse Culvert, Tusmore Drain Outfall.

	Fabric	Description	No	%	Wt (g)	%	Eve	%
Native	GR1	soapy grog-tempered	483	28.5	10174	38.5	256	22.5
	GR2	sandy grog-tempered	47	3	1028	4	16	1.5
	GR3	shell and grog-tempered	206	12	3242	12	117	10.5
	GR4	sandy grog with shell, flint	250	14.5	3225	12	29	2.5
	GR5	orange-red grog-tempered	68	4	770	3	204	18
	GRSA	sandy with sparse grog	12	★	71	★	0	0
	SH1	shelly ware	134	8	1805	7	196	17.5
	SH2	sandy with sparse shell	151	9	1882	7	113	10
	SH3	sandy, common shell	128	7.5	1594	6	44	4
	SH4	sparse fine limestone/shell	123	7	1484	5.5	32	3
	SH5	shell and limestone	2	★	23	★	5	★
	FE1	sandy with red-brown iron	1	★	88	★	0	0
	FE2	smooth, fine with iron grains	3	★	18	★	3	★
	SA1	sandy with iron, rare calcareous	12	★	83	★	6	★
	SA2	fine sandy, rare calcareous	12	★	79	★	0	0
	SA3	black sandy, some calcareous	13	★	90	★	10	★
	SA4	black sandy, iron stained quartz	1	★	39	★	0	0
	CA1	calcite-tempered	9	★	201	★	0	0
	ORGR	organic-tempered with limestone	4	★	58	★	1	★
	ORCA	organic with calcareous frags	6	★	83	★	0	0
	OO	unidentified crumbs	14	★	23	★	0	0
Roman	SGSAM	South Gaulish samian	1	★	19	★	0	0
	GREY1	fine grey ware	7	★	62	★	0	0
	OXID2	oxidised sandy ware	6	★	64	★	0	0
	WW2	fine white ware	4	★	23	★	0	0
	PNK GT	pink grog-tempered ware	6	★	175	★	100	4
TOTAL			**1703**	**100**	**26403**	**100**	**1132**	**100**

Table 4.2: Summary of pottery from Silverstone Fields Farm (★ = less than 1%).

OXF WH: Oxfordshire white ware (Tomber and Dore 1998, 174; Young 1977; 2000)

Forms: mortaria (Young 1977, types M6, M22), flagon, bowls (ibid type W33, W53), everted rim necked jar (ibid type W6).

Sites: Brackley Hatch 4, Syresham, Shacks Barn Farm, Great Ouse Culvert.

OXF RE: Oxfordshire fine grey ware (Tomber and Dore 1998, 173; Young 1977; 2000).

Forms: No featured sherds.

Sites: Brackley Hatch 4, Great Ouse Culvert.

OXF OX: Oxfordshire oxidised ware (Young 1977; 2000).

Forms: No featured sherds.

Site: Silverstone 2.

OXF PA: Oxfordshire parchment ware (Tomber and Dore 1998, 174; Young 1977; 2000).

Site: Great Ouse Culvert.

ROB SH: late Roman shelly ware (Tomber and Dore 1998, 212)

Form: Jars.

Site: Great Ouse Culvert.

VER WH: Verulamium white ware (Tomber and Dore 1998, 154).

Forms: Butt beaker.

Site: Brackley Hatch 4.

Fine wares (excluding samian)

MICA: A thin walled dark orange ware with a finely micaceous paste and a mid grey inner core. The surface is covered in a thin gold mica slip.

Forms: Flat rim bowl.

Sites: Brackley Hatch 4, Syresham, Biddlesden Road Bridge.

GLAZE: A dark orange, fine, fairly soft, fabric with no visible added temper. The exterior surface is a paler orange. The interior surface has a thin clear, semi-glossy glaze or orange appearance. The character of the fabric would suggest this may be a British glazed ware as opposed to a post-medieval ware but the only examples, from a posthole, were not associated with any other material to confirm dating.

Form: Open form.

Site: Silverstone 3.

SILVERTONE FIELDS FARM (SFF)

Introduction

A total of 1703 sherds of pottery weighing 26.4 kg were recovered, largely dating to the middle to late Iron Age. In addition there was a small amount of fired clay amounting to some 46 fragments. A summary of the fabrics recorded can be found in Table 4.2.

Pottery was recovered from 78 separate contexts in some 50 individual features. The assemblage is reasonably well-preserved for an essentially later prehistoric assemblage with an overall average sherd size of 15.5 g. Despite this, there are no obvious complete profiles. Most of the groups are quite small and the larger assemblages suggest a certain degree of redeposition.

Iron Age

The main fabrics present in the group are fossil-shell-tempered wares (31.5% by sherd count), grog-tempered wares (62.6%) and sandy wares (2%) accompanied by a small number of other fabrics, notably organic (vegetable) - tempered ware, two ferruginous wares (FE1-2) and a calcite-tempered ware (CA1). Most of the pottery assemblage from the features appears to date to the middle Iron Age. The preponderance of grog-tempered wares might suggest continuation into the later Iron Age. Forms are typically slightly globular or round-bodied jars. Decoration is rare. The coarser shell-tempered fabric along with at least two vessels with finger-tipped rims might hint at an early Iron Age presence or a phase of occupation dating to the very beginning of the middle Iron Age phase, traditionally taken to date from the fourth to second centuries BC.

The boundary ditch of the trapezoidal enclosure (Enclosure 2) produced quite a small group of material comprising some 65 sherds, 837 g. The substantial part of a complete shouldered jar (fabric SH4) missing most of its rim but with a diameter of around 140 mm came from 27 (28), and several sherds from a rounded bowl from 77 (78) (Fig 4.1, 9). The sherds comprise almost equal quantities of grog tempered and shelly ware and would appear to be typical of the earlier middle Iron Age.

The first phase of Enclosure 1, thought to be contemporary with Enclosure 2, produced just 19 sherds, 128 g, in quite fragmentary condition, and one large fragment of fired clay. The fabrics comprise a mixture of grog and shelly wares in which the former accounts for 69% by sherd count. One sherd of calcite-gritted ware (CA1) was also present. The only other sherds of this fabric from the site came from pit 183 within Structure 1, and pit 180. A middle Iron Age date would fit this material.

Of the other features on the site, the earlier assemblages, perhaps contemporary with the outer enclosure, appear to be associated with Structure 2 along with pit 56 and possibly pits 65, 126 and 164. Structure 2 produced 93 sherds all exclusively shelly wares (fabrics SH1, SH3 and SH4). The sherd size is relatively large and several of the sherds appear to derive from the same vessels. The group of eight sherds from pit 56 includes a jar with a slashed top. Pit 65 with just 12 sherds also includes a jar with a slash-decorated rim. Pit 126 produced just six shell-tempered sherds and pit 164 just two coarse shell-tempered sherds.

The roundhouse gullies associated with Structures 1 and 3 produced small assemblages of 21 and 11 sherds respectively, more typical of the middle Iron Age proper. Amongst the material from Structure 1 are several sherds from a single very large jar (Fig 4.1, 5) and one sherd with vertical scoring. Structure 3 had one sandy ware sherd and a shelly ware handle. Most of the pits in and around Structure 1 and from the clusters along the eastern side of the site appear to date to this phase. In total 32 pits produced 628 sherds of pottery, of which only 10 had

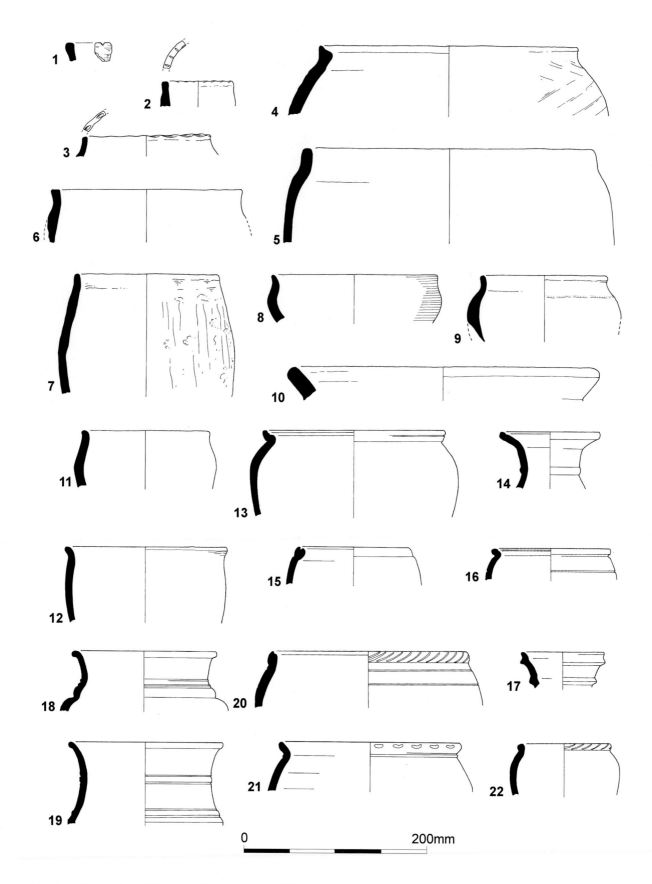

Fig. 4.1: Pottery from Silverstone Fields Farm, 1-22.

assemblages exceeding 10 sherds (63, 65, 75, 86, 89, 146, 148, 183, 204 and 212). Of particular note is a group of 79 sherds from pit 146 which includes a number of jars with a burnished finish and several sherds from single vessels, for example, Figure 4.1, 7. Pit 206 contained one small sandy sherd with part of an incised chevron and pit 217 has a grog-tempered sherd with incised decoration. A join was observed between pits 86 and 89. One jar from pit 75 showed evidence of paddle beating during manufacture presumably to consolidate the coils (Fig 4.1, 4).

Very little material was recovered from the quarries, just five sherds from 53, all typical middle Iron Age fabrics. The only other middle Iron Age features on the site to produce pottery were gullies 169 and 210. An organic-tempered jar and a sandy ware jar came from 169 alongside the more typical grog and shell and shelly wares and just a single shelly ware from gully 210.

Phase 2 of Enclosure 1 yielded a large assemblage of pottery with 821 sherds weighing 15,031 g (Fig 4.1, 10-22). The material was generally well preserved with an average sherd weight of 18 g. A substantial amount of this assemblage, some 503 sherds came from the terminal 100, mainly from the upper fill (101). The only primary fill to produce pot was 94 with six grog-tempered sherds (fabric GR2). The remaining material was largely recovered from the middle fills. The vessels are all native wares, mainly shell or grog-tempered ware but include wheel-turned vessels, suggesting a date in the late first century BC or first century AD.

The upper fills produced the largest group of material – fill 101 itself some 740 sherds, 90% of the total assemblage from this phase of ditch. This material is again predominantly native in character but a small number of more Roman types suggest that the enclosure was probably abandoned around AD 60-5. In particular, 101 produced a single sherd of South Gaulish samian, the only piece from the site, and fragments of a white-ware butt beaker (as Camulodunum type 113) of British origin. Six sherds of wheelmade grey sandy ware from 101 and two flagons in more local grog-tempered fabrics (Fig 4.1, 14 and 17) reinforce a mid to late first-century AD date. A few channel rim jars are also present in shelly and sandy fabrics and a number of large storage jars in grog-tempered fabrics. Several of the storage jars have simple incised or burnished line decoration. The proportion of grog-tempered ware far outweighs the shelly ware, for example in the group from 100, grog-tempered ware accounts for 83% by sherd count (86% by weight) and shelly ware for 14% by count (12.5% by weight). A small number of sherds in more typical earlier-middle Iron Age fabrics are also present, presumably redeposited from the earlier phase of the enclosure.

Material from features within Enclosure 1 was sparse but one pit, 115, with just grog-tempered sherds may belong to the later Iron Age-early Roman phase of the enclosure.

Catalogue of illustrated sherds (Fig 4.1)

In the following catalogues the context information is presented as: Feature and number, phase (where appropriate), Cut number (where appropriate), context number in parentheses.

1 Rim fragment with an incised notch on rim edge. Form: ?E1/12. Fabric SH4. Pit 56 (57).

2 Small handmade jar or small bowl. Form E1. Fabric GR3. Pit 65 (66).

3 Handmade jar, possibly a biconical form with a finger-depressed rim. Form: B1/5. Fabric SH3. Residual in Enclosure 1, 121 (122).

4 Large handmade vessel with a bevelled internal rim. Form C3. Fabric SH3. Pit 75 (76).

5 Large handmade, slightly shouldered vessel. Smoothed exterior surfaces, possibly originally burnished. Form C1. Fabric GR3. Structure 1, 49 (50).

6 Wide-mouthed jar or bowl with a coil break. Form C2. Fabric SH2. Pit 212 (214).

7 Slack-bodied ovoid jar with a roughly smeared finish. Form C1. Fabric GR4. Pit 146 (147)

8 Squat rounded bowl with a highly burnished exterior finish. Form D1. Fabric SH2. Pit 95 (139).

9 Globular-bodied jar with a smooth exterior finish. Blackened rim zone. Form B1. Fabric SH2. Enclosure 2, Ditch 77 (78).

10 Large handmade jar with a sharply everted rim. Form N13. Fabric GR1. Enclosure 1.2, 121 (122).

11 Handmade rounded jar with a slight lip. Form C4a. Fabric GR1. Enclosure 1.2, 44 (45).

12 Handmade jar with a burnished finish. Form C1. Fabric GR3. Enclosure 1.2, 37 (33).

13 Handmade, wheel finished channel-rim jar. Form K7. Fabric SH1. Enclosure 1.2 107 (32).

14 Flagon in an orange grog-tempered fabric with a grey core. Form O13. Fabric GR5. Enclosure E1.2, 198 (200).

15 Handmade channel rim jar. Form K7. Fabric GR3. Enclosure 1.2, 107 (31).

16 Wheelmade channel rim jar. Form K7. Fabric SH1. Enclosure 1.2, 107 (32).

17 Wheelmade flagon. Form O10. Fabric GR5. Enclosure 1.2, 39 (41).

18 Wheelmade necked, cordoned jar. Form J4. Fabric GR1. Enclosure 1.2, 100 (101).

19 Handmade, wheel finished carinated bowl with girth grooves. Form L4a. Fabric GR5. Enclosure 1.2, 100 (101).

20 Handmade lid-seated jar with light diagonal slashing on the exterior rim. Form K12. Fabric SH1. Enclosure 1.2, 100 (101).

21 Handmade, wheel finished jar with impressions around the outer rim. Form K13. Fabric SH2. Enclosure 1.2, 100 (101).

	Fabric	Description	No	%	Wt (g)	%	Eve	%
Native	GR1	soapy grog-tempered	117	11	1053	9	47	11
	GR2	sandy grog-tempered	34	3	317	3	5	★
	GR3	shell and grog-tempered	222	20	2930	25.5	93	22
	GR4	sandy grog with shell, flint	30	3	454	4	5	★
	GR5	orange-red grog-tempered	1	★	5	★	0	0
	GR6	sandy with sparse grog	2	★	55	★	0	0
	SH1	shelly ware	72	6.5	810	7	42	10
	SH2	sandy with sparse shell	180	16.5	1978	17	114	27
	SH3	sandy, common shell	74	7	712	6	15	3.5
	SH4	sparse fine limestone/shell	48	4.5	512	4.5	5	★
	SH5	shell and limestone	91	8	1530	13	55	13
	SH6	coarse shell and limestone	8	★	454	4	18	4
	SH5/FE	iron-rich shell and limestone	2	★	12	★	2	★
	SH00	miscellaneous other shell	8	★	103	1	0	0
	L1	limestone-tempered	1	★	3	★	1	★
	SA1	sandy with iron, rare calcareous	13	1	125	1	22	5
	SA2	fine sandy, rare calcareous	4	★	33	★	0	0
	SACA	sandy with calcareous grains	4	★	61	★	0	0
	ORG1	organic-tempered	6	★	34	★	0	0
	ORCA	organic with calcareous frags	3	★	47	★	0	0
	OO	unidentified crumbs	164	15	234	2	0	0
Roman	SAM	samian	1	★	1	★	0	0
	GLAZE	?British glazed ware	3	★	6	★	0	0
	OZID2	oxidised sandy ware	2	★	6	★	0	0
	GREY1	grey sandy ware	3	★	44	★	0	0
	PNK GT	pink grog-tempered ware	2	★	12	★	0	0
Total			1095	100	11531	100	424	100

Table 4.3: *Summary of pottery from Silverstone 3 (★ = less than 1%).*

22 Small wheel-turned jar with a beaded rim decorated with light diagonal slashing on the exterior. Form: K9. Fabric SH1. Enclosure 1.2, 100 (101).

SILVERSTONE 3 (SL3)

Introduction

The archaeological work at Silverstone 3 resulted in the recovery of 1095 sherds of pottery weighing 11.5 kg, largely dating to the middle Iron Age. In addition there is a small amount of fired clay amounting to some 18 fragments, eight Roman sherds and two pieces of Roman tile. A summary of the pottery recorded is in Table 4.3.

Pottery was recovered from 95 separate contexts deriving from over 52 individual features. The assemblage is quite fragmented with an overall average sherd size of 10.6 g. There is at least one complete reconstructable profile and several instances of multiple sherds coming from single vessels.

Iron Age

The main fabrics present in the group are fossil shell-tempered wares, shell and grog, and grog-tempered wares accounting for 44%, 20% and 17% by sherd count respectively. Small amounts of other types, for example sandy, limestone-tempered and organic-tempered wares, are also present. Most of the pottery assemblage appears to date to the middle Iron Age. These are typified by slightly globular or round-bodied jars with simple undifferentiated rims. Decoration is rare. Several of the sherds have a burnished finish or show evidence of vertical scoring or wiping. One sherd from Enclosure 5 (ditch 2007) was decorated with two incised parallel grooves and a sherd from Enclosure 4 (ditch 2002) may also show traces of decoration (Fig 4.2, 24). One bodysherd from 2118 (the post-medieval structure) had a wall perforation. Two sherds, from Structure 3 (gully 2026) and pit 2085, had been fashioned into counters. Only one rim was present with finger-tipped decoration (pit 2089). At least three handle fragments were present, mainly from jars. An almost complete jar was recovered from pit 2108 (Fig 4.2, 31).

Although the stratigraphic sequence hints at a complex history of use of the site most of the individual assemblages are too small and too limited, both typologically and in terms of distinctively different wares, to show any obvious trends through the suggested sequences. The largest assemblages were recovered from the fills of enclosure ditches 2002 (Enclosure 4), 2023 (Enclosure 3) and 2051 (Enclosure 1), with 109, 133 and 298 sherds respectively. Together these account for 49% of the total assemblage.

Northern Area

Amongst the early features defined in the northern area (Phase 1) is ditch 2014 with a small group of 15 sherds, mostly shelly wares with two grog-tempered sherds. At least two simple rim jars are present. Possibly contemporary with this is ditch 2011 with just 12 shelly ware sherds. Ditch 2016 produced a larger assemblage of 75 sherds. The more varied composition of this latter group with 63% shell, 25% grog and shell, 5% sandy and 7% grog-tempered ware would support a slightly later date compared to the other ditches.

In Phase 2, ditch 2009 (Structure 5) produced 51 sherds, 17% grog and 83% shelly, the latter including a handled jar. Ditches 2005 and 2006 also produced small groups of 32 and six sherds. Ditch 2005 had a number of typical middle Iron Age jars and sherds with vertical scoring. For Structure 4, possibly of a later phase, gully 2008 also contained a very small assemblage of just six sherds, while of 11 sherds came from ditch 2004, all shell or shell and grog-tempered. Gully 2013, possibly a replacement of 2004, was without pottery.

In Phase 3, ditch 2012 (Enclosure 5) contained twelve sherds, including vertically scored sherds typical of middle Iron Age assemblages and examples of grog-tempered fabrics GR1 and GR4, grog and shell (GR3), and shelly wares SH1, SH2 and SH4. Ditch 2010 (Enclosure 5) produced just 14 sherds and three fragments of fired clay, one of which had a wattle impression. The pottery showed the familiar mix of grog and shelly wares. The recut, ditch 2001, produced just three sherds in fabric GR3 and Ditch 2007 a total of 20 sherds basically indistinguishable in terms of form and fabric composition from the previous groups.

In Phase 4, ditch 2003 produced a single sherd in fabric SH3. By contrast Enclosure 4 (ditch 2002) produced 109 sherds. In terms of fabric composition these comprised 11% grog, 5% grog and shell, 3.5% sand and calcareous, 1% limestone and 79.5% shelly ware by sherd weight.

Of the six pits in the northern zone only 2018 and 2019 produced pottery, but with just one and six sherds respectively little can be said other than that they are broadly contemporary with the enclosure ditches.

Middle Area

Structure 3 (gullies 2025 and 2026) yielded a small group of ten sherds among which was a loop handle from a jar (fabric GR3). A much larger assemblage was recovered from Enclosure 3 (ditch 2023) with 133 sherds. Several jars and bowls, some burnished, featured in this group (Fig 4.2, 25-30). In terms of fabric composition the assemblage comprised 25% grog, 22% grog and shell, 50% shelly ware and 3% unsorted crumbs by sherd weight. Structure 2 (gully 2029) produced 18 sherds of typical middle Iron Age pot, one vessel showing vertical wiping marks.

Of the twelve postholes defined in this area, only 2032 and 2041 produced middle Iron Age pottery, just six and two small sherds respectively. Posthole 2043 produced three small sherds of glazed ware, presumed to be early Roman. Five of the eight pits forming the pit alignment contained very small groups of pottery, again the same range of material as seen in the other features.

Southern Area

Enclosure 1 (Ditch 2051) produced the largest single group of pottery, some 298 sherds, along with 18 fragments of fired clay. In terms of fabric composition the group comprised 10.5% grog, 29% grog and shell, 1% organic, 54.5% shell and 5% other. The assemblage was quite well fragmented with an average sherd weight of just 7.5 g suggesting that the ditches were not receiving fresh rubbish. The form and fabric ranges again support a middle to late Iron Age date for this enclosure. Two wheel-thrown Roman greyware sherds came from the upper fill, possibly suggesting a general abandonment of this feature in the later first century AD.

The early pit, 2108, contained a single, but broken vessel in fabric SH6 (Fig 4.2, 31). Pit 2083 contained nine sherds, of which two are joining wheel-turned grog-tempered sherds, alongside typical middle Iron Age pieces. The former suggest a date in the later Iron Age and, if the relationship with 2051 is correct, are presumably intrusive.

Five gullies of Structure 1 - 2054, 2056, 2060, 2064 and 2066 - contained small groups of mainly unfeatured pottery in typical middle Iron Age fabrics. Only one posthole, 2072, contained pottery. Of the other features within Enclosure 1, small assemblages of pottery were associated with gully 2097 and pits 2084, 2085, 2090 and 2093. Pit 2089 (possibly part of a second pit alignment) contained ten sherds, among which was a shelly ware jar with a finger-tipped rim which might suggest this is an earlier feature. Pit 2085, with just five sherds, had a grog-tempered sherd of late Iron Age type fashioned into an oval counter. Pit 2090 had a tiny sherd of oxidised sandy ware of Roman character which may have been intrusive alongside 30 Iron Age sherds.

The only other assemblage of note came from pit 2099. This contained 28 sherds from a single large grog and shell-tempered jar (fabric GR3) (Fig 4.2, 35) along with a jar in fabric SA1 and sherds of ORCA, GR1 and SH4.

Roman

Thirteen sherds of Roman date were present. Two from Enclosure 1 (ditch 2051) and one from pit 2090 may be intrusive in features of prehistoric date. Three glazed sherds of possible Roman date came from posthole 2043, south of Structure 3. Two further sherds were recovered from the post-medieval structure 2118, along with four Iron Age sherds, three from modern features 218 and 406 in the evaluation, and two unstratified.

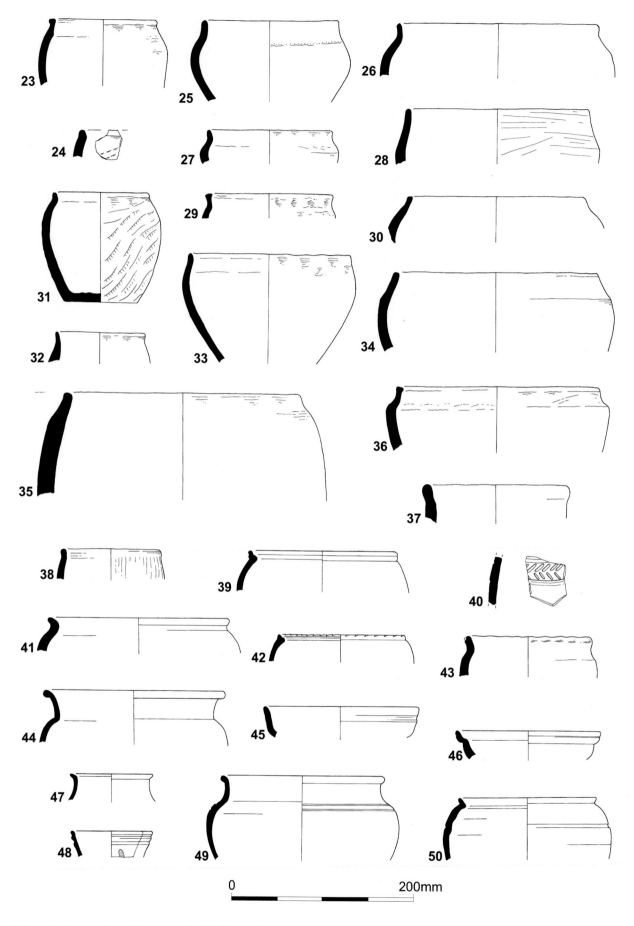

Fig. 4.2: *Pottery from Silverstone 3, 23-35; and Silverstone 2, 36-50.*

Post-medieval pit 2117 produced one fragment of probable Roman tile, a piece of combed hypocaust tile came from 1186 and a fragment of imbrex was present amongst the surface material. The incidence of sherds is insufficient to suggest Roman use of the site but may hint at such a site in the locality.

Catalogue of illustrated sherds (Fig 4.2)

23 Jar with a slightly rounded rim and internal collar. Sooted exterior. Form C4a. Fabric SH2. Ditch 2016 (1417).

24 Small, slightly beaded rimsherd with possible decoration. Two discontinuous parallel lines cross the sherd. Form C9. Fabric SH2. Enclosure 4 (1286).

25 Round-bodied bowl with sooting on the upper exterior rim. Form D1. Fabric SH5. Enclosure 3 (1269).

26 Wide-mouthed jar with pitted dark grey surfaces where shell has leached out. Form B1. Fabric SH5. Enclosure 3 (1268).

27 Small round-bodied bowl. Fabric GR3. Form D1. Enclosure 3 (1268).

28 Bowls with horizontal wiping marks. Form D1. Fabric SH2. Enclosure 3 (1268).

29 Jar/ bowl with a slightly internally expanded rim. Form B4b. Fabric GR3. Enclosure 3 (1268).

30 Wide-mouthed jar/ bowl with a smoothed interior. Form D1. Fabric GR1. Enclosure 3 (1268).

31 Several sherds from a small jar with patchy red-brown to dark black brown firing. Diagonal finger smoothing on the exterior. Form C1. Fabric SH6. Pit 2108 (1314).

32 Jar with a slightly tapered rim. Light orange-brown with a black core. Form C1. Fabric SH2. Pit 2116 (1266).

	Fabric	Description	No	%	Wt (g)	%	Eve	%
IRON AGE	SH5	shelly ware	16	2	127	1.5	5	1
	SH6	coarse shell and limestone	43	5.5	450	5	18	2
	SH7	sandy dense fine limestone/shell	10	1	100	1	17	3
	SST	sandstone etc	9	1	53	*	5	1
	GR3	grog and shell-tempered	89	11	901	10.5	15	2.5
	SA1	sandy	1	*	2	*	0	0
	SA2	fine sandy	12	1.5	112	1.5	13	2.5
	FECA	ferruginous with calcareous	3	*	29	*	0	0
	ORCA	organic with calcareous	2	*	27	*	0	0
ROMAN								
Import	CGSAM	Central Gaulish samian	2	*	55	*	0	0
Regional	OXF OX	Oxfordshire oxidised ware	1	*	3	*	0	0
Local	GR1	soapy grog-tempered	34	4	1013	12	31	5.5
	GR2	sandy grog-tempered	12	1.5	198	2	0	0
	GR4	sandy grog with shell, flint	17	2	264	3	0	0
	GR5	orange-red wheelmade, soapy	65	8	656	7.5	61	11
	GR6	very sandy, sparse grog	6	*	89	1	-0	0
	GREY2	grey sandy ware	2	*	113	1.5	27	5
	GREY4	black sandy ware with buff core	56	7	563	6.5	46	8
	GREY6	very sandy, sparse grog	2	*	12	*	15	2.5
	GREY8	well-fired grey sandy ware	15	2	143	1.5	58	10.5
	OXID1	fine oxidised ware	21	2.5	77	1	16	3
	WW1	sandy white ware	14	1.5	122	1.5	14	2.5
	PNK GT	pink grog-tempered ware	23	3	372	4.5	0	0
	SH!	shelly ware	179	22	1359	16	129	23
	SH2	sandy with sparse shell	113	14	1238	14.5	33	6
	SH4	shell and limestone, hm	37	4.5	307	3.5	36	6.5
Unknown	GREY	miscellaneous grey	13	1.5	51	*	17	3
	CRUMBS	unidentified crumbs	14	1.5	20	*	0	0
TOTAL			811	100	8456	100	556	100

Table 4.4: *Summary of pottery from Silverstone 2 (* = less than 1%).*

33 Wide-mouthed bowl. Form D1. Fabric SH2. Enclosure 1 (1223).

34 Round-bodied bowl with a very slight shoulder carination. Form A1. Fabric SH1. Enclosure 1 (1302).

35 Large slack-sided ovoid-bodied jar. Form C1. Fabric GR3. Pit 2099 (1137).

SILVERTONE 2 (SL2)

Introduction

The archaeological work (evaluation and excavation) resulted in the recovery of 848 sherds of pottery weighing 8.5 kg and largely dating to the middle to late Iron Age and early Roman periods. In addition there was a small amount of fired clay and tile amounting to some 23 fragments.

Pottery was recovered from 31 separate contexts deriving from 28 individual features (Table 4.4). The assemblage is quite fragmented with an overall average sherd size of 10 g. There are no obvious complete profiles present.

Iron Age

The main fabrics present in the group are fossil shell-tempered wares and grog-tempered wares. Small amounts of other types, for example sandy ware, organic-tempered ware, a ferruginous fabric and a sandstone-tempered ware are also present. The shell-tempered component is the largest group accounting for 47% by sherd count of the total assemblage followed by grog at 26.4%. The shell-tempered group globally includes both Iron Age and early Roman material.

Features which appear to contain exclusively material of middle Iron Age date include Phase 1 of Structure 1, and nearby pit 1074. In addition, the line of the pits along the south side of the enclosure appear to be contemporary. In particular, pits 1000, 1031, 1034, 1037, 1041, 1046 and 1052 all produced small groups of pottery.

The second phase of Structure 1 (ditch 1063) produced a much larger assemblage of pottery amounting to some 164 sherds. The presence of sherds of a wheel-turned, grog-tempered, necked bowl suggests that this ditch was abandoned in the early years of the first century AD.

Although the ditch appears to date to the later Iron Age much of the material is middle Iron Age in character. The proportion of shelly ware is quite high (Fabrics SH2 and SH6) accounting for 66% of the group. This may represent redeposited material from the earlier phase or more likely shows a continuation of the middle Iron Age traditions into the later Iron Age. The overall average sherd size for the material from 1063 is 9.9 g compared to 7.0 g for the material from 1082, perhaps arguing against a high level of redeposition. Several jars came from 1063 but these are present in both grog and shelly wares.

Late Iron Age/Early Roman

At least 151 sherds of Roman wares were present. This refers specifically to wares of Romanised form, fabric and technology and excludes the large number of grog and shell-tempered sherds which chronologically also belong in this period.

The enclosure ditches 1006, 1023, 1048 and 1050 produced a large assemblage of pottery amounting to some 451 sherds. Most of this came from the east and north ditches (1048 and 1050). The assemblage comprises mainly late Iron Age 'native' wares in shelly and grog-tempered fabrics which probably continue to be used in rural areas up into the second century AD. Both fabrics include channel rim jars, a distinctive local type particularly common on the first century AD.

A small proportion of more Romanised wares and two sherds of samian indicate a date in at least the second half of the first century AD or even possibly the early second century AD. The sandy wares comprise grey, black and white wheelmade wares, the latter including a bowl with traces of red-painted decoration from ditch 1050. Also present are a few sherds of the local soft, pink, grogged ware, which seems to have developed out of the late Iron Age grog tradition.

Two pits appear to belong to this phase of activity, 1016 and 1059 along with the tree hole 1061. Pit 1004, cut by ditch 1023, also contained a mixture of Iron Age and later material. This pit appears to respect the earlier pit alignment and it is possible that the later pottery, two sherds of sandy ware, is intrusive.

Catalogue of illustrated sherds (Fig 4.2)

36 Handmade wide-mouthed jar with slight sooting on the outer rim. Form B4b. Fabric SH2. Structure 1, Ditch 1063 (1064).

37 Handmade wide-mouthed vessel. Form D(1). Fabric SH2. Structure 1, Ditch 1063 (1064).

38 Small handmade jar with vertical smoothing marks. Form C1. Fabric ORGR. Structure 1, Ditch 1063 (1064).

39 Wheelmade lid-seated jar. Form B7. Fabric SH1. Enclosure Ditch 1048 (1058).

40 Bodysherd with a zone of incised decoration. Fabric GRSA. Enclosure Ditch 1048 (1049).

41 Handmade, wheel-turned everted rim jar with a slightly sooted exterior. Form I4. Fabric SH. Enclosure Ditch 1048 (1058).

42 Wheelmade channel rim jar with notched rim edge. Form B7. Fabric GR3. Ditch Enclosure 1048 (1049).

43 Handmade jar with slight finger depressions around the rim. Form B5. Fabric SH2. Ditch 2/4, = 1021 or 1023.

44 Wheelmade necked jar. Form I4a. Fabric GR5. Structure 1, Ditch 1063 (1064).

45 Wheelmade dish. Form M1. Fabric GREY4. Pit 1059 (1060).

	Fabric	Description	No	%	Wt (g)	%	Eve	%
Native	GR1	soapy grog-tempered	84	17	1047	21	45	17
	GR2	sandy grog-tempered	5	1	68	1.5	13	5
	GR3	shell and grog-tempered	117	23	996	20	58	22
	GR4	sandy grog with shell, flint	19	4	280	5.5	0	0
	GR5	orange-red wheelmade, soapy	3	★	18	★	0	0
	SH1	shelly ware	85	17	728	14.5	44	16.5
	SH2	sandy with sparse shell	89	18	985	20	37	14
	SH3	sandy, common shell	2	★	16	★	3	1
	SH6	coarse shell and limestone	57	11.5	493	10	37	14
	SA1	sandy with iron, rare calcareous	13	2.5	84	1.5	17	6
	SA2	fine sandy, rare calcareous	3	★	91	2	2	★
	SST2	mixed temper with sandstone	1	★	22	★	7	2.5
	ORCA	organic with calcareous frags	9	2	78	1.5	0	0
	Misc	unidentified crumbs	13	2.5	25	★	0	0
Roman	OXIDF	fine oxidised ware	1	★	4	★	3	1
	PNK GT	pink grog-tempered ware	1	★	2	★	0	0
TOTAL			**502**	**100**	**4937**	**100**	**266**	**100**

Table 4.5: Summary of pottery from Biddlesden Road Bridge (★ = less than 1%).

46 Dish with an internal ledge. Form M10. Fabric SH1. Pit 1059 (1060).

47 Beaker. Form I3. Fabric GREY6. Enclosure Ditch 1050 (1051).

48 Small whiteware bowl with orange-red painted decoration. Form H10. Fabric WW1. Enclosure Ditch 1050 (1051).

49 Wheelmade necked bowl. Form F4a. Fabric GREY2. Pit 1016 (1017).

50 Wheelmade round bodied jar with an internally bevelled rim. Form K3. Fabric SH1. Pit 1016 (1017).

BIDDLESDEN ROAD BRIDGE (BRB)

A total of 502 sherds of pottery weighing 4.9 kg were recovered, largely dating to the middle and late Iron Age. In addition, there is a small amount of fired clay amounting to some six fragments and one piece of Roman tile.

Pottery was recovered from 69 separate contexts, deriving from at least 49 individual cuts contributing to 20 defined features. The number of associated sherds is thus quite low. The assemblage is quite fragmented with an overall average sherd size of 9.8 g. There are no complete profiles and only 47 rim sherds present in the total assemblage. A summary of the fabrics recorded can be found in Table 4.5.

Iron Age

The main fabrics present in the group are fossil-shell-tempered wares and grog-tempered wares, of which there are almost equal amounts. These include wares of early, middle and late Iron Age date. A small number of other wares were noted, for example, a sandstone-tempered ware (SST2), sandy ware (SA1, SA2) and an organic and calcareous-tempered ware (ORCA).

?Early-middle Iron Age

On the basis of the pottery, one of the earliest features on the site appears to be curvilinear ditch 2. This produced just 12 unfeatured sherds, all in fabric SH6 for which a provisional date of early or early-middle Iron Age is given on the basis that the sherds are coarse fossil shell. This feature was cut by linear ditch 1 with ten sherds of fabrics SH1, SH2 and GR3, again potentially indicative of an early date in the early or middle Iron Age. Gully 3 also cut by ditch 1 produced no pottery. Slot 1007, close to Ditch 2, also produced nine sherds of fabric SH6. The roundhouse gullies of Structures 4 and 5 similarly yielded very small unfeatured groups. From Structure 5 came one sherd of grog-tempered ware while four sherds of grog-tempered ware, four shelly wares, two grog and shell-tempered wares (GR3) and a fragment of Roman tile came from gully 6. The latter is presumably intrusive. Pits 1252 and 1261 with, between them, 12 shelly wares could also date to the early-middle Iron Age.

Mid-later Iron Age

Structure 2 produced the largest group of material, comprising 122 sherds which seem to suggest a middle to late Iron Age date. The group includes globular bodied simple everted rim jars in grog and shell-tempered fabrics (GR3) and shelly wares SH2 and SH6. A jar from context 1276 (Phase 2) is identical to, or the same vessel as one from 1234 (ditch 11) (see below). If the high percentage

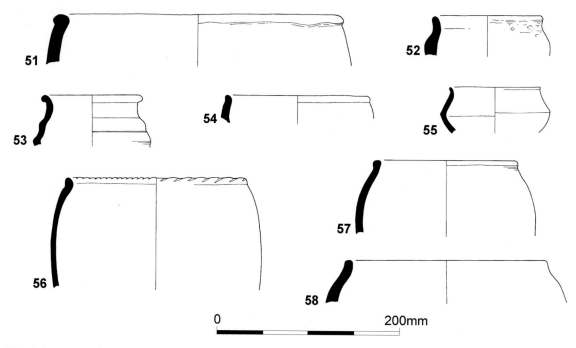

Fig. 4.3: *Pottery from Biddlesden Road Bridge, 51-58.*

of shelly ware and shell and grog-tempered ware against grog-tempered (fabric GR1) and the presence of fabrics ORCA can be regarded as chronologically valid, then it might suggest this structure predates Structure 1.

Ditch 25 and gully 14 (Structure 3) similarly suggest a middle Iron Age date. Ditch 25 contained 15 sherds, including a jar in fabric SST2 alongside fabric SH1 and GR1. Gully 14 with 14 sherds had an association of fabrics GR3, SH1 and SA2. The absence of grog-tempered wares could indicate a potentially earlier date for this feature,

Structure 1 produced one of the larger assemblages from the site, some 80 sherds, 920 g. These included a number of jars in fabric SH2 and in grog-tempered fabrics GR1 and GR2, both handmade and wheel-turned forms. The forms are typical 'Belgic' style dating to the later Iron Age/ early Roman period, for example, necked cordoned jars, and beaded rim types (Fig 4.3, 51-3). A number of shelly wares show greater affinity to middle Iron Age traditions suggesting some residual material, the perpetuation of early traditions or a mid to later Iron Age origin to the enclosure. Some contamination of deposits is evident with a post-medieval sherd. A jar rim in a fine oxidised Roman fabric from the upper fill (1315) could also be intrusive or could indicate a date of abandonment of the later phase ditch in the early Roman period (first century AD).

Curvilinear ditch 8, possibly associated with Structure 1, contained a small group of 21 sherds among which are three jars with simple rims also typical of the later Iron Age period. Pits 1115 and 1119 (Group 10), although small, contained a channel-rimmed jar alongside 'Belgic' type grog-tempered wares, and thus may be contemporary with Structure 1.

Ditch 11 (Structure 3) produced an assemblage of 32 sherds, all exclusively grog-tempered fabrics (GR1-GR4).

The only featured sherds were from an ovoid jar with a slightly beaded rim similar to Figure 4.3, 54. A late Iron Age date is thus likely for the feature. Pits 1239 and 1011 produced small groups, notably a small slackly carinated cup from pit 1011 (Fig 4.3, 55).

Ditch 12 (Structure 3) also produced a small fairly undistinguished assemblage of 11 sherds of grog and shelly wares (GR3, SH1, SH2), probably dating to the later Iron Age. Ditch 17, which cut ditch 11, produced a similar size of assemblage of 31 sherds from four separate contexts. The latest material appears to be a shelly ware jar with diagonal lines on the rim and a wheel-finished grog-tempered jar, which together suggest a later Iron Age or early Roman date. An identical jar was recovered from furnace 1, which was cut by ditch 17. Sixteen sherds were recovered from this furnace, a mixture of shell, and grog-tempered wares including at least one wheelmade vessel.

Although the site appears to have gone through several phases of use the pottery suggests that most of these could be relatively short-lived and that most of the activity dates to the middle and later Iron Age. The lack of many distinctive later Iron Age types could suggest that there is little change in pottery development, or that this phase of use on the site was fairly non-intensive or of a non-domestic character.

Roman

Although the site was probably occupied in the first century AD only one sherd specifically of Roman type was present, from a post-medieval furrow. Wheelmade wares, when present, were in local native grog or shell-tempered fabrics. A fragment of probable Roman tile was recovered from gully 6 (Structure 4) which otherwise appears to be Iron Age in date. The evidence thus suggests that the site may have been abandoned sometime around or before the middle of the first century AD.

	Fabric	Description	No	%	Wt (g)	%	Eve	%
IRON AGE	SH1	shelly ware	49	4	406	3	23	2
	GR1	grog-tempered ware	3	★	38	★	0	0
	GR3	grog and shell-tempered	47	4	179	1.5	0	0
	SA2	sandy	7	★	76	★	0	0
ROMAN Import								
	CGSAM	Central Gaulish samian	8	★	81	★	42	3.5
Regional	DPR BB1	Dorset black burnished ware	4	★	30	★	0	0
	LNV CC	Lower Nene Valley colour-coat	1	★	10	★	0	0
	OXF WH	Oxfordshire white ware	21	2	326	2.5	176	15
	OXF WHM	Oxfordshire mortaria	3	★	96	★	7	★
Local	GR1	soapy grog-tempered	87	7	1630	12.5	11	1
	GR3	shell and grog-tempered	18	1.5	198	1.5	6	
	GR4	sandy grog with shell, flint	1	★	7	★	0	0
	GR5	orange-red wheelmade, soapy	18	1.5	249	2	0	0
	GR6	very sandy, sparse grog	4	★	60	★	0	0
	GR7	whiteware grog-tempered	14	1	189	1.5	0	0
	GR8	sandy grog-tempered	100	8.5	2062	16	98	8.5
	GREY1	fine grey ware	41	3.5	324	2.5	76	6.5
	GREY2	grey sandy ware	200	17	1585	12	151	13
	GREY4	black sandy ware with buff core	2	★	30	★	22	2
	GREY7	black sandy ware	19	1.5	149	1	43	3.5
	GREY8	well-fired grey sandy ware	29	2.5	305	2.3	71	6
	GREY9	Nene Valley grey ware	24	2	270	2	35	3
	MICA	mica-slipped oxidised ware	2	★	20	★	5	★
	OXID1	fine oxidised ware	78	6.5	741	5.5	35	3
	OXID2	sandy oxidised ware	176	15	1259	9.5	218	18.5
	WW1	sandy white ware	116	10	1777	13.5	115	10
	PNK GT	pink grog-tempered ware	9	★	128	1	0	0
	SH1	shelly ware	60	5	350	2.5	8	★
	SH2	sandy with sparse shell	3	★	13	★	0	0
	SH3	sandy, common shell	8	★	54	★	3	★
	SH4	shell and limestone, hm	2	★	50	★	0	0
Unknown	GREY	miscellaneous grey	22	2	230	2	0	0
	OXCC	oxidised with colour-coat	2	★	10	★	10	1
	WWCC	white ware with colour coat	4	★	71	★	16	1.5
	WW	miscellaneous white sandy	1	★	3	★	1	★
	MORT	unclassified mortaria	2	★	49	★	0	0
	MISC	miscellaneous	2	★	18	★	0	0
TOTAL			1187	100	13073	100	1172	100

Table 4.6: Summary of pottery from Area G Syresham (★ = less than 1%).

Catalogue of illustrated sherds (Fig 4.3)

51 Large wide-mouthed vessel. Form C4a. Fabric SH2. Structure 1, Cut 1328 (1326).

52 Handmade, small necked bowl. Form G1. Fabric SH6. Structure 1, Cut 1328 (1326)

53 Wheelmade necked bowl/jar. Form G4a. Fabric GR1. Structure 1, Cut 1318 (1315).

54 Handmade ovoid jar. Form C1. Fabric SH2. Structure 1, Hollow 1150 (1149).

55 Handmade carinated cup. Form A4a. Fabric SH2. Pit 1011 (1010).

56 Handmade barrel-shaped jar with a burnish in the interior and exterior surfaces. Form C4a. Fabric GR3. Structure 2, Cut 1385 (1384).

57 Handmade barrel-shaped jar with a slashed rim. Form C4ab/12. Fabric SH1. Furnace 1, Pit 1073 (1072).

58 Handmade wide-mouthed jar. Form C1. Fabric GR1. Furnace 1, Pit 1073 (1072).

SHACKS BARN FARM (SHB)

The evaluation resulted in the recovery of 83 sherds of pottery weighing 1474 g. Sherds were associated with eleven contexts, three of which, 2704 (ditch 2774), 2706 (pit 2775) and 3620 (gully 36100) probably date to the middle Iron Age period and yielded a total of 39 sherds. One of these sherds is Roman and presumed to be intrusive. The remainder of the assemblage dates largely to the Roman period (first to third centuries). The only imports are a sherd of Oxfordshire white ware mortarium (Young 1977, form M22) and a sherd of Central Gaulish samian.

Illustrated sherd (Fig 4.4)

59   Handmade, slightly shouldered jar. Form C3. Fabric SH6. Pit 2775 (2706).

JUNIPER HILL (JH) WB M40 Ch6305

A small assemblage of some 45 sherds weighing just 158 g was recovered from context 7, pit 6. The material was very fragmentary and consists of a mixture of shell-tempered ware and grog-tempered ware. The latter appears to be a wheel-finished, necked, cordoned, bowl suggesting a possible date in the later Iron Age for this group.

SILVERSTONE 4 (SL4)

A small assemblage of just nine sherds (89 g) was recovered from the watching brief. This includes three sherds of middle Iron Age date from Pits 3 and 5, and late second to third century Roman wares from pits 7 and 9. The latter includes two sherds of Lower Nene Valley colour-coated ware. The unstratified material contains two Roman sherds (PNK GT).

COTTISFORD TURN (TCT)

A small group of 16 very abraded sherds weighing just 40 g was recovered from the main fill of Ditch 178 (103) and pits 130 and 162. The material is difficult to date closely other than probably later prehistoric. All the sherds appear to be shell-tempered, including fabric SH6, which could be regarded as diagnostic of the early-middle Iron Age.

TUSMORE DRAIN OUTFALL (TDO)

A small assemblage of 114 sherds (1308 g) was recovered from four contexts. Two contexts, 5 and 7, both fills of Ditch 6, containing 24 and 23 sherds respectively, have proved difficult to date with confidence. The fabric range is slightly different to the typical Iron Age material elsewhere on this project. There are three main fabrics present, one containing finely crushed fragments of calcined bone; one containing a mixture of fine grog and shell, the latter

represented by flat voids; and a micaceous ware with grog, organic matter and ferruginous inclusions. The latter sherds from context 7 show internal sooting. The only featured sherds are one rim from context 5 and one body-sherd with a single circular finger-impression showing the nail line. On balance, the group probably dates to the early Iron Age (D Jackson pers comm). Recent work has identified small quantities of Iron Age bone-tempered pottery from assemblages in the Thames Valley, in particular Yarnton (A Barclay pers comm).

The possible posthole, 118, produced a single Roman grey ware, while context 1, the topsoil, contained 66 sherds all of Roman date. This group includes Central Gaulish samian, Oxfordshire colour-coated ware, Nene Valley grey ware and local pink grogged ware, which together suggest occupation dating to the later second and third centuries

Illustrated sherd (Fig 4.4)

60   Handmade, expanded rim jar. Form B3/4 ab. Fabric GR3. Ditch 6 context 5.

CPO WB SL Ch7420

Illustrated sherd (Fig 4.4)

61   A single unstratified sherd from a grog-tempered bowl (form D6) was recovered. The vessel is typical of the late Iron Age or early Roman period.

SYRESHAM, AREA G

Introduction

A total of 1187 sherds of Iron Age and Roman pottery weighing c 130 kg was recovered. Eleven per cent of this, some 131 sherds (1444g), came from the watching brief in Field C. The remaining pottery, from the trench excavations, comprises a mixture of Iron Age ware, later Iron Age/early Roman native wares and Roman material proper. The watching brief assemblage similarly comprises a mixture of Iron Age and Roman material with one medieval and three post-medieval pieces. A summary of the Iron Age and Roman fabrics can be found in Table 4.6.

Pottery was recovered from nine of the total 32 trenches excavated; a total of 32 individual contexts. The assemblage was only moderately well preserved with an overall average sherd size of 10.5 g. The sherds were fairly abraded in appearance and colour-coats did not survive well. The sherd size is relatively low, especially for Roman wares, which tend to be more robust. There was some variability between contexts. Several joins were apparent among material from the same contexts.

Iron Age

All the pottery recovered from Field A (trenches 4, 5, and 6), a total of 100 sherds, appears to date to the Iron

Age. Forty-four of these sherds derive from the base of one closed vessel from a buried soil (619) in trench 6. Apart from the vessel from 619, the sherds are generally quite small (average 6.5 g) and abraded. The pottery was associated with just two features, enclosure ditches 412 and 516, and linear gully 620.

The group includes at least six rims of which one, from gully 620 (603) may have surface finger-nicking but the rim is very fragmentary. The other vessels, all jars, suggest fairly globular or round-bodied vessels with simple undifferentiated inward-turned rims in shell or grog-tempered fabrics. There were no decorated pieces although some of the sherds displayed a burnished finish. A further four grog-tempered sherds occur in ditch 1147 (Field C) suggesting a later Iron Age date for this feature.

The fabrics basically fall into two groups: grog-tempered and shelly. A date in the middle to late Iron Age (fourth to second/first century BC) might be proposed for much of this assemblage based on the rim morphology. The jar base from 619 is less easy to date; the fabric is very soapy, with grog-tempering. The exterior is orange with a black core and interior, a feature characteristic of early prehistoric material. The walls however, are quite thin. It may thus be contemporary with the other Iron Age material.

Roman

Most of the assemblage derived from trenches across Fields B, C, D and E appears to date from the later first century AD through to the third century. The principal fabrics are grog-tempered wares, accounting for 16.6% of the total assemblage, and various grey and oxidised sandy wares together accounting for 4.8%. Recognisable traded wares include eight sherds of Central Gaulish samian, four sherds of Dorset black burnished ware, Oxfordshire white ware including mortaria, and Nene Valley grey ware and mortaria. Pottery was recovered from trenches 9, 10, 11, 22, 23 and 31.

A single sherd of PNK GT came from the buried soil (903) in trench 9 for which a second or third century date is possible. The greatest concentration of material by far came from trench 10 in Field C, some 861 sherds, 72% by sherd count of the total assemblage. The most substantial features in the trench, ditch 1043, produced quite a modest assemblage of 38 sherds. Forms include whitewares imitating samian form Dragendorff 30 (cf. Young 1977, type W53), one of which probably had a colour-coat, several grog-tempered wares and some grey sandy wares, probably one of the Nene Valley greywares and a greyware flat-rim bowl. The forms might suggest an early second-century date for this feature. Ditch 1147 (trench 11) also produced a modest assemblage of 30 sherds. The only featured sherd was a Nene Valley grey ware bowl, as Camulodunum (Cam) form 37 (Bidwell and Croom 1999, 469) which has quite a broad timespan through the second into the early third century. The group also includes various grog-tempered sherds, seven shelly wares and five

grey sandy wares. The grog and shelly wares, if not residual, could suggest an earlier rather than later date.

The complex of shallow gullies in the central area of trench 10 produced much larger groups of pottery. The earliest stratigraphically, gully 1038, contained 243 sherds, 2261 g. Within the group are three sherds of Central Gaulish samian, Oxfordshire white ware, including mortaria, and various oxidised and reduced grey sandy wares. Forms in the latter two groups include reeded rim bowls, flat rim bowls, lids, shallow dishes, cornice rim beakers and an Oxfordshire white ware jar (Young 1977, form W33). Of particular note are three very worn sherds (Fig 4.4, 66-8) from a bowl made in a mould imitating a decorated samian bowl. The sherds are in a fine off-white fabric and are very worn with no surviving colour-coat. The faint relief patterns suggests that the design is quite a faithful copy with figures and motifs (?palmettes) within defined zones. No parallel is known for the production of imitation samian in the area although the nature of the paste could well suggest local production rather than an import. By contrast to the enclosure ditch(es) grog-tempered wares are low in number, just five sherds, four from a storage jar, and shelly wares are absent. A date around the mid second century would encapsulate the wares present.

Gully 1037, cutting 1038, yielded 124 sherds, 1893 g. In contrast to gully 1038 the sherds were in better condition and generally larger in size, an average of 15 g (as opposed to just 9 g in 1038). The range of material showed a number of similarities with reed-rim bowls, flat-rim bowls everted-rim jars and lids. A slightly later date for the group is suggested by an indented greyware beaker, a Dorset black burnished ware plain-rimmed dish and a ring-necked Oxfordshire whiteware flagon (Young 1977 type W6), placing the assemblage overall into the mid to later second century. Also present is a Central Gaulish samian cup, Dragendorff type 33 with a broken stamp]TERNIF.

Gully 1036, cutting 1037, had a smaller assemblage of 60 sherds (622 g) in a similar state of fragmentation to those in gully 1038, at 10 g. This also had a grey ware bowl (Cam type 37), a whiteware cornice rim beaker and a greyware plain-rimmed dish amongst other jars, bowls and beakers. Chronologically it is quite close to gully 1037 and a date in the later second century may fit this group. The latest gully in the sequence, gully 1039 produced the largest assemblage, some 301 sherds, 2711 g, again quite well fragmented with an average sherd weight of 9 g. In terms of fabric and form composition it is quite similar to the other groups and thus not much later in date. Imports include four sherds of Central Gaulish samian and Oxfordshire whiteware mortaria. Amongst the finewares are two sherds from a mica-slipped flat-rim dish and a sherd from a beaker with roughcast decoration. Oxidised sandy wares are well represented with lids, cornice-rim beakers, everted-rim jars and dishes. Some of the oxidised and whiteware sherds have faint traces of a colour-coated finish.

	Fabric	Description	No	%	Wt (g)	%	Eve	%
ROMAN								
Import	CGSAM	Central Gaulish samian	3	★	50	★	2	2
Regional	LNV CC	Lower Nene Valley colour-coat	1	★	30	★	0	0
	OXF RE	Oxfordshire grey ware	1	★	6	★	0	0
	OXF BW	Oxfordshire burnt white ware	1	★	24	★	0	0
	OXF WHM	Oxfordshire whiteware mortaria	6	1.5	213	3	11	12.5
	OXF RS	Oxfordshire colour-coated ware	15	4	122	1.5	0	0
	OXF RSM	Oxfordshire cc mortaria	13	3.5	218	3	12	13.5
	OXF PA	Oxfordshire parchment ware	2	★	33	★	0	0
Local	GROG	grog-tempered ware	1	★	10	★	0	0
	GR3	grog and shell-tempered	1	★	32	★	0	0
	GR7	grogged whiteware	2	★	27	★	0	0
	GREY1	fine grey ware	20	5	600	7.5	20	23
	GREY4	black sandy ware with buff core	16	4	281	3.5	5	5.5
	GREY5	speckled hard grey sandy	7	2	57	★	0	0
	GREY7	black sandy ware	2	★	26	★	0	0
	GREY8	well-fired grey sandy ware	25	6.5	387	5	0	0
	GREY9	Nene Valley grey ware	12	3	274	3.5	11	12.5
	OXID2	sandy oxidised ware	12	3	78	1	0	0
	WW1	sandy white ware	7	2	74	1	0	0
	PBK GT	pink grog-tempered ware	204	53.5	5148	64.5	10	11.5
	SH1	shelly ware	9	2.5	65	1	0	0
	ROB SH	late Roman shelly ware	12	3	142	1.7	17	19
Unknown	GREY	miscellaneous grey	7	2	87	1	0	0
	MISC	miscellaneous	3	1	14	★	0	0
TOTAL			**382**	**100**	**7998**	**100**	**88**	**100**

Table 4.7: *Summary of pottery from Great Ouse Culvert (★ = less than 1%).*

Trench 11 produced a small group of 30 sherds from ditch 1147 with a mixture of grog-tempered and shelly wares alongside a grey sandy ware bowl (Cam form 37), suggesting a date in the early second century at the earliest, although as noted already this form is quite long-lived.

Trench 22 produced a very small assemblage from gully 2280, some 12 sherds, all unfeatured. The fabrics, GR5, SH1 and OXID2 are all types current in the first to second centuries. A particularly unusual group of material was recovered from trench 23, feature 2384, which probably represents a dump of kiln waste within a kiln structure. The group of 75 sherds were mainly white or pink wares with sparse grog-tempering (fabric GR2). Also present were 20 whiteware (fabric WW1). The sherds gave the impression of poor firing with grey patches on some sherds. The vessels included a cordoned, necked jar, a sharply everted rim jar and some unusual reeded rims. One jar had rows of decoration comprising impressed crescents (Fig 4.4, 64). No other wares occurred with this group to assist dating and at present it is provisionally dated to the early second century. The fabric greatly resembles that associated with the kilns investigated at Brackley Hatch 4. Eight fragments of kiln bars were also recovered from this feature.

An adjacent context from the same trench, ditch 2385, produced a sharply carinated bowl or cup in a grog- and limestone-tempered ware and a 'Belgic' grog-tempered sherd. These would also be consistent with a first century date. Gully 2387 produced a small mixed group of 12 sherds, mostly grog-tempered and probably of second-century currency.

The remaining pottery was unstratified. Trench 31 produced a single grog-tempered bodysherd from the topsoil. The watching brief collection of material from Field C produced a mixture of grog, shell and grey wares generally reflective of the material seen elsewhere with a general date range extending from the later Iron Age through to the second century.

Discussion

The assemblage shows occupation dating back to the middle Iron Age, with reoccupation of the site from perhaps in the late Iron Age or early first century AD. The bulk of the assemblage dates to the second and possibly early third centuries AD. There does not appear to be any evidence of continuity of occupation, on the basis of the pottery assemblage, between the Iron Age and

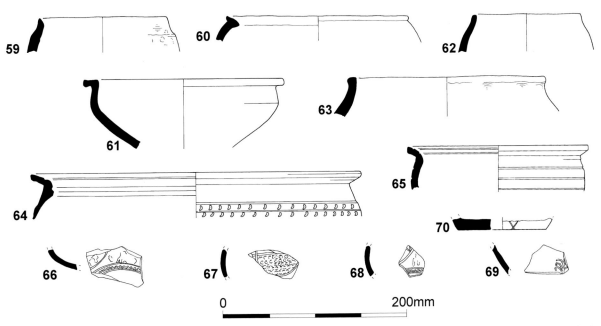

Fig. 4.4: *Pottery from Shacks Barn Farm, 59; Tusmore Drain Outfall, 60; WB SL Chainage 7420, 61; Area G Syresham, 62-68; Great Ouse Culvert, 69-70.*

the subsequent first-century AD occupation. The small amount of pottery dated provisionally to the first century AD is the most difficult to be certain of, both in terms of dating and whether it should be seen as discrete from the Roman occupation proper. There is no evidence of occupation dating to the later Roman period (mid third to fourth centuries).

The assemblage is a fairly modest one in terms of status in that it only contains a small quantity of imports and few fine wares. The impression is that of a rural domestic assemblage where locally made storage jars and domestic wares dominate.

Catalogue of illustrated sherds (Fig 4.4)

62 Handmade barrel-shaped jar. Form C1. Fabric GR1. Ditch 412 (407).

63 Handmade wide-mouthed jar with a roughly smoothed finish. Form C1. Fabric SH2. Ditch 412 (407).

64 Wide-mouthed bowl with a grooved rim and decorated with two extant rows of impressed crescents. Pink in colour. Form D10/7. Fabric GR8. Kiln 2384 (2302).

65 Bowl with an everted grooved rim and decorated with girth grooves. Orange-pink in colour. Form D10/7. Fabric GR8. Kiln 2384 (2302).

66-8 Three very worn bodysherds from a single bowl made in a mould imitating samian. The design appears quite complex embodying several components paralleled on imported samian. Made in a very fine off-white fabric (WW2). Gully 1038 (1011).

GREAT OUSE CULVERT (GOC)

The archaeological work resulted in the recovery of 382 sherds of pottery weighing 8 kg exclusively dating to the later Roman period. In addition there is a small amount

of ceramic building material and fired clay amounting to some 18 fragments.

Pottery was recovered from just eight contexts with a large collection of unstratified material, which effectively accounts for 74% of the recorded assemblage (Table 4.7). The assemblage is quite well preserved with an overall average sherd weight of 20.9 g, although the sherds generally appear quite worn and slightly abraded. There are no complete profiles.

The assemblage mainly comprises wares of local origin, in particular soft pink-grogged wares (PNK GT) in both handmade and wheelmade forms and local grey sandy wares. Continental imports are limited to three sherds of Central Gaulish samian. The latest wares present are sherds of late Roman shell-tempered ware (ROBSH) and several later fourth-century products of the Oxfordshire industries including colour-coated ware, burnt white ware, parchment ware and mortaria. Recognisable forms include Young (1977) types M22, C48, C71 and colour-coated mortaria.

Of particular note are two sherds with graffiti. One is a basesherd with a small X incised into the edge (Fig 4.4, 70) from the unstratified material. The second sherd, from context 3, the buried soil, has a small floral motif scratched into the sherd after firing (Fig 4.4, 69).

A small amount of ceramic building material is also present including at least two tegulae, one imbrex and one fragment of combed box flue.

Catalogue of illustrated sherds (Fig 4.4)

69 Bodysherd in a fine hard white fabric with a pictorial graffiti scrathed into the surface after firing. Fabric WW2. Context 3.

	Fabric	Description	No	%	Wt (g)	%	Eve	%
Import	CGSAM	Central Gaulish samian	3	★	16	★	0	0
	SGSAM	South Gaulish samian	1	★	24	★	0	0
Regional	DOR BB1	Dorset black burnished ware	4	★	36	★	6	★
	LNV CC	Lower Nene Valley colour-coat	3	★	14	★	0	0
	OXF WH	Oxfordshire white ware	34	1	449	1	68	2
	OXF RE	Oxfordshire grey ware	5	★	49	★	0	0
	OXF RS	Oxfordshire colour-coat	4	★	76	★	7	★
	VER WH	Verulamium white ware	22	1	186	★	0	0
Local/native	GR1	soapy grog-tempered	219	9	3763	8	123	4
	GR3	shell and grog-tempered	77	3	1697	4	164	6
	GR4	sandy grog with shell, flint	8	★	290	★	18	★
	GR5	orange-red wheelmade, soapy	117	5	1719	4	248	8.5
	GR6	very sandy, sparse grog	29	1	494	1	113	4
	GR7	whiteware grog-tempered	213	9	2837	6	294	10
	GR8	sandy grog-tempered (kiln)	584	24	19744	43	732	25.5
	GRL	grey ware with fine calcareous	86	3.5	1443	3	208	7
	GREY1	fine grey ware	56	2	538	1	57	2
	GREY2	grey sandy ware	80	3	709	1.5	23	1
	GREY3	fine grey ware with red core	6	★	45	★	14	★
	GREY4	black sandy ware with buff core	10	★	91	★	39	1
	GREY5	grey speckled ware	17	★	101	★	5	★
	GREY6	fine silky grey ware	11	★	70	★	7	★
	GREY7	black sandy ware	30	1	265	★	0	0
	GREY8	well-fired grey sandy ware	52	2	579	1	63	2
	GREY9	Nene Valley type grey wares	53	2	780	2	52	2
	MICA	mica-slipped oxidised ware	2	★	5	★	0	0
	OXID1	fine oxidised ware	17	★	61	★	15	★
	OXID2	sandy oxidised ware	27	1	119	★	36	1
	PNK GT	pink grog-tempered ware	238	10	4703	10	133	5
	SH1	shelly ware	209	8.5	2487	5.5	210	7
	SH2	sandy with sparse shell	96	4	1645	3.5	206	7
	SH3	sandy, common shell	39	1.5	257	★	10	★
Unknown	GREY	miscellaneous grey	12	★	144	★	17	★
	WW1	miscellaneous white sandy	27	1	203	★	5	★
	WW2	fine white ware	1	★	4	★	0	0
	MISC	miscellaneous	9	★	66	★	0	0
	crumbs		32	1	56	★	0	0
TOTAL			**2433**	**100**	**45765**	**100**	**2873**	**100**

Table 4.8: *Summary of Roman fabrics from Brackley Hatch 4 (★ = less than 1%).*

70 Base of a black sandy ware jar. Fabric GY4. A cross has been incised onto the base of the wall. Unstratified.

BRACKLEY HATCH 4 (BH4)

Introduction

The excavation resulted in the recovery of 2433 sherds of Roman pottery weighing 45.8 kg. Pottery was recovered from 34 separate contexts, some 26 individual features. A particularly large group of material was recovered from ditch 35 effectively accounting for 37% of the total assemblage. A further substantial group of material came from the two kiln structures, 61 and 66, accounting for another 18% of the assemblage, and Ditch 48 with a further 14%. The remaining 29% spread across the other contexts has resulted in a number of small groups, some with no obviously chronologically diagnostic material.

The condition of the sherds is variable with some exceptionally well preserved pieces, including at least three profiles, and some slightly more abraded material. The average sherd size of 19 g reflects this good preservation, particularly where much of the grog-tempered material is quite soft and easily abraded.

Most of the pottery assemblage from the features appears to date to the later first, second and third centuries.

The group is a very conservative one dominated by local products with few imported wares, thus making dating of some of the smaller groups tentative (Table 4.8). The coarse ware assemblage can basically be divided into three groups: shell-tempered ware, grog-tempered wares and sandy wares, which account for 12%, 65% and 16% of the assemblage respectively.

Amongst the wares imported to the site are four sherds of samian, four sherds of Dorset black burnished ware, twenty-two sherds of Verulamium white ware, at least two Oxfordshire mortaria, Oxfordshire whiteware and four sherds of Oxfordshire colour-coated ware. Other regional products include three sherds of Lower Nene Valley colour-coated ware, and a considerable amount of grey ware probably from the Nene Valley industries. Two sherds of mica-slipped vessel from posthole 27 may be local or imported.

Description of pottery kiln material
Most of the pottery recovered from the kilns appears to be one ware type, albeit with minor variations. This is a sandy textured grog or clay-pellet tempered ware, mainly in oxidised ware (fabric GR8). The consistency of the group plus the presence of clearly over-fired material strongly suggest that these groups are representative of the material produced from these kilns. In total 370 sherds were recovered from the kilns. The sherds were relatively large, with an average sherd weight of 48 g and an estimated vessel equivalence of 702. A number of other fabrics were also present and it is unclear whether these include other products on the site or slightly further afield. One fabric, GRL, may be waster material as it is highly fired, but the other sherds show no signs of being kiln waste.

The pottery produced in the kilns is likely to have been oxidised as a completely sealed atmosphere necessary for reduction would have been more difficult to maintain. Indeed, most of the sherds from the kiln pits are oxidised. Amongst the pottery sherds was some thick-walled 'vessel' in the same fabric with crude internal finger-smearing. It is uncertain whether this is material connected with the kiln structures, a saggar or some other form of portable kiln furniture, or if it is from a large, crude vessel.

The pottery recovered from the kilns comprised a mixture of jar and bowl forms (Fig 4.5, 71-85). Several of the jars had channel rims and the bowls included one with a reeded rim and cordoned body. Also present were larger storage-type jars and three white shallow dishes or platters loosely copying moulded imported types. Many of the vessels, although wheelmade, are quite thick-walled and suggest the use of a fairly slow wheel. Jars account for 87.5% of the total group by EVE, bowls for 8.5% and dishes for 4%.

Slightly sandy grog-tempered wares, often generically referred to as soft pink grogged wares, are very common in the later first to second century onwards in the area. The ware probably developed out of the 'Belgic' grog-tempered tradition. The technology associated with these wares suggests perhaps that the potters were probably producing wares for a very local market. The vessels are difficult to date closely. The shallow dishes and storage jars can be paralleled with wares produced in the Weekley and Rushden kilns (Jackson and Dix 1986-7; Woods and Hastings 1984) dated to the post-conquest period. Some of the associated wares in the kilns are perhaps of later first century date, for example Fig 4.6, 92. The cordoned carinated bowls and dishes (Fig 4.6, 86-7) also find parallel with the material produced at Weekley (Jackson and Dix 1986-7, fig 21). Provisionally therefore, without any independent dating evidence, a date perhaps in the later first century AD may be appropriate for this group.

The same fabric occurs throughout most of the other features investigated reflecting the broad contemporaneity of much of the assemblage. In particular, an over-fired storage jar was recovered from ditch 35.

Other features
The largest assemblage from the site is that associated with ditch 35, some 909 sherds, 12,943 g in weight. The average sherd size for the group is 14 g. In terms of composition the ditch assemblage comprises 60% grog, 23% shelly ware and 17% sandy wares. The latter includes 13 sherds of Verulamium white ware and seven sherds of Oxfordshire white ware. The form repertoire on the basis of the rims is limited to just jars (79.5%) and bowls (20.5%). Most of the wares would appear to date to the second century, to a certain extent supported by the relatively high presence of shelly wares which tend to be superseded by grog-tempered wares from the second century. There are one or two sherds, notably a roulette-decorated Verulamium white ware butt beaker of first-century origin. Most of the shelly wares here are fabric SH2, mainly featuring as channel rim jars.

Ditch 35 cut ditch 48, which also contained a moderately substantial assemblage of 341 sherds. Of particular note in this group was a plain rimmed Dorset black burnished ware dish, an Oxfordshire white ware flagon and mortaria (Young 1977, type M6), Nene Valley grey ware, some potentially later pink grogged ware and an indented colour-coated Lower Nene Valley ware beaker. These might suggest that this ditch was abandoned in the later 2nd century, or even early 3rd century. On the basis of these potentially later sherds, it is possible that there was some intrusive material from Ditch 35. The assemblage from ditch 48 comprised 12% shelly ware, 57% grog-tempered wares and 31% sandy or other wares. The sherd size was similar to the pottery in ditch 35, with an average sherd weight of 12 g. In terms of vessel composition 85.5% comprised jars, 3% bowls, 3% mortaria and 8.5% flagon. Ditch 35 was in turn cut by quarry pit 45 which produced a small group of 39 sherds, in slightly more fragmented

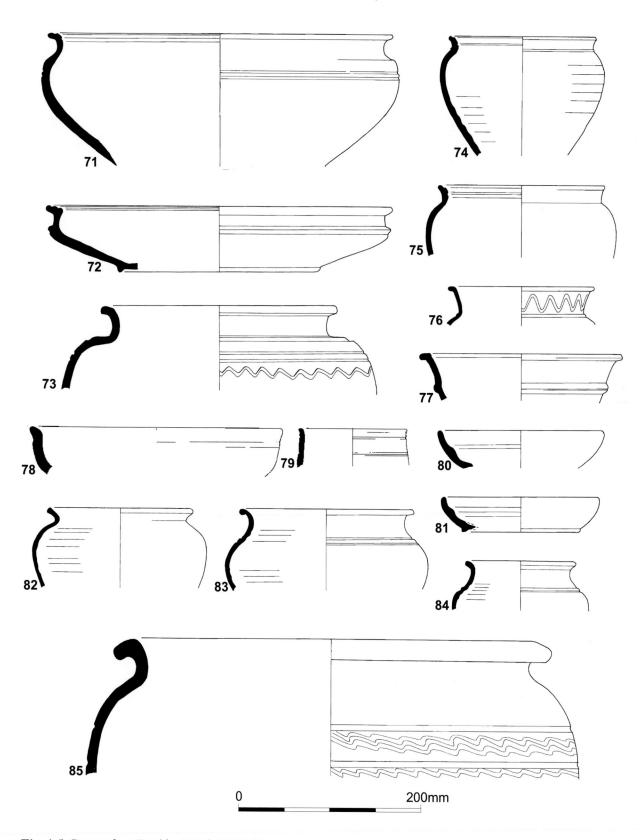

Fig. 4.5: Pottery from Brackley Hatch 4, 71-85.

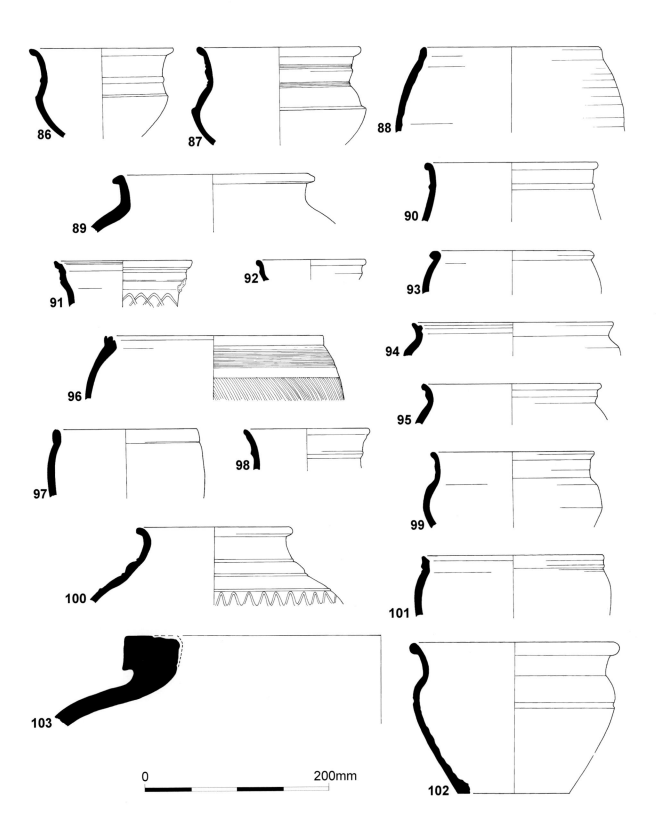

Fig. 4.6: *Pottery from Brackley Hatch 4, 86-103.*

condition with a mixture of shell, grog and sand sherds but with nothing diagnostically late.

Ditch 48 cut a shallow curving gully (41) to the south which contained just three pink grog-tempered sherds, potentially of second-century date. The remaining groups of pottery, largely recovered from pits, postholes, gullies and ditches, were quite small. Ditches 9 and 76 would appear to contain material typical of the later second or third centuries. Some kiln lining was noted in ditch 9 but whether this should be seen as redeposited or evidence of ongoing pottery production in the locality is difficult to say.

The subsoil (layer 22) contained a grooved rim Dorset black burnished ware bowl and a sherd of Nene Valley colour-coated ware indicative of third century activity in the area. A moderately large assemblage of 261 sherds from the underlying colluvium (layer 23) sealed the cut features at the southern margin of the site (particularly ditches 11, 14, 35 and 48). With the exception of four post-medieval sherds the layer contains a mixture of sherds reflective of the material within the underlying features. The sherd size is not appreciably different to the feature fills at 13.5 g, suggesting little ongoing soil disturbance of the deposits. The latest Roman pieces include a sherd of Oxfordshire colour-coated ware (Young 1977, form C51) and an Oxfordshire white ware mortarium (ibid, form M22) suggesting a later third or early fourth-century terminus post quem. The only other late Roman material came from the general overburden, represented by a single sherd of an Oxfordshire colour-coated bowl (Young 1977, type C75) traditionally dated to the period AD 325-400, and a sherd of Nene Valley colour-coated ware. Of particular note from the unstratified material was an exceptionally large storage vessel or dolium in the local pink-grogged ware (Fig 4.6,103).

Catalogue of illustrated sherds (Fig 4.5: Kilns 61 and 66)

71 Large necked bowl with a slightly moulded rim and girth grooves. Form H10. Fabric GR8. Kiln 61 (62).

72 Large shallow bowl with a reeded rim and carinated, cordoned body. Form H11. Fabric GR2. Kiln 61 (62).

73 Large necked storage jar decorated with a single wavy tooled line. Form I4a. Fabric GR8. Kiln 61 (62).

74 Cordoned short-necked jar. Form K. Fabric GR8. Kiln 61 (62).

75 Necked jar with internally moulded rim. Form K10. Fabric GR3. Kiln 61 (65).

76 Necked cordoned jar decorated with a lightly tooled wavy line on the neck. Form I4a. Fabric GR7. Kiln 61 (65).

77 Bowl with a girth cordon and slightly flattened rim. Form H6. Fabric GR8. Kiln 61 (62).

78 Shallow bowl with a slightly out-turned lip. Form H4. Fabric GR8. Kiln 61 (65).

79 Small bowl or wide-mouthed beaker with girth grooves. Form L10. Fabric GR1. Kiln 61 (65).

80-1 Shallow dishes loosely copying moulded forms. Form M4. Fabric GR8. Kiln 61 (62).

82 Jar with sharply everted rim. Form K. Fabric GREY5. Kiln 66 (69).

83-4 Necked cordoned jars. Form I4a. Fabric GREY5. Kiln 66 (69).

85 Large storage jar decorated with a band of wavy combing. Form N. Well fired fabric GR8 although with a reduced core. Kiln 66 (69).

Catalogue of illustrated sherds (Fig 4.6)

86 Wheelmade carinated, cordoned bowl. Form L4a. Fabric GR3. Ditch 35 (54).

87 Wheelmade carinated cordoned bowl. Form L4a. Fabric GR8. Ditch 35 (54).

88 Wheelmade barrel-shaped jar. Form C1. Fabric GR3. Ditch 35 (36).

89 Wheelmade necked jar. Fabric I4a. Overfired fabric GR8. Ditch 35 (36).

90 Large ?carinated, cordoned bowl. Form H/L4a. Fabric GR8. Ditch 35 (36).

91 Light grey sandy ?tankard with a handle scar. Decorated with tooled wavy lines. Form L10. Fabric GREY. Ditch 35 (36).

92. Bowl with a concave mouth. Form H4a. Fabric GREY4. Ditch 35 (36).

93 Rolled rim jar. Form C4a. Fabric GR8. Ditch 35, (2/7).

94 Wheelmade jar/bowl with moulded interior rim. Form H10. Fabric SH1. Slighted sooted exterior. Ditch 48 (50).

95 Necked jar. Form I4a. Fabric GR7. Ditch 48 (50).

96 Wheelmade channel rim jar with a groove on the upper rim surface. Horizontal rilling below the rim and diagonal fine combing on the body. Form C7/10. Fabric SH1. Ditch 35 (2/7).

97 Wheelmade grooved rim jar. Form C7. Fabric SH2. Ditch 35 (2/7).

98 Wheelmade bowl. Form L4a. Fabric GR8. Burnished exterior. Ditch 35 (2/7).

99 Necked bowl. Wheel-turned. Form F4a. Fabric SH1. Ditch 35 (2/7).

100 Necked cordoned jar decorated with a zone of tooled wavy line. Form J4a. Fabric GR5. Ditch 35 (2/7).

101 Wide-mouthed jar or bowl. Form H120. Fabric GR7. Ditch 35 (2/7).

102 Necked jar. Form F4a. Fabric GREY9. Ditch 59 (60).

103 Dolium. Fabric PNK GT. Unstratified.

Ceramic building material

In addition to the fired clay there were approximately 50 fragments of ceramic building material. This was generally only small fragments not easily identifiable to type although at least two tegulae were noted (pits 24, 72). Many of the fragments came from colluvium layer 23.

DISCUSSION

Although the county of Northamptonshire is rich in archaeological remains dating to the Iron Age and early Roman periods there is still much work required on refining our understanding of the ceramic sequence throughout this period. To a certain extent this requires some large, stratified, well-preserved assemblages to establish the fabric and form sequences. The material recovered from the A43 sites is slightly piecemeal and in many cases multi-phase, making precise dating within broad phases difficult. This is partly a result of the perpetuation of two basic fabric traditions, the use of shelly clays or addition of shell temper and the use of grog/ argillaceous inclusions. Without diagnostic sherds dating is very difficult on the basis of small groups of unfeatured sherds. Whilst there is the possibility that the use of the different clays is the result of functional rather than chronological differences, the occurrence of the same forms across different fabric groups suggests otherwise. The persistence of the use of shell and grog is more likely to be a cultural factor tied in with available local resources. The lack of distinctiveness combined with the small samples and lack of stratigraphic relationships also makes it difficult to determine whether the assemblages represent continuums or there are hiatuses present.

Early Iron Age (sixth to third centuries BC)

Evidence of early Iron Age occupation on the sites examined along the A43 is sparse. On the basis of other sites excavated in the locality dating to the sixth to fourth/ third centuries BC diagnostic pottery would be expected to include carinated bowls or jars and the use of finger-tipping on the rims or finger depressions on the bodies of vessels and expanded rims. Excavated assemblages of this period include Gretton (Jackson and Knight 1985) and Wilby Way (Blinkhorn and Jackson 2003), several sites in the Milton Keynes area, for example, Pennyland-Hartigans (Knight 1993), and Fenny Lock (Ford and Taylor 2001). The fabrics recorded at Gretton, considered to date to the later Bronze Age-early Iron Age transition and to the early-middle Iron Age are divided into two groups: one with abundant shell (encapsulated within fabrics SH1-6) with variants containing variable mixtures of other materials; the other a shell with grog/natural argillaceous inclusions and other materials (broadly equivalent to GR3) (Jackson and Knight 1985, 76). Sites along the A43 which have produced some evidence hinting at earlier Iron Age activity could include a carinated cup from Biddlesden Road Bridge (Fig 4.3, 55), a finger-depressed bodysherd from Tusmore Drain Outfall, and finger-tipped jars from Silverstone Fields Farm and Silverstone 2. There have been no examples of incised decorated vessels in the Chinnor-Wandlebury style (Cunliffe 1991, A.11). The Gretton early Iron Age assemblage also includes handled jars, examples of which have been noted at Silverstone Fields Farm,

Biddlesden Road Bridge, Silverstone 2 and Silverstone 3 but the form could be considered to continue into the middle Iron Age period. At Twywell the use of finger-tip decoration is common on rims and seems to be typical of the area from around the fourth century BC (Harding 1975, 70). It need not, therefore, be indicative of an early date.

Middle-late Iron Age (late third to first centuries BC)

Pottery of this date is very common in Northamptonshire and the surrounding region and it is likely that most of the Iron Age assemblages from the A43 fall into this period of occupation. Other contemporary sites include Weekley (Jackson and Dix 1986-7), Wilby Way (Blinkhorn and Jackson 2003), Hunsbury hillfort (Fell 1936) and Twywell (Jackson 1975), Moulton Park and Blackthorn (Williams 1974). To the south, a mid to late Iron Age enclosure has been excavated near Bicester (Cromarty et al 1999) and middle-late Iron Age material has come from various sites in the Milton Keynes area (eg Wavendon Gate (Williams et al 1996); Fenny Lock (Ford and Taylor 2001); cf also Marney 1989; and Waugh et al 1974)). The Iron Age assemblages tend to include long-lived forms and diagnostic forms and decoration are rare in most assemblages. It is also possible that differences in ceramic assemblages between some sites may reflect social or functional distinctions rather than chronology (Kidd 1999). Most published sites appear to make the distinction between pre-'Belgic' and 'Belgic' pottery, the latter representing in essence the later Iron Age but continuing in many instances well into the first century AD.

The middle Iron Age pottery from Northamptonshire is characterised by plain, rounded or ovoid jars and open bowls with a general lack of definitive features. Most of the vessels from the A43 sites are plain with no surface finish; a small number show a burnished finish. A few sherds with scored decoration also occur but again these are rare. There appears to be quite a range in vessel size from small to large. The absence from the A43 of any obvious decorated wares or clear imports from outside the region may be a reflection of the status of the sites involved. This is in complete contrast to the later Iron Age assemblage from the settlement site at Weekley which produced large quantities of 'La Tène' decorated pottery and imported wares from Glastonbury (Jackson and Dix 1986-7). Twywell produced a single decorated bowl and some sherds with curvilinear decoration came from Moulton Park and Blackthorn (Williams 1974, figs 14 and 35). Sites with clear Middle Iron Age occupation along the A43 include Silverstone 2 and Silverstone 3, Shacks Barn Farm and Area G Syresham. Slightly later occupation, from the middle to later Iron Age, is suggested for Biddlesden Road Bridge, Silverstone Fields Farm and perhaps Silverstone 2. The slightly higher preponderance of coarser shell-tempered fabrics at Silverstone 3 might

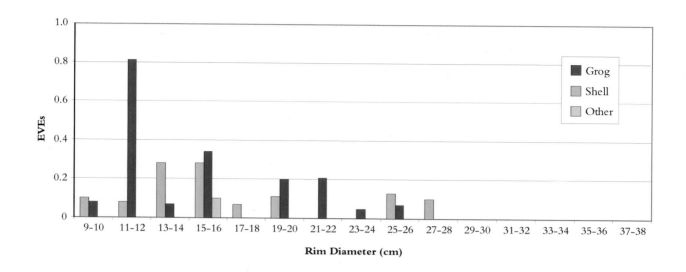

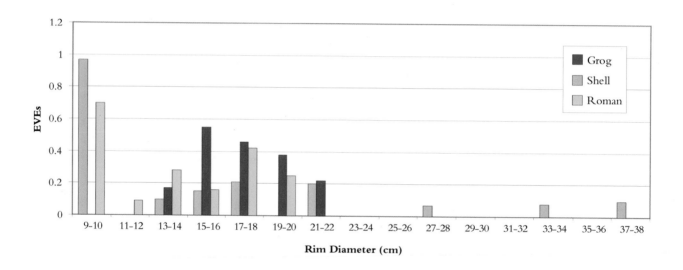

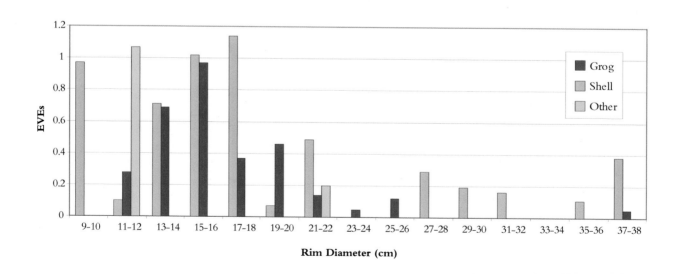

Fig 4.7: *Frequencies of vessels by rim diameter for grog-tempered, shell-tempered and other fabrics. Silverstone Fields Farm, Silverstone 2, Silverstone 3 and Biddlesden Road Bridge.*

hint at an earlier phase of Iron Age compared with, for example, Silverstone Fields Farm. There are a number of slight differences between the fabrics from these two sites which might suggest slightly different dates of occupation or the exploitation of different clay sources for the pottery. In general, the assemblages from these sites matches well with those from Twywell, Moulton Park and Blackthorn and the coarse pottery assemblage of Weekley (Jackson and Dix 1986-7, CP1).

Sites which appear to continue into the later Iron Age or span the later Iron Age-early Roman period include Biddlesden Road Bridge, Silverstone Fields Farm, and Silverstone 2. Occupation appears to have ceased at Silverstone 3 before the 'Belgic' phase and possibly Shacks Barn Farm and Syresham, although the assemblages from the latter sites are very small. Vessels include handmade and wheel-turned forms in which channel rim jars, necked, cordoned jars, carinated cordoned bowls in grog or shelly ware are present. Fabric GR5 is very typical of the period along with GR1 and SH1.

Roman

The Roman assemblage is not large and is mainly confined to Area G Syresham, Great Ouse Culvert and Brackley Hatch 4. Most of the other sites produced small amounts of Roman pottery. Only two Roman sherds came from Biddlesden Road Bridge, which cannot be taken as evidence for Roman use of the site, and it is likely that occupation here ceased in the later Iron Age/early Roman period. Silverstone Fields Farm produced 23 sherds of Roman pottery, 1% of the total assemblage, but within this group was one sherd of South Gaulish samian and four white ware butt beaker sherds suggesting a terminus post quem for the site around AD 60/70. It would seem that the effects of Roman culture were just beginning to appear in the assemblage around this date, coinciding with the apparent abandonment of the site.

At Silverstone 2, Roman pottery proper was more prolific but may not have arrived at the site until the late first/early second century, the later Iron Age fabric types perhaps continuing through into the later first century AD but with some wheel-turned or wheelmade vessels gradually appearing alongside the Roman greywares and samian. If there was a hiatus between the late Iron Age occupation and that where Roman wares are present, it would be extremely difficult to identify on the basis of the pottery alone. The absence of anything obviously of later date suggests that this site was probably abandoned in the early second century. At Silverstone 3 only eleven sherds of Roman pottery were recorded, again 1% of the total assemblage, suggesting that just as Romanisation was becoming manifest the site was abandoned.

A similar picture is demonstrated at Weekley where a much larger Roman assemblage was recovered but occupation seems to have ended in the early-mid second century AD (Jackson and Dix 1986-7). Most of the post-conquest wares appear to be local indigenous products,

the only imports being a small sherd of Claudio-Neronian samian, two sherds of terra nigra and a whiteware butt beaker.

The discovery of two kilns with associated pottery from Brackley Hatch 4 and another at Area G Syresham is of some note. Northamptonshire shows one of the highest densities of pottery kilns dating to the first and early second centuries of anywhere in Britain, as well as amongst the earliest evidence of the use of surface kilns in Britain (cf Swan 1984, maps 4 and 14). The greatest density occurs to the north-east of Towcester, the only known kilns to the south-west, in the immediate area of the A43 sites being Wood Burcote, Syresham (ibid, 145) and Biddlesden (Woods et al 1981). There are no published details of the pottery from these latter two kiln sites. Several pottery kilns dated to the second half of the first century AD were excavated at Weekley (Jackson and Dix 1986-7) and one of similar date from Weston Favell (Bunch and Corder 1954). The kilns were all of single flue updraught design with associated portable kiln furniture in the form of kiln bars. The pottery from Weekley was made from local clays to which grog or shell was added. The vessels were handmade and finished on a wheel or turntable. Forms made include channel rim jars in shelly ware, large storage jars, carinated bowls and dishes imitating moulded imported forms and butt beakers (Jackson and Dix, fig 21; cf Woods and Hastings 1984, 98-105).

The Brackley Hatch 4 and Area G Syresham vessels appear to be entirely indigenous in their development. Although the vessels are wheel-thrown, the forms do not show any direct continental influence as seen on the products from Weekley and Rushden (Woods and Hastings 1984). The sandy, grog-tempered fabric appears to be a development out of the 'Belgic' grog-tempered later Iron Age traditions and is one seen across a wide area including Buckinghamshire (Marney 1989). The sandier nature of the clays might suggest the exploitation of different clay beds but the use of grog as an additive persists, whereas in other areas, such as the south-east of Britain, it is substantially replaced by sandy wares. It appears to be intermediate between the Iron Age grog-tempered tradition and the later Roman tradition represented by fabric PNK GT, which is found in enormous quantities on sites in the Midlands from the end of the second century onwards. A similar fabric was probably produced at several different sites so it would be extremely difficult to identify on macroscopic grounds whether products from Brackley Hatch 4 and Syresham were reaching other sites in the immediate locality.

Vessel function

Figure 4.7 a-c illustrate the range of measurable diameters present for the four larger later prehistoric sites, Silverstone Fields Farm, Silverstone 2, Silverstone 3 and Biddlesden Road Bridge. The measurements are expressed as the sum total of the estimated vessel equivalents (EVE) for each of the diameter ranges shown on the horizontal axis. The bars distinguish the two main fabrics present, shelly ware and grog-tempered ware with a third column for other fabrics. The exercise was undertaken to explore two lines of enquiry. First, the question could be asked, are there any differences between the shelly wares and the grog-tempered wares in terms of vessel function which might be reflected in the size range of the vessels made? It has been suggested that the diameter of a vessel broadly equates with the volume or capacity of that vessel (Woodward and Blinkhorn 1997). Second, different sized vessels might reflect different site functions; for example, a large number of large capacity vessels could indicate larger scale storage of foodstuffs, as has been suggested at Wilby Way (Blinkhorn and Jackson 2003). A change from smaller to larger vessels through time could indicate changes in serving and eating habits from communal to individual eating vessels or vice versa. Unfortunately, the data available from the A43 sites are too limited to form a statistically valid sample on a chronological basis. Silverstone Fields Farm produced 73 measurable rims, a total 10.13 EVEs; Silverstone 2, 35 rims, 4.59 EVEs; Silverstone 3, 34 rims, 3.35 EVEs and Biddlesden Road Bridge, 24 rims, 2.27 EVEs. The samples were thus considered globally for each site and slightly different trends were evident. The assemblage from Silverstone 3 is largely of middle Iron Age date. Both the two main fabrics feature across the diameter range, that is from 9 cm up to 26 cm diameter, with one larger grog-tempered vessel at 28 cm. The shelly wares show a higher incidence of smaller vessels whereas the grog-tempered wares show a fairly even occurrence across the range. Broadly speaking, the greatest number of vessels occur between 12 and 16 cm. At this site shelly wares (and shell and grog) formed 64% of the assemblage and grog 17%. At Biddlesden Road Bridge almost equal amounts of grog and shelly ware were present with a date range from the early through to the later Iron Age. In contrast to Silverstone 3 there was a greater range of size present, with vessels up to 36 cm in diameter but with a lack of vessels between 24 cm and 34 cm. The range was also slightly more spread out. Again, shelly wares dominate the smaller end but are replaced by grog-tempered wares in the 14-18 cm range, taking over again between 20 and 24 cm. At Silverstone Fields Farm the pattern is again slightly different, with perhaps a greater representation of larger vessels between 26 and 38 cm mainly in grog-tempered wares. In contrast to the other two sites, grog-tempered wares also dominate the smaller end of the range but the two wares are fairly evenly matched between 14-16 cm. At this site, grog-tempered wares account for 62% overall compared to 31.5% shell, perhaps accounting for the greater incidence across the graph. Finally, at Silverstone 2, where shell was 47% and grog 26.4%, the grog wares again dominate the two extremes of the spectrum with vessels at 10 cm through to 38 cm. The shelly wares mirror quite closely the Roman wares proper, perhaps an indication of the later date of much of the shelly wares from this site. The range is more focussed between 10 and 22 cm with just a small number of larger wares. At present, without

a great deal of more intensive analysis across a greater spectrum of sites and with assemblages where the samples are large enough to analyse by period, the data produced from these sites are difficult to interpret. The main point to emerge is that there are differences, particularly with Silverstone 3 which has no very large measurable vessels. Grog-tempered wares tend to be used to produce a greater range of vessel sizes, possibly a reflection of the greater plasticity of the clay with the grog additive, whereas shelly wares tend to be used for smaller diameter vessels. It could be suggested that the early assemblages show a more restricted diameter range which increases considerably in the middle to later Iron Age to become more restricted again in the early Roman period.

POST-ROMAN POTTERY

Summary

The post-Roman pottery from the excavations comprised a miscellaneous collection of 83 medieval and post-medieval sherds. The figure excludes the fieldwalking collections from the earlier stages of fieldwork. The material has been catalogued, without detailed identification, by Jane Timby with a fuller report on the material from Wood Burcote Bridge by Paul Blinkhorn retained in archive.

Wood Burcote Bridge

The pottery assemblage, recovered during the Watching Brief, comprised 38 sherds (597 g). All were effectively unstratified. The majority was of seventeenth or eighteenth-century date and was quantified using the Northamptonshire County Ceramic Type Series. Most of the pottery was Staffordshire Manganese Glazed Ware of 1680-1760 (CTS F413), with smaller amounts of Red Earthenwares, Staffordshire Slipware, Tin-Glazed Earthenware, Iron-glazed Coarsewares and Late English Stoneware.

Other sites

Of the other sites, most of the medieval and post-medieval pottery came from Brackley Hatch 4 where 20 sherds came from modern soil and colluvial layers. A further 15 sherds of post-medieval pottery came from Silverstone 3 and four from Silverstone 2, all largely from intrusive features. Smaller amounts came from other sites.

POTTERY KILN FURNITURE
J Timby and T Hylton

Introduction

Pottery kiln furniture, comprising mainly bars, slabs and possible fragments of kiln structures, was recovered from Brackley Hatch 4 and Area G Syresham. These sites also included the truncated remains of pottery kilns dating to the early Roman period and there can be little doubt

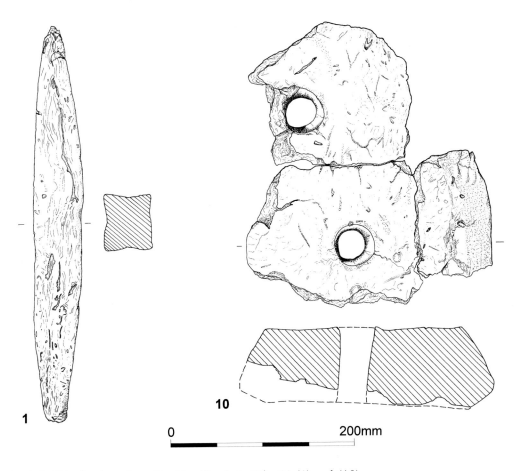

Fig. 4.8: Kiln furniture from Brackley Hatch 4, Kiln 61 (1) and (10).

that the furniture is associated with the excavated kilns, or similar features very close by.

Brackley Hatch 4

In addition to the pottery from the site, a substantial quantity of fired clay was recovered amongst which were a large quantity of fragments presumably from the kiln structure. Some show a slight curvature suggesting kiln lining. Of particular note are 73 fragments from kiln bars with tapered ends and square cross-section made from local clay heavily tempered with coarse organic matter. These represent portable kiln furniture and would have radiated out around a central pedestal to form a temporary kiln floor, which would be dismantled and reused. At least one complete example was recovered measuring 430 mm in length with a cross-section 60 mm by 55 mm (Fig 4.8, 1). Examples of kiln bar were recovered from contexts 62, 65, 68 and 69, the fills of the kiln chambers and rake-out pits. Also present from 65 and 68 in particular were several perforated slab fragments either from a floor, which would have been an integral component of the kiln, or perhaps more likely in view of the bars, from moveable perforated clay plates. Perforated plates have been noted on several sites in the Welland/Nene and Ouse valleys, and in particular examples have been published from Blackmore Thick, Southwick and Camp Hill, Northants

and Elstow, Beds (Swan 1984, 65). Small kilns such as these are generally built on the ground surface or in a shallow scoop leaving little archaeological trace.

There are two basic fabric types:

1   Pale orange to grey in colour, hard to touch, very abrasive. Few inclusions, sometimes sand-tempered with coarse organic matter, sometimes heavily, most probably straw/grass.

2   Pale buff/pink in colour, relatively soft to touch (almost soapy). Few inclusions, no organic tempering, most probably natural clay.

All the kiln bars were manufactured from variations of Type 1 fabric

Variations of fabric Type 1 dominate the assemblage. This particular fabric type appeared to have been used for all the kiln bars from the kilns (contexts 62, 65, 68 and 69), perforated floor from 65 (the fill of the rake-out pit of Kiln 61) and most of the fragments of kiln lining (from 65, 68 and 69). Fabric Type 2 occurred only in 62, the firing chamber of Kiln 61 and diagnostic fragments indicate that it had been used for perforated floor, kiln lining and four concave fragments.

119

Catalogue

Portable kiln furniture, Brackley Hatch 4

1   Kiln bar, complete. Square cross-section with tapered terminals. Length: 430mm Width: 60 x 55mm Weight: 1.056kg.
Kiln 61 (62) (Fig 4.8).

2   Kiln bars (fragments). Eighteen individual fragments with square cross-sections and tapered ends, no apparent joins. Length: up to 255mm Width: 50-60mm Weight: 5.935kg.
Kiln 61 (62).

3   Kiln bars. Thirty-six individual fragments. Four pieces join together to form parts of two incomplete kiln bars measuring c 260mmm in length. The expanded sections of the kiln bar fragments range from 55-60mm in width. Weight: 13.305kg.
Kiln 61 (65).

4   Kiln bar. Incomplete, square cross-section with tapered ends. Length (incomplete): 330mm Width: 60 x 60mm Weight: 1.069kg.
Kiln 61 (65).

5   Kiln bars. Nineteen individual fragments, no apparent joins. Length: up to 220mm Width: 60 x 60mm Weight: 3.691kg.
Kiln 66 (68).

6   Kiln bars. Two fragments. Length: up to 190mm Width: c 50 x 50mm Weight: 1.035kg.
Kiln 66 (69).

Kiln Structure

7   Kiln lining. Six flat fragments furnished with a single flat/smoothed surface and rough underside. Dimensions up to c 120 x 85mm Thickness: 17mm Weight: 0.842kg.
Kiln 61 (62).

8   ?Kiln lining. Four concave fragments which display similarities to imbrex. Fragments measure up to c 120 x 110mm Thickness: 25mm Weight: 11.386kg.
Kiln 61 (62).

9   ?Perforated floor. Four pieces with vestiges of tapered circular perforations, diameter: c 40mm. Fragments measure up to: 160x 90mm Thickness: 17mm Weight: 0.960kg.
Kiln 61 (62).

10   ?Perforated floor. Three large fragments which join together to form a piece of possible perforated floor furnished with a vestige of the outer edge and two complete circular perforations slightly tapered. Dimensions: 300 x 280 x 90mm. Perforations – Diameter: 45mm Weight: 4.012kg.
Kiln 61 (65) (Fig 4.8).

11   ?Perforated floor. Four fragments with vestiges of circular perforations. Fragments measuring up to 220 x 130 Depth: 70mm Weight: 1.689kg.
Kiln 61 (65).

12   ?Kiln lining One large fragment with flat surface and folded down along one edge. Dimensions: 180 x 230x 40mm Weight: 1.695kg.
Kiln 66 (68).

13   Kiln lining. Thirty-two amorphous fragments, furnished with one smoothed flat surface and rough underside. Fragments measure up to c 100 x 90mm Weight: 1.863kg.
Kiln 66 (68).

14   Twenty-three amorphous fragments of kiln lining some with a single smoothed surface. Fragments measure up to c 110 x 80mm Weight: 0.915kg.
Kiln 66 (69).

Miscellaneous

15   One flat undiagnostic amorphous fragment. Dimensions: 75 x 75 x 10mm Weight: 0.081kg.
Ditch 9 (10).

16   One fragment of fired clay, possibly kiln lining. Dimensions: 95 x 60 x 30mm Weight: 0.120kg.
Ditch 11 (12).

17   Six small amorphous fragments of fired clay. Measuring up to 30 x 20 x 15mm Weight: 0.028kg.
Pit 45 (46).

18   Two fragments of lining with smoothed flat surfaces. Measuring up to 75 x 73 x 10mm Weight: 0.192kg
Pit 45 (46).

Area G Syresham

Feature 2384 (trench 23) was interpreted as the truncated base of a pottery kiln. It was dated to the later first or second century AD. In addition to a group of probable kiln waster pottery (Timby, above), eight fragments of kiln bars were recovered, three of which join together to make a square-section bar with tapered ends (dimensions 40 x 40 mm; incomplete length 225 mm).

Catalogue

19   Kiln bar. Three fragments join together to form almost half a kiln bar. Length (incomplete): 225mm Width: 40 x 40mm Weight: 0.425kg.
Kiln 2384 (2302).

20   Kiln bar. Seven fragments, although not joining, appear to come from the same kiln bar. Length (incomplete): c 150mm Weight: 0.246kg.
Kiln 2384 (2302).

COINS

I Meadows (Roman) and M Curteis (Iron Age and post-medieval)

Introduction

A small collection of twenty-one coins was recovered from excavations on the project. Most were Roman, with the majority coming from the midden site at Great Ouse Culvert (13 coins). Brackley Hatch 4 also yielded four Roman coins. All are common third and fourth-century types. Two late Iron Age coins came from the outer enclosure ditch at Silverstone 2. These are of greater interest but were poorly preserved. A Rose Farthing of c 1640 came from Silverstone 3. This is an unremarkable find in itself, but provides dating evidence for the posthole structure near the entrance to the Iron Age enclosure.

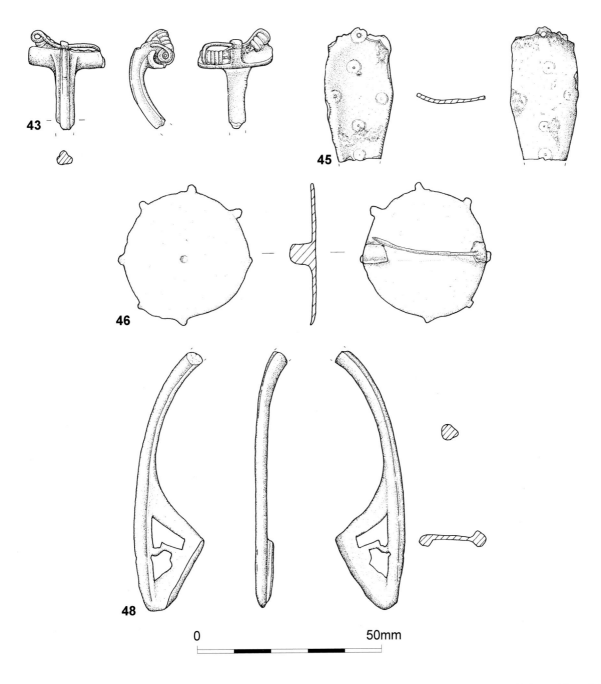

Fig. 4.9: Copper alloy objects from near Silverstone 2 (43); Brackley Hatch 4 (48); Great Ouse Culvert (4) and (46).

Iron Age catalogue

Silverstone 2

21 Iron Age AE unit.
    Very corroded. The module and cupped nature of the coin would suggest that it is a late Iron Age issue by the tribes of the Eastern coin series (ie belonging to the Catuvellauni/Trinovantes). Probably attributable to Tasciovanus. Diameter: 12 mm Weight: 0.55 g.
    SF (Small Find No) 14, Enclosure Ditch 1050 (1051).

22 Iron Age plated silver unit.
    Very corroded. Mechanical cleaning revealed evidence of silver plating over a copper alloy core. The coin of this plating and module would suggest that it is a type attributed to the Western coin series (ie belonging to the

Dobunni). Plated coins of this type are comparatively common around the Catuvellauni/Dobunni boundary, with a notable concentration of finds at Evenley. Diameter: 12 mm, Weight: 0.77 g.
SF15, Enclosure Ditch 1048 (1049).

Roman catalogue

Great Ouse Culvert

23 AE coin of Valens (364–378). The reverse is SECVRITAS REIPUBLICAE with victory advancing left. Mint mark CONST and OF 1. Closer dating not possible. SF1, buried soil (3.)

24 AE3 coin of Constantine 1 (307–337). The reverse is GLORIA EXERCITVS, 2 soldiers and 2 standards

121

type. The mint mark starts with T and is possibly Treveri. SF2, buried soil (3).

25 AE3 coin, possibly of Constans (337-350). The reverse is VICTORIAE DD AVGG Q NN with 2 victories facing and holding wreaths.
SF3, buried soil (3).

26 Half a copper alloy coin, probably a centenionalis of Constans (337-350). The obverse is poor but the reverse shows the stern of a galley with seated figure and the feet of a standing figure.
SF5, buried soil (3).

27 AE3 CONSTANTINOPOLIS issue (post-330).
SF7, buried soil (3).

28 AE3 coin of Constantius II (337-361). The reverse is GLORIA EXERCITVS, two soldiers and two standards type.
SF8, buried soil (3).

29 A copper alloy AE4 Divine Constantine commemorative issue, quadriga on reverse (post-337).
SF9, buried soil (3).

30 AE4 coin of Crispus (317-326), reverse illegible.
SF10, unstrat.

31 A copper alloy minimus of fourth-century type. Diameter: 7 mm.
SF11, buried soil (3)

32 AE3 coin of the House of Constantine. The reverse shows two victories facing holding a wreath. Generally illegible.
SF12, buried soil (3)

33 AE4 coin, probably a barbarous fourth-century copy of a GLORIA EXERCITVS, two soldiers one standard issue.
Chainage 3570, unstrat.

34 AE3 coin, illegible.
Chainage 3600, unstrat.

35 A copper alloy coin of the House of Constantine, barbarous minimus.
Chainage 3600, unstrat.

Brackley Hatch 4

36 AE3 coin of Constantius II (337-361). Reverse illegible owing to corrosion.
SF3, unstrat.

37 A copper alloy flan, now illegible, of a third to fourth century coin.
SF4, unstrat.

38 A copper alloy minimus, probably of later fourth-century date. Severely corroded and illegible. Diameter: 7 mm.
SF50, unstrat.

39 A copper alloy coin of the Gallic empire. Possibly an antoninianus of Gallienus (253-268) but severely corroded.
SF51, unstrat.

Post-medieval catalogue

Silverstone 3

40 A copper alloy Rose Farthing of Charles I (c 1640).
SF2, Structure 2118, posthole 1122 (1121.)

41 A copper alloy Farthing or trade token of the seventeenth century. Diameter: 15 mm.
SF16, Ditch 1051 (superficial).

NON-FERROUS METAL OBJECTS
I Meadows with a contribution by D Mackreth

Introduction

A small collection of twenty-one objects of copper alloy and lead was recovered. Many of these are of medieval, post-medieval or unknown date and are of little archaeological interest. The remaining items include scraps of copper alloy sheet, most unidentifiable, and four Roman brooch fragments; one from Great Ouse Culvert, two from Brackley Hatch 4, and one found during the Watching Brief from north of Silverstone 2 [Chainage 7490].

Iron Age and Roman catalogue

Silverstone Fields Farm

42 A fragment of copper alloy sheet of uncertain date and function. 33 x 13 mm.
SF13, Pit 215 (216).

WB SL Chainage 7490 (hedgerow north of Silverstone 2)

43 A copper alloy Roman brooch of head and spring type dating to the second half of the first century AD.
Unstrat. (Fig 4.9).

Shacks Barn Farm

44 Twisted copper wire ear-ring of late Roman type. Thickness of wire 2 mm.
SF1, Ditch 36103 (3607).

Great Ouse Culvert

45 A copper alloy strap-end fragment comprising two thin sheets, broken at each end, and both decorated with ring and dot motifs. Possibly originally lancet shaped (Clarke 1979). Late Roman. Length: 35 mm Width: 18 mm thinning at one end to 12 mm.
SF6, buried soil (3). (Fig 4.9).

46 Disc brooch (D Mackreth).
The pin is hinged. The plate is essentially circular and had eight projections of which one is missing and two or three more are incomplete. The original intention was to have projecting circles, but the edges defining the circle next to the main plate have not been finished using a file, leaving the shape of each somewhat indistinct. There is a hole in the middle to hold a separately made mount, probably once enamelled. Unstrat. (Fig 4.9).
The commonest circular brooch with projections and a hinged pin is a variety of a large family whose distinguishing mark is the use of bifurcated terminals and/or a central circular recess containing a beaded annulus around a hole for an attachment. In the last respect, the present brooch should be a relation. The

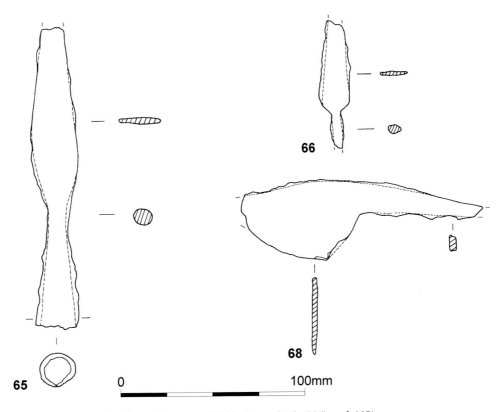

Fig. 4.10: *Iron artefacts from Silverstone Fields Farm (65), (66) and (68).*

dating is from the conquest into Neronian times, although one from Castleford is a reminder that they could also survive into the 70s (Cool and Philo 1998, 51, fig 13,99) and perhaps a better terminal date for all would be 75/80, even if very few indeed occur in lands taken into the province from the early 70s. There are not enough like the present item to be sure that this should be regarded as a separate type, as opposed to being merely a member of a loose group. However, there is nothing here which insists that it could belong in any way to the second century, and a date before 100, if not 80, is to be preferred.

Area G Syresham

47   A flat lead square, one edge chamfered. 25 mm x 34 mm x 8 mm. Undiagnostic. SF9, Gully 1039 (1023).

Brackley Hatch 4

48   The copper alloy catch plate and part of the bow of a brooch. A single rib runs down each side of the bow. The catch plate is perforated by two geometric holes. Length: 71 mm long. Second half of first century AD. SF5, unstrat. (Fig 4.9).

49   The triangular copper alloy catch plate of a brooch. Length: 28 mm. Second half of first century AD. SF6, unstrat.

Post-Roman and miscellaneous catalogue

Silverstone 3

50   A fragment of plain copper alloy sheet. 16 mm x 12 mm. Unknown date. SF12, unstrat.

Silverstone 2

51   A fragment of a copper alloy object with incised diagonal lines as decoration. The piece formed part of a spherical object, probably a post-medieval crotal bell. 21 mm x 14 mm. SF15, Enclosure Ditch 1048 (1058).

52   A strip of copper alloy which has been cut or clipped from a larger piece. 100 mm x 5 mm. Unknown date. SF17, unstrat.

Great Ouse Culvert

53   A lead shot/ball with flashing around the casting seam. Diameter: 12 mm. Post-medieval. SF4, Gully 8 (11).

Biddlesden Road Bridge

54   Part of a cast copper alloy crotal bell. A late example with 'petal' decoration around the lower portion. It appears to have the cast letter G. Post-medieval. SF1, furrow (1101).

55   A copper alloy buckle fragment. Cast pronged element preserving part of the loop and a fragment of the pin. Length: 32 mm. Medieval/post-medieval. SF3, subsoil (1001).

56   A large lump of cast lead, perhaps a piece of recycled lead. Ovate in shape, 85 mm x 46 mm x up to 10 mm. Unknown date. SF4, furrow (1101).

57   A lead aulnager's wool/cloth seal. The piece preserves what appears to be the intertwined initials A M. Diameter: 19 mm. Medieval. SF5, furrow (1101).

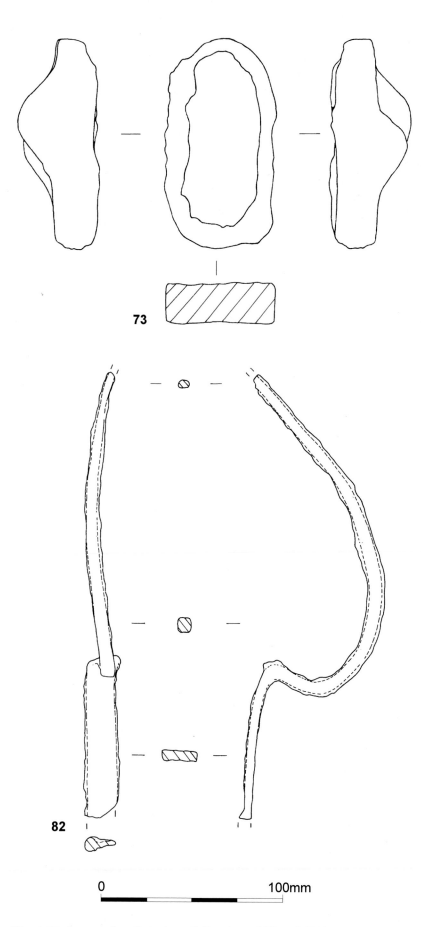

Fig. 4.11: *Iron artefacts from Area G Syresham (73) and (82).*

58   A lead cylindrical cup of unknown function. Diameter: 17 mm Height: 20 mm. Unknown date.
SF6, subsoil (1001).

59   Two fragments of copper alloy, both thin sheet metal. A single nail hole in the smaller piece suggests that it may have once been fixed to another object. Larger piece 40 mm x 19 mm, smaller piece 17 mm x 14 mm.
SF7, furrow (1101).

60   A copper alloy bell fragment with white metal, probably tinning, both inside and out. The piece is part of the lower edge and flare of the campanulate form. It had an original diameter of 50 mm. 38 mm x 20 mm. Unknown date.
SF10, unstrat.

Brackley Hatch 4

61   The upper part of a spherical copper alloy crotal bell which has come apart around its middle. The item is domed in shape. The surface shows no sign of decoration. Diameter: 35 mm Height: 14 mm. Surmounted by an oval loop, 10 mm x 5 mm. Medieval/post-medieval.
SF1, unstrat

62   A lump of copper alloy which may be described simply as an ingot. 20 mm x 20 mm x 10 mm. Unknown date.
SF2, unstrat

IRON OBJECTS
I Meadows and T Hylton

Introduction

There were a limited number and range of iron objects from the excavations. Some of the Iron Age and Roman sites yielded remarkably little from archaeological contexts, particularly in view of the fact that a metal-detector was used regularly. There were no iron finds at all from Silverstone 2 and Brackley Hatch 4, and just two stratified items each from Biddlesden Road Bridge and Silverstone 3. A much larger group of finds came from the Roman midden at Great Ouse Culvert, while the trenches at Area G Syresham yielded 14 items from Roman contexts. The range of finds was, however, unremarkable on both sites, with nails predominating. In this light, the group of six artefacts from the upper fill of the late Iron Age/early Roman enclosure ditch at Silverstone Fields Farm is noteworthy. They included a spearhead and two blades.

In the following catalogue only material from archaeologically significant contexts, or stray items which may be archaeologically significant, are listed. A note is made of other finds where the catalogue is retained in archive.

Silverstone 3

63   A curved rod, sub-square in section. 117 mm x 4 mm.
SF13, Enclosure 4, ditch 2002 (1284).

64   Nail. Length: 28 mm.
SF14, gully 2017 (1004).

Silverstone Fields Farm

65   A near-complete spearhead comprising a socket, 50 mm long and up to 19 mm in diameter, tapering to a short waist 8 mm below the blade. The blade survives to a length of 94 mm, but the tip is missing. The iron shows no signs of bending and must have been broken off cleanly. Total length 160 mm. Blade width up to 24 mm.
SF2, Enclosure 1 (101). (Fig 4.10).

66   An object comprising a blade, 48 mm long tapering from 16-17 mm wide, and a tang or socket. The piece may be a knife with a central tang, or an arrowhead. Total length 65 mm.
SF4, Enclosure 1 (101). (Fig 4.10).

67   A pointed stem tapering from 4 mm across to the point. The piece could be part of a pin, buckle tongue or staple. Length 28 mm.
SF5, Enclosure 1 (101).

68   A blade with a curved back and cutting edge 60 mm x up to 38 mm, with a tang 60 mm long which continued the line at the back of the blade. Its function is unclear but its small size suggests it was a craft tool rather than for agriculture. Total length 120mm.
SF7, Enclosure 1 (100). (Fig 4.10).

69   Corroded nail or staple. Length: 36 mm.
SF8, Enclosure 1 (100).

70   Bar tapering to both broken ends. Probably the back of a joiner's dog or staple. Length: 85 mm Width: maximum of 11 mm, tapering to 5-6 mm.
SF11, Enclosure 1 (101).

Biddlesden Road Bridge

71   Bar, slightly curved and broken at one end. Perhaps a metal collar. 60 mm x 10 mm x 5 mm thick.
SF8, Structure 2 ditch 27 (1276).

72   Rod, square in cross section. 70 mm x 5 mm.
SF12, Structure 1 ditch 7 (1312).

Area G Syresham

73   A collar or band, 25 mm wide and forming an oval with an internal diameter of 90 mm x 40 mm. 8 mm thick and slightly squared at one end, rounded and 4 mm thick at the other. From the upper edge of each long side the strip has a nearly central triangular extension, giving the strip a width of 41 mm. It may have covered a wooden shaft.
SF3, gully 1038 (1041). (Fig 4.11).

74   Strip, not identifiable.
SF6, gully 1037 (1012).

75   Nail. Square-sectioned shank (now bent) with large flat sub-circular head. Length: 45 mm.
SF7, gully 1037 (1012).

76   Nail. Fine, square-sectioned shank, flat sub-circular head, terminal bent. Length: 37 mm.
SF8, gully 1036 (1035).

77   Possible nail. Square-sectioned shank, flat head. Length: 53 mm.
SF10, gully 1037 (1039).

78   Parallel-sided strip, D-shaped cross-section, bent at right angles. 34 mm x 20 mm. SF11, gully 1039 (1019).

79   Four hobnails with domed heads. Length: 12 mm.
SF12, trench 10, unstrat.

Debris Class	Weight (g)	% of total
Tap Slag	19,481	25.5
Furnace Slag	42,100	55.1
Un-diagnostic	2,509	3.3
Smithing Hearth Base	5,326	7.0
Hammer scale	3	0.0
Refractory	6,640	8.7
Ore /ore preparation	51	0.1
Natural	261	0.3
Non-metallurgical	1	0.0

Table 4.9: *Weight of debris by major class.*

80 Two objects: a rectangular-sectioned bar 72 mm x 12 mm x 2 mm; and nail shank 42 mm long.
SF13, gully 1037 (1012).

81 Parallel-sided strip. 68 mm x 17 mm.
SF16, ditch 1147 (1103).

82 A latch lifter. The shaft, 90 mm x 17 mm x 2 mm thick, is bent at right-angles and swept upward into the 7 mm square-sectioned prong which straightened and tapered towards the point. A similar example came from Borough Hill, Daventry, Northants (Manning 1985, Plate 38, O12).
SF19, gully 1039 (1019). (Fig 4.11).

83 A nail with a square-sectioned shank tapered to a fine point, flat sub-circular head. Length: 47 mm.
SF20, gully 1039 (1019).

84 A nail with a square-sectioned shank, flat sub-circular head. Length: 56 mm.
SF21, gully 1037 (1030).

Great Ouse Culvert

85 An assortment of dome-headed hobnails of various sizes, possibly derived from a single shoe.
Buried soil (3).

86 A collection of nine complete carpentry nails 25-40 mm long, each with a flattened head. There were also 12 other fragments of both heads and shanks.
Buried soil (3).

87 A possible T-shaped tile clamp with a shank 50 mm long and two arms 18 mm and 10 mm long.
Buried soil (3).

Post-medieval and unknown contexts

The most substantial collection of post-medieval ironwork came from Wood Burcote Bridge. The collected assemblage comprises twelve complete and fragmentary horse shoes, two large square-headed bolts (probably from a building or cart) and 38 nails and nail fragments.

Two horseshoes came from overburden at Tusmore Drain Outfall, together with three other iron objects which may also have been post-medieval.

In addition to the stratified material at Great Ouse Culvert, a collection of unstratified metal-detected finds were retained. Most were carpenters' nails and there was also a small cleat and a ring. Some or all of this material may be Roman. A few unstratified pieces from Area G Syresham may also be Roman since they came from the same trench as most of the Roman material.

At Silverstone 3 the post-medieval features pit 2117, posthole 2043 and Structure 2118 yielded a few nails and a staple. At Silverstone 1 a nail came from silts overlying the cobble road surface. Superficial deposits at Biddlesden Road Bridge also yielded a corroded iron object and a wedge for splitting wood (SF11). Although not dated this latter item seems likely to be medieval or later.

IRON SLAG
C Salter
with a contribution by A Chapman

Introduction

The identification of the type of activity carried out on a ferrous metallurgical site can be quite problematic for some periods. This is due to the complex nature of the iron production process and the similarity of the by-products from the various production stages. The iron production and manufacture can be classified into five stages: smelting, bloom smithing, billet smithing, artefact manufacture, and finally repair and recycling. The actual physical processes involved at most stages are the same, welding and forging, but the proportion of time spent welding compared with forging tends to decrease as the metal moves from raw product to finished object. Therefore, most stages of the iron manufacturing process can produce the full range of debris types; it is just the relative proportions of the various types of debris that change with the stage of manufacturing being undertaken. To some extent, the size of the pieces of debris may also decrease depending on what was being manufactured. The one process that does produce a distinctive debris type is smelting, and it can generate large

Group	Location	Features
Group 1	Northern edge of site	Pit and gully groups 9 and 10; gully 22
Group 2	Southern furnace area	Furnace 1; Furnace 2; ditch 17
Group 3	Furnace 3 area	Furnace 3; 'industrial deposit' 24; gully 26; pit group 28
Group 4	Central area	Structure 1, ditch 7; Structure 2, ditch 27; gully 1208,
Unassociated	Other areas of site	

Table 4.10: *Slag distribution by group.*

Debris Type	Unstratified	1	2	3	4	Un-associated
Tap Slag	913	2716	5778	8631	972	586
Furnace Slag	734	11964	18777	7627	1799	1083
Un-diagnostic	50	1010	533	1647	275	25
Smithing Hearth Base		3225	530	1571		
Hammer scale		1				2
Ore /ore preparation				51		
Hearth/furnace	282	2460	794	1609	160	304
Natural				30		231
Non-metallurgical		1				

Table 4.11: Debris type by feature groups (weight in grammes).

quantities of characteristic tap slag. However, iron smelting at some periods and in some areas of the country used a variety of non-slag tapping techniques. Recent evidence seen by the author suggests that the pattern of use of slag tapping and non-slag tapping techniques is much more complex throughout the history of bloomery iron smelting than has previously been considered the case.

The metallurgical debris from the Iron Age site at Biddlesden Road Bridge has been shown to confirm this pattern of complexity, which is explored in this report. The results suggest that the recording and analysis of most iron-smelting sites in the past has not been done in sufficient detail to enable comparisons to be made. The particular importance of the site at Biddlesden Road Bridge is that it represents the earliest use of slag tapping technology in the Midlands, if not southern Britain. Further evidence of slag tapping technology came from the early Roman smelting furnace at Area G Syresham.

Biddlesden Road Bridge

Methodology
This report is based on a simple sorting, classifying and weighing of the debris. The archive catalogue uses a more detailed classification scheme for the furnace slag than is used in this report. The more detailed classification is based on the furnace slag morphology, which is thought to reflect the position of the slag in the furnace when slag movement ceased. The basic classification used for this report is given in Tables 4.9 and 4.11 with the definition of these debris types retained in archive. Once the initial classification had been carried out, samples representing the various types of slag from two iron working areas (Groups

	Feature Group			
Slag Ratio	1	2	3	4
Tap/Furnace	0.23	0.31	1.13	0.54
Smith/Tap	1.19	0.09	0.18	–

Table 4.12: Ratios of slag types between feature groups.

2 and 3, below) were cut, mounted in epoxy resin, polished and examined under the optical microscope. From these polished samples a smaller set was selected for further analysis using the Scanning Electron Microscope (SEM) and Energy Dispersive X-ray analysis (EDX).

Nature of bloomery iron production
The early history of iron smelting technology is very much bound up with the size of the furnace and the way in which the slag was removed from the furnace. The size of the furnace controlled the heat balance within the furnace, with small furnaces losing a much higher proportion of their heat through the furnace walls than larger ones. The way in which slag was removed controlled the size of the bloom that formed, and hence the amount of iron that could be produced during a single smelt. If the slag were not removed, it would build up in the base of the furnace and gradually surround the bloom. This would limit air access to any charcoal remaining in the base of the furnace, in turn the base of furnace would cool. This cooling of the base of furnace raises the level at which slag becomes too viscous to flow away, so that eventually the slag blocks the tuyères and the smelting process ceases.

The quality of the ore used, and the capacity of the furnace below the level of the tuyères, limited the production of such a furnace. Clearly, if there is a larger volume into which the slag can drain before it cools the base of the furnace, then the furnace can be run for longer before smelting ceases, and hence a larger bloom can be produced. The quality of the ore in terms of its iron content is important because in the bloomery furnace the main flux for the unwanted elements present is iron oxide. Thus, the greater the quantity of impurities present, and silica in particular, the greater the amount of iron from the ore is lost to the slag to flux the impurities. Hence, a greater the volume of slag produced for a given volume of metallic iron. This means that a high quality ore would produce a greater weight of metallic iron before smelting ceased due to a build-up of slag than would be the case with a poor quality ore.

Another way to increase the size of the metallic bloom was to remove the slag from the base of the furnace by periodically tapping it out. It was generally thought that the change from the use of non-slag tapping furnaces to slag tapping occurred during the Late Iron Age in south-east England and became fully developed throughout England and Wales during the Romano-British period. But evidence from Wales and the south-west of England show the continued use and development of non-slag tapping furnaces well into Roman period. Unfortunately it is very difficult to develop a detailed picture of the geographical and chronological development of iron smelting through the Iron Age and Romano-British Period due to the poor state of preservation of most furnaces that have been excavated. The almost total absence of descriptions of smelting debris on reported but unexcavated slag spreads, as well as the lack of dating evidence on many the sites, are further drawbacks. For example, of the 213 sites reported by Bellamy, Jackson and Johnston in the Rockingham Forest area, 112 were undated, only 6 were given an Iron Age attribution, and the dating of one of these was uncertain (Bellamy et al 2000-1). The middle to late Iron Age date range of the Biddlesden Bridge Road site makes it an important addition to our knowledge of the early British iron industry. The regional importance of the site is further increased as it appears to have been using slag tapping furnaces.

The material

The categories of material examined are presented in Table 4.9. The presence of tap slag immediately indicated that this set of debris was likely to be the result of iron smelting activity. However, the amount of tap slag was less than half the weight of the furnace slag.

The ratio of furnace slag (slag retained within the furnace at the end of the smelting operation) to tap slag (the slag run out of the furnace during the smelt) is one of the important indicators of how efficiently the furnace was being run. For a given ore and furnace construction (internal diameter and number of tuyères), the greater the tapping ratio (weight of tap slag to furnace slag), the greater the amount of iron that could accumulate as a bloom.

Using the limited number of smelting sites with comparable data, this ratio was shown to be relatively low compared with Roman sites, such as those in the Weald and Forest of Dean. This may indicate that the iron smelters at Biddlesden Road Bridge had yet to learn the optimum furnace conditions for maximum iron production.

Spatial distribution

There were three main areas of the site yielding metallurgical debris and a fourth yielding a small amount. These have been designated Context Groups 1, 2, 3 and 4.

Looking at the distribution of the slag types across the site, there appear to be some interesting patterns shown by Tables 4.11 and 4.12. Context Group 4 consisted of only a couple of kilograms of debris from the centre of the site and as such may only be material from tertiary contexts (redistributed material). The quantity and location of the material in Groups 2 and 3 indicates that it is likely to be either primary or secondary deposits of material produced by the associated furnaces (Furnaces 1 and 2 in the case of Group 2 and Furnace 3 in the case of Group 3). The source of the material in Group 1 is not immediately clear. It may represent a different sort of activity from that of Groups 2 and 3. Its ratio of tap slag to furnace slag is much lower than the other groups, and the proportion of smithing hearth debris is higher. Perhaps this represents debris from the fettling of the unwanted slag from the bloom and the initial forging of blooms into a billet or bar.

There is a marked difference in the ratio of tap slag to furnace slag between Groups 2 and 3, with the Group 3 debris containing a much higher proportion of tap slag. It would seem that Furnace 3 was being run much more efficiently in terms of the quantity of iron produced, if not its quality. It has been suggested that there was a major increase in iron production some time during the latter part of the middle or late Iron Age. The possible differences in technology between Groups 2 and 3 on this site might well reflect this increase in the production of iron.

The Furnace Lining

One of the problems that iron smelters appeared to have had was with the integrity of the furnace wall. A number of pieces of refractory lining and slag show that the slag was working its way through the clay lining, and that pieces may have been spalling off the wall. The slag seems

	Na2O	MgO	Al2O3	SiO2	P2O5	SO3	K2O	CaO	TiO2	Cr2O3	MnO	FeO
Normal												
463	0.4	0.8	12.7	75.4	0.6	0.3	1.6	0.2	0.8	0.1	0.1	7.0
Light refractories												
426	0.5	0.3	6.9	82.9	0.8	0.2	2.7	0.4	0.8	0.0	0.0	4.4
440	0.4	0.2	6.1	86.0	0.4	0.2	2.0	0.2	0.8	0.0	0.1	3.5

Table 4.13: *Composition of normal and lighter coloured furnace lining.*

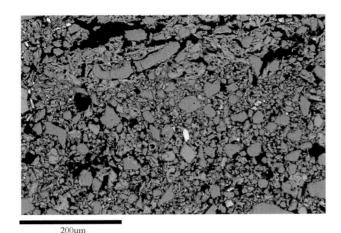

200um

Fig. 4.12: *Normal sandy and clay refractory fired to terracotta red colour. Showing a mass of small angular and sub-rounded silica grains in clay matrix. The bright grain in centre of field is a monazite (Cerium/ Lanthanum Phosphate). Sample OX463.*

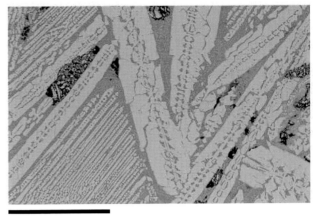

200um

Fig. 4.15: *A typical microstructure of a furnace slag from context group 2 with large primary fayalite laths and a matrix of hercynite and 'glass'.*

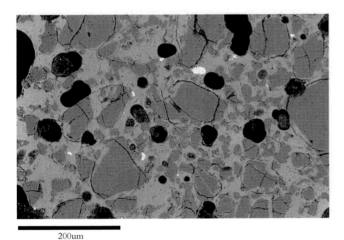

200um

Fig. 4.13: *Microstructure of lighter coloured refractory, with higher proportion of large silica grains. Sample OX 440.*

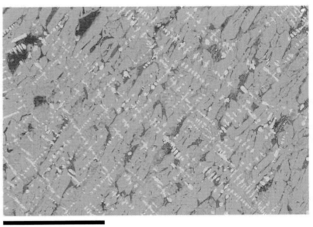

200um

Fig. 4.16: *A typical slag of context group 3, with fine, light-coloured free oxide dendrite in a ground mass of fayalite (mid-grey) and hercynite (lighter grey) outlined by dark glass.*

200um

Fig 4.14: *Lighter coloured refractory. Sample OX426.*

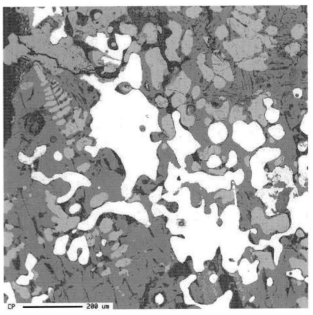

CP   200 um

Fig. 4.17: *Showing poorly consolidated metal (white) surrounded by slag with high free iron oxide content (midgrey) and fayalite with hercynite with occasional pools of glass.*

to be penetrating along cracks in the lining rather than attacking the furnace lining as a whole. Analysis of the hearth lining was undertaken to determine if the clay had been modified in any way to make it more suitable as a furnace refractory.

A number of relatively large fragments of vitrified hearth lining were recovered or could be re-assembled. However, relatively few of these were consistent with having come from the Furnaces 1 and 2, in that they were flat or had radius of curvature very much greater than these furnaces. Only one of the larger pieces had a curvature similar to that of these furnaces, with a radius of curvature between 215 and 250mm. Most showed none or very little curvature, and some of the furnace bottoms showed that the furnace wall on the blowing side was nearly flat. This could be consistent with coming from the flat face of the truncated furnace Furnace 3 (pit 1096) which would seem to have a D-shaped construction. Whereas, the furnace bottom (Lab ref. Ox-341) from the rake pit of Furnace 1 clearly shows a flat vertical face in contact with furnace lining.

Another possible explanation could be that these relatively flat regions were the result of furnace wall erosion in the area of the tuyère/air blast hole. However, there is no indication of this in Furnaces 1 and 2.

Some of the furnace lining fabrics were unusual for early iron-smelting furnaces. Usually the furnace lining consisted of local clay made more refractory, if necessary, by the addition of suitable quartz sand. At the Biddlesden Road Bridge site, there were a number of features which suggest that there were problems with the furnace lining and the way that the furnace was run. There seemed to have been excessive penetration of slag into the clay lining (possibly due to the low viscosity of the slag or high furnace running temperatures). Some of the furnace lining was perfectly normal, consisting of a dark vitrified layer, overlying a dark grey reduced-fired sandy clay, in turn overlying a red oxidising-fired sandy clay. However, a number of other samples of furnace lining were a very light colour, even though they had clearly been fired close to vitrification. Light-coloured fired hearth or furnace lining often indicates a more refractory material than the standard clay sand mix, due to a lower iron content (iron acts as a flux reducing the melting point of the clay). A number of samples were selected to determine the reasons for the difference between the light firing clay and the standard material and to determine whether the use of the lighter coloured material was deliberate.

The normal clay lining seen in sample Ox-463 (Fig 4.12) shows a ground mass of small silica grains with a few larger grains in the fired clay matrix. Towards the interior of the furnace this structure transformed very rapidly, within one or two millimetres, to one in which the structure consisted of iron-rich slag penetrating cracks in the lining, or where the very fine silica grains had fully reacted with the slag leaving only the large silica grains in a matrix of crystalline or semi-glassy slag.

This is very different from the structures seen in the light-coloured furnace lining material (Figs 4.13 and 4.14). The matrices of these samples were vitrified to great depth, several centimetres, so that very little of the fired but un-vitrified clay material remained to be examined. Therefore it is impossible to know whether these vitrified materials contained the same proportion of very finely divided silica and other minerals as seen in the normal lining. However, it is clear from the analysis that the proportion of silica present was higher in the light-coloured linings, and that the iron content was lower (Table 4.13).

Thus, separation of the refractories on the basis of their appearance in the hand sample does seem to be based on their chemistry, and seems rather, to some extent, to reflect their microstructure. Although the differences in the chemistry are not very great, in the normal lining there was a higher proportion of small silica grains which could be much more readily attacked and dissolved by the iron-rich slag than could the larger grains seen in the light-coloured lining. In addition, the higher concentration of iron oxides already present in the clay matrix of the normal lining would add to the process of furnace lining degradation.

The Slag – detailed examination

Macroscopic Observations

By fitting together various pieces of slag from the interior and exterior of the furnaces it was possible to get an impression of the relative position of the slag masses. These seem to show the furnace slag resting on the clay base of the furnace. The tap slag flowed out over a drop of a few centimetres (the base of the slag flows seem to drop between 40 and 80 mm immediately after leaving the tapping opening). It is not clear how this fits with the illustrated furnaces where there is no obvious tapping arch at the base of the furnace, even though the furnace lining from context 1078 (Ox-396), the fill of ditch 25, is consistent with coming from such an arch. It is probable that the tapping arch was destroyed when the furnace was broken open, or that this particular piece of furnace lining came from an unexcavated furnace off site.

The furnace bottom from the raking pit 1073 of Furnace 1 may also explain some of these inconsistencies. It appears to have tap slag on the top of the hearth lining adhering to the top of the slag. This would suggest that the iron smelters were having difficulty removing the slag. (In this case, it seems that they could not remove all of the bloom as there is evidence of metallic iron incorporated in part of the upper surface.) It would seem that instead of cleaning the furnace, they simply moved the tapping hole, and presumably the blowing hole, higher up the shaft of the furnace.

Another explanation is that this site represents a transition between a middle Iron Age non-slag tapping iron-smelting tradition, and the late Iron Age slag-tapping furnaces. However, the number of well-excavated, recorded and dated Iron Age iron smelting sites is so limited that it is impossible to build a consistent national or regional history of iron smelting technology at this point. A number of recent unpublished finds from southern England appear to be evidence for a slag tapping tradition in the earliest parts of the Iron Age.

Microstructural Observations

All the polished sections of a number of samples of slag from Groups 2 and 3 were examined, as well as a few from other contexts. In all cases the main mineralogical component was the iron silicate fayalite (Fe_2SiO_4), together with the spinel-hercynite $FeAl_2O_4$, and a potassium-alumina rich glassy component. The one mineralogical component that is normally present in most smelting slag, iron oxide, either in the form of wüstite (FeO) or magnetite (Fe_3O_4) also a spinel, was generally absent from the slag from Group 2. The seminal papers by Morton and Wingrove (1969 and 1972) on the mineral components of bloomery iron smelting slag indicate that when rich ores were used the slag had free iron oxide present. The slags from rich ore of the Roman and medieval periods were seen to lie in slightly different regions of the silica (SiO_2) - wüstite (FeO) - anorthite ($CaAl_2Si_2O_8$) ternary phase diagram (Morton and Wingrove 1972, 487), with the Roman slag plotting closer to the FeO corner than the medieval slag. However, when leaner ores were used, the compositions plotted further toward the anorthite corner of the diagram. The Biddlesden Bridge Road slag compositions lie between Morton and Wingrove's medieval slag produced from rich and lean ores. This, and the relatively low level of calcium recorded, is consistent with use of ores from the local glacial gravels rather than a more distant calcareous ore.

Most of the tap slag and the furnace slag from Group 2 had, at the most, very low levels of free iron oxide (wüstite or magnetite) present. In some of the furnace slag there were fine dendrites of a phase that had morphology very similar to that seen with iron oxides. But their reflectance was much lower than would be expected for either magnetite or wüstite. On analysis, these proved to be the spinel, hercynite. In most of the samples hercynite was a common minor phase, sometimes forming eutectic structures with fayalite. The only region in which free iron oxides were regularly observed in Group 2 slags was on, or close to, the air contact side of tap slags (Fig 4.15). This near-absence of free iron oxides is unusual. Most Roman and Iron Age iron smelting slag tends to have some free iron oxide as this helps to reduce the melting point, and decrease the viscosity of the slag.

The slags from Group 3 were more 'normal', as most contained moderate to a high proportion of free iron oxides (Fig 4.16). However, hercynite was still present in all samples, whereas Morton and Wingrove only reported it to be occasional in Roman bloomery slag.

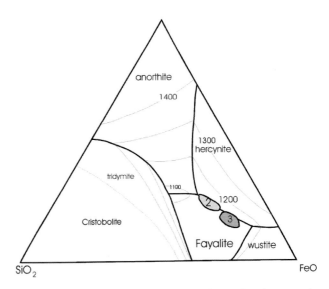

Fig. 4.18: *Tenary FeO-SiO2 Anorthite plot showing the regions where the slags from composition groups 2 and 3 fall. (After Morton and Wingrove 1972).*

Thus, although there is some overlap between the slag from Groups 2 and 3, there was a clear trend in the types of microstructure seen in the slag. The Group 2 slags had a low proportion of free iron oxide, and frequent hercynite, whereas the Group 3 slags, in general, had free iron oxide present in moderate amounts. Looking at the $FeO-SiO_2$-Anorthite ($CaAl_2Si_2O_8$) ternary phase diagram the iron-oxide-free slag compositions would fall close to the low melting region on the boundary between the fayalite and hercynite fields (Fig 4.18). Although the chemistry of the slag is more complex than can be described by the $FeO-SiO_2$-Anorthite phase diagram, with significant concentrations of potassium and phosphorus, the microstructures seen closely fit with those that would be expected. If the slag compositions were plotted on the alternate $FeO-SiO_2-Al_2O_3$ diagram suggested by Morton and Wingrove (1972), they would plot well in the hercynite field. Thus, the slag would have massive primary hercynite, rather than the primary fayalite with a secondary fayalite/hercynite eutectic actually observed. Given that the $FeO-SiO_2$-Anorthite seems to be the most appropriate diagram to interpret the structures, it also means that there is no significant difference in the melting points of the slag from the two context groups. Ignoring the effects of the other elements present, all the slag compositions measured would melt in the range 1100°C to 1150°C. Most of the additional elements - sodium, potassium and phosphorous - are likely to reduce the melting point still further. So the possibility that the slag composition of the Group 2 slag was such that the melting point of the slag was sufficiently high to make slag tapping more difficult, can be ruled out. There is not likely to be much difference between the average melting points of the two slag groups. Therefore, the difference proportions of slag types and microstructures must be due to the way in which the furnaces were run.

It seems likely that the furnace supplying the slag in Group 2 was being run at a lower temperature but under more reducing conditions than that of Group 3. That is, the Group 2 furnace was not being blown so hard as the Group 3 furnaces. It was initially thought that the furnaces associated with Group 3 were the ones that were being used more efficiently, as there was a greater ratio of tap slag to furnace slag. However, the internal structure of the slag indicates that the loss of iron into the slag was around 5% less for the material from Group 2 if the same ores were being used, even though the proportion of slag tapped out of the furnace was less.

The evidence from both the macroscopic and microstructural examination of the slag suggested that the Group 3 furnace was being run at a higher temperature than the furnaces represented by Group 2. To get to higher temperature it is necessary to blow air into the furnace faster in order to burn more charcoal in a given time. However, this can result in the atmosphere becoming less reducing, hence the increased proportion of free iron oxide present. Running the furnace hotter means that the slag will be easier to tap out, as in general the higher the temperature of the slag above its melting point the less its viscosity. Running at a higher temperature will also make the smelting reactions proceed faster, which in turn means an increased rate of iron production, as long as the losses of metallic iron to the slag in the form of free iron oxides are not excessive.

The other problem associated with running the furnace at a higher temperature is that the furnace lining will be attacked and eroded by the slag much more rapidly. This is exactly what the bulk slag evidence suggested, with excessive penetration of the furnace lining by slag. To counteract this it would be necessary to use a more refractory furnace lining. The presence of the light coloured furnace lining fragment from Group 3 suggests that the master smelter had sufficient knowledge of his materials and their properties to find a clay with lower iron content and mix in sand with a higher proportion of larger sand grains, to make such a refractory.

This raises question as to why there was a change in the way the furnaces were run. The two possibilities that come to mind are:

- The smiths wanted to change the quality of the metal that they were producing; either a metal with fewer slag inclusions, or that the more reducing bloomery was producing a steel rather than iron.

- They wanted to produce metal more quickly.

The metallic iron

Slag with high concentration of metallic iron was recovered from contexts in both Groups 2 and 3. These were mounted and polished for optical examination. The metallic iron when etched with nital showed a simple slow cooled grain structure with no evidence for any carbon or phosphorus content. It is likely that the metal may not be representative of the metal produced on this site. All the samples show the iron poorly consolidated (Fig 4.17), surrounded by slag with a high free iron oxide content. In addition, it is clear that in places metallic iron has been oxidised back into wüstite. Sample Ox-348 had an unusual juxtaposition of structures. One part of the sample consists of small blebs of ferritic iron in matrix of slag with a high free iron oxide content. The slag structure in the areas with metallic iron is relatively coarse, suggesting that the material had cooled slowly in a furnace. However, in other regions of the same sample the structure consisted of very fine iron oxide and fayalite dendrites with a thin surface oxide scale. This structure is typical of a tap slag that has cooled quickly outside the furnace in contact with air. The two structures are not compatible. Thus it seems likely that a fragment of bloom was lost during removal of the bloom from the furnace, or fell off during bloom-forging, or was simply not considered worth consolidating. As some stage the piece was dumped in the slag tapping channel where it was then enveloped in a flow of tap slag during a later smelt.

It is likely that these metal samples are from the outer parts of the bloom which are normally decarburised in the smelting furnace as shown by the smelting experiments carried out by the Crews and analysed by Salter (Crew and Salter 1997). The samples, unfortunately, do not help to determine whether the use of two ways of running the furnaces was a deliberate attempt to produce iron with a higher carbon content, or purely a result of two slightly different smelting traditions.

The iron ore

It is generally assumed that the iron smelting sites along the Jurassic ridge would use the same ores that were of economic importance in the late nineteenth and twentieth centuries. That is, the Middle Lias Marlstone Rock Band in the Banbury area, and the Northampton Sand of the Inferior Oolite Series. The Northampton Sand Ironstone is usually a sideritic chamositic oolite and limonitic oolite, but the region of twentieth-century exploitation of the ore field was limited by lateral passage into ferruginous sandstone or by its absence beneath younger strata (Hains and Horton 1969, 105). In the region under consideration the Northampton Sand Ironstone thins and disappears under the Lower Estuarine series to the south and west of Northampton. This has the result that the nearest exposures of the Northampton Sand Ironstone are about 5 km away to the north-east of Silverstone. Thus, the iron smelting site at Syresham is outside the area where one might expect the development of an iron extraction industry.

A number of pieces of possible iron ore were trapped beneath flows of tap slag. One other sizeable piece of ironstone conglomerate was also recovered with the slag. A large number of the possible trapped ore samples proved to be hearth lining type material covered by a thin layer of post-deposition iron rich minerals. However, a number of the samples proved to be fragments of iron ores. Samples trapped in slag from contexts 1053 (feature 1054), 1108 (gully 1109), and 1371 (pit 1372) were examined. These consisted of two different rock types. The first was more or less pure iron oxide with very little or no other minerals present. The second consisted of ferruginous sandstones with angular to sub-rounded quartz grains and minor amounts of other detrital minerals. Neither showed any evidence of the presence of ooliths, and very little evidence of any fossil material.

The ironstone conglomerate from context 1082 (ditch 25) consisted of bands of ill-sorted siliceous sand and chert-like pebbles. The sand grains like those from the ore trapped in the tap slag flows consisted of a mixture of angular and sub-rounded grains and made up about 25% of the cross-section area (excluding the pebbles) in the sandy band. The other band consisted mainly of iron oxide with two distinct structures. The matrix consisted of almost pure iron oxides surrounding oval regions of iron oxide, surrounding small inclusions of what appeared, under the optical microscope, to be clay-like material. Only an occasional quartz grain was observed in some of these iron-oxide-clay regions. It is thought likely that this rock originally consisted of a conglomerate of rock fragments represented by the chert-like pebbles, sand and marl clasts. The original matrix and most of the marl fragments having been replaced by iron oxide during weathering. Although the sample size of the trapped ore fragments was rather too small to be totally sure, they could have come from broken up fragments of a rock similar to the conglomerate.

In summary, all the ore fragments examined were of sufficient quality, that is the iron to silica ratio was high enough, for them to have been used as a bloomery iron ore. It is also clear from the lack of oolitic material and presence of large amounts of quartz that the material was not derived from the Northampton Ironstone. It is thought likely that this material was the result of local weathering and enrichment in iron of material initially derived from the Lias Marlstone, and deposited in the vicinity by glacial activity. The enrichment processes are likely to have occurred where such material was deposited in situations suitable for the formation of local hard pans.

Area G Syresham
A Chapman and C Salter

A total weight of 19.3 kg of slag was recovered from five separate contexts. Contexts 1039 (gully 1037), 2202 (gully 2280) and 2310 (the raking pit of Furnace 2386) contained large fragments of tap slag and a limited amount of furnace slag (total weight 7.5kg). On some of the material from 2310 patches of fired clay from the furnace lining were adhering to the tap slag. Context 2306, from the furnace itself, contained two large fragments (total weight 10.3 kg) from a single furnace bottom. When joined together it could be seen that the furnace bottom had a flattened oval plan with a long axis of 400 mm and short axis length of 240 mm, and an overall depth of about

180 mm. One of the longer sides was flattened and had hearth lining adhering to it, and no fossilized charcoal impressions. The rest of the perimeter and base of the furnace bottom showed flows of slag through a bed of charcoal. It is clear that the slag was tapped out of the furnace from the base of the flattened side. The slag here was massive and dense, like tap slag, whereas elsewhere it was of a 'flow through fuel' furnace slag morphology. The section showed a relatively flat undersurface sloping away from the tapping hole, and a concave upper surface. The concave upper surface represents the depression in which the bloom formed. This was 180 by 170 mm across and the bloom was likely to be at least 75 mm thick (if it did not protrude above the level of the surrounding slag). There were also a number of unusual impressions in the upper surface of the furnace bottom towards the tapping side. On the left side there were two square section holes (15mm), one of which was at least 38mm deep. Both show wood impressions preserved in the slag. These holes must have been made late in the smelting operation otherwise the wood would have burnt out and the slag filled the holes. It is likely that these were formed either in an unsuccessful attempt to clear the tap hole from the inside, or whilst attempting to manipulate the bloom whilst still hot. The shape of the furnace bottom suggests that the furnace was blown by two tuyères opposite each other at right angles to the tapping hole.

The term tuyère is used here to describe the hole through which air was blown into the furnace. However, it is unlikely that tuyeres in the strict sense (independent clay pipes) were used, it is more likely that the furnace was blown by holes through the furnace lining.

It is possible to estimate the likely weight of iron in the bloom produced during this smelt on the basis of the size of the depression and the estimates of density blooms from experimental reconstructions carried out by Peter Crew (pers comm). Using a rough density of 5 g cm-3, the weight of the bloom would be around 7 kg, although a considerable proportion of this metal would be lost during the forging from a bloom to a billet to a bar to final artefact (Crew 1991).

Context 1204 (a plough furrow) contained a single 'cake', weighing 1.5 kg, which was a large smithing hearth bottom, also certainly formed during the initial high temperature forging of the bloom into a malleable billet of iron.

The material from the site therefore clearly indicates that iron smelting and the initial forging of the bloom was carried out in the area.

OTHER FINDS
I Meadows and T Hylton
with a contribution by H E M Cool

Introduction

A small collection of artefacts made from stone, antler, bone and glass were recovered from five sites. The Iron

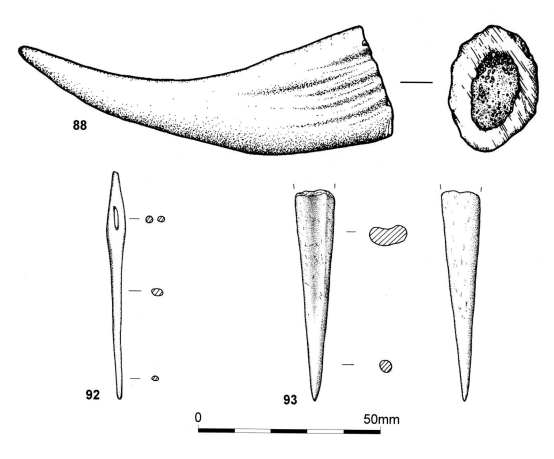

Fig. 4.19: *Antler and bone artefacts from Silverstone 3 (88); Silverstone Fields Farm (92) and (93).*

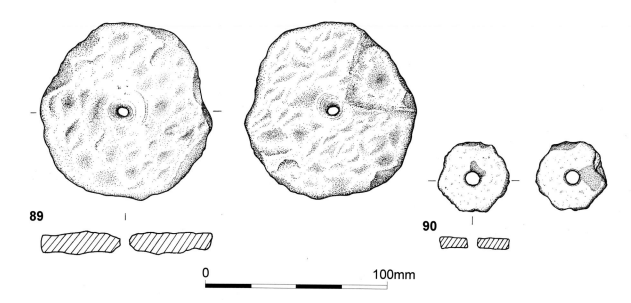

Fig. 4.20: *Limestone disc, Silverstone 3 (89) and spindle whorl, Silverstone Field Farm (90).*

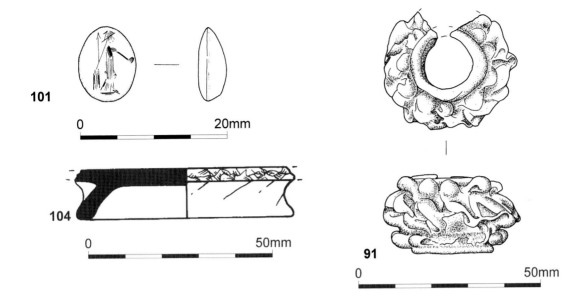

Fig. 4.21: *Glass ring, Silverstone Fields Farm (91); Jasper intaglio, Area G Syresham (101); Base of glass bowl, Area G, Syresham (104).*

Age glass ring from Silverstone Fields Farm (91) and the Roman jasper intaglio from Area G Syresham (101) are unusual and of particular interest. Other more common items included bone pins and quernstones.

Silverstone 3

88 Sawn antler tine. The point is smooth and burnished but it is not known whether this was done during the life of the deer or through the subsequent use of the object. Function unknown. Length: 105 mm Width 24 mm x 32 mm across at the sawn end. SF1, Enclosure 1 ditch 2051 (1020). (Fig 4.19).

89 Limestone disc with well-dressed edges and a single perforation diagonally through the centre. This would preclude its use as a spindle whorl. It may have been a pot lid or weight. Unknown date. Diameter: 90 mm Thickness 15 mm.
SF5, unstrat. (Fig 4.20).

Silverstone Fields Farm

90 Spindle whorl made from a coarse Roman potsherd base. Diameter: 37 mm x 30 mm Thickness 6 mm. The central drilled perforation is 8 mm wide.
SF3, Enclosure 1 (200). (Fig 4.20).

91 Blue cobalt glass ring with raised blobs and swags. Diameter: 35 mm. Guido's Type 8 Exotic Iron Age (1978, 71). Dated to the first century BC in the example from Vieux Passage in Brittany. A very similar example comes from Boxford, Berkshire. The design is found on continental glass armlets which suggests it might be an import (J Henderson, pers comm).
SF6, pit 204. (Fig 4.21).

92 Bone needle made from a sliver of long bone which had become highly polished, presumably through use. Length: 61 mm. Head 9 mm long above the eye and up to 7 mm wide. The eye is 7 mm long and a little over 1 mm wide. Below the eye the stem tapers from 6 mm to a point.
SF9, pit 146 (148). (Fig 4.19).

93 Bone point broken at one end. It has a highly burnished tip, presumably through use. Possibly a pin beater used

in weaving. The surviving length 55 mm and the broken end 11 mm x 5 mm in section.
SF10, pit 183 (185). (Fig 4.19).

94 Incomplete piece of bone which shows signs of having been trimmed to a point. At the opposite end to the point a small hole, 3-4 mm in diameter, has been drilled into one side but not the other.
SF12, pit 146 (147).

95 Rotary quern fragment of Millstone Grit. The piece preserves part of a concave smooth grinding surface indicating that this was the upper stone, the complete diameter of which would have been about 300 mm. The fragment measures 105 mm x 90 mm x 40 mm.
SF15, Enclosure 1 (101).

Shacks Barn Farm

96 Small block of bituminous shale, possibly worked, but eroded. Unknown date. 30 mm x 25 mm x 10 mm.
SF2, pit 1748 (1706).

97 Splinter of animal long bone with two knife-cut notches. 59 mm x 12 mm.
SF3, ditch 3186 (3104).

98 Quern fragment of Millstone Grit. Probably Roman.
SF4, trench 38, unstrat.

Biddlesden Road Bridge

99 Saddle quern fragment in glauconite sandstone. The fragment preserved part of the grinding surface and the lip that developed along one edge. 210 mm x 170 mm and 80 mm thick.
SF13, ditch 17 (1151).

100 Rubbing stone in two pieces from a fine-grained quartzitic pebble. 250 mm x 160 mm and 50 mm thick.
Ditch 1 (1185).

Area G Syresham

101 Carnelian intaglio. The stone is convex on both surfaces, most strongly on the reverse. Engraved on

the surface is a standing figure with the right hand leaning on a shield and the left holding out a libation bowl. A shallow mark denotes a spear resting against the right shoulder. The head is shallowly incised, but would appear to be helmeted. The figure is Minerva, a popular image for use on intaglios. Close dating is difficult, but a date before the late second century AD, when flat cut stones became more common, is likely. (Zienkiewicz 1987).

SF2, gully 1037 (1012). (Fig 4.21).

102 Bone pin shaft fragment broken at both ends. Length: 35 mm.

SF4, gully 1038 (1041).

103 Bone pin shaft fragment, tapering toward one end and slightly flattened at the other. Length: 50 mm.

SF5, gully 1037 (1039).

104 Glass bowl base fragment (H E M Cool) Dark yellow/brown in colour. Flat base; applied true base ring with diagonal tooling marks and a trace of post-technique scar. Side grozed. Base diameter: 60 mm.

SF18, ditch 1147 (1106). (Fig 4.21).

The fragment comes from a tubular-rimmed bowl (Price and Cottam 1998, 78). In general the type was in use from the mid first to the mid second century AD, but the dark colour of this example makes a first century date more likely. The side of the vessel has been deliberately trimmed so that the base became a disc of glass. This re-use might have prolonged the life of the object into the second century.

CHAPTER FIVE
HUMAN SKELETAL MATERIAL

Introduction

Human bone was recovered from two sites. Most came from the Iron Age settlement at Silverstone Fields Farm where a group of five partial and near-complete infant skeletons were found in the later phase of Enclosure Ditch 1. An analysis of these forms the main subject of this chapter. At Brackley Hatch 4 a fragment of adult human cranium (75 x 35 mm in size) came from the colluvial silt (23) near to and overlying ditch 35. This fragment is not datable, but, in common with the other finds from the site, it seems likely to be Roman. It was probably redeposited from a burial in one of the sections of ditch on the site or from outside the excavation area. Little more can be said of this fragment.

The infant bones from Silverstone Fields Farm came from burials discovered during the course of excavation. Four individuals were found in sections excavated as part of the initial sampling strategy. The complete excavation of the enclosure ditch by machine resulted in the discovery of another skeleton. Two of the skeletons were found to be virtually complete. It is unclear whether the incompleteness of the other skeletons was a result of selection at burial or of recovery biases. On balance the latter explanation may be the correct one as infant bones, particularly neonatal ones, are tiny, fragile and notoriously difficult to see. Complete recovery is likely only in the most favourable circumstances even where most of the bone survives in the soil.

One of the burials (Burial 1) was found to comprise two skeletons. The individuals had presumably been buried together at the same time. None of the individuals was associated with other finds or grave goods, except perhaps Burial 5 which lay close to, and just below, bones from a partially articulated cattle carcass. It is possible that the two depositions were connected in some way.

In this report Burial and Skeleton (SK) numbers are interchangeable.

INFANT BURIALS FROM SILVERSTONE FIELDS FARM
T Anderson

The material

Human foetal/neonatal human skeletal material was recovered from the later phase of the late Iron Age/Early

Roman enclosure ditch (Enclosure 1). One burial (Burial 1) contained two individuals, here classed as SK1a and 1b. As such, five individuals were available for analysis. Two skeletons were practically complete (SK1a; 2). One individual was represented by limb bones; scapulae; rib fragments and cranial fragments (SK3). The least complete was SK5, in which, only the right ilium; upper femur and the left side of the skeleton were recovered. SK1b, is represented by limb bones and cranial fragments. In general, the bones are solid and well-preserved and only minor reconstruction of damaged fragments was required. Based on the definitions in Fazekas and Kósa (1978), supplemented by data in Bass (1987: 212-13, 233) and Schutkowski (1989), measurements of all the available intact bones are presented as Appendix 2.

Age

An approximate age at death could be calculated for each skeleton, based on limb bone (diaphyseal) lengths (Appendix 2, Table 1). Four skeletons could be classed as full-term foetal (37-42 gestational weeks). One individual (SK1b) was slightly smaller, but was still within the size range for full-term (33-39 weeks). The detailed data in Fazekas and Kósa 1978 suggests similar ages: SK1b appears to be 36-40 weeks, and the other skeletons are larger than full-term (40 weeks).

An accurate chronological age assessment (ie foetal or new born) based solely on bone size is handicapped by the fact that there is variation in the size of foetuses and neonates. A small skeleton may represent a premature birth or a young infant that is failing to thrive. A larger skeleton may represent a post-term foetus rather than neonate or young infant.

The humero-tibial ratio and the crural index suggest that SK1b is foetal (gestational age of less than 40 weeks). The indices of the other skeletons would all support foetal or neonate (Appendix 2, Table 2). The length :breadth ratio of the basilar portion of the occipital bone in SK2 (86.8) would be compatible with a full term foetus (Fazekas and Kósa 1978, table 45), whereas the index (79.5) of SK1a, would suggest a neonate or young infant (Scheuer and Black 2000, table 5.4).

Examination of the developmental maturity of the bones may also give clues to the chronological age. In two individuals (SK1a; 2) fusion of the petromastoid and squamotympanic portions of the temporal, with the fusion line still visible, would suggest that both are neonate or infant rather than foetal (Scheuer and Black 2000, 83).

Unerupted deciduous teeth crowns were recovered in two individuals (SK1a; 2). The crowns of the central upper incisors are almost complete (Appendix 2, Table 3) which would support an age of c new born - 3 months (van Beek 1983, table 1).

Sex

Various attempts, based on pelvic morphology, have been made to sex foetal and neonatal skeletal material (Fazekas and Kósa 1978; Molleson 1993; Schutkowski 1989, 1993; Weaver 1980). Based on the indices produced by Schutkowski (1989), the three skeletons with intact ilia (Sk1a; 3; 5) display certain male characteristics (Appendix 2, Table 4). However, most workers consider that pelvic sexual dimorphism, including the morphology of the greater sciatic notch, is insufficiently expressed to be a reliable indicator of foetal or neonatal sex (Boucher 1955, 1957; Holcomb and Konigsberg 1995; Mittler and Sheridan 1992; Scheuer and Black 2000, 342).

In this small sample of unsexed skeletons, limb bone robusticity does not show dimorphism (Appendix 2, Table 5). The very slight sexual dimorphism in modern limb bone proportions at known chronological age (Appendix 2, Table 2) is of limited value in archaeological samples of undocumented age. In one skeleton (SK1a) the length and the mesio-distal width of the developing incisor crowns are larger than the mean dimensions for modern fully formed incisor crowns (Appendix 2, Table 3). However, this is not diagnostic evidence for a male individual.

Pathology

In clinical practice, prematurity, congenital malformations, infections, birth trauma, chromosomal abnormalities as well as maternal complications are all associated with neonatal deaths (Kalousek and Gilbert-Barnes 1997). There was no evidence for any pathology or abnormality on the available bones. In the smallest skeleton (SK1b) the brachial and the crural indices suggest that the lower arm and the upper leg were slightly shorter than normal (Appendix 2, Table 2). However, this probably represents slight variation in normal growth rather than a pathological condition.

Comparative material

In certain later Iron Age cemeteries, infant and child burials are quite rare (Whimster 1981, 89). There is some evidence that infants were buried within Iron Age buildings (Collis 1977a). In southern Iron Age Britain infants were frequently placed in partly filled ditches (Collis 1977b; Philpott 1991, 97; Whimster 1981). Indeed, according to Whimster, the primary silting of enclosure ditches were "an appropriate or convenient burial place for children dying in the first weeks or months of life ", (Whimster 1981, 28).

The tradition of infants being buried in ditches continues into the Roman period (Dolby 1969a, 248; Goodburn 1979, 323; Oliver and Applin 1978, 80-81; Woodward and Steer 1936, 85). On rural sites especially, infants were being buried with little ceremony in the vicinity of dwellings or outbuildings (Anderson and Andrews, archive; Philpott 1991, 98). Numerous examples occur at villa sites (Ashcroft 1934; Cocks 1921; Frere 1984, 322; Johnston 1972; Leech 1981; Philpott 1991, 97-98; Price and Watts 1980; Scott 1999, 110-113; Stead and Rigby 1986, 38, 393).

In the Roman period, the only burials permitted within city walls were children who had not cut their deciduous teeth (Pliny). This accounts for the numerous infant graves found within Roman towns (Kj?lbye-Biddle 1995, 211; Philpott 1991, 97-98; Wheeler and Wheeler 1936). At Ancaster, two probable still-births (one aged 28 weeks) were buried under the floor of a building (Cox 1989, 11).

Consequently, many urban cemeteries contain relatively few infant burials (Philpott 1991, table 17; Whytehead 1986). However, at Poundbury, in the later Roman period, neonates and foetuses, including the non-viable and the still-born, as well as smaller than average babies, were buried within formal cemeteries (Molleson 1993, 171-181). This was in contrast to the late Iron Age and early Roman periods, when neonates and infants were buried in close proximity to the settlement; occurring in ditches (SK273); within buildings (SK1249; 1371; 1376; 1379; 1380; 1383; 1386; 1387-1394) and in construction trenches (SK253) (Farwell and Molleson 1993, 13; 253; 260; 300; 301; fig. 5).

In certain cases, such as the public bath house at Wroxeter (Kenyon 1938, 188) and Springhead, where two of the burials were decapitated (Penn 1960), infants appear to have been sacrificed as foundation deposits. The discovery of infant burials within forts (Frere 1988, 433; Hooper 1975; Philp 1966, 7; Philpott 1991, 97) suggests the deliberate disposal of unwanted babies born to native women from the local vicus.

Based on the age-distribution of large numbers of perinatal skeletons, it has been suggested that infanticide was practised in Roman Britain (Mays 1993). It is true that still-births and also some neonatal deaths are related to premature delivery (Kalousek and Gilbert-Barnes 1997). These would tend to present archaeologically as skeletons of slightly younger gestational age. However, many natural neonatal deaths and cases of infanticide will occur at an identical age. Also, variation in foetal bone size and growth means that it is not possible to determine the exact gestational age of individual skeletons.

As such, in the absence of skeletal manifestation of a non-lethal deformity, it will be very difficult to reach a definite diagnosis of infanticide. Clues may be obtained from the location of the burial and the lack of respect that has been assigned to the interment (Smith and Kahlia 1992). However, it must be remembered that many infanticides may not have been buried at all. It is possible that the majority of unwanted children were abandoned rather than murdered (Boswell 1988, 41-45). There is also both archaeological and documentary evidence for infants being drowned (Wicker 1999).

Conclusion

Based solely on limb bone size, four skeletons could be classed as viable full-term foetal or new born. One individual (SK1b) was slightly smaller, but could still represent a slightly smaller than average, or a premature new born. Detailed examination of bone ratios, skeletal maturity and dental development, suggest that SK1a and 2 may be new born rather than foetal. Certain pelvic measurements suggest that three skeletons (SK1a, 3 and 5) may be male. Also, the teeth crowns in the former are quite large. However, such criteria are considered insufficient to diagnose sex with certainty.

There was no evidence for cause of death on the available bones. Slight variation in limb proportions in the smallest skeleton are considered to be in the bounds of normality rather representing underlying pathology. The burial of neonates and infants outside formal cemeteries, in ditches and in close proximity to settlements, is well known in the late Iron Age and early Roman period. As such, these articulated burials displaying no skeletal evidence of congenital deformity or deliberate mutilation appear to favour perinatal death from natural causes rather than infanticide or ritual sacrifice.

CHAPTER SIX
ECONOMIC AND ENVIRONMENTAL EVIDENCE

THE ANIMAL BONES
K Deighton

Introduction

A total of 70.5 kg of animal bones was analysed from the five sites producing the largest assemblages – Silverstone 3, Silverstone 2, Silverstone Fields Farm, Biddlesden Road Bridge and Brackley Hatch 4. The first four sites are broadly contemporary middle to late Iron Age settlements, while the settlement at Brackley Hatch 4 dates to the second to third centuries AD.

Methodology

Bone was sorted into identifiable and recordable fragments according to selected anatomical units (Halstead 1985, after Watson 1979). Non-identifiable fragments were counted and are included in Table 6.1. The numbers of ribs and vertebrae were noted but these elements were not recorded to species level. Skeletons were recorded but not included in quantification to avoid species bias. Identifications to species, where possible, were made with the aid of Schmidt (1972) for large mammals, while bird bone identification follows Serjeantson and Cohen (1996). Recording follows Halstead (1985) and uses minimum anatomical unit (MinAU) whereby each bone is held to have a proximal and a distal half, which were recorded separately or recorded as absent. Any matching fragments from the same context were rejoined and where more than one fragment belonged to the same anatomical unit, only the one with the most information was recorded. This procedure lessens the likelihood of over-recording due to the fragmentation of elements.

A calculation of the minimum number of individuals (MNI) by selected anatomical element per species was also made (Appendix 3, Tables 1 - 5). This has been summarised to give an overall quantification of MNI by site (Table 6.2).

For each identifiable bone fragment the following were recorded; element, taxon, proximal fusion, distal fusion, side, modification, butchery and fragmentation. Butchery follows Binford (1981). Pathologies are described after Baker and Brothwell (1980). Ageing for cattle follows Halstead (1985) after Payne (1973) and for ovicaprids follows Payne (1973). Fusion follows Silver (1969). Material from sieved samples was also included (9 samples producing animal bone) but this added little to the final analysis.

Results

Preservation
Fragmentation was high and this was mostly the result of old breaks. The proportion of unidentifiable bone was 40-44 % for the Iron Age sites (Table 6.1) but far lower (9%) for Brackley Hatch 4 where a low frequency of weathering was also noted. Concretions of minerals were seen on occasional bones from Silverstone 3 and Biddlesden Road Bridge. Canid gnawing was moderate (ranging from 0.8%-9.2% of identified bones) and a single example of digested bone was noted.

Butchery and burning
The frequency of butchery was low for all sites, being observed on only 51 bones, most of them cattle or cattle-sized. The generally good surface condition of the bone suggests butchery evidence was not obscured by surface damage, and so this paucity of evidence could be due to the use of boning out as a method of dismembering carcasses. Chopping marks were observed on 13 bones. Some ribs appeared to have been chopped into sections, which could suggest their use in soups and stews. Evidence for dismembering and possible filleting were also seen along with some indeterminate knife marks.

The frequency of burned bone was very low at only 0.5% of total fragments (ie 15 fragments). The nature of the charring suggested burnt debris (even charring of entire fragments) rather than charring during roasting (fragments charred at ends).

Pathologies
There were only three pathological elements identifiable. Silverstone 2 yielded a cattle third molar with an uneven

Taxon	Common name	SL2 (%)	SL3 (%)	SFF (%)	BRB (%)	BH4 (%)
Equus	Horse	14 (2.6)	13 (1.9)	30 (2.2)	17 (4.2)	5 (7.2)
Bos	Cattle	108 (20.0)	152 (22.7)	152 (11.2)	116 (28.6)	24 (34.8)
Ovicaprid	Sheep/goat	102 (18.9)	145 (21.6)	375 (27.6)	39 (9.6)	18 (26.0)
Sus	Pig	13 (2.4)	17 (2.5)	52 (3.8)	14 (3.4)	3 (4.3)
Canid	Dog	2 (0.37)	1 (0.2)	4 (0.3)	3 (0.7)	1 (1.4)
Cervid	Deer	-	-	5 (0.4)	3 (0.7)	-
Ovic/cap	Sheep/goat/roe	-	1 (0.2)	34 (2.5)	2 (0.4)	-
L.ungulate	Horse/cow/red	53 (9.8)	53 (7.9)	18 (1.3)	34 (8.4)	6 (8.7)
S.ungulate	Sheep/goat/roe/pig	9 (1.67)	14 (2.0)	144 (10.6)	3 (0.7)	10 (14.5)
Avis	Bird	-	-	3 (0.2)	-	-
Indet		239 (44.3)	273 (40.8)	542 (39.9)	175 (43.1)	6 (8.7)
Total		**540**	**669**	**1358**	**406**	**69**

Table 6.1: Animal bone; summary of taxa by site (MinAU). **Key:** Ovic/cap = Ovicaprid/Capreolus capreolus.

wear pattern. At Silverstone 3 an ovicaprid metatarsal showed exostosis on one side and at Brackley Hatch 4 a similar condition was noted on a cattle first phalanx. The two latter pathologies could be indicative of osteoarthritis due to stress on joints or old age. Indeed, the third pathology could be indicative of the use of the animal for traction.

Frequency of Species

All the sites were characterised by the two main domesticates, cattle and sheep. These accounted for between 65% and 75% of identified species. There were smaller quantities of pig and horse and also occasional dog bones from each site. Deer (probably red deer *Cervus elaphus*)) was found at two sites and bird bones from one. Table 6.1 presents the overall quantities and relative frequencies of species calculated according to the minimum anatomical unit, and Table 6.2 calculations of the minimum numbers of individuals. Comparisons between the two tables show very similar proportions of species when the unidentified elements are omitted, despite low numbers of individual animals calculated in Table 6.2. Elements recorded for individual sites are presented in Appendix 3 Tables 1 – 3.

Skeletons

BRACKLEY HATCH 4. HORSE SKELETON (ENCLOSURE DITCH 35, CONTEXT 70/71).

Most elements are present although the skull is severely fragmented. All long bone ends appear to be fused and mandibular teeth are well worn suggesting an animal of 20-40 years (Levine 1982). No evidence of butchery was noted, which, along with intact burial suggests no carcass utilisation.

SILVERSTONE FIELDS FARM. PARTIAL CATTLE SKELETON (ENCLOSURE I DITCH, BURIAL 4, CONTEXT 45).

Approximately three-quarters of the animal was present. The elements comprised ribs, vertebrae, tibias, radii, ulna, teeth and mandible fragments. The remains were partly articulated, noticeably several of the vertebrae and leg bones, but there appeared to be some dispersal of the remains. The articulated remains may originally have been limited to ribs and vertebrae with lower leg bones as separate deposits. The mandible fragments would have been non-articulating and a range of bones of other taxa (ie horse, sheep/goat, pig) were also present in the group, indicating a rather heterogeneous assemblage.

Taxon	Common name	SL2	SL3	SFF	BRB	BH4
Equus	Horse	1	1	2	1	3
Bos	Cattle	6	10	8	9	2
Ovicaprid	Sheep/goat	7	12	25	3	3
Sus	Pig	1	2	4	3	1
Canid	Dog	1	1	1	1	1
Cervid	Deer	1		1		
Avis	Bird			2		
Total		**17**	**26**	**43**	**17**	**10**

Table 6.2: Animal bone; summary of taxa present by minimum number of individuals (MNI).

Key: SL2 - Silverstone 2; SL3 – Silverstone 3; SFF - Silverstone Fields Farm; BRB - Biddlesden Road Bridge: BH4 - Brackley Hatch 4.

The condition of the teeth and the fact that the long bones present are completely fused suggests a mature animal. Measurements from the long bones suggest a large animal by Iron Age standards (Reynolds 1979, table 8 appendix). There was an absence of sexing criteria. The bones exhibited no obvious signs of butchery. The remains were very close to an infant burial and could represent a "side of beef" ritual deposit.

A partial cattle skull from the northern terminal of Enclosure 1 (context 102) is also worth noting. It showed evidence both of possible pole-axing and the subsequent skinning or removal of horn from cores (fine cut marks near base of horn cores). This could be related to the remains in context 45 as the bone elements are not duplicated, but it is not certain.

Age of slaughter

There are insufficient data available for meaningful calculations of herd slaughter patterns. Tooth-wear analyses were carried out for cattle at Biddlesden Road Bridge (n=6), and for sheep/goat at Silverstone 3 (n=6) and Silverstone Fields Farm (n=26). The results are shown in Appendix 3 Tables 6, 7 and 8.

Fusion data is presented in Appendix 3 Tables 10–12. This class of data is rough and prone to inaccuracies due to the many gaps and overlaps it entails. It is generally used to confirm patterns seen in tooth wear analysis rather than as evidence for age patterns on its own. Unfortunately, in this instance little light is shed on toothwear data as much of the fusion was indeterminate.

Discussion

Silverstone 2

The assemblage was dominated by cattle and sheep/goat with a slight preponderance of cattle (20% to 18.9%) according to MinAU calculations (Table 6.1). The relative proportion of sheep/goat increases over cattle using MNI

calculations (Table 6.2). However, if the number of 'large' and 'small' ungulates are included the dominance of cattle/cattle-sized animals is reinforced. Horse, pig and dog were the only other animals recorded, all in small numbers.

The small size of the assemblage makes body part analysis tentative. For cattle slightly higher numbers of humerus and tibia are present compared with other bones (Appendix 3 Table 1). Although these bones have a relatively high meat yield, it is possible that their dominance reflects the preservation of these relatively robust bones, rather than it being a pattern of consumption or discard. For sheep/goat tibia dominate, as they do on all the sites, while for pig the emphasis on long bones probably reflects preservation bias. There is nothing to suggest specialised activity on site (eg primary butchery, kitchen waste, selective consumption) and the remains generally indicate non-specialised patterns of processing and consumption.

Two neonatal elements were present, one sheep/goat and one cattle. This is more than on the other sites, but insufficient to suggest a greater emphasis on livestock rearing here.

Silverstone 3

Like Silverstone 2, the assemblage is dominated by cattle and sheep/goat with a slight preponderance of cattle (22.7% to 21.6%) according to MinAU calculations (Table 6.1) but a slight increase in sheep/goat when MNI are considered (Table 6.2). 'Large' ungulates are more common than 'small' ones, suggesting that the preponderance of cattle is increased when these data are taken into account. Horse, pig and dog are again present, but in small numbers.

There are high numbers of cattle humeri and radii (Appendix 3 Table 2). When elements are compared on Brain's (1981) preservation index (Figure 6.1), where elements are placed in order of durability, the proximal tibia, proximal humerus and proximal and distal radii appear to be over-represented. This is particularly remarkable when

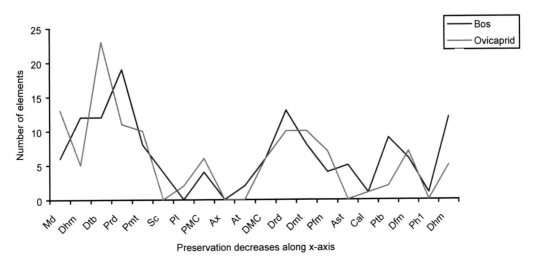

Fig. 6.1: *Silverstone 3, Preservation of Bos and Ovicaprids.*

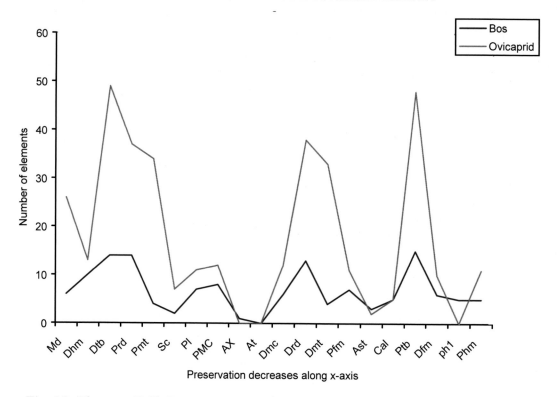

Fig. 6.2: *Silverstone Fields Farm, Preservation of Bos and Ovicaprid.*

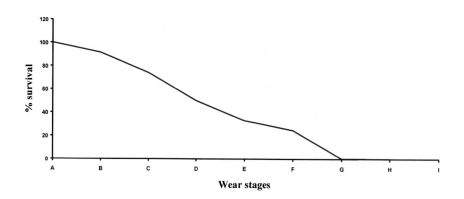

Fig. 6.3: *Silverstone Field Farm, Survival pattern of Ovicaprid based on tooth eruption and wear (from 29 mandibles).*

the high frequency of fragmentation is taken into account as these bones are more likely to fragment and be rendered unidentifiable. Binford's (1978) meat utility index shows that both tibia and humerus have a relatively high meat yield. This suggests that the assemblage has a component which was the by-product of consumption rather than of primary butchery. The radius has a moderate meat yield and a high value for this element is more problematic. It is possible that joints of beef brought to site comprised whole limbs, rather than disjointed ones, but if this were the case an over-representation of femora might also be expected.

Some difference is seen between the cattle and sheep/goat in terms of body part representation in that the pattern for cattle is less erratic. This is possibly due to size

differences in the carcasses resulting in a greater overall preservation and/or recovery of cattle bones.

The sheep/goat herd structure is difficult to define as there was little data for age estimates. Only six andibles could be assigned to age categories but tooth-wear analysis from this sample suggests that animals were slaughtered at a range of ages (Appendix 3 Table 7). A single cattle neonatal element was noted.

Silverstone Fields Farm

This site produced the largest bone assemblage. It is dominated by sheep/goat in very large proportions (about half the identifiable assemblage). The proportion of cattle is about 18% of the identifiable assemblage whether the MinAU or MNI figure is used. If the 'large ungulate' and 'small ungulate'and 'ovicaprid' figures are added to the numbers of cattle and sheep/goat respectively, the dominance of sheep/goat is emphasised, amounting to 68% of the identifiable bones. In contrast, the cattle/cattle-sized component amounts about 20%. The proportions of horse, pig and dog are similar to those on the other Iron Age sites.

This was the only site to produce evidence for birds, which included a pigeon (*Columba* sp.) and an indeterminate bird species. Deer was represented by tibia, metacarpal and phalanx fragments. It cannot be said for certain that this represents one animal. When compared with Brain's (1981) preservation index, body part analyses for sheep/goat and cattle suggest an over-representation of tibia and distal radius (Fig. 6.2). This may be due to selection for consumption.

There was little data for age estimates. Tooth wear analysis for sheep/goat, based on 26 mandibles, shows animals slaughtered in their prime (between 1 and 3 years, which covers Payne's (1973) optimum of 18-30 months), and seems to suggest husbandry primarily for meat (Fig. 6.3 and Appendix 3 Table 8). A single neonatal ovicaprine element was noted.

Biddlesden Road Bridge

This site had a relatively small assemblage of animal bone. It was dominated by cattle (over 50% of the identifiable assemblage) with a smaller proportion (17%) of sheep/goat (Tables 6.1 and 6.2). The dominance of cattle is further emphasised when the 'large ungulate' and 'small ungulate' categories are considered. Pig, dog and deer are also represented.

The assemblage was small for body part analysis, but there is a possible over-representation of the proximal radius of cattle (Appendix 3 Table 5). Ageing criteria were sparse, with tooth wear analysis for cattle possible on only six mandibles (Appendix 3 Table 6). Four of these animals were classified as senile and may have been slaughtered at the end of their useful lives. Two neonatal elements, both ovicaprid, were noted.

The small size of the bone assemblage appears to reflect the general paucity of finds and charred plant remains from the site. It is possible that this was due to the settlement's specialised nature as an iron smelting site and therefore not primarily engaged in agricultural production.

Brackley Hatch 4

This was the smallest of the assemblages with only 69 elements recovered. In view of this, comments are particularly tentative. The assemblage is dominated by cattle but with sheep/goat and the other principal domesticates also present. The high proportion of cattle is a typical feature of Roman sites. It has been suggested that this is the result of increased liverfluke infestation among sheep (Robinson and Wilson 1983). It can be noted, however, that sheep are more prominent when MNI is considered (Table 6.2). The nature of the assemblage may have been

affected by the pottery-making function of the site (or at least the excavated part of it), which perhaps relegated its agricultural functions. The body-part data (Appendix 3 Table 4) does, however, suggest the presence of butchery waste (eg mandibles, pelvis) and it is possible that this was a peripheral area of the site where waste might have been disposed (Wilson 1985). The horse burial (above) may also be seen as an act of disposal in a peripheral area. Horse burials are sometimes seen as ritual or 'special' deposits (Hill 1996), although there is no particular treatment in the present example to suggest this, other than the obvious point that it was buried intact rather than as food debris.

Inter-site comparisons

The data collected and analysed offer some opportunity to compare the animal bone assemblages from four Iron Age sites which were in more or less contemporaneous use – Silverstone 2, Silverstone 3, Silverstone Fields Farm and Biddlesden Road Bridge. The three Silverstone sites are, moreover, within half a kilometre of each other and may represent different aspects of essentially the same settlement or economic unit. The Roman site at Brackley Hatch 4 yielded a quite meagre faunal assemblage which may not be typical of the settlement as a whole.

Levels of bone preservation are similar on all sites despite a range of different burial environments. Canid gnawing, weathering and burning are at a similar low frequency for most sites, although a slightly higher level of weathering is seen at Silverstone 2. This may be due to the lower number of features available for deposition, and hence a greater degree of middening. The general low levels of weathering and canid gnawing suggest burial followed deposition fairly rapidly. The low frequency of burning suggests this was not a preferred or consistent method of disposal and was the result of casual activity.

Fragmentation is high for all sites, but the lack of evidence for butchery suggests this is not the result of heavy-handed butchery techniques. Equally, it would not seem to be due to trampling, as low levels of gnawing and weathering suggest that the bone was not left exposed. Fragmentation may therefore be the result of compaction following burial. While the evidence of butchery was low overall, a slightly higher level is seen at Biddlesden Road Bridge, perhaps because of the dominance of cattle here.

The larger faunal assemblages come from sites which are more likely to have been on open ground, namely Silverstone 2, Silverstone 3, and Silverstone Fields Farm, which were all situated on a limestone ridge. There may have been more pasture here than at the ironworking and pottery making sites of Biddlesden Road Bridge and Brackley Hatch 4, which may well have been situated in more wooded areas. All sites are, however, dominated by the two principal domestic animals, cattle and sheep. Wild species are scarce and only two sites (Silverstone Fields Farm and Bidddlesden Road Bridge) have deer.

Occasional bird bones came from Silverstone Fields Farm, and are not seen anywhere else.

Differences in the dominance and relative proportions of the major domesticates are seen between the sites. Silverstone 2 and Silverstone 3 show very similar species profiles with roughly equal proportions of cattle and sheep/goat. At Silverstone Fields Farm, however, a much higher proportion of sheep/goat is found and Biddlesden Road Bridge is dominated by cattle. Proportions of pig are consistently low at all sites. Unlike the other domestic species, pigs have no secondary products (ie nothing you can get without killing them) and they may not have been favoured for rearing. It is also worth noting that pig bones have the poorest preservation of the major domesticates (Stallibrass 1985) and may therefore have been more common than the surviving evidence indicates. The high levels of fragmentation on all sites would not, however, have discriminated against the identification of pig bones.

The different proportions of the main domesticates between the sites is of some interest. While the Iron Age sites are broadly contemporary, it is possible that there were slight chronological differences, so that the dominance of sheep at Silverstone Fields Farm reflected an earlier date than the other Silverstone sites, while Biddlesden Road Bridge, with a preponderance of cattle, was later than the others. This fits with a general national trend which shows an increase in cattle over sheep in the Roman period (Robinson and Wilson 1983). On the present sites, this explanation would, however, suggest a quite rapid change in species composition.

Alternatively, variations in environment might be a factor, although this seems likely only for Biddlesden Road Bridge. Here a less open and more wooded or marginal land would favour cattle over sheep because of their ability to browse. The three Silverstone sites are so closely adjacent that the surrounding environment would have been the same for each. In this instance, there may well have been functional differences between the sites which are reflected in the faunal assemblages. The most obvious explanation for the variation relates to the animals' non-meat products, so it can be hypothesised that wool was a specialised commodity at Silverstone Fields Farm, while milk and hides may have been more significant at the other sites.

Comparisons of the results of body part analysis are somewhat inconclusive due to the small samples at each site and the difficulty of explaining variations. The larger samples at Silverstone 3 and Silverstone Fields Farm enable a comparison of preservation index results (Figures 6.1 and 6.2). Both sites show similar patterns of bone preservation for ovicaprids and cattle, with an apparent over-representation of some bones. This may imply some selection of meat in favour of consumption at both sites, although other explanations are possible.

Comparisons of herd structures between the sites were not possible due to a lack of suitable age at death data. All sites (except Brackley Hatch 4) have very low numbers of neonates. From this it is not possible to say whether any of the sites specialised in breeding.

Comparisons with other sites

While the faunal assemblages at the Iron Age sites show some inter-site variations, they all generally fall within the ranges found on other sites in the county and further afield (Robinson and Wilson 1983; Hambleton 1999). The small Roman assemblage from Brackley Hatch 4 is also fairly typical in the lower proportion of sheep/goat in this period, and it has been suggested this is the result of increased liverfluke infestation and the flooding of meadowland (Robinson and Wilson 1983). However, the overall quantities here are low and it is not clear that the assemblage is typical of the site as a whole.

The dominance of cattle seen at Biddlesden Road Bridge does not seem to be common on Iron Age sites, but is seen at Great Houghton near Northampton which had a larger assemblage (Deighton 2001). There is also a slight dominance of cattle at Sywell (Thompson 2001) although the assemblage here was small and was affected by a large number of broken cattle skull bones, so that the proportions of cattle and sheep/goat may have been similar (op. cit., table 5, MNI).

The dominance of sheep at Silverstone Fields Farm would seem to be a pattern more usual for the region and other parts of southern Britain. In Northamptonshire it is seen at Brigstock (Field 1983), Hardingstone (Gilmore 1969), Wakerley (Jones 1978) and Weekley (Whatrup and Jones 1988). At Brigstock the sample may have been biased by a group of 164 bones from five sheep in a single pit, and the overall balance of animal husbandry may have been more even, like Silverstone 2 and Silverstone 3. Weekley, in the middle Iron Age phase, shows similar percentage of ovicaprids to Silverstone Fields Farm, amounting to 62% of identified bones (Whatrup and Jones 1988). Cattle accounted for just 13%, outnumbered by pig (22%) on this site. Sheep were also more numerous than cattle at Twywell (Harcourt 1983) by a ratio of 2.5:1 (using MNI), and at Hardingstone (Iron Age Enclosure site) by a ratio of 43% to 35% based on NISP (Gilmore 1969, 52-53, table II). As far as one can tell, the relative proportions of sheep/goat and cattle do not seem to be dependent upon the site 'type'. In all cases the animals would appear to have been kept primarily for meat within a broad-based subsistence strategy. Age ranges include occasional neonates as well as more elderly animals. The different proportions of the main domesticates therefore seem to reflect slightly different emphases rather than discrete specialisms. The subtle differences in the relative proportions of species on the present project probably reflect these emphases which appear to have a counterpart in the charred plant remains (Carruthers, below). However the paucity of the faunal data does not allow a more detailed inter-site comparison of herd structures to enable the subject to be explored more fully.

The lower numbers of pig and horse bones are also typical of Iron Age sites. Red deer are occasionally present, as they were at Silverstone Fields Farm and Biddlesden Road Bridge, and suggest no reliance on hunting. Similarly, the few bird bones recovered at Silverstone Fields Farm are not uncommon in Iron Age assemblages. The occasional presence of dog is typical of Iron Age sites (eg Great Houghton). Intact dog burials are found on some sites and are occasionally numerous (eg Twywell). Whatever the reason for this, it is apparent that the species' economic value was becoming disassociated from its value for meat.

CHARRED PLANT REMAINS
WJ Carruthers

Introduction

The five principal sites on the project – Silverstone 2, Silverstone 3, Silverstone Fields Farm, Biddlesden Road Bridge and Brackley Hatch 4 – were sampled for environmental remains. One hundred and twenty-seven soil samples were taken from a range of features. This report discusses the results from an examination of the charred plant remains in thirty-one of the samples.

Methodology

Ten litre subsamples from sixty-two of the samples were processed by Northamptonshire Archaeology staff using standard methods of flotation (using a Siraf tank fitted with 500 micron meshes for both the flots and residues). The dried floats were assessed by Karen Deighton (NA 2002). On the basis of the assessment report and discussions with the Project Director, the author selected thirty-one samples for full analysis. Although none of the assessment samples had been very productive, it was hoped that comparisons could be made between the five settlement sites in terms of environment and economy.

Tables 6.3 – 6.7 present the results of the analysis. Nomenclature and most of the habitat information follow Stace (1997).

State of preservation

Much of the charred grain was recovered in a poor state of preservation, being vacuolated (puffed up), impregnated with mud and/or fragmented. For this reason several grains have been identified as 'cf.' Triticum sp. etc., and numbers of indeterminate cereals grains are high in many samples.

Vacuolation occurs when grain is charred at high temperatures. It makes the cereals more fragile and prone to fragmentation. Redeposition of charred material is also likely to increase fragmentation. The low concentrations of charred plant remains in most of the samples suggest that much of the material consisted of redeposited background domestic waste. This means that only general information about the range of crops grown can be recovered, rather than more specific details about crop processing activities and crop husbandry. However, despite the absence of well-preserved assemblages, some small differences can be seen between the sites that could prove to be significant when more excavations are carried out in the area. The results of the analysis are discussed site by site, after which some conclusions are drawn.

Soils

The three adjacent Silverstone sites were located on a limestone ridge. The Iron Age iron-smelting site at Biddlesden Road Bridge was on a gravelly glacial outcrop and the Roman pottery-manufacturing site at Brackley Hatch 4 was on clay.

Silverstone 2

Nine samples from pits, a posthole and ditches were examined from this Iron Age settlement site. Phasing for these features ranged from Iron Age Phase 1 to late Iron Age/early Roman period.

Most of the charred plant assemblages from this site were dominated by grain, the overall ratio of grain to chaff to weed seeds being 13:2:3. However, sample 2 from pit 1000 produced larger amounts of chaff. The ratio of charred remains from this feature (roughly 2:2:1; see General Discussion below) suggests that either crop processing waste had been mixed with processed cereals, or that the waste from processing spikelets of hulled wheat had been present.

This site stands apart from the other four in producing larger quantities of barley than wheat in most of the samples studied. This is discussed further below (see Tables 6.3 – 6.7). In the author's experience of Iron Age sites in southern and central England, hulled wheats are usually the dominant cereals recovered, although barley is often present in small quantities in a wide range of contexts. This type of low concentration but widespread occurrence is likely to indicate the use of barley for fodder. This is partly because fodder cereals are less likely to become charred in large-scale drying accidents, as they did not have to be fully processed. More importantly, hulled wheats would probably have come into contact with fire on a day to day basis, whilst being removed from their spikelets prior to cooking. Fodder cereals, however, could well have become widely distributed around a site as waste fodder and dung, and then been burnt amongst sweepings and other types of domestic waste.

The fact that on this site a fodder crop was more dominant than grain for human consumption could indicate that this site leaned more towards a pastoral economy than the other sites. In this case, hulled wheats for human consumption may have been traded and brought onto the site as cleaned spikelets. Wheat grains and arable weeds would then be comparatively rare on this site, since the wheat would be too highly valued to waste, and some of

Taxa	Sample	2	4	8	10	13
	Context	1001	1036	1045	1009	1064
	Feature	1000	1034	1044	1008	1063
	Feature type	Pit	Pit	Pit	Posthole	Ditch
	Phase	MIA	MIA	MIA	MIA	MIA
CEREALS						
Triticum aestivum-type (bread-type free threshing wheat grain)					cf. 1	
Triticum dicoccum/spelta (emmer/spelt wheat grain)		7	1	3	cf. 1	5
Triticum sp. (NFI wheat grain)						
Hordeum sp. (hulled barley grain)		6	2		17	39
Avena sp. (wild/cultivated oat grain)						1
Cf. Secale cereale L. (cf. rye grain)					cf. 1	
Indeterminate cereals		22	1	6	63	93
CHAFF						
Triticum spelta L. (spelt glume base)		3		2		
Triticum cf. dicoccum (cf.emmer glume base)		4				
Triticum dicoccum/spelta (emmer/spelt glume base)		27		1	2	2
Triticum dicoccum/spelta (emmer/spelt spikelet fork)		4				
Hordeum sp. (barley rachis frag.)		1				
Avena sp. (oat awn frag.)		+				
Cereal-size culm node						1
WEEDS						
Chenopodiaceae embryo			1			
Montia fontana L. (blinks seed) BGw						1
Silene cf. vulgaris Garke (bladder campion seed) DGo						1
Fallopia convolvulus (L.)A.Love (black bindweed achene)						3
Rumex sp. (dock achene) CDG		1				1
Polygonum aviculare (knotgrass achene) CD						1
Brassica/Sinapis sp. (mustard, charlock etc. seed) CD★			1			
Trifolium/Lotus sp. (clover/trefoil seed) DG		3			3	7
Vicia/Lathyrus sp. (small seeded (2-3mm) weed vetch/tare) CDG				2		
Hyoscyamus niger L. (henbane seed) Dn		1				
Odontites verna/Euphrasia sp. (red bartsia/eyebright seed) CD		1			1	
Galium aparine L. (cleavers nutlet) CDHW					7	10
Carex sp. (sedge nutlet) MPd		3			1	1
Bromus sect. Bromus (chess caryopsis) ADG		9		3	1	1
Lolium perenne-type Poaceae (3mm, elongate) DG		1				
Poaceae (small seeded grass caryopsis) CDG					1	
NFI tuber frag.					1	
Total charred remains		93	6	17	100	167
Sample size		10	10	10	20	10
Fragments per litre		9.3	0.6	1.7	5	16.7

Table 6.3a: Charred plant remains from Silverstone 2.

Key: All remains are charred unless in [ ] brackets = mineralised.
NFI = not further identified ; + = occasional (not quantified).
Habitat Preferences: A = arable; C = cultivated; D = disturbed/wasteground; G = grassland; H = hedgerows; M = marsh/bog; P = ponds, rivers, ditches; W = woods.
Soil preferences: d = damp to wet; n = nutrient-rich; o = open.

Sample	15	17	19	21
Context	1083	1051	1049	1058
Feature	1082	1050	1048	1048
Feature type	Ditch	Ditch	Ditch	Ditch
Taxa Phase	MIA	LIA/ER	LIA/ER	LIA/ER
CEREALS				
Triticum sp. (NFI wheat grain)	cf. 3			
Hordeum sp. (hulled barley grain)	31	1		
Indeterminate cereals	31		3	
CHAFF				
Triticum dicoccum/spelta (emmer/spelt glume base)		2	2	
WEEDS				
Montia fontana L. (blinks seed) BGw			6	
Brassica/Sinapis sp. (mustard, charlock etc. seed) CD★				1
Vicia/Lathyrus sp. (small seeded (2-3mm) weed vetch/tare) CDG	1		1	
Odontites verna/Euphrasia sp. (red bartsia/eyebright seed) CD		1		
Galium aparine L. (cleavers nutlet) CDHW			2	
Carex sp. (sedge nutlet) MPd				1
Total charred remains	**66**	**4**	**14**	**2**
Sample size	20	10	10	10
Fragments per litre	3.3	0.4	1.4	0.2

Table 6.3b: *Charred plant remains from Silverstone 2.*

Key: NFI = not further identified.
Habitat Preferences: C = cultivated; D = disturbed/wasteground; G = grassland; H = hedgerows; M = marsh/bog;
P = ponds, rivers, ditches; W = woods.
Soil preferences: d = damp to wet.

the weed seeds would have already been removed from the spikelets prior to trading. The occupants of the site would have prepared the hulled wheat piecemeal, as suggested by Hillman (1981), producing a waste product that was predominantly glume bases, spikelet forks and weed seeds. This type of waste could have been fed to the livestock, or used as tinder to light fires.

Both emmer (*Triticum dicoccum*) and spelt (*T. spelta*) wheat appear to have been grown or brought onto the site, but it was not possible to determine the relative importance of these two hulled wheats because of the poor state of preservation of most of the chaff remains. Other possible minor crops tentatively identified were bread-type wheat and rye. Rye is not commonly found prior to the Roman period, and even in Roman times was probably only grown in small quantities where the soil was too poor to support other cereal crops. However, several Iron Age sites, such as Stafford (Moffett 1987), have produced occasional grains of rye. It may have been growing as a weed at this time, or as an early bite crop (ie grazed green in spring), in which case few seeds would be found in the charred plant record. Bread-type wheat is often recovered in small quantities from Iron Age sites, but it is not until the Roman period that large deposits are found.

All of the weed taxa present on this site are commonly found in charred plant assemblages from other sites of this date, and few are specific enough in their habitat requirements to provide information about soils and crop husbandry. Cleavers (*Galium aparine*) seeds were relatively frequent in posthole 1008, and were also notably common in the samples from Silverstone Fields Farm. The significance of this is discussed in the Silverstone Fields Farm section below. Damp ground indicators include blinks (*Montia fontana* ssp. *chondrosperma*) and sedges (*Carex sp.*). The presence of these taxa could indicate the cultivation of wetter land close to Silverstone Brook but the remains could also have been charred amongst hay or dung. Damp ground taxa were recovered in small numbers from all of the A43 sites except Biddlesden Road Bridge.

Silverstone 3

Four samples from middle Iron Age pits and ditches were examined from this site. The assemblages were fairly small (less than 1 fragment per litre of soil processed in three of the four samples), consisting of a few cereal grains, occasional chaff fragments (four emmer/spelt glume bases) and a few common weeds of cultivated and disturbed soils. They probably represent background levels of general domestic waste, such as cereal contaminants picked out of the grain prior to grinding or cooking, and spilt food remains swept up from floors and thrown into the fire.

The evidence shows that emmer and/or spelt wheat was cultivated, in addition to hulled barley and possibly a little bread-type wheat. The hulled wheat glume bases were too poorly preserved to identify them beyond emmer/

	Sample	4	5	7	23
	Context	1280	1056	1268	1036
	Feature	2022	2046	2023	2051
	Feature type	Pit	Pit	Ditch	Ditch
Taxa	Phase	2-3	1	MIA	MIA
CEREALS					
Triticum aestivum-type (bread-type free threshing wheat grain)			cf.1		
Triticum dicoccum/spelta (emmer/spelt wheat grain)		5	3	4	
Hordeum sp. (hulled barley grain)		4	2	1	1
Indeterminate cereals		8	1	2	2
CHAFF					
Triticum dicoccum / spelta (emmer / spelt glume base)		1		3	
WEEDS					
Rumex sp. (dock achene) CDG		3			
Trifolium/Lotus sp. (clover/trefoil seed) DG		1	2	1	
Hyoscyamus niger L. (henbane seed) Dn		1			
Galium aparine L. (cleavers nutlet) CDHW				1	
Eleocharis subg. Palustres (spike-rush nutlet) MPd		2			
Carex sp. (sedge nutlet) MPd		2		1	
Bromus sect. Bromus (chess caryopsis) ADG		28		5	
Poaceae (small seeded grass caryopsis) CDG		5		1	
Total charred remains		**60**	**9**	**19**	**3**
Sample size		30	40	40	40
Fragments per litre		2	0.2	0.5	0.1

Table 6.4: *Charred plant remains from Silverstone 3.*

Key: NFI = not further identified.
Habitat Preferences: A = arable; C = cultivated; D = disturbed/wasteground; G = grassland; H = hedgerows; M = marsh/bog; P = ponds, rivers, ditches; W = woods.
Soil preferences: d = damp to wet; n = nutrient-rich.

spelt, but since spelt and emmer wheat were identified at Silverstone 2 and Silverstone Fields Farm it is likely that both species were grown on all three sites.

A few weeds of damp to wet soils were present in the sample from pit 2022, including spike-rush (*Eleocharis* subg. *Palustres*) and sedge (*Carex* sp.), suggesting either that the cereals had been grown in the vicinity of damp soils, or that hay from damp meadows had been mixed in with the cereal waste.

The most notable fact about this site is that chess seeds (*Bromus* sect. *Bromus*) were particularly frequent in the sample from pit 2022. They were also common in most of the samples from Silverstone Fields Farm, particularly the rich sample from pit 75. This large-seeded grass was a common weed of arable in the past and appears to be particularly characteristic of Iron Age and Roman charred cereal assemblages. Godwin (1975) suggests that it was introduced as a weed of spelt wheat, which would explain its predominance during the Iron Age and Roman periods since those were the main periods of spelt cultivation. Being a large-seeded grass it is difficult to separate from the crop using sieves. Although some authors have suggested that it may have been grown as a crop in its own right (Hubbard

1975) there is, as yet, no archaeobotanical evidence of this. A predominantly chess deposit was recovered from a fourth-century feature at Prickwillow Road, Ely (Carruthers 2003), but because it was present amongst crop processing waste it was considered to be more likely to represent a serious weed infestation than a crop. It is possible that chess was tolerated as a weed, since the grain is large and edible. The fact that it is sometimes numerous in deposits of crop processing waste suggests that either some of the seeds were small enough to be removed by a fine meshed sieve during processing, or that it was being selectively hand-picked from the crop. It would be interesting to see how different quantities of chess affect the taste and cooking qualities of spelt to help to answer this question. Campbell (2000) suggests that at Danebury chess may have been tolerated or even encouraged amongst fodder crops during the early and middle Iron Age when autumn sowing was practised. When spring sowing was introduced in the later Iron Age at Danebury, this is thought to have favoured oats, which flower later than chess. Because cultivated oats begin to appear amongst archaeobotanical assemblages at this time it is difficult to say whether oats were simply taking over the niche that chess had formerly occupied as a

Taxa	Sample	11	12	13	14	15
	Context	104	185	149	132	168
	Feature	75	183	146	129	166
	Feature type	Pit	Pit	Pit	Pit	Pit
	Phase	M-LIA	M-LIA	M-LIA	M-LIA	M-LIA
CEREALS						
Triticum aestivum-type (bread-type free threshing wheat grain)					Cf. 1	
Triticum dicoccum/spelta (emmer/spelt wheat grain)		14	2		4	6
Triticum sp. (NFI wheat grain)		12			2	
Hordeum sp. (hulled barley grain)		6	1		5	
Avena/Bromus sp. (oat/chess grain)		1				
Indeterminate cereals		63	2	1	7	
CHAFF						
Triticum spelta L. (spelt glume base)		40	2	2	4	2
Triticum dicoccum / spelta (emmer / spelt glume base)		38	2	4		4
Triticum dicoccum / spelta (emmer / spelt spikelet fork)		5	4			
T. dicoccum /spelta (emmer/spelt rachis frag.)		5				
Hordeum sp. (barley rachis frag.)		1				
Avena sp. (oat awn frag.)		+				
Cereal-size culm node		1				
Cereal-sized culm base		1				
WEEDS						
Chenopodium album L. (fat-hen seed) CDn			1		1	
Montia fontana L. (blinks seed) BGw		1				1
Rumex sp. (dock achene) CDG		1			1	
Polygonum aviculare (knotgrass nutlet) CD			1			
Brassica/Sinapis sp. (mustard, charlock etc. seed) CD★			Cf. 1			
Trifolium/Lotus sp. (clover/trefoil seed) DG		6	1			3
Vicia/Lathyrus sp. (small seeded (2-3mm) weed vetch/tare) CDG		3			1	
Cf. Daucus carota L. (cf. wild carrot mericarp) Gc★		3				
Lithospermum arvense L. (field gromwell nutlet) ADGoc		3				1
Plantago laceolata L.(ribwort plantain seed) Go					1	
Veronica hederifolia L. (ivy-leaved speedwell seed) CDWoH		1				
Odontites verna/Euphrasia sp. (red bartsia/eyebright seed) CD		2	1			1
Galium aparine L. (cleavers nutlet) CDHW		8	1	1	3	
Lapsana communis L. (nipplewort achene) DHWo		1				
Tripleurospermum inodorum (L.)Schultz-Bip. (scentless mayweed achene) CD		6				
Carex sp. (sedge nutlet) MPd		1	1			
Bromus sect. Bromus (chess caryopsis) ADG		114	3	10	7	4
Lolium perenne-type Poaceae (3mm, elongate) DG		1				
Poaceae (small seeded grass caryopsis) CDG		3			1	1
Mineralised nodules		[++]		[+]		
Total charred remains		338	19	22	38	23
Sample size		30	40	40	20	20
Fragments per litre		11.3	0.5	0.6	1.9	1.2

Table 6.5a: *Charred plant remains from Silverstone Fields Farm.*

Key: All remains are charred unless in [ ] brackets = mineralised.

NFI = not further identified ; + = occasional (not quantified) ; ++ = several (not quantified).

Habitat preferences: A = arable; C = cultivated; D = disturbed/wasteground; G = grassland; H = hedgerows; M = marsh/bog; P = ponds, rivers, ditches; S = scrub; W = woods.

Soil preferences: c = calcareous; d = damp to wet; n = nutrient-rich; o = open.

	Sample	16	17	18	19
	Context	62	58	134	17
	Feature	61	56	133	16
	Feature type	Pit	Pit	Pit	Gully
Taxa	Phase	MIA	MIA	MIA	MIA
CEREALS					
Triticum aestivum-type (bread-type free threshing wheat grain)					1
Triticum dicoccum/spelta (emmer/spelt wheat grain)			1	1	
Hordeum sp. (hulled barley grain)		1	3	3	2
Indeterminate cereals		5	6	1	5
CHAFF					
Triticum spelta L. (spelt glume base)		2	2		2
Triticum dicoccum / spelta (emmer / spelt glume base)		9	6		1
Avena sp. (oat awn frag.)		+			
Cereal-size culm node					1
WEEDS					
Stellaria media (L.) Villars (common chickweed seed) CD					1
Rumex sp. (dock achene) CDG		4			1
Trifolium/Lotus sp. (clover/trefoil seed) DG		3			
Vicia/Lathyrus sp. (small seeded (2-3mm) weed vetch/tare) CDG		5		1	
Hyoscyamus niger L. (henbane seed) Dn		1			
Galium aparine L. (cleavers nutlet) CDHW		1			1
Valerianella dentata (L.) Pollich (narrow-fruited corn-salad seed) AD			1		
Bromus sect. Bromus (chess caryopsis) ADG		2	6		
Lolium perenne-type Poaceae (3mm, elongate) DG					
Poaceae (small seeded grass caryopsis) CDG		2	1		
Mineralised nodules				[+]	
Mineralised worm cocoons				[7]	
Total charred remains		**35**	**26**	**13**	**15**
	Sample size	20	20	20	20
	Fragments per litre	1.8	1.3	0.7	0.8

Table 6.5b: *Charred plant remains from Silverstone Fields Farm.*

Key: All remains are charred unless in [ ] brackets = mineralised.
NFI = not further identified ; + = occasional (not quantified).
Habitat Preferences: A = arable; C = cultivated; D = disturbed/wasteground; G = grassland; H = hedgerows; W = woods.
Soil preferences: n = nutrient-rich.

tall, cereal-sized weed, or if their increase relates to changes in agricultural practices. No obvious increase in oats was seen on the A43 sites until the Roman period.

Silverstone Fields Farm

Nine samples, from middle to late Iron Age pits and a gully, were examined. This site produced a large number of pits, many of which were probably used for storage, although they were shallower than the classic 'beehive-shaped'

storage pits. In contrast, Silverstone 2 and Silverstone 3 had virtually no pits of this nature.

Eight of the samples produced low concentrations (all less than two fragments per litre) of cereals, chaff and weed seeds. These assemblages are likely to represent background levels of burnt domestic waste. One sample, however, produced a more concentrated deposit that consisted either of crop processing waste mixed with some grain, or of waste from processing cereals still in spikelets or ears. The ratio of grain to chaff to weed seeds in this sample (sample

	Sample	4	5	7	11
	Context	1028	1072	1091	1091
	Feature	1029	1073	1092	1092
	Feature type	Pit	Furnace Pit	Hollow	Hollow
Taxa	Phase	M-LIA	M-LIA	M-LIA	M-LIA
CEREALS					
Avena/Bromus sp. (oat/chess grain)					1
CHAFF					
Triticum spelta L. (spelt spikelet fork)				1	
Triticum dicoccum / spelta (emmer / spelt glume base)					1
WEEDS					
Urtica urens L. (small nettle achene) CDn				1	1
Corylus avellana L. (hazelnut shell frag.) HSW					1
Chenopodium album L. (fat-hen seed) CDn				1	3
Atriplex patula/prostrata (orache seed) CDn					1
Polygonum aviculare L. (knotgrass achene) CD				1	
Rumex sp. (dock achene) CDG				1	1
Malva sp. (mallow nutlet) DG					1
Crataegus monogyna Jacq. (hawthorn fruit stone) HSW		1			
Galeopsis tetrahit L. (common hemp-nettle nutlet) ADWod					1
Valerianella dentata (L.) Pollich (narrow-fruited corn-salad seed) AD				2	2
Lapsana communis L. (nipplewort achene) DHWo					1
Tripleurospermum inodorum (L.)Schultz-Bip. (scentless mayweed achene) CD				1	1
Bromus sect. Bromus (chess caryopsis) ADG			2		
Lolium perenne-type Poaceae (3mm, elongate) DG					1
Poaceae (small seeded grass caryopsis) CDG				2	1
Total charred remains		**1**	**2**	**10**	**17**
Sample size		30	20	20	20
Fragments per litre		0.03	0.1	0.5	0.9

Table 6.6: *Charred plant remains from Biddlesden Road Bridge.*

Key: Habitat Preferences: A = arable; C = cultivated; D = disturbed/wasteground; E = heaths; G = grassland; H = hedgerows; M = marsh/bog; S = scrub; W = woods.
Soil preferences: d = damp to wet; n = nutrient-rich; o = open.

11, context 104, lower fill of pit 75) was 32:30:50, and both small and large weed seeds were frequent. Few straw-sized culm nodes were recovered, suggesting that at least the early stages of processing (removal of straw and coarse weeds; Hillman 1981) had been carried out, reducing the crop to spikelets and weed seeds. However, straw is one of the first elements to be destroyed on charring (Boardman and Jones 1990), so differential preservation could have affected the results.

As at Silverstone 3, the cereals present were primarily emmer/spelt wheat and hulled barley, with small amounts of bread-type wheat. Spelt was positively identified from a higher percentage of emmer/spelt glume bases than at Silverstone 2 (47% compared with 12%), but this could relate to better conditions of preservation rather than increased spelt cultivation. It is worth noting that emmer glume bases are more fragile and difficult to identify with

certainty, which means this taxon is probably under-represented in the archaeobotanical record, particularly in poorly preserved assemblages.

Apart from the high occurrence of chess in samples from this site, as noted in the Silverstone 3 section, cleavers was common, being recovered from seven of the nine features. Cleavers is said to be an indicator of autumn sowing (Reynolds 1981). Spelt wheat is a hardy crop that is likely to have been autumn-sown on the fertile soils of the limestone ridge, and any of the other cereal crops found on the A43 sites could also have been autumn sown. It should be noted that the presence of indicators of autumn sowing does not rule out the practice of spring sowing also taking place. At Danebury spring sowing is thought to have been introduced in the late Iron Age (Campbell 2000).

Cleavers is also a plant of fairly nitrogen-rich soils (Hill *et al.* 1999), indicating that the soils being cultivated

Sample	Ev1	Ev2	2	3	4
Context	2/8	2/7	65	68	69
Feature	35	35	61	66	66
Feature type	Ditch	Ditch	Kiln Pit	Kiln	Kiln Pit
Taxa / Phase	2	2	2it	2	2
CEREALS					
Triticum aestivum-type (bread-type free threshing wheat grain)	Cf.2		Cf.2		
Triticum dicoccum/spelta (emmer/spelt wheat grain)	36	32	1	1	
Triticum sp. (NFI wheat grain)	13				
Hordeum sp. (hulled barley grain)	14	Cf.3	2	4	6
Avena sp. (wild/cultivated oat grain)	7	1		2	5
Avena/Bromus sp. (oat/chess grain)		1			5
Cf. Secale cereale L. (cf. rye grain)	Cf.1		Cf.2		
Indeterminate cereals	77	23	4	1	15
CHAFF					
Triticum dicoccum / spelta (emmer / spelt glume base)			12	3	
WEEDS					
Chenopodium album L. (fat-hen seed) CDn					2
Atriplex patula/prostrata (orache seed) CDn					2
Chenopodiaceae embryo					1
Montia fontana L. (blinks seed) BGw				2	
Rumex sp. (dock achene) CDG	3				2
Primulaceae (scarlet pimpernel etc. seed)			1		2
Crataegus monogyna Jacq. (hawthorn fruit stone) HSW					
Trifolium/Lotus sp. (clover/trefoil seed) DG				1	1
Vicia/Lathyrus sp. (small seeded (2-3mm) weed vetch/tare) CDG	12	1	1		
Cf. Daucus carota L. (cf. wild carrot mericarp) Gc★					Cf.3
Galeopsis tetrahit L. (common hemp-nettle nutlet) ADWod					1
Plantago laceolata L.(ribwort plantain seed) Go					1
Plantago major L.(greater plantain seed) DGo					1
Odontites verna/Euphrasia sp. (red bartsia/eyebright seed) CD			1		
Galium aparine L. (cleavers nutlet) CDHW	1	1			
Valerianella dentata (L.) Pollich (narrow-fruited corn-salad seed) AD					1
Tripleurospermum inodorum (L.)Schultz-Bip. (scentless mayweed achene) CD			3	1	20
Asteraceae NFI embryo					13
Eleocharis subg. Palustres (spike-rush nutlet) MPd	1				
Carex sp. (sedge nutlet) MPd	1				
Bromus sect. Bromus (chess caryopsis) ADG	1		2	2	5
Lolium perenne-type Poaceae (3mm, elongate) DG	8	1	1		
Poaceae (small seeded grass caryopsis) CDG		2	9	2	3
Total charred remains	177	65	41	19	89
Sample size	20	20	40	40	40
Fragments per litre	8.9	3.3	1.0	0.5	2.2

Table 6.7: *Charred plant remains from Brackley Hatch 4.*

Key: NFI = not further identified.

Habitat Preferences: A = arable; C = cultivated; D = disturbed/wasteground; G = grassland; H = hedgerows; M = marsh/bog; P = ponds, rivers, ditches; S = scrub; W = woods.

Soil preferences: c = calcareous; d = damp to wet; n = nutrient-rich; o = open.

Total % abundance of identifiable cereals	barley	all wheats
Silverstone 2	82	18
Silverstone 3	40	60
Silverstone Fields Farm	32	68
Brackley Hatch 4	25	75

Table 6.8: Percentage abundance of cereals. Barley was the dominant crop at Silverstone 2, contrasting with the greater abundance of wheat at the other Iron Age sites, Silverstone 3 and Silverstone Fields Farm, and the Roman site Brackley Hatch 4.

% of samples where present	barley	all wheats
Silverstone 2	67	56
Silverstone 3	100	75
Silverstone Fields Farm	78	78
Brackley Hatch 4	100	80

Table 6.9: Percentage of samples where present. Despite the greater abundance of barley compared to wheat at Silverstone 2, barley was present in more samples at the other sites, albeit as a low proportion of cereals present.

Site	G: Ch: W
Silverstone 2, overall ratio	13 : 2 : 3
Silverstone 2, sample 2, pit 1000	35 : 39 : 19
Silverstone 3	8 : 1 : 13
Silverstone Fields Farm	2 : 2 : 3
Silverstone Fields Farm, sample 11, pit 75,	32 : 30 : 50
Biddlesden Road Bridge	1 : 2 : 27
Brackley Hatch 4	19 : 1 : 8

Table 6.10: Grain: Chaff:Weed ratios. The two richest samples (Silverstone 2, sample 2 and Silverstone Fields Farm, sample 11), with high proportions of chaff, probably represent the charred waste from crop processing.

were fairly fertile. It is not possible to determine whether fertility was being increased by manuring, although it is interesting to see that a few mineralised worm cocoons and 'nodules' (unidentified spheroids generally found in mineralised assemblages, see Carruthers 1989) were present in three samples from this site. The residues of these samples (11, 13 and 18) were scanned for mineralised seeds but none was found. Mineralisation usually occurs in highly organic and moist deposits such as cess pits, but it can also be found in midden-type deposits such as the late Bronze Age deposit at Potterne, Wiltshire (Carruthers 2000). Small quantities of mineralised remains have been recovered from other Iron Age sites on calcareous soils, eg Maiden Castle, Dorset (Palmer and Jones 1991) and Brighton Hill South, Basingstoke (Carruthers 1995). It is uncertain whether these represent seeds that had become mineralised *in situ* within organic waste deposited in the pits, or whether the remains had originally been preserved

in middens and then became mixed in with redeposited waste.

There were a few other charred indicator weeds of nutrient-rich soils present, such as fat hen (*Chenopodium album*) and henbane (*Hyoscyamus niger*), although this group was not quite as frequent as on Biddlesden Road Bridge and Brackley Hatch 4. There were also a few indicators of wet soils, ie. blinks seeds (*Montia fontana*) and sedge (Carex sp.) nutlets.

Biddlesden Road Bridge Iron Age settlement and iron smelting site

The four samples examined from this site were all very poor in charred plant remains, with no sample attaining even one fragment per litre. All of the remains except one hawthorn seed (*Crataegus monogyna*) and two chess caryopses came from the samples from the industrial refuse hollow 24, 1092, samples 7 and 11. The hawthorn seed may provide evidence for one source of fuel for the furnaces. There appears to have been no cereal processing waste used as tinder, since the furnace pit 1073 produced only two chess grains.

Cereal remains were particularly scarce, with only one possible grain (oat/chess) and two chaff fragments being recovered. The weed species were all general weeds of disturbed and cultivated ground, and many of them were indicators of nutrient-enriched soils, such as nettles, docks and members of the Chenopodiaceae family. These plants may have been growing on or around the industrial refuse, rather than representing crop processing waste.

In the author's experience, iron working sites often produce very few charred plant remains, apart from charcoal. Since cereal processing waste does not appear to have been burnt in the furnace, and the waste deposited on the midden did not contain charred cereals, it is likely that any cereal-based food consumed by the workers on this site had been prepared elsewhere. In addition, the amount of time required to grow and harvest arable crops may not have fitted in well with a settlement specialising in metalworking, so the economy of this site may have been primarily pastoral rather than arable. Unfortunately, without detailed pollen work it is difficult to determine the arable/pastoral balance, since absence of charred cereal remains could also be attributed to sampling or preservation biases.

Brackley Hatch 4

Five samples were examined from this Roman pottery-making site. These included an enclosure ditch, ditch 35 (evaluation samples 1 and 2), and samples from the rake-out pits and firing chambers from two pottery kilns, Kiln 61 (rake-out pit sample 2) and Kiln 66 (firing chamber sample 3 and rake-out pit sample 4). The abundant pottery associated with these features dated primarily from the later first to early third centuries AD.

155

The enclosure ditch (35) produced two samples containing primarily charred grain, at a ratio of 7:0:1 grain to chaff to weed seeds. This probably represents processed grain discarded amongst household waste, since pottery was abundant in this feature. Emmer/spelt wheat was the predominant cereal, with frequent hulled barley grains and small amounts of cf bread-type wheat, wild/cultivated oats and cf rye. The weeds were general weeds of cultivated and disturbed soils, all of which had been recovered from some of the other sites discussed above. There was also a small number of damp to wet ground taxa such as sedge and spike-rush. The clay soils of this site may have made the ditches damp enough to support these taxa, or the plants could have grown as weeds in damp areas of arable land.

The pot kiln firing chamber and rake-out pits did not produce particularly rich samples, but the overall ratio of grain to chaff to weed seeds (3 : 1 : 5), suggests that crop processing waste had probably been used as kindling. The sparse grain included all four taxa found in the enclosure ditch, although barley was a little more frequent than emmer/spelt this time. Most of the weed seeds were general weeds of cultivated and disturbed soils, with quite a few of the taxa favouring nutrient-rich soils.

General Discussion

Because only a few, fairly poor samples have been examined from each site, comparisons need to be viewed with caution. However, some tentative suggestions have been made in the hope that future archaeological investigations in the area can add to the discussion.

Emmer and spelt wheat appear to have been the dominant cereals on three of the four sites, but on Silverstone 2 hulled barley was more frequent (the fifth site, Biddlesden Road Bridge, produced only one chess/ oat grain). Table 6.8 shows the data in terms of percentage of identifiable grains, ie abundance.

However, when occurrences of wheat and barley are examined by number of samples in which they are recorded, ie presence, (Table 6.9) differences between the sites are less obvious. These figures illustrate the common finding that barley is often present in low numbers on Iron Age sites, but in a high percentage of samples.

As discussed above (Silverstone 2), this probably relates to the importance of livestock at Silverstone 2, in comparison with the other sites on the limestone ridge, Silverstone 3 and Silverstone Fields Farm. Although only one sample from Silverstone Fields Farm was reasonably productive, the abundance of possible storage pits on this site suggests that it had been producing more grain for human consumption (ie mainly emmer and spelt) than the other two Silverstone sites. The other two sites, Brackley Hatch 4 and Biddlesden Road Bridge, produced fewer, poor samples, so comparisons are difficult. The Iron Age smelting site at Biddlesden Road Bridge produced so few cereal remains that it is probable that the charred weed seeds relate to the burning of hay and domestic waste as

tinder rather than crop processing activities. The Roman pottery-making site produced mainly grain, with some evidence for the cultivation of oats and possibly rye as minor crops. Cereals may have been brought onto the site as processed grain, since very few chaff fragments were present.

It should be remembered that one accidental burning of a fodder store could create misleading results if the remains were spread around a number of features. This highlights the importance of widespread, detailed sampling. There is also some evidence to show that barley was being consumed by humans during the Iron Age, since the gut of Lindow Man contained emmer, spelt and barley (Holden 1986). However, as Greig (1991) points out, the last meal of a ritually killed man may not be typical of the Iron Age diet as a whole.

Evidence from snail analysis at Silverstone 2 and Silverstone Fields Farm (Mark Robinson, below) shows that these sites on the limestone ridge were set within open countryside, so it is likely that much of the area was put to arable cultivation and pasture. The local soils would have been well-suited to the cultivation of wheat and barley. Bread-type wheat is better suited to heavier clays than light soils, although there was no clear evidence from these samples that its cultivation increased on the heavier soils or with time. It occurred in small numbers on all four cereal-producing sites and was probably a minor crop through the Iron Age and Roman periods.

Oats were only positively identified from the Roman site, Brackley Hatch 4, although it was not possible to determine whether they were wild or cultivated because no oat chaff (in particular the floret bases) was preserved. There is some evidence to suggest that oats were a minor crop during the Iron Age (eg Fifield Bavant, Helbaek 1953), but their incidence greatly increases during the Roman period, particularly around military sites, since they were valued as horse fodder.

As with oats, rye is occasionally found in Iron Age deposits but is more frequent on Roman sites. It is difficult to determine whether the single cf. rye grain at Silverstone 2 was a weed, occasional crop or contaminant from Roman activities on the site. Two of the Roman samples produced poorly preserved cf. rye grains, so it is possible that rye was a minor crop at this time. Oats would be well-suited to the heavier clay soils of site Brackley Hatch 4, and rye is a useful crop on poor soils.

There is little evidence to demonstrate that cereals were being grown at Biddlesden Road Bridge, although negative evidence for charred plant remains should be used with caution. However, of the fifteen samples assessed from this site, only three produced a single cereal grain each (Deighton, in NA 2002). As suggested above, cereal growing may not have been compatible with the iron smelting industry on the site.

Of the 62 samples assessed, only two samples produced reasonable quantities of chaff; Sample 2 from Pit 1000 at Silverstone 2 and Sample 11 from Pit 75 Silverstone Fields

Farm. Table 6.10 shows ratios of grain to chaff to weed seeds.

Because the two richest samples produced roughly equal quantities of grain and chaff: it is possible that these two pits had contained the burnt remnants of stored grain still in spikelet form, or perhaps whole ears of wheat. However, experimental charring by Boardman and Jones (1990) has shown that grains survive charring to a much greater extent than glume bases, so the original composition of the samples would have been much richer in chaff. The deposits may, therefore, represent the charred waste from processing spikelets or ears of wheat. Unfortunately, rachis fragments are even less likely to survive charring than glume bases, so it is not easy to tell whether spikelets or ears were present. Whole-ear deposits would have contained more weed seeds of all sizes, being at an earlier stage in the processing. The high ratio of weed seeds in Sample 11 is mainly due to the large number of chess seeds present. This large-seeded grassy weed would have been difficult to separate from the crop at all stages of processing. Because the two rich samples produced higher proportions of large, rather than small weed seeds (see Stevens 2003), it is likely that the crops were being stored as semi-cleaned spikelets, as suggested by Hillman (1981). Of course, if mixed waste from a variety of sources had been deposited in the pits, it would be even more difficult to unravel the evidence.

All of the remaining samples discussed for this report produced little more than background domestic waste. This type of assemblage may be derived from floor sweepings, hand-picked cereal cleanings, redeposited hearth material etc, ie material spilt or discarded during general domestic activities. The Roman kiln samples may contain some remnants of crop processing waste used to light the kilns

Although the charred plant assemblages from these five sites were not large, small differences can be seen between the sites. Some of these differences can be related to site function or period, and others, such as the dominance of barley on one of the Silverstone sites, appear to indicate differences in the arable/pastoral balance between adjacent

sites. It would be useful to carry out further archaeobotanical investigations in the area to clarify the picture.

CHARCOAL FUEL DEBRIS FROM BIDDLESDEN ROAD BRIDGE AND BRACKLEY HATCH 4

R Gale

Introduction

This report includes the analysis of charcoal deposits recovered from industrial features at Biddlesden Road Bridge (seven samples from iron smelting furnaces and nearby features) and Brackley Hatch 4 (four samples from pottery kilns). Both sites were located close to what became the medieval forest of Whittlewood. The aim of the study was to identify the type and character of the fuel used for these industrial processes and to obtain environmental data.

Methods

Bulk soil samples were processed by flotation and sieving using 500-micron meshes. The resulting flots and residues were sorted by hand to isolate the larger fragments. The iron smelting features produced considerably larger amounts of charcoal than the pottery kilns, although much of the smelting debris was very comminuted. Charcoal fragments measuring >2 mm in radial cross-section were considered for species identification.

The condition of the charcoal varied from firm and well preserved to poor and friable. Standard methods were used to prepare the samples for examination (Gale and Cutler 2000). The anatomical structures were examined using incident light on a Nikon Labophot-2 microscope at magnifications up to x400. The taxa identified were matched to reference slides of modern wood. When

Sample	Context	Description	Pomoideae Hawthorn group	Prunus blackthorn	Quercus oak	Ulmus elm
2	1061	Furnace 2 raking pit	-	-	75h, 64s	-
5	1072	Furnace 1 raking pit	1	5r	14h/u, 20s	-
6	1084	Ore-roasting pit	-	-	21h/u, 81s	-
7	1091	Industrial dump F24	-	-	6h, 8s	-
12	1104	Pit F18	-	1	52h/u, 111s	-
15	1312	Ditch F7	2	-	26h, 5s	1
17	1124	Hearth 1127	-	-	69h, 41s	-

Table 6.11: Biddlesden Road Bridge: Late Iron Age iron-working fuel debris – charcoal identification.

Key: h = heartwood (oak only), r = roundwood (diameter 9mm), s = sapwood (oak only), u = unknown maturity (oak only). The number of fragments identified is indicated.

Sample	Context	Description	Fraxinus ash	Quercus oak
1	62	Kiln 61 firing chamber	–	8s
2	65	Kiln 61 raking pit	–	4s
3	68	Kiln 66 firing chamber	–	2s
4	69	Kiln 66 raking pit	1	3h/u, 4s

Table 6.12: Brackley Hatch, BH4: Charcoal analysis of fuel debris from early Roman pottery kilns.

Key: h = heartwood (oak only), r = roundwood (diameter <20mm), s = sapwood (oak only), u = unknown maturity (oak only). The number of fragments identified is indicated.

possible, the maturity of the wood was assessed (i.e. heartwood/ sapwood).

Results

The taxa identified are presented in Tables 6.11 (Biddlesden Bridge Road) and 6.12 (Brackley Hatch) and discussed below. Classification follows that of *Flora Europaea* (Tutin *et al.* 1964-80). Since anatomical differences between related genera of members of the Pomoideae (*Crataegus, Malus, Pyrus* and *Sorbus*) are too slight to allow secure identification to genus level, they are included as a group entry. When a genus is represented by a single species in the British flora, this is named as the most likely origin of the wood, given the provenance and period. But it should be noted that it is rarely possible to name individual species from wood features, and exotic species of trees and shrubs were introduced to Britain from an early period (Godwin 1956; Mitchell 1974). The anatomical structure of the charcoal was consistent with the following taxa or groups of taxa:

Biddlesden Road Bridge

Charcoal was examined from the raking pits of Furnaces 1 and 2 (contexts 1072 and 1061). The former produced a huge quantity of charcoal (484 g), most of which was too comminuted for examination. Identified material consisted entirely of oak (*Quercus sp.*), both sapwood and heartwood, probably from fairly wide roundwood/ cordwood. Oak was also the dominant fuel in Furnace 2, although here small quantities of blackthorn (*Prunus spinosa*) roundwood (diameter 9 mm), the hawthorn/ *Sorbus* group (Pomoideae) and charred hazel nutshells were also present.

Oak (*Quercus sp.*) heartwood and sapwood was also recovered from pit 1085 (context 1084) and an industrial dump, Feature 24. Supplementary uses of the pit - either for cooking or for dumping domestic debris - were suggested by the presence of bone.

Oak (*Quercus sp.*) was also dominant in deposits from pit 1105 (Pit and Gully group 18) and ditch 7 of Structure 1 (contexts 1104 and 1312). Other taxa identified included blackthorn (*Prunus spinosa*) in pit 1105 and the hawthorn/

Sorbus group (Pomoideae) and elm (*Ulmus* sp.) in ditch 7. The oak fragments probably derived from fairly wide roundwood or largewood. Growth rings up to 5 mm in width (recorded in fragments from the pit) indicated origins from moderate to fast-grown wood.

Charcoal deposits in Hearth 1127 also consisted entirely of oak (*Quercus* sp.), from fairly wide roundwood or cordwood.

Brackley Hatch 4

Charcoal was examined from the firing chambers and raking pits of early Roman pottery kilns 61 and 62. The deposits were comparatively sparse in all contexts (62, 65, 68 and 69) but indicated the common use of oak (*Quercus* sp.), probably mostly from fairly wide roundwood. Ash (*Fraxinus excelsior*) was also recorded from the raking pit in Kiln 66. Kiln 61 included fast-grown oak with growth rings up to 7 mm wide.

Discussion

The sites at Biddlesden Road Bridge and Brackley Hatch 4 were located on Boulder Clay areas near Syresham and Whitfield respectively, on the western edge of what subsequently became the medieval Forest of Whittlewood. The excavated area at Biddlesden Road Bridge included three furnaces dated to around the first century BC and, although there was the possibility of further associated features in the immediate vicinity, the production capacity of the iron industry here is thought to have been low and probably short-lived. Evidence from the early Roman pottery kilns at Brackley Hatch 4 suggests that these activities were also small scale. It is sometimes thought that this type of industry operated on a seasonal basis. At both sites the contemporary environment was clearly considered sufficiently wooded to sustain these industries.

Fuel deposits from the iron smelting furnaces and pit appear to have been similar in character and consisted of oak (*Quercus* sp.), probably from fairly wide roundwood/ cordwood. Similarly, the fuel used for pottery firing was also supplied mainly from oak poles/cordwood. The main differences between fuel supplies would have been the use of charcoal by the iron industry and firewood (probably lengths of roundwood) by the potters.

There was insufficient evidence, however, to establish whether coppice or naturally grown trees provisioned the charcoal burners/ firewood gathers. Fast-grown oak recorded from pit 1105 at the iron-smelting site, and Kiln 61 at the pottery production site, could be interpreted as either from non-woodland trees (ie with little or no competition from adjacent tree growth) or poles from managed woodland. At present, there is little evidence to suggest widespread industrial activities were focused in this area, but if a number of industrial enterprises such as these were based in neighbouring woodland locations on a long-term basis, it is possible that coppiced stock was managed from a relatively early period.

Extant woodland and topographical features in Whittlewood Forest demonstrate the extensive management regimes of the medieval period (Marren 1992). It is almost certainly due to the difficulty of ploughing the heavy clay soils that woodland tracts in this region escaped the widespread deforestation that occurred throughout much of Northamptonshire (ibid). In the present day only 5% of the county remains wooded: predominantly in Rockingham Forest in the north, and Whittlewood and Salcey Forests and Yardley Chase on the southern and south-eastern borders (ibid).

Buckingham Thick Copse, sited near Whittlebury, a short distance north-east of the industrial sites discussed here, is probably the most representative of extant medieval woodmanship in the region and illustrates the character of the contemporary climax woodland. The lime-rich clay soils typically support ash/ maple (*Fraxinus/Acer*) woodland, interspersed with oak (*Quercus*) and crab apple (*Malus*). These species now occur as ancient coppice stools and pollards and also include sweet chestnut (*Castanea sativa*), an exotic species probably introduced in the medieval period (or earlier). Immediately north of Brackley Hatch 4, the naming of Hazelborough Wood suggests that hazel (*Corylus avellana*) was frequent, although this may reflect medieval or later management practices. With the exception of chestnut, it is probable that the status and distribution of tree species named here was similar in the Iron Age and Roman periods.

It is clear from the fuel deposits that oak was specifically selected for these industrial processes in favour of either ash or maple, which, presumably, would have been more readily available. All three species provide high calorie fuel, although the denser wood of oak heartwood is longer lasting. When burning, oak tends to split along the multiseriate rays, thereby increasing the surface area in contact with free atmospheric oxygen which, in turn, may enhance the temperature of the heat source. The apparent absence of hazel in the fuel deposits is also of interest, given the proximity of the site to woodland likely to have supported this taxon, eg at Hazelborough Wood, and especially since charred nutshells were included in the fuel debris in Furnace 1 raking pit at the iron-smelting site. This could imply:-

1   That hazel was more important for other uses.
2   That the abundance of oak rendered hazel less desirable.
3   That hazel was not readily available (the nuts may have been brought in from elsewhere).

There are no published data available for fuel analyses from contemporary iron-working or pottery sites in this region and comparatively few from elsewhere in Britain. Those available tend to indicate a preference for oak (usually including heartwood), either used as the sole fuel but sometimes in combination with other species. For example, at Riseley Farm, Hampshire (Gale 1991-3), and Quidney Farm, Norfolk (Gale 2000), where fuel consisted entirely of oak. In contrast, at Watchfield, Oxfordshire (Gale in Birbeck forthcoming), Creeton, Lincolnshire (Cowgill in preparation), and Hatton-Silk Willoughby (Rackham *et al.* 1999) oak formed the principal fuel, supplemented by a range of other species.

Conclusion

The analyses of industrial fuel debris (charcoal) from an Iron Age iron-smelting site and early Roman pottery kilns has indicated the almost exclusive use of oak (*Quercus* sp.) from fairly wide roundwood, poles or cordwood. Although there was some evidence of fast-grown wood, the charcoal was too comminuted to assess whether it originated from managed or naturally growing woodland. Both industries probably operated on a small-scale local basis.

The sites were located in woodland on clay soils on the western fringes of what became the medieval Forest of Whittlewood. Climax woodland typically consisted of ash/maple interspersed with oak. It is therefore significant that oak appears to have been specifically selected for use as fuel in preference to commoner species.

LAND SNAILS
M Robinson

Introduction

The length of the A43 on the Northamptonshire/ Oxfordshire border under consideration crosses Jurassic limestones and calcareous clays. They sometimes give alkaline soils in which shells survive well but deeper profiles over them tend to be circumneutral so are not always conducive to the survival of mollusc remains. The brashy nature of the limestone can present problems of interpretation for land snails because some species which are usually characteristic of woodland can also find favourable conditions in the interstices to the rubbly fill of archaeological features.

Samples were taken for molluscan analysis from five sites. The contexts sampled were mostly the fills of Iron Age ditches and pits from pit alignments. Floats from these samples were assessed and two sites, Silverstone 2 and Cottisford Turn, were found to have molluscan assemblages with the potential for more detailed analysis, while the assessment results from some of the other sites were of more limited use.

Methods and Results

Each mollusc sample, 1 litre in volume, was broken up in water and any shells which floated were poured off onto a 0.5 mm mesh and dried. The residue was also sieved over a 0.5 mm mesh and dried. The floats were sorted under

		Minimum Number of Individuals									
Molluscs	**Sample** **Context**	**2** 1001	**3** 1036	**5** 1047	**7** 1045	**12** 1064	**14** 1083	**18** 1049	**19** 1049	**20** 1058	**21** 1058
Carychium cf. *tridentatum* (Risso)		-	1	-	1	-	-	10	-	-	-
Lymnaea truncatula (Müll.)		-	-	-	-	-	-	-	1	-	-
Cochlicopa sp.		1	3	-	1	3	-	1	1	-	-
Vertigo pygmaea (Drap.)		1	1	-	1	-	2	1	-	-	-
Pupilla muscorum (L.)		1	1	-	1	4	2	4	16	-	-
Vallonia costata (Müll.)		-	4	-	1	2	-	13	2	-	-
V. pulchella (Müll.)		1	-	-	1	-	-	1	-	-	-
V. excentrica Sterki		2	1	-	3	8	5	18	13	-	-
Vallonia sp.		1	6	-	1	2	1	43	17	-	-
Acanthinula aculeata (Müll.)		-	1	-	-	2	-	3	-	-	-
Punctum pygmaeum (Drap.)		-	-	-	-	-	-	3	-	-	-
Discus rotundatus (Müll.)		1	-	-	-	-	-	1	-	-	-
Vitrina pellucida (Müll.)		-	1	-	-	-	-	2	-	-	-
Vitrea cf. *contracta* (West.)		-	6	-	2	2	-	1	-	-	-
Nesovitrea hammonis (Ström)		-	-	-	-	-	-	2	1	-	-
Aegopinella pura (Ald.)		-	1	-	-	-	1	2	-	-	-
A. nitidula (Drap.)		-	1	-	1	1	-	4	2	-	-
Oxychilus cellarius (Müll.)		-	5	1	4	-	-	2	1	-	-
Cecilioides acicula (Müll.)		+++	+++	-	+++	+++	+++	-	-	-	-
Macrogastra rolphii (Turton)		-	-	-	-	-	-	4	-	-	-
Cernuella virgata (da Costa)		1	-	-	1	-	1	-	-	-	-
Helicella itala (L.)		2	-	-	-	2	2	-	5	-	-
Trichia hispida gp.		-	5	-	-	6	4	69	22	4	-
Cepaea sp.		-	-	1	-	-	-	-	-	-	-
Total excluding *Cecilioides acicula*		**11**	**37**	**2**	**18**	**32**	**18**	**184**	**81**	**4**	**0**

Table 6.13: Molluscs from Silverstone 2. **Key:** + present 1-5, ++ some 6-10, +++ many 11+.

a binocular microscope for shells, which were identified. The results are given in Table 6.13 for Silverstone 2 (Site SL2) and Table 6.14 for Cottisford Turn (Site TCT), nomenclature following Kerney (1999). The small burrowing snail *Cecilioides acicula* was very numerous in some of the samples but has been excluded from the totals because it was likely to have been intrusive.

Silverstone 2

The pits

Samples 2, 3, 5 and 7 were from the line of middle Iron Age pits. Shells were sparse in most of the samples but shells of species characteristic of dry, open conditions were present in all the samples except sample 5, which contained only two shells. *Cernuella virgata*, which is regarded as a medieval introduction, was present in samples 2 and 7. This suggests that the snail assemblages in them were not entirely stratigraphically secure. However, this species was absent from sample 3 from context 1036, which contained the highest concentration of shells. Open-country species, particularly *Vallonia costata*, were well represented. Two shade-loving species, *Vitrea* cf. *contracta* and *Oxychilus*

cellarius, were also well represented, but there was not a full woodland fauna. These two species also thrive in a rock-rubble habitat. Therefore, the interpretation placed on the molluscs from sample 3 is that the pit was surrounded by open conditions and some shade-loving snails lived amongst rubble in the pit bottom. It is also likely that such conditions prevailed in and around the other pits.

Structure 1, the ring ditches

Sample 12 from context 1064 and sample 14 from context 1083 were from the roundhouse enclosure ditches. Shells of dry-ground open conditions predominated, particularly *Vallonia excentrica* and *Pupilla muscorum*, but *Vertigo pygmaea*, *Vallonia costata* and *Helicella itala* were also present. This suggested that conditions in the vicinity of the penannular ditches were open.

The enclosure ditch

Samples 18, 19, 20 and 21 were from a column through the sediments of the enclosure ditch. Shells were almost absent from samples 20 and 21 from context 1058, the lower fill to the ditch. However, there were high concentrations

		Minimum Number of Individuals					
Molluscs	**Sample**	*11*	*12*	*13*	*14*	*15*	*16*
	Context	103	103	103	115	115	115
Carychium tridentatum (Risso)		46	122	9	81	5	3
Lymnaea truncatula (Müll.)		-	-	1	-	-	-
Cochlicopa sp.		2	3	2	-	-	1
Vertigo pygmaea (Drap.)		7	2	2	6	3	-
Pupilla muscorum (L.)		5	5	-	6	3	-
Vallonia costata (Müll.)		3	-	-	-	-	-
V. excentrica Sterki		31	9	1	22	6	1
Vallonia sp.		14	6	6	8	5	-
Acanthinula aculeata (Müll.)		4	7	-	2	1	-
Ena obscura (Müll.)		2	3	-	2	1	-
Punctum pygmaeum (Drap.)		5	3	1	2	4	1
Discus rotundatus (Müll.)		-	1	1	3	-	-
Vitrina pellucida (Müll.)		-	-	1	-	-	-
Vitrea cf. *contracta* (West.)		13	62	17	6	32	1
Nesovitrea hammonis (Ström)		1	-	-	1	1	-
Aegopinella pura (Ald.)		10	9	1	3	1	1
A. nitidula (Drap.)		4	4	1	4	3	-
Oxychilus cellarius (Müll.)		-	1	3	-	6	-
Cecilioides acicula (Müll.)		++	+	+	+	+	-
Clausilia bidentata (Ström)		1	1	-	1	-	-
Helicella itala (L.)		-	-	-	5	1	-
Trichia striolata (Pfeif.)		3	1	-	4	2	-
T. hispida gp.		6	10	6	15	7	1
Cepaea sp.		1	1	1	3	1	-
Total excluding *Cecilioides acicula*		158	250	53	174	82	9

Table 6.14: Molluscs from Cottisford Turn.

Key: + present 1-5, ++ some 6-10.

of shells in samples 18 and 19, from context 1049, the upper fill. The open-country species, *Pupilla muscorum* and *Vallonia excentrica*, were numerous and there were few shells of shade-loving species in sample 19 from the bottom half of context 1049. A single example of the amphibious mollusc *Lymnaea truncatula* perhaps represented an episode when there were puddles of standing water in the ditch bottom. Shells of open-country species, particularly *V. costata* and *V. excentrica*, still predominated in sample 18, from the upper half of context 1049 but they had been joined by species of shaded habitats. The most numerous of these was *Carychium* cf. *tridentatum* but *Acanthinula aculeata*, *Aegopinella nitidula* and other species of Zonitidae were also present. They did not comprise a rock-rubble fauna, so it is likely that some tall herbaceous vegetation or a little scrub had become established in the top of the ditch. Shells of *Trichia hispida* gp. were abundant in both samples from context 1049, but they can occur in a wide range of terrestrial habitats.

The results suggested that the initial silting of the ditch was rapid, so the concentration of shells was low. With the lower part of context 1049, the sedimentation rate was

Fagaceae	*Quercus* sp., oak
Oleaceae	*Fraxinus excelsior* L., ash
Rosaceae	Subfamilies:
Pomoideae	which includes *Crataegus* sp., hawthorn; *Malus* sp., apple; *Pyrus* sp., pear *Sorbus* spp., rowan, service tree and whitebeam. These taxa are anatomically similar; one or more taxa may be represented in the charcoal.
Prunoideae	*Prunus spinosa* L., blackthorn.
Ulmaceae	*Ulmus* sp., elm.

slower and was occurring against a background of open conditions. By the time the upper part of context 1049 was being deposited, it is likely that the ditch had become somewhat overgrown with tall herbaceous vegetation, a little scrub or spreading shrubs from a hedge alongside it. This may have been a result of the abandonment of the site. However, more general conditions remained open.

Silverstone 3

Snails were almost absent from a column through the fill of a middle Iron Age ditch cut into clay.

Silverstone Fields Farm

Snails were almost absent from a column through the fill of the ditch of Enclosure 1 on limestone. In contrast, a sample from the lower fill of an earlier phase of this ditch contained a small assemblage of the open-country molluscs *Pupilla muscorum*, *Vallonia costata* and *V. excentrica*.

Brackley Hatch 4

Shells were almost absent from a Roman ditch on this site.

Cottisford Turn

The ditch segments

High concentrations of shells were present in samples 11, 12 and 13 from ditch 178 (cut 103). The most numerous species included both dry-ground open-country snails, such as *Vallonia excentrica*, and shade-loving species such as *Carychium tridentatum* and *Vitrea* cf. *contracta*. While *V. contracta* also occurs in a rock-rubble habitat, *C. tridentatum* requires the shelter of tall grass, scrub or woodland. All three species were present in sample 13 from the bottom of the ditch but *C. tridentatum* and *V.* cf. *contracta* predominated. The highest concentration of shells was in sample 12 from the middle fill of the ditch. Almost half the shells were *C. tridentatum* and *V.* cf. *contracta* was the next most abundant. Other shade-loving species included *Ena obscura*, *Acanthinula aculeata* and *Aegopinella pura*, none of which are rock-rubble species. Open-country species, including *Pupilla muscorum* and *Vallonia excentrica*, comprised less than 10% of the total number of individuals. *C. tridentatum* was the most numerous species in sample 11, the top sample from the sequence but open-country species comprised around 40% of the total shells. The most numerous of them was *V. excentrica* but *Vertigo pygmaea* was also present.

While the number of *Vitrea* cf. *contracta* in the samples was perhaps enhanced by the brashy fill of the ditch, there was also a strong element suggestive of shady vegetation, particularly in the middle of the sequence. There was evidence that conditions became more open at the top of the sequence. One interpretation of the ditch sequence would be of mixed partly open, partly shaded conditions on the site, with areas of scrub and areas of grass. However, the results could also have been given by the ditch running alongside an overgrown hedge in an otherwise open landscape.

The Pit Alignment

Samples 14, 15 and 16 comprised a sequence through pit 115, one of the pits of the alignment. Sample 16, from the bottom of the pit, contained few shells. The concentration of shells was much higher in Sample 15 from the middle of the pit. *Vitrea* cf. *contracta* predominated but various other shade-loving species were present including *Carychium tridentatum* and members of the Zonitidae. Open-country species were not as abundant as the shade-loving species but included *Vertigo pygmaea*, *Pupilla muscorum* and *Vallonia excentrica*. Shells were particularly numerous in Sample 14 from the top of the pit, *C. tridentatum* being by far the most abundant. Open-country species made up 27% of the total shells from the sample. They included *Helicella itala* as well as the three species noted for Sample 15.

Although some of the individuals of *V.* cf. *contracta* perhaps lived amongst the interstices of the rubble fill to the pit, the sequence of increasing shell concentration in the samples showed that the pit filled slowly and developed its own fauna of snails. Species such as *C. tridentatum* probably thrived in the shaded conditions provided by the pit itself and vegetation growing in it. The open-country species were probably from the area around the top of the pit. It is uncertain the degree to which scrub, or perhaps even a hedge on the alignment of the pits, was present.

Overview

The results of the molluscan analyses are useful in providing palaeoenvironmental information on the middle Iron Age of the Jurassic limestones and clays of the Northamptonshire/Oxfordshire border, an area which has previously been little studied. They suggested open conditions with some scrub, although it is possible that the scrub was in the form of hedges. The two sites examined in detail, Silverstone 2 and Cottisford Turn, both had pit alignments, which were perhaps related to the clearance and division of the landscape for organised agricultural exploitation. Sequential analysis of samples from one pit showed that after digging, it remained open and silted slowly. There has been debate as to whether pits in pit alignments were virtually backfilled immediately after digging, used for planting trees or left open to serve as boundary markers.

CHAPTER SEVEN
GENERAL DISCUSSION

CHRONOLOGY

Earlier prehistoric activity

There was very little evidence of earlier prehistoric activity within the areas investigated. The fieldwalking surveys yielded 89 flints from all fields surveyed (about 287 ha) and a further 72 were recovered from the excavations. No earlier prehistoric features were found and all the flintwork was residual in later features or the ploughsoil. There is little that can be deduced from this material other than that it probably represents a background scatter relating to activity of an ill-defined nature mainly in the Neolithic and Bronze Age periods.

Two microliths from Silverstone 3 and a single microlith from Silverstone Fields Farm are the only evidence for Mesolithic activity from the project. It is not clear whether these are characteristic of the earlier or later Mesolithic. On a county-wide scale it is thought that Mesolithic habitation sites show a preference for light, well-drained soils (Phillips 1999), although the landscape as a whole would have been used extensively in the highly mobile Mesolithic economy. Mesolithic sites, including 'core areas', are known from the claylands of Leicestershire (Clay 2002, 46), and it is worth mentioning that the hunter-gatherer economy is unlikely to have been as strongly influenced by the character of the substrata as farming would have been. It is possible that the favoured sites would have been at the boundaries of ecological zones, and there is some evidence from Leicestershire that hunting camps were on the fringes of the claylands (ibid, 110). Proximity to water and topographic prominence are thought to have been influences on site locations in Northamptonshire and Leicestershire (ibid, 109-110; Phillips 1999).

The largest group of worked flint from the excavations - the collection of 56 pieces from Silverstone 3 - proved to be a more homogeneous assemblage than most, and generally characteristic of the earlier Neolithic. The distribution of sites in the earlier Neolithic period shows a similar pattern to the Mesolithic and the evidence is similarly sparse (Clay 2002, 111; Chapman 1999). Recent interpretations suggest that there was not a major reorientation of the economy toward farming in the earlier Neolithic and that

a substantial hunter-gatherer element was retained (Barrett 1994). The nature of the Mesolithic/Neolithic transition in Northamptonshire is at present poorly understood and in need of re-assessment (Chapman 1999). Within this general framework the flintwork from Silverstone 3 can be seen as representing part of a light and probably an activity-specific occupation in a fairly typical location on the upper valley slope, close to a water source, and on the interface of clay and permeable limestone substrata. There is insufficient evidence to suggest the nature of this occupation.

The lack of discrete concentrations of flintwork from the remainder of the route is noteworthy. Even the limestone and gravel substrata in the Oxfordshire section of the route failed to reveal any evidence of earlier prehistoric occupation (23 flints came from the 260 ha covered by fieldwalking between Barley Mow roundabout and the M40). While excavations would undoubtedly recover more evidence, it does not seem that the permeable geology in itself was the particular attraction for settlement. Perhaps of more importance were factors such as water, visibility, ecological variety and communications.

Iron Age settlement

Iron Age chronology is acknowledged to be problematic due to the long-lived nature of ceramic forms, the frequent absence of diagnostic decoration on pottery and uncertainty over the nature of fabric variations. To these factors can be added the imprecision of the calibration of radiocarbon dates in this period. These factors have a bearing on the chronological refinement of the Iron Age evidence on the current project.

Early Iron Age settlements are not common in the region and firm evidence for any activity predating around 400 BC proved elusive. The single shallow ditch at Tusmore Drain Outfall yielded a pottery assemblage with rather unusual fabrics which, on balance, probably dates to the early Iron Age, and this would seem to be the earliest evidence found for Iron Age activity. The pottery included a bone-tempered ware which is rare, although not unique in Oxfordshire. The 47 sherds from the ditch, together with some iron slag and animal bones, suggest that there was settlement in the vicinity. The wider geophysical survey failed to define this, possibly due to the shallow and scattered nature of the associated features which tend to characterise sites of this period. Consequently, little can be said about the occupation here.

The pit/segmented ditch alignment at Cottisford Turn, 1.3 km north-east of Tusmore Drain Outfall, was probably slightly later in date. The few fragments of pottery appear to be shell-tempered and later prehistoric in character, while a radiocarbon determination gave a date range of 386–200 cal BC (95% confidence level, 2227+/- 40 BP, NZA 16362). The pit alignment therefore belongs to the earlier part of the middle Iron Age and conforms to the pattern of land boundary definition in Northamptonshire where this type of monument may be the first manifestation of the extensive agricultural landscapes which develop from the middle Iron Age and into the Roman period (Kidd 1999). The later segmented ditches at Cottisford Turn were shown to be deliberately sited in relation to the pits and are unlikely to post-date them significantly.

Pit alignments were also investigated at Silverstone 3 and Silverstone 2 where they were associated with Iron Age settlements. In each case they were thought to be relatively early features, but this could not be established conclusively. At Silverstone 3, the pits were characteristically over 1.5 m wide and 0.5 m or less deep, with flat bases, and formed an alignment on the northern side of a large enclosure (Fig 2.2). They were without stratigraphic relationships and yielded pottery which was similar to that from other features, but the pits do appear to have formed a land boundary that may have predated the settlement. The alignment can therefore be seen to have defined the orientation of the large enclosure, and perhaps the settlement as a whole, although insufficient of the wider picture was examined to be sure.

At Silverstone 2, this argument was more convincing since the pits shared a common alignment with the southern boundary of the large enclosure, and three were cut by a later phase of the boundary ditch (Figs 2.14 & 2.15). Small groups of pottery were again not chronologically diagnostic, and it is unclear to what extent the pits predated the other features on the site.

Pit alignments are quite common in the county (136 have been recorded, primarily by aerial survey) and have been shown, in some instances, to cover large distances (Kidd 1999). Their frequency suggests that they would not have been major boundaries such as tribal or territorial divisions. At Wollaston they are interpreted as dividing the landscape into blocks of land into which Iron Age settlement was inserted (Meadows 1995), and this may be a common pattern. The dating of pit alignments is often problematic, even when the features are excavated, although late Bronze Age/early Iron Age pottery has come from Gretton and Ringstead (Jackson 1974; 1978) and a radiocarbon date of 800–410 cal BC (95% confidence, 2510+/-70BP, Wk-9171) has been obtained from an alignment at Gayhurst,

near Newport Pagnell, Buckinghamshire (Chapman forthcoming). Where they occur with settlements, they are normally earlier. The pit alignments on the present project, while imprecisely dated, were certainly infilled at a rather later date than these quoted examples and there is no indication that they were especially long-lived features with substantially earlier origins. The pits themselves were unremarkable, but it can be mentioned that they were not the rectangular pits which characterise some of the alignments in the county and may be an earlier type (cf Jackson 1978). There was also little indication of edge weathering to suggest that they were open for any great length of time, although rock rubble snails came from pits at both Silverstone 2 and Cottisford Turn, which indicates a certain amount of natural infilling. It seems inherently likely that the chronology of these features varied according to local patterns of land exploitation. It is possible to speculate that the sites of Cottisford Turn, Silverstone 2 and Silverstone 3 were all at some distance from long-established areas of settlement, which archaeological work to date suggests were in the major river valleys of the region, and that formalised land-division was therefore relatively late.

The dates of occupation of the Iron Age sites on the present project are also imprecise. There are a few pottery sherds with diagnostically early features, including a carinated cup from Biddlesden Road Bridge and jars with finger-tipped impressions from Silverstone Fields Farm and Silverstone 2, but these only hint at early activity, rather than help to define it. On the whole, the relatively simple layouts, to these sites in particular, indicate a fairly short occupancy and it must be doubted that there are any real indications of settlement before the fourth century BC. The Iron Age sites, then, are broadly contemporaneous, with the ceramic evidence and the radiocarbon dating indicating occupation from around 300 BC into the first century AD. A slightly earlier end date is suggested for Silverstone 3 due to the absence of any 'Belgic' elements in the pottery assemblage, but it is far from clear that slight differences in ceramic assemblages reflect chronology rather than social or functional distinctions.

The end dates for occupation at all the Silverstone sites present certain problems of interpretation. The radiocarbon samples were chosen to date relatively late phases in the occupation at each of these sites, but they all produced dates earlier than would have been expected from the stratigraphic-ceramic contexts. At Silverstone 3, the sample (a cattle radius) came from the upper fill of the ditch of the large enclosure, a deposit which was interpreted as post-dating the demolition of an internal bank, and therefore one of the latest phases of occupation. Notwithstanding the absence of any characteristic late Iron Age pottery, the date range of 357–182 cal BC (95% confidence, 2191+/-40BP, NZA 16358) appears too early for the infilling of the ditch. It is probable that the bone itself had been redeposited, perhaps from a nearby rubbish midden, and that the date reflects the more general period of occupation. This interpretation receives some support from the pottery in this fill, which was generally fragmented. This suggests that the ditch did not receive fresh rubbish after the banks were slighted, but that the abandonment of the enclosure, and perhaps the settlement itself, was marked by a general levelling of the site. The date of the abandonment of occupation therefore remains unclear, but it does not seem to have been later than the first century BC. However, if the two Roman sherds from the ditch fills are contextually sound, there remains the possibility that the site was not levelled until the first century AD, after a long period of abandonment. The recovery of 46 sherds of Roman pottery from the fieldwalking survey also needs to be taken into consideration. This was a significant concentration in terms of initial site identification, outnumbering the Iron Age sherd count by a factor of two. It seems that there was Roman activity on or near the site which is difficult to account for on present evidence, although a particularly dense manuring scatter is one possible interpretation.

At Silverstone 2, the radiocarbon sample (a cattle axis) came from the main fill of a later phase of the central roundhouse ring ditch (Fig 2.14, Structure 1). This deposit contained pottery of mainly middle Iron Age character, with some later material. It was thought possible, on the basis of the large shelly ware component, that much of the pottery had been redeposited from the earlier phase of ditch, although the large size of the sherds argues against this. The date of 378-196 cal BC (95% confidence, 2215+/-40BP, NZA 16359) is very similar to that from Silverstone 3 and, given the late Iron Age component of the pottery assemblage, earlier than expected. It seems either that the ditch was a long-lived feature which was not cleaned out over its lifetime, or that there was a significant amount of redeposited material within it. This ring ditch was probably not finally infilled until the first century BC, the lack of Roman pottery, which was found elsewhere on the site, arguing against a later date. The Roman pottery came mainly from the eastern and northern arms of the outer enclosure ditch, including a relatively large group of 37 sherds from a lower fill. Significant quantities of Roman pottery also came from two peripheral pits. The pottery is of general first-century AD date, possibly extending into the second century. This would indicate that the enclosure was a later feature than the ring ditch, at least on its eastern and northern sides. There is less evidence that the southern side was as late, although the probably intrusive Roman sherds in a pit and a ditch seem likely to have come from the latest phase of a gully. This boundary might therefore be contemporary with the eastern and northern ditches despite being of a different character. In this connection, mention may be made of the stray finds of a Roman brooch and a pottery sherd from the modern hedgerow north of Silverstone 2, which came from the vicinity of a small enclosure, which, while undated, would not be out of place in a Roman context (Fig 2.1).

Roman pottery also came from Silverstone Fields Farm, but only from the latest fill of the smaller enclosure and only in very small quantities (Fig 2.20). The pottery included a sherd of South Gaulish samian and fragments of a white-ware butt beaker, suggesting a mid to late first-century AD date for the final infilling. The radiocarbon date from the middle fill of this ditch was rather earlier at 339-326 and 202-60 cal BC (95% confidence, 2126+/-40BP, NZA 16360). The date came from a cattle tibia within a group of partly articulated bones (burial 4) and is unlikely to have been redeposited. There is no difficulty with accepting a first or even second-century BC date for the burial, which is supported by the associated pottery, but the Roman pottery in the later fill indicates that there was a lengthy period of activity running into the first century AD. The discrepant dating between the middle and upper fills suggests that the final infilling was not a single event related to site clearance, but an accumulation over time. Activity elsewhere on the site appears to have been limited as none of the excavated pits produced an assemblage which can be ascribed to this date. Alternatively, it is possible that there were functional or social distinctions which meant that diagnostically late Iron Age material (such as wheel-turned and non-local pottery) became deposited exclusively in the enclosure ditch.

The end date for the Biddlesden Road Bridge settlement is less problematic and the generally middle to late Iron Age character of the pottery assemblage (which included some diagnostic types such as neck-cordoned and bead-rimmed jars) is confirmed by the calibrated date of 52 cal BC to cal AD 84 (95% confidence, 1988+/-40 BP, NZA 16361) from a late ditch (Fig 2.36, Ditch 17). The absence of Roman pottery probably means that the site was abandoned before the later first century AD.

The other fragmentary Iron Age and Roman occupations at Shacks Barn Farm and Area G, Syresham do not appear to show continuity between the two periods. It seems likely that the Roman occupation at the latter site was set out in fields of first or second-century date, although the evidence is too incomplete to allow further speculation.

A review of the dating from these Iron Age settlements indicates that they were broadly contemporaneous and followed a similar pattern of foundation in the third or fourth century BC and abandonment in the first century BC or first century AD. This was presumably the result of economic and social changes at these times although it is uncertain whether these forces operated at a more than local scale. At a regional scale there does not seem to be a clear pattern of development, although it has been claimed that most Iron Age settlements and landscapes "continued to evolve rather than display radical change well into the Roman period" (Kidd 1999), and there are examples such as Weekley (Jackson and Dix 1986-7), and Wakerley (Jackson and Ambrose 1978). There are, however, many exceptions such as Twywell (Jackson 1975), Crick (Chapman 1995, BUFAU 1998, Foundations Archaeology 1999) and Wilby

Way (Thomas and Enright 2003). At Crick it appears that the large (12 ha) sprawling Iron Age settlement was replaced in the early Roman period by smaller enclosed units on slightly higher ground, although it is at present unclear whether this represented a radical break with the earlier settlement or was similar to the shifting which had taken place before. The reverse pattern, of small Iron Age settlements coalescing in the Roman period, may be present at Earls Barton Quarry (NA 2003). At Wilby Way, the 5 ha agglomerated settlement seems to have been completely abandoned before the first century AD, with the possible exception of the D-shaped 'defended' enclosure, the fill of which contained some 'Belgic' and early Roman pottery (Windell 1981). In some cases it is possible to see a break in individual settlements within a broadly stable landscape – for example at Wollaston (Meadows 1995). In the Brigstock survey, the evidence of surface finds suggested a major discontinuity between the middle Iron Age and the 'Belgic'/Roman periods (Foster 1994, 46–50).

These examples indicate the need for detailed local studies within the region together with an assessment of the impact of the Roman conquest and administration upon native settlement and economy. The discontinuity seen on the present project may be a local variation related to the presence of Watling Street a few kilometres to the north and the Towcester to Alchester road, which passed close by the Silverstone sites. No dating was obtained from the small section of road examined.

Roman settlement

The framework for establishing the chronology of Roman settlement in the region is relatively secure, except for the later fourth to fifth centuries when, as elsewhere, there is a lack of reliably dated artefacts. However, the present project produced only fragmentary settlement evidence and there is little that can be said about the chronology of any of the Roman sites encountered. The second and third-century occupation at Brackley Hatch 4 clearly relates to a much larger settlement whose chronological parameters remain unknown (Fig 2.53). The few early Saxon potsherds retrieved during fieldwalking here are intriguing but of unknown significance. The midden deposit at Great Ouse Culvert yielded predominantly later Roman material, including later fourth-century pottery and coins. The nature of the presumed settlement nearby is unknown. At Tusmore the surface pottery was mostly of second and third century date, but the chronology of the Roman settlement remains undefined.

THE NATURE OF THE IRON AGE SETTLEMENT

Middle Iron Age settlements are commonly found across the county and, while most have been recorded in the Nene and Ise valleys, this distribution undoubtedly reflects the pressures of modern development and the responsiveness

of the soils here to aerial prospection. As the present project has shown, they are also common in the south-west of the county. The forms of Iron Age settlement are varied. Following Knight's typology of settlement groups (excluding hillforts) they may be broadly classified as open, enclosed or agglomerated (that is to say settlements with groups of enclosures but not bounded overall (Knight 1984: Kidd 1999)). At present, however, it is unclear to what extent settlement morphology reflects differences in function or social organisation. Several different forms of Iron Age settlement were revealed on the project and there are certainly some similarities to sites elsewhere, with regard both to overall forms and the individual elements with the settlement.

The sites on the present project comprised: an agglomerated settlement with few pits at Silverstone 3; an open settlement with numerous pits at Silverstone Fields Farm; an enclosed settlement with few pits at Silverstone 2; an open settlement with few pits at Biddlesden Road Bridge; and small enclosures at Shacks Barn Farm and Area G, Syresham.

Silverstone 3

Settlement form

The settlement appears to be a small one, a little over 1 ha in size (Figs 2.1 & 2.2). The site phasing is somewhat speculative, but it has been suggested, largely by analogy with other sites, that an alignment of pits on the northern side of the large enclosure may have formed the initial phase (although alternatively, the alignment was laid out in respect to the enclosure, with the pits perhaps used for grain storage). The pit alignment does not seem to cross the settlement, and it is possible that the settlement was founded at the limit of this particular land division. There were also pits within the enclosure, although they were of a different character. One was cut by the enclosure ditch (or at least by the later eroded edge) and others near the ditch edge would have pre-dated the ditch, if it is assumed to have had an internal bank.

The smaller enclosures, which were themselves of several phases, lay on the northern side of the boundary, and included at least four gullies encircling roundhouses, and another roundhouse, probably of four phases, lay to the south of this line, within the larger enclosure. The grouping of settlement to the north of a larger enclosure has a close similarity to the site at Finmere in Oxfordshire (Holbrook et al 2002) where the enclosure was also apparently inserted into a pre-existing settlement.

Structure 1

This roundhouse lay within the larger enclosure, but its position, within 3-4 m of the enclosure ditch, may indicate that it was not contemporary, since a continuous internal bank would have impinged upon it. It can be noted, however, that at Wootton Hill Farm, Northampton a roundhouse lay in a very similar position with respect to the enclosure ditch (Jackson 1988-9, fig 5). It is therefore possible that the roundhouse at Silverstone 3 was contemporary with the large enclosure, as seems to have been the case at Wootton. A further difficulty is that the roundhouse entrance (or perhaps just one of the entrances) appeared to face the ditch in the later phases of construction, which would have made access awkward, to say the least. A possible compromise interpretation of the sequence would see the enclosure sited in relation to an existing roundhouse, so that the bank could have been constructed to avoid the house altogether. Certainly, the multiple roundhouse rebuildings could be accommodated within a relatively long time frame, allowing a version of this structure to have existed throughout the lifetime of the settlement.

The interpretation and phasing of the gullies forming structure 1 has proved difficult. While a four-phase structure, with gullies representing both wall lines and eaves drainage, has been shown, there was no real distinction between the two types of feature evident in their forms or fills. The pattern of features is superficially similar to that of Hut Circle B found at Great Doddington (Windell 1981) within the 'defensive' enclosure. Here a fairly central roundhouse is marked by concentric rings of what is interpreted as an outer drainage gully, which would have been about 15 m in diameter, and two shallower internal wall slots. It is not clear why there should have been two walls, but it is possible that there was more than one phase to the structure or that the structure was of an unusual type.

Enclosure 1

The large enclosure had internal dimensions of about 40 m by 55m, and an area of about 0.22 ha. Apart from the few pits, which may all have been earlier, the roundhouse was the only feature within the excavated part, and the geophysical survey does not show any substantial features further west, although there could clearly have been small features. The enclosure ditch was large, 4-5 m across and about 2 m deep, and the enclosure bears some similarity to a group of Iron Age enclosures which have been called defended (Dix and Jackson 1989). This group includes Wakerley (Jackson and Ambrose 1978), Aldwincle, Enclosure E (Jackson 1977), Stanwell Spinney, Enclosure A (Dix and Jackson 1989, Appendix II), Weekley, Enclosures C and E (Jackson and Dix 1986-7), Wootton Hill Farm, Northampton (Jackson 1988-9), and Great Doddington (Windell 1981). The similarities are worth examining. The enclosure's commanding position, with an extensive view in at least one direction, is common to many of the examples cited, as is its relatively small size and the scarcity of internal features, particularly pits. The enclosure ditch itself is deep (2 m) but not massive, and probably could not be construed as defensive on its own. The size of the internal bank is a problem which is difficult to resolve, but it may not have been substantial if Structure 1, just inside the entrance, were contemporaneous. The example

of Wootton Hill Farm suggests, however, that, contrary to what is claimed for most sites, a bank may have been constructed which did not require a wide corridor inside the ditch. The absence of evidence for a gateway sets this enclosure apart from most examples quoted by Dix and Jackson (1986-7, 162-3). While a case can be made for a rectangular structure at the entrance, the postholes were tiny, and bear no comparison to the post trenches of the apparently standard timber gateways at Wakerley, Enclosure A, Aldwincle, Stanwell Spinney, Weekley and Wootton Hill Farm. Gateways have, however, been recognised at the entrances to other enclosures, such as Wakerley, Enclosure B, which is thought to have been for stock, and Clay Lane, Enclosure 1, which was clearly a homestead and for which no defensive function has been suggested (Windell 1983, 38).

The scarcity of internal features, common to most of the examples mentioned, means that there are few clues to aid an assessment of the function of this type of site. This scarcity can be read as an indication that these enclosures were for restricted use, which, together with the imposing nature of ditch and bank, may suggest a residence for someone of unusual status. There is, however, nothing in the nature of the finds from this enclosure to suggest that it was of high or distinctive status, and this is a situation common to all the examples mentioned, with the possible exception of Weekley; but even here the unusual pottery profile, which comprised a high proportion of decorated and imported wares, is a characteristic of the earlier date (ceramic phase 1), rather than something associated with the later 'defended' enclosures. The most that can be said is that the enclosures at these sites represented a phase of site development, where a particular location, including a house or small group of houses, became emphasised through being enclosed by a relatively deep ditch. Rather than indicating a need for defence, it is possible that this reflects a more subtle need to emphasise the significance of a particular space through imposing architecture. A primarily defensive function is questionable purely on the limited area enclosed since this might carry the implication that only a limited number of inhabitants were protected. Alternatively, the enclosure may have been suitable as a refuge for all the inhabitants of the settlement on an occasional basis. It is difficult to evaluate this suggestion when the number of inhabitants of the settlement during the relevant phase is unknown. Furthermore, it is unclear whether the defensive role envisaged for this enclosure might have extended to the nearby inhabitants at Silverstone Fields Farm and Silverstone 2.

The absence of diagnostically late Iron Age pottery makes it unlikely that this enclosure was inhabited beyond the mid first century BC. Some of the evidence supports the suggestion that the bank was deliberately levelled and the ditch subsequently backfilled at the end of the occupation. Wootton Hill Farm was probably of a similar date, the enclosure clearly pre-dating a 'Belgic' phase of occupation. While there was no evidence from the ditch itself that it had been deliberately infilled, it was apparent that the later ditches on the south-western side occupied the position of the earlier bank indicating that the earthwork had been levelled by this time (Jackson 1988-9, 14-15). The date of Aldwincle, Enclosure E would appear to have been similar, with 'Belgic' pottery occurring only in the upper silts which were thought to represent a levelling of the enclosure after the occupation inside it had ceased (Jackson 1977, 15). The enclosure at Great Doddington was less securely dated, for while it was thought to be contemporary with the 'late pre-Belgic' occupation inside it, the ditch apparently yielded first/second-century Roman pottery which led the excavator to suggest that it not been finally backfilled until the early Roman period (Windell 1981, 68). Further examination of this ditch in the Wilby Way excavations failed to clarify the date, although the ditch would seem to have been relatively late in the occupation sequence (Thomas and Enright 2003). Enclosure B at Wakerley would seem to have been filled, perhaps deliberately, in the late Iron Age as a few 'Belgic' forms were present in the upper fill (Jackson and Ambrose 1978, 121-122). This enclosure was immediately replaced by another to the north (Enclosure A) of very similar form, and indeed almost its mirror image. A sequence of enclosures was also found at Weekley, where a deep-ditched enclosure of late Iron Age date, Enclosure E, was replaced by another 'defended enclosure', Enclosure C (Jackson and Dix 1986-7, 50). Enclosure E is reported to have contained some Roman pottery in the ditch immediately below apparently redeposited bank material, while Enclosure C contained first/second century material in the ditch fill. The foregoing indicates the problems of arriving at reliable dates for these enclosures, perhaps particularly their date of use, since it is characteristic that their lower fills contain few, if any diagnostic finds. It must be doubted, however, that they can be seen as an exclusively late Iron Age phenomenon. Both Silverstone 3 and Wootton Hill Farm were without diagnostically late pottery in their excavated sections, and would appear to have been abandoned in the first century BC. Enclosure B at Wakerley, with late Iron Age pottery, would seem to be of similar or slightly later date, while Enclosure A at Wakerley and Enclosure C at Weekley were almost certainly used in the first century AD.

Silverstone Fields Farm

Settlement form

The settlement here appears to have been genuinely small (less than 0.5 ha). There were no obvious features outside the area cleared for excavation, although under the conditions of the watching brief when the site was discovered it is possible that small features, such as posthole structures, may have been missed. There were also relatively few intercutting features, implying no great longevity to the settlement.

One of the earliest features was the trapezoidal outer enclosure which contained most but not quite all of the settlement (Fig 2.20). It was defined by a shallow gully that may have held a timber palisade, although there was no evidence for post placements within it. The earliest phase of settlement at Hartigans, Milton Keynes was thought to have been defined by palisade enclosures (Williams 1993, 179-81) and at Twywell, Enclosure B was inserted into a pre-existing settlement which included what was interpreted as a palisade (Jackson 1975, 36). The Twywell example appears to find a parallel at Silverstone Fields Farm where the later phase of the inner enclosure cut the trapezoidal enclosure.

Pits

Silverstone Fields Farm shares other similarities with Twywell, particularly with regard to the relatively high number of pits. At Twywell there were about 180 found, and the true number was undoubtedly higher. At Silverstone Fields Farm there were about 80. This difference may be accounted for by the larger size of the settlement at Twywell, or to the longevity of occupation (which probably started in the third or fourth century BC). The settlement here included perhaps as many as ten roundhouses defined by gullies as well as more peripheral enclosures. The pits at Twywell were generally larger than those at Silverstone Fields Farm. A comparison has been made of the dimensions of the 87 pits in pit group A at Twywell with the 35 excavated pits at Silverstone Fields Farm (Table 7.1). The 'grain-storage' pits from Pennyland, Milton Keynes (ie those pits over 0.6 m deep) have also been included for comparison.

Depth (m)	Number of pits					
1.5 - 1.8				*2*		
1.2 - 1.5			5	**2** *2*	1 **1**	*2*
0.9 - 1.2		3	5	14 *2*	3 **1** *3*	*1*
0.6 - 0.9		3 **1**	19 **2**	13 **2** *2*	2 **1** *3*	
0.3 - 0.6		4	8 **9** *1*	5 **3**	**2**	
0 - 0.3	**3**	**1**	**5**	**4**		
Diameter (m)	0.3 - 0.6	0.6 - 0.9	0.9 - 1.2	1.2 - 1.5	1.5 - 1.8	1.8 - 2.1

Table 7.1: *Comparison of pit dimensions at Twywell (underline), Silverstone Fields Farm (bold) and Pennyland (italic).*

The median depth of the Twywell pits lay in the range 0.6-0.9m (42%) while there were a significant number in the range 0.9-1.2 m (29%). By contrast, 77% of the Silverstone Fields Farm pits were less than 0.6 m deep. This contrast may be due to functional differences, although there was little to indicate what these might be. Neither the forms nor fills of the pits were distinctive enough to allow a clear cut classification. Indeed, none of the pits at Silverstone Fields Farm was clay-lined, a form identified at Twywell and at Pennyland as a type of shallower pit which may have been used for water-storage or -heating (see also Knight 1984, 100-14, for a classification and discussion of pit types). Iron Age pits are commonly interpreted as being for the storage of grain and perhaps other foodstuffs. This seems the probable function of many of the Twywell pits although the excavator disfavoured the grain storage hypothesis due to the overall paucity of charred grain (Jackson 1975, 66). It can be argued, however, that the contents of pits seldom relate to their primary function, and the lack of charred grain in this instance reflected processes of taphonomy. In more recent times it has become common to interpret Iron Age pits of cylindrical, barrel or beehive shape as grain stores, although normally only when they are conspicuously large and therefore efficient (Knight 1984, 110-2). It is likely that they would have been for storing seed grain since grain for consumption would have been needed on a regular basis and re-sealing a partly emptied pit results in significant grain loss (ibid).

At Pennyland a class of grain-storage pit was identified, apparently principally from shape and dimensions, with little evidence of carbonised grain (Williams 1993, 41). The class comprised pits about 1.0-1.75 m in diameter and 0.60-1.35 m deep and usually of cylindrical or barrel profile (Williams 1993, table 3). At Silverstone Fields Farm eight of the 35 excavated pits fall into this category, although another seven have been classified as potential grain stores using a minimum depth of 0.45 m as the chosen parameter. All these pits were circular or oval in shape with near-vertical, or sometimes slightly undercut, sides and flat bases. They do not form a cohesive group, however, since some of the shallower pits also have these characteristics and the distinction between grain-storage pits and other pits is therefore somewhat arbitrary. It is, nevertheless, considered that the shape of the pits, which includes a certain uniformity of design, was a deliberate choice. It can be noted, for instance that the features interpreted as quarry pits were usually of a different form, with sloping sides and more irregular or concave bases. It therefore appears that the cylindrical shape and flat base of the class of potential storage pits was intentional (and not simply due to the ease of cutting the local limestone in this manner), and it can be suggested that the shallower features of this type had a similar element of design about them, whatever their function might have been.

Shallow pits, such as most of those at Silverstone Fields Farm, are inefficient as grain stores since the volume of the pit in relation to the area of pit wall should be high to minimise the proportion of grain lost (Reynolds 1974). It is sometimes suggested that the depth of Iron Age pits is usually determined by the geology and height of the watertable - pits on the chalklands, for instance, generally being deeper than those on the less stable gravels and clays (Knight 1984, 108; Williams 1993, 39). However, it is clear that the geology at Silverstone Fields Farm was as suitable for digging pits as that at Twywell, and more suitable than at Pennyland, and it is probable that other factors influenced pit forms. Elsewhere the author has speculated that relatively shallow pits may also have been dug for grain storage and in these cases efficiency of storage may have been a less important factor than amount of seed grain available or required for the individual or community (Mudd 1993). From this perspective, the smaller average size of pits at Silverstone Fields Farm, compared for instance with Twywell, may have been largely determined by the size of the settlement, and more specifically its arable component.

Enclosure 1

The small enclosure was devoid of features apart from four shallow pits (Fig 2.20). This type of relatively small, apparently empty enclosure is frequently interpreted as a corral for stock and has a number of regional and national parallels. Closely similar examples come from Pennyland, Enclosures 1 and 2, both of which are only slightly larger (Williams 1993). They also share the characteristic of having entrances near the corners which has the practical advantage of helping to funnel stock. Enclosure 2 at Pennyland can also be seen to have been inserted into the corner of a ditched land division containing roundhouses, like the enclosure at Silverstone Fields Farm. The cropmark evidence of the site at Stanwell Spinney shows a similar arrangement of a small enclosure tucked into the corner of a larger one (Dix and Jackson 1989, fig 10.6). A similar enclosure was also found at Hartigans (Enclosure 00) which, at about 18 m by 15 m was nearly identical in size to the Silverstone Fields Farm enclosure (Williams 1993, 181). With enclosures of this size it is difficult to envisage an internal bank, which would have reduced the available interior still further, and at Silverstone Fields Farm this arrangement seems unlikely since the second phase ditch was dug on the inside of the earlier ditch, at least in part. An external bank was suggested at Pennylands (ibid, 19) although, since the later ditches were dug outside the earlier ones in both enclosures, this is not convincing. It is possible that ditch spoil was used to raise the level of the surface inside the enclosure generally, a situation which could account for the lack of internal features surviving at the level of the stripped surface. However, there is no indication from any examples of platform material either surviving as a mound, or having been ploughed into the tops of the ditches, so it may be more likely that the spoil was taken elsewhere.

Infant burials

Whether or not the small enclosure was a stock corral, the presence of five perinatal infant burials within the later phase of the ditch implies that the enclosure had another significance of some sort. These were the only human remains from the site (or indeed from any of the Iron Age sites). The burials moreover were all from the same phase in the site's occupation, four of them occurring at the base of the upper fill or within the middle fill (half a metre or so below ground level), and the fifth, retrieved from modern spoil, probably in this location also. It is highly unlikely that they had been inserted at a later stage and the interments are likely to have taken place within a relatively short space of time - conceivably as part of the same event. There is no indication from the bones that the deaths were the result of anything other than normal mortality, although there is no doubt that infanticide could have been carried out without any bone trauma being involved. The reason why infanticide might have been practised remains essentially guesswork, but the most likely context was perhaps as an 'aversion sacrifice' (Green 2001, 128) undertaken as a response to stress, such as war and famine, in order to placate divine powers. Whatever the actual cause of death, the infants must have been drawn from a wider community than the site itself. This, and the fact that the burial of infants, as much as adults, was an exceptional rather than normal rite in the Iron Age of this region, serves to emphasise the particular significance of this location.

Burial rites in the Iron Age have been shown to have been highly variable. Excarnation, sometimes with the subsequent burial of body parts, is thought to have been the normal rite (Cunliffe 1995; Carr and Knussel 1997; Green 2001, 129), although there are examples of complete inhumations, apparently for a minority. Burials of perinatal infants have been reported from Owslebury where the rite was present in the third to second centuries BC, but seems to have been more prevalent in the first century BC (Collis 1977b). Here 10 newborn infants were found in first-century BC contexts, seven of them as a group. The unusual infant mortality profile, which included a disproportionate number of neonates, suggested that infanticide may have been practised (ibid).

A closer parallel comes from Wakerley where nine infant burials, likely to date to the late Iron Age, were reported as coming from the top of the ditch of Enclosure B (Jackson and Ambrose 1978, fig 7). In view of the varying and sometimes shallow depth of this fill, at least some of the burials might have come from the base of this deposit, and hence in a similar position to those at Silverstone Fields Farm, or, alternatively, had been inserted at a later date during the Roman occupation on the site. Five other infants were buried elsewhere on the site, although here the dating is also insecure. The number of infants in the enclosure ditch is remarkable in view of the fact that only about 10% (21 m) of its length appears to have been excavated. The number and location of the

infant burials at Wakerley and Silverstone Fields Farm suggests the possibility that there was a similar structure to deposits and sequence of events at both sites which deserves examination.

At Wakerley it was suggested that the upper fill, which was a clearly anthropogenic soil, represented a deliberate levelling of the site prior to the abandonment of Enclosure B and its replacement by Enclosure A (ibid, 121). The infant burials might then be seen within the context of a ritual act of closure. This suggestion has received detailed consideration by Gwilt in a re-examination of the site from the perspective of social and symbolic aspects of enclosure definition through material culture (Gwilt 1997). He found it difficult to decide between the alternatives of rapid versus gradual accumulation, but tended to favour the latter, seeing the effectively abandoned enclosure being marked as a place of significance by the continued deposition of material culture (ibid, 159-160). The infant burials can also be seen as part of this expression, perhaps as a reciprocal gesture to the spirits of the underworld to ensure the continued fertility of the earth and/or domestic animals (Green 2001, 129). The burials at Silverstone Fields Farm invite a similar interpretation. In this case it seems unlikely that the upper fills, while containing nearly half the pottery recovered from the site, were deposited rapidly as a levelling layer. They contained late pottery, including some early Roman sherds, while the radiocarbon date from the partial cattle carcass (burial 4) immediately above infant burial 5 indicated that the burials should have taken place shortly after 200 cal BC. This indicates a long period of accumulation in the upper part of this ditch.

Special deposits

Like Enclosure B at Wakerley, there are also indications that the Silverstone Fields Farm enclosure was a place of other significant deposits. A partial cattle carcass was deposited close to one of the infant burials on the southern side of the enclosure. It cannot be known whether this was a deliberate association or whether the cattle bones were regarded as more than butchery waste. However, it can be seen as a structured deposit in the sense defined by J D Hill by reason of its contextual associations and human agency (Hill 1996). A cattle skull (the cranial vault) had been deposited in the secondary fill of the northern ditch terminal. While it is not possible to say whether the skull belonged to the same animal, this may be a possibility as there were no bones duplicated from the two deposits. The northern terminal also contained a large quantity of other finds, including over 60% of the pottery from this phase of ditch (Fig 7.1). The terminal also yielded all the iron finds from the site, comprising a spearhead, two blades, a staple or joiner's dog, and two unidentifiable stem fragments. From the same location a fragment of rotary quern made from Millstone Grit was the only item of this nature from the site. There can be little doubt that this pattern was not a random one. It seems likely that this side of the enclosure (ie the northern, or right hand

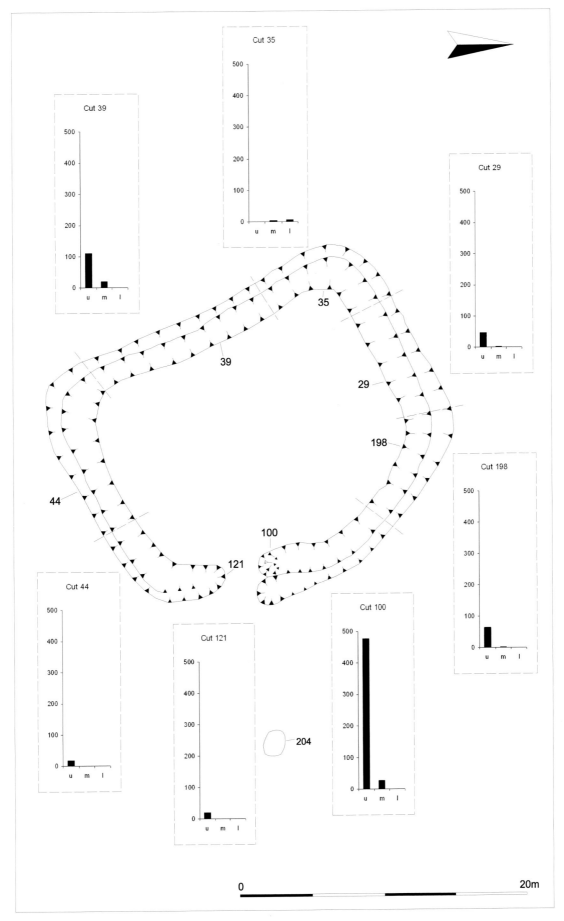

Fig. 7.1: *Silverstone Fields Farm Enclosure 1, Pottery quantification for excavated sections, upper (u), middle (m) and lower (l) fills.*

side looking towards the enclosure) was considered the appropriate place for the deposition of material. This may be seen as part of a symbolic patterning associated with the 'special' nature of the enclosure, connected with its function as an animal corral.

At Wakerely, Enclosure B was also seen as a probable stock enclosure due to the apparent absence of contemporary internal features. Gwilt saw a preference for the deposition of finds, including carinated bead-rimmed and decorated sherds in the southern ditch section of the enclosure (Gwilt 1997, 157-60; figs 15.2 & 15.3). At Hartigans, Enclosure 00, also probably for stock, the preponderance of finds almost exclusively from the ditch terminals is mentioned (Williams 1993, 183), particularly from the northern arm where the material included a human skull fragment and femur at the base of the ditch. No quantification is presented in the published report, although nearly half the illustrated pottery from this enclosure (17 out of 37 sherds) comes from the northern terminal, section J (ibid, 233-235). A similar pattern can be surmised from the published evidence from Twywell, Enclosure B, where 10 of the 13 illustrated sherds from this enclosure come from the eastern, left-hand terminal looking toward the entrance (Jackson 1975, 81-3, section BIII). This may have been a stock enclosure (the corner entrance is suggestive), although some of the pits and post-built structures may have been contemporary with its use. There is therefore some suggestion that the symbolic significance of these enclosures was reflected in the deposition of finds at the entrance, particularly to one or other side. Such a generalisation is based on a rather superficial reading of the evidence, however, and deserves the kind of detailed contextual treatment accorded by Gwilt to Wakerley.

There is little to indicate that material was deposited in significant locations in other parts of the Silverstone Fields Farm site. The roundhouse gullies were very shallow and finds were few. The pits generally yielded an assortment of material with no groups which appeared to be unusual. The only possible exception was a pit which contained the decorated blue glass ring (Fig 4.21, 91), together with a few sherds of pottery. This pit was very shallow and unlikely for that reason to have been used for storage. It is possible that it had been dug specifically to receive the ring, although it can be noted that neither the ring nor any of the associated pottery formed a complete object and there is nothing, other than its intrinsic rarity to suggest that the ring was deposited deliberately. The ring has a close parallel with one illustrated from Boxford, Berkshire (Guido 1978, fig. 23.7) and the similarity of the raised swag design to that on continental glass armlets suggests that the item may have been imported (C Henderson, pers comm). It is also possible that this pit was sited significantly in relation to the inner enclosure, lying opposite the entrance. In common with the roundhouse gullies to the south, the enclosure entrance faces just north of east, an alignment which may have had symbolic significance, although in

these cases the alignments fall between the sun's positions at the equinox and midsummer sunrise (Oswald 1997, fig. 10.4) and any significance which may have been attached is far from clear.

Silverstone 2

Form of settlement

The settlement here was contained within a large enclosure, measuring 60 m north-south by 120 m east-west (Fig 2.14). The density of occupation inside would seem to have been sparse, and the absence of storage pits genuine. There was a funnel entrance in the south-west corner, as well as a smaller enclosure in the north-west, defined by a substantial ditch. It is likely that one of the functions of the site was to contain stock.

Boundaries

The pits in the alignment did not cross the site and, if these were a primary feature, it appears that the enclosure was laid out at the limit of this particular land division. It is likely that the pit alignment was replaced as a boundary by the earliest phase of gully to the south. Both this gully and the subsequent one, were shallow and with somewhat irregular bases and may have held timber palisades. This interpretation is less likely for the third phase of gully, which had a relatively broad base. Its shallowness, when compared with the ditches on the northern and eastern sides, is not easily explicable, particularly if it was intended to control domestic animals. One can perhaps envisage a bank and/or hedgerow along the southern boundary.

The northern and eastern enclosure ditches were substantial, but not massive and would have been suitable for controlling stock. The only indication of a bank came from a single section where a deposit of bluish clay underlay the upper silting on the eastern (outer) side.

Structure 1

The roundhouse ditch was the only excavated evidence of habitation within the enclosure, although there are hints from the geophysical survey of at least one further building further west. It is possible that the site was only occupied by a single household. The orientation of the roundhouse to the north-east is very similar to those at Silverstone Fields Farm. In common with many examples from other parts of the country, the house almost perversely faces away from the enclosure entrances, which were on the southern and south-western sides.

Biddlesden Road Bridge

Settlement size and location

The settlement here appears to have been a small one and features were not dense. It was shown to be about 100 m wide east to west, but extended outside the survey and excavation area for an unknown distance to both the north and south (Figs 2.35 & 2.36). Being sited towards the southern margin of an outcrop of glacial gravel in an area dominated by Boulder Clay, it is probable that the settlement would not have extended a great deal further south. The gravel outcrop was shown to be more extensive to the east and it appears that the settlement either had no need to expand in this direction, or the land here was required for other uses. The settlement was bounded on its western side by a ditch, and although this was not the earliest feature here, it is possible that the settlement had always been constrained on this side either by the less favourable clay geology in this direction, or by existing land usage.

While ostensibly sited on an outcrop of freer-draining ground, the experience of excavating the site during the winter months showed that the groundwater rose very quickly after rain and the site was susceptible to flooding. It can be noted that the field to the north has the name 'Water Furrows' and it therefore appears that this condition is not a recent one. In contrast to the Silverstone sites, the settlement here may have been in a somewhat unfavourable location. This, however, is not an uncommon phenomenon in the Iron Age. There are many examples of small sites on clay geology and more extensive settlements are also found, such as the open settlement at Covert Farm, Crick, spread across at least 8 ha of clay and gravel geology (BUFAU 1998) and the nearby settlements at The Long Dole and The Lodge (NA 1995). In the present state of knowledge it is unclear whether these settlements on apparently unfavourable ground included types which were occupied only seasonally.

Roundhouses

The main foci of residence on the site were two substantial roundhouses (Fig 2.36; Structures 1 and 2), with at least two smaller roundhouses as subsidiary structures to the south (Structures 4 & 5). Both the main structures were of two principal phases. Structure 1 possessed a C-shaped enclosure with an entrance facing south-east, which was replaced by a narrower entrance facing north-east. The south or south-west facing entrance to Structure 2 also appears to have been narrowed in its second phase. The ditch of Structure 2 contained a large assemblage of pottery which in its range of fabrics was different from the pottery from the ditch enclosing Structure 1. It is possible that the differences are chronological, although they might reflect slight social or functional differences between a related pair of buildings. There is no indication from other finds that these buildings were functionally distinct and they are perhaps best seen as domestic houses. Groups of two or more roundhouses are frequently found on sites of this period, although it is rarely possible to determine whether they were contemporaneous or, if they were, whether there were functional differences between them. Pairings do not appear to be a recurring pattern. At Bancroft, Milton Keynes, the linking of two or more roundhouses by drainage ditches suggested small contemporaneous groups of buildings, but this was noted to be an unusual feature

(Williams and Zeepvat 1994, 50). A possibly analogous example comes from Clay Lane, Earls Barton, where an enclosure contained two roundhouse ditches, one being the slightly larger of the two. Other, more rectangular structures, toward the front of the enclosure, may have been for storage (Windell 1983). The orderly arrangement of structures here suggests that they would have been contemporaneous. At Aldwincle (Jackson 1977), a likely interpretation of the structures within Enclosure E is that a pair of roundhouses was replaced by another pair, although it is not certain that one house did not replace the other in sequence. On this site there was also no repeated spatial relationship between the houses, although one of each pair can be seen to have been slightly larger than the other, an observation which is applicable to Structures 1 and 2 at Biddlesden Road Bridge.

Structure 3

This complex of gullies seems to represent a series of small structures in this part of the site, with perhaps a small roundhouse or other structure to the south and an adjacent enclosure to the north. It is tempting to see them as associated with smithing, as has been claimed for paired semi-circular structures at Great Oakley (Jackson 1982) and other sites, but there is no indication that they were connected with ironworking in any form. A cattle skull, found in the northernmost terminal would seem to have been a deliberate placement and suggests some symbolic significance. Near the southern terminal a small pit contained part of a carinated cup (Fig 4.3, 55). This was a unique find and may also have had symbolic significance.

Iron smelting furnaces

The truncated remains of three iron smelting furnaces lay toward the southern margin of the site. They were of a simple shaft type. Although more furnaces may exist outside the excavated area, the small overall quantity of slag indicates production on a local domestic scale. The furnaces have similarities with the 'Type 2' sunken shaft furnaces at Wakerley, although there are some differences (Jackson and Ambrose 1978). The Wakerley furnaces were in relatively deep (0.4-0.7 m) but narrow pits, with little room for the clearance of slag in the base of the pit. In contrast, the Biddlesden Road Bridge shafts were less than 0.4 m deep and had large oval pits dug alongside for clearing the slag and ash. The Wakerley furnaces of this type were also characterised by an arch in the base of the pit. The reason for this feature is unclear but it may have been to induce updraught in the shaft. The problem of accounting for the depth of the pit and the arch at the base of this type of furnace has been discussed (ibid, 163-4). The arch would not, it appears, have helped drain slag away, and there was no evidence of slag-tapping on this type of furnace. By contrast, there is clear evidence from the analysis of the slags that tapping was being undertaken at Biddlesden Road Bridge. The tapping slag was concentrated in the features near furnace 2, suggesting that this was a slag tapping furnace. Elsewhere tap slag was less common and 'furnace slag' (ie slag retained within the furnace at the end of the smelting operation) dominated. There was no arch evident in the Biddlesden Road Bridge furnaces, although so little remained of furnace 3 that the form of the structure above the base of the pit is open to question. With the better evidence from furnaces 1 and 2, it seems that the shafts were broken open at the end of the smelting to extract both the slag and iron bloom. There was also no evidence of multiple use at Biddlesden Road Bridge, unlike some of the examples from Wakerley where the furnace pit was re-lined. The simpler bowl-furnaces at Wakerley (Type 1) do not seem to have been re-lined and it is possible that this was only undertaken on the larger furnaces to save the trouble of digging a new pit.

Pit and Gully features

A number of pit and gully features had an overall similarity of form which suggests that they were associated with iron working, and they also contained relatively large amounts of iron working debris, although their specific function is not known. Some of these features contained a higher proportion of smithing hearth bases than other groups, and for this reason it can be surmised that they had a function relating to smithing rather than smelting. There are two possibly similar features at Great Oakley (Jackson 1982, fig 4) one of which contained a piece of slag as well as dark, charcoal-flecked soil. These were described as irregular pits which may have been quarry scoops. It seems unlikely, however, that ironstone erratics within the Boulder Clay would have been prospected for in this manner. The local ore is mainly ironstone nodules of the Ironstone Junction Band which outcrops in the valley sides of the region (Bellamy et al 2000-1). It therefore seems possible that these features had some connection with the iron-making process.

No channel hearths or ore-roasting pits were identified. The function of channel hearths is a subject of debate (Jackson and Ambrose 1978; Jackson 1979) but, the normal absence of iron-working residues in these features suggests they may have been charcoal pits or clamps. Ore-roasting would not have been necessary using secondary ore, as seems to have been the case at Biddlesden Road Bridge.

Shacks Barn Farm and Area G, Syresham

Form of settlements

The geophysical surveys and evaluation trenches at these sites yielded too little information to be sure of the nature of the Iron Age settlements. In both cases, however, the lack of identified features in the blanket geophysical reconnaissance and the absence of features in adjacent trenches and geophysical grids, impose parameters on the scale of occupation. At Shacks Barn Farm, the enclosure ditches, which occupied a gentle south-west facing slope were of moderate dimensions (c 0.5-1.0 m deep). It is

unlikely they extended far to the west and a site of up to 0.25 ha seems a reasonable estimate. This still leaves plenty of scope for an enclosure or groups of enclosures and other features in this area.

At Area G, Syresham, the small sub-rectangular enclosure was shown to have been accompanied by shallower external features (Fig 2.49). Again, the absence of features in the surrounding surveyed area would suggest an upper limit to the site of about 0.25 ha, although this only applies to the field in question and it is possible that features lay in the unsurveyed field to the east. A generally wider and more diffuse occupation also cannot be discounted, particularly if it comprised small features such as gullies and postholes rather than ditches.

IRON SMELTING AT BIDDLESDEN ROAD BRIDGE

Iron production in the Iron Age

The identification of a small Iron Age settlement undertaking iron smelting is of some significance in regional terms. The dating of the furnaces here is fairly securely pre-Roman on the basis of pottery and radiocarbon. Although pottery was sparse from the furnaces themselves, and was present in only two of them, the absence of Roman pottery from anywhere on the site argues against a continuation of activity into the later 1st century. A middle or late Iron Age date can therefore be accepted.

Definitive evidence of iron production in this period in the region is surprisingly rare, and generally suffers from an inadequate characterisation of iron working residues and a lack of secure dating. The frequently quoted examples of bowl furnaces and sunken shaft furnaces at Wakerley (Jackson and Ambrose 1978) lack conclusive dating evidence. The bowl furnaces were considered likely to be of first-century BC date on typological grounds (ibid 163). Iron slag (not, however, identified to type) was recorded from a middle Iron Age pit and ditch, and this may be evidence of smelting at this stage (ibid 172). There is also some evidence for early Iron Age smelting using a bowl furnace at Great Oakley (Jackson 1982), although again the furnace itself was not directly dated, and an Iron Age or early Roman furnace was excavated at Harringworth (Jackson 1981). The type of sunken-shaft furnaces at Wakerley were considered likely to date to around the first century AD, based on limited pottery and stratigraphic grounds, and the assumption of the typological development of the furnaces. There are no other examples of Iron Age smelting furnaces known in Northamptonshire. It seems likely, however, that there was iron smelting undertaken in or near the hillfort at Castle Yard, Farthingstone since smelting slag from there, derived from a tapping furnace, has been metallurgically analysed (Knight 1986-7). The slag is said to have derived from the rampart of the defences, although, since the excavations from which the material was collected were carried out in the early nineteenth century, there is inevitably some doubt as to its contextual reliability. That said, there is no record of later occupation on the site and an Iron Age date would seem a reasonable assumption on that basis. It was not possible to determine the source of ore.

The assertion that Hunsbury hillfort, Northampton was an important iron production centre does not stand up to scrutiny (contra Ehrenreich 1985 & 1994; Schrufer-Kolb 1999). There were understandably no metalworking residues retrieved in the archaeological salvage during the nineteenth-century ironstone quarrying, and there is only the note that there was 'a considerable amount of slag' (Fell 1936, 95). There was then further speculation that the hillfort was sited to take advantage of the outcrop of ironstone. It is possible that the slag referred to was fuel ash or smithing slag rather than smelting slag. Fuel ash slag can occur in considerable quantities on Iron Age sites of all types. The large quantity of iron artefacts found on the site include some possible blacksmithing tools (chisels, wedges, files and hammers) as well as two billets or 'currency bars' and nine pieces identified as billet fragments (Ehrenreich 1985, 163-186). However, these do not in themselves indicate that the iron was produced there, and, indeed, this interpretation fits uncomfortably with Ehrenreich's own analysis showing that only 37% of the sampled Hunsbury artefacts could have been made with the local (ie. phosphoritic) ore (ibid, fig 5.1). A very similar range of iron objects was recovered at Danebury (Selwood 1984; Cunliffe and Poole 1991). Here, analysis of the slag indicated that little or no smelting was carried out and that blacksmithing, while practised, was only small-scale activity (Salter 1991, 414).

More recent investigations of the defences at Hunsbury have not been able to clarify activities carried out within the fort, although it is interesting to note the amount of burnt stone (both limestone and ironstone) found within the rampart along with the charred remains of the timber revetments (Jackson 1993-4a). In places the ironstone had been subjected to intense heat, 'sufficient for slag to form ... It is assumed that it is debris associated with the burning of the box rampart' (ibid, 14). This is another possible derivation of 'slag' at this site. Investigations around Hunsbury Hill have also failed to provide sound evidence of Iron Age smelting (Jackson 1993-4b). At Hunsbury Hill Farm the association of Iron Age pottery with slag looks unconvincing given the presence of an Anglo-Saxon smelting furnace on the site (ibid, 36-7). Similarly, at Hobby Close an Anglo-Saxon ditch contained slag, so that the slag found 'in the area of' what were interpreted as Iron Age 'quarry pits' may involve a tenuous linkage. The iron slag claimed for Briar Hill in the Iron Age phase (Knight 1984, 166) has since been identified as fuel ash (Bamford 1985, 51).

In general, the failure to identify types of slag makes Knight's survey of the material from the Nene and Ouse basins (Knight 1984) of limited value in assessing the evidence for iron production. In a recent survey of early iron smelting in the Rockingham Forest area, Bellamy and others list a small number of potential sites, but the identifications tend to be based on the association of surface finds of pottery and slag (Bellamy et al 2000-1). Associations of pottery and slag also come from other parts of the county (Hall 1982), but firm evidence of Iron Age iron production is genuinely sparse. In view of the amount of positive evidence now coming to light for Saxon smelting in the region (of the 15 new dates published by Bellamy et al, at least nine are Saxon and the rest medieval), it appears inherently likely that a number of the undated or poorly dated sites are more likely to be Saxon than Iron Age. Other overviews of the region have tended to focus on the Roman and later industry which is known to have been large and extensive (Condron 1997; Schrufer-Kolb 1999; Foard 2001). That this was rooted in the Iron Age may be a correct assumption, but it has yet to be demonstrated.

Methods of production

The indication that both slag tapping and non-slag tapping technologies were being employed at Biddlesden Road Bridge adds to the importance of the site. In technological-evolutionary terms this may indicate a stage in the development of iron production which saw the iron smelters developing slag tapping techniques, presumably to increase output. It should be noted, however, that there was no discernible chronological dimension to these differences; tap slag and furnace slag were found together in a number of contexts, including a stratigraphically early pit that contained 3.6 kg of tap slag. As an alternative, it is therefore possible that the iron smelters were using different methods for slightly different ends. It is possible, for instance that the non-slag tapping furnaces would have been more suitable for the production of steel due to the lower temperature and more reducing atmosphere (Salter, this volume).

It is highly likely that bloom smithing, reducing the bloom to a billet of relatively pure iron, was also undertaken on the site. This may have been concentrated closer to the buildings in the northern part of the site. The slags from here comprised a higher proportion of smithing slag than elsewhere. The enigmatic pit and gully features may have been associated with smithing (eg. where an anvil was placed). If so, smithing (or at least a stage of smithing) would appear to have been an outdoor activity. There is no evidence that smithing was carried out in either of the roundhouses. This contrasts with the situation at Bryn y Castell, Gwynedd, where, although smelting was undertaken outside and at the southern edge of the enclosure, a distinctive snail-shaped building at the northern end of the enclosure contained smithing debris (Crew 1986, fig.1). At this site bloom smithing also seems to have taken place on the site of one of the smelting furnaces after it had gone out of use. It is possible that here and at Biddlesden Road Bridge the processes of bloom smithing, billet/bar smithing and artefact production were undertaken in different locations, although the evidence is difficult to disentangle.

There was no evidence that charcoal was produced on site although it is possible that above ground clamps have simply not left any trace. It is perhaps likely that charcoal would have been produced within or adjacent to woodland, as it was in the medieval period, since it is easier to transport than the equivalent in wood (Sims and Ridge 2000, 37). The charcoal was found to consist almost entirely of oak and it is probable that oak was selected in preference to other wood such as ash and maple. The wood seems to have been fairly large roundwood (as opposed to timber). It has not been possible to determine whether this was from managed or natural woodland. It has been suggested that managed woodland would have been necessary to support the large scale iron production in Roman times in places such as the Weald and Rockingham Forest (Rackham 1993, 41) and Cleere has estimated that it would have needed 24 acres of coppice woodland to produce a ton of iron per year (quoted in Foard 2001, 86). Whatever the situation in the Roman period, it seems unlikely that production on a small scale, such as that at Biddlesden Road Bridge, would have made woodland management strictly necessary and more ad hoc harvesting might be envisaged.

It has been suggested that the combination of sources of iron ore and of wood in close proximity was the determining factor in the location of early iron industry in Northamptonshire (Bellamy et al 2000-1, 106; Foard 2001, 70). The significance of these factors is more difficult to gauge in the Iron Age than the later periods, when production came to be on something approaching an 'industrial' scale. It can perhaps be assumed that there was a local outcrop of secondary ore near the Biddlesden Road Bridge settlement. This seems to have been used in preference to ironstone ore, whose nearest outcrop is 5 km away, north of Silverstone. It is not known whether the secondary ore was preferable because of its ease of smelting (it did not need roasting), or the location of the ironstone was not known about, or the choice was based on some other factor. The availability of fuel may also have been significant in the choice of settlement location, although this is also unknown. The evidence does however indicate that iron production here was essentially a household-based industry or craft, and similar in that sense to the mode of production typical of the Iron Age subsistence strategies in the wider area.

The discovery of another iron smelting furnace, this time almost certainly early Roman in date, in a trial trench at Area G, Syresham, raises questions concerning the continuity, and indeed the overall extent, of iron production in this area. It is possible that it was practised on a number of settlements in the Iron Age and early Roman periods, although this can only be confirmed by further fieldwork. It can be noted that the small scale of production resulted in a lack of surface slag and no clear depiction of furnaces in the magnetometry surveys in these areas. Iron production is likely to be difficult to prove without excavation. It is further possible that iron and pottery production were linked in the Iron Age, as they appear to have been in the Roman period at Syresham. This has been suggested in general terms for the Roman period in the region when, despite the emergence of much larger regional centres, both were largely rural industries (Condron 1997).

ROMAN POTTERY PRODUCTION AT BRACKLEY HATCH 4

Two pottery kilns dating to the later first/second century AD were excavated at Brackley Hatch 4. The kilns were badly truncated and only a shallow circular firing chamber and oval rake pit survived in each instance. These features contained portable kiln furniture in the form of bars and also fragments of perforated clay slab. The kiln furniture was found as backfill in the firing chambers, rake pits and adjacent ditches rather than abandoned in situ, so a reconstruction of the kiln relies on analogies with other sites where the evidence was better preserved.

The kiln bars are examples of the well-known type of temporary floor and would have radiated from a central pedestal (Woods 1974; Swan 1984, fig VIII). The fragments of perforated slab may also have been moveable supports or an integral part of the kiln. A slab is partly reconstructable (see Fig 4.8) showing that it had two parallel long edges which are slightly chamfered. It could therefore only have been fixed to the kiln structure at the ends, if at all. The piece appears too large and thick to have been the sort of plate thought to have been used to span gaps between kiln bars (cf Swan 1984, fig VIII), but it may have been used to separate layers of pots in the kiln. This seems the likely function of a perforated slab from Kiln IV, Elstow, where the furniture seems to have been abandoned and to have collapsed in situ (ibid, plate 22). Alternatively, it may have formed the lintel to the flue, as shown by the plan of a similar type of kiln at Biddlesden (Woods et al. 1981, figs 22.5 & 22.9), where it is classified as a 'perforated fire-bar Type 5' (ibid, 384). A drawing of this piece (ibid, fig 22.7 A) shows the width to have been identical to that found at Brackley Hatch 4. There is insufficient length surviving from Brackley Hatch 4 to determine whether it had the same curvature as the illustrated piece. This piece would have been removable to gain access to the kiln for raking out. It is not clear why perforations would be needed for a piece in this position. Woods et al suggest, as an alternative, that it may have been used as another type of kiln bar within the body of the kiln. If this is correct it would indicate that two slightly different types of kilns were operating at Brackley Hatch 4. This is clearly possible, and it is by no means certain that the kiln furniture found relates exclusively to the excavated kilns. There may have been a number of other kilns nearby. The extended magnetometer survey (Fig 2.53) shows the site to have been large. It can be noted that the excavated kilns did not show up clearly on this survey so the likelihood of further kilns on the site is difficult to assess. It is impossible to judge the nature and status of the settlement as a whole from the small area examined.

The kilns were of a type which Swan has called 'La Tene-derived', and which are particularly common in the Upper Nene region (Swan 1984). Most of the pottery recovered from the kilns was an oxidised, sandy grog-tempered ware and the presence of over-fired vessels indicates that this was the material produced in the kilns (Timby this volume). The pottery produced comprises mainly jars and some bowls. These seem to have developed out of the 'Belgic' grog-tempered tradition, and although wheel-thrown, do not show any of the direct continental influence found for instance at Rushden and Weekley. The pottery tradition is therefore small-scale and very local. It was perhaps not linked to the impact and demand of the Roman army, as seems to have been the case with pottery development near urban areas (Swan 1984, 8).

The discovery at Brackley Hatch 4 adds to the picture of early Roman kiln distribution in south-west Northamptonshire (ibid, maps 4 & 14). Known kiln sites are more common north-east of Towcester, but this may reflect the greater amount of archaeological work undertaken around Northampton. The discovery of a similar kiln in a trial trench at Syresham, Area G (which adds to the three others already recorded in this area) suggests that the industry may also have been common in the Buckinghamshire border region, which is archaeologically less well known. The reason for this distribution has not been explored in any detail. Clearly the presence of the necessary raw materials – clay, water and fuel – was not the only factor, and may not have been a particularly significant one since these resources must have been widespread. Later pottery production on a large scale, at centres such as the lower Nene valley, would have entailed a greater pressure on these resources, particularly on wood for fuel. It has been suggested that managed woodland must have been used to supply the industry, although there is little evidence of this from either the nature of carbonised wood samples or from the presence of woodland boundaries in this period (ibid, 7). It is possible, however, that the 'concave' settlement boundaries at Brackley Hatch 4 (Fig 2.53) were woodland rather than field boundaries.

The carbonised wood from the kilns at Brackley Hatch 4 showed a dominance of oak roundwood. It was unclear whether this was coppiced or naturally grown wood, but it seems to have been selected from what would have been a greater range of available trees, among which ash may have been dominant. In any case, it appears that managed woodland would not have been necessary to sustain the small scale pottery industry in the early Roman period, although the demand for wood would have been greater for iron smelting which needed charcoal as a fuel. The average conversion factor of wood to charcoal has been estimated at 7:1 (Sim & Ridge 2002, 37). The extent of iron smelting in this region is, however, unknown and the single furnace

found at Syresham, Area G is the only recorded Roman furnace here to date. It appears unlikely that the iron industry hereabouts was ever substantial, and it is clear that the Roman industry became concentrated in the ironstone areas of what later became Rockingham Forest (Bellamy et al 2000-1; Foard 2001). In the first century AD the iron industry in south-west Northamptonshire was probably similar in scale to the pottery industry, a development from the Iron Age tradition, and essentially local.

The reasons for the location of pottery production in this region is not known, although in general terms the location of production centres, particularly the major ones, has received a certain amount of attention. Although analyses have often focused on questions of resources and marketing (Woods 1974; Swan 1984), Millett has argued that the production and distribution of pottery was determined to a great extent by social and political structures (Millett 1990, 167-174). Hence, locations of the industry may have been influenced by pre-Roman territorial organisation, with boundary zones of tribes, and the later *civitates*, particularly favoured (ibid, fig. 68). The location of the Upper Nene industries on the fringes of Catuvellaunian territory might therefore have been closely associated with the structure of late Iron Age/early Roman social and political organisation. While there is some indication that potters in the Roman world were of a particularly low status, it is almost certainly too simplistic to equate this with a peripheral tribal location. It is sometimes speculated that the potters who used portable kiln furniture might have been itinerant, but this is far from certain and the portable elements may have been more related to the ease of building and re-building kilns than the movement of potters from site to site (Swan 1984, 58). The derivation of this type of kiln is often seen within the context of continental ('Belgic') influences, which included the use of the potter's wheel for the production of wares of 'Belgic' character. The precise nature of this influence is still a matter for debate and an enquiry into the status of potters is a subject requiring far more research than the scope of this report.

SETTLEMENT AND ECONOMY

Investigations into the nature of rural Iron Age settlement are frequently confronted with difficulties of chronology and the general poverty of material remains. The differences in settlement size and morphology often suggest variations in social and economic organisation, such as differing specialisms, statuses and social practices, while the archaeological evidence can turn out to be meagre, banal or ambiguous. The sites on the present project suffer from many of the limitations of undiagnostic pottery, the paucity of non-ceramic finds, and the inconclusive nature of economic evidence. However, as a starting point, it has been noted that several different forms of Iron Age settlement were revealed which are likely to have been socially and functionally distinct and can be compared as far as the evidence allows. It is also significant that three sites lay within about 500 m of one another and it is possible that, despite a clear spatial separation, these might be part of the same settlement and reflect different social and economic aspects of it (Fig 7.2). With this in mind, an examination of these sites may offer the opportunity of recognising the constituent parts of both agglomerated and more dispersed settlement forms in the region.

Settlement morphology

Silverstone Fields Farm shows an obvious contrast with the other Iron Age settlements in the quantity of pits. This element is often taken as an indication that grain storage was important, although there are frequent indications that storage may also, or alternatively, have been above ground on sites lacking many pits. On these sites a high water-table is frequently cited as a reason why underground storage was not suitable. Where this was not an issue it seems that the reasons were mainly functional, although the importance of pits as a receptacle of symbolically-charged deposits may also have been a factor in their presence. The possible stock enclosure at this site was relatively small and suggests a minor interest in this aspect of the economy. At Silverstone 2, the large and sparsely settled enclosure provides an obvious contrast. If it was not intended to control a large number of animals it is difficult to envisage a function for it. With the caveat that less than 50% of the site has been examined, it seems that grain storage pits were not a significant element and that houses were not common. The nature of the settlement at Silverstone 3 is more difficult to assess on morphological grounds. It was sited at the interface of limestone and clay substrata and the lack of pits may be accounted for by the ground's unsuitability for underground storage. Although there were clear elements to the site's structure, it was not possible to ascertain the purpose of the individual enclosures. Some may have been for animals, human habitation, or agricultural or craft activities. There were the sites of several roundhouses. The main enclosure is similar to others which have been called 'defended' and this in itself may imply that it was of high status. The settlement at Biddlesden Road Bridge lacked storage pits and does not seem to have been enclosed. The presence of iron smelting furnaces may imply that the site was a specialised one, perhaps not primarily engaged in agriculture.

Pottery and chronology

Accepting the problems with defining the chronology of the sites, on balance it is probable that the Iron Age settlements at Silverstone and Biddlesden Road Bridge were contemporaneous, at least during the main phases of occupation. The chronological difficulties are bound up with the problem of deciding whether variations in pottery types are sensitive indicators of chronological change or more to do with the function and status of sites. It is

possible, for instance that the slightly higher proportion of shell-tempered pottery from Silverstone 3 reflects an earlier date for the site, when compared with Silverstone 2 and Silverstone Fields Farm, where grog-tempered wares are in the majority, or it may relate to the types of vessels used. It is also possible that both factors are involved, with the site perhaps having an earlier origin than the others (although jars with finger-tipped decoration suggest that there are early elements in both the Silvestone Fields Farm and Silverstone 2 assemblages).

The Roman pottery from the large enclosure ditch at Silverstone 2 indicates activity in the post-conquest period which is barely present at Silverstone 3 or Silverstone Fields Farm. This activity is limited, however, and may indicate no more than backfilling at this time.

The inter-site comparison of vessel function, using rim diameter and vessel fabric as variables (see Fig 4.7), suffers from a small sample size, but there are slight variations between sites which may have been significant. In general the size classes of vessels are similar to those found at Wilby Way (Blinkhorn and Jackson 2003) with commonest rim diameter modes in the 120-180 mm range. There does, however seem to be a spread of larger vessels from 250 to 380 mm in diameter, which does not seem to correspond to the larger vessel mode of 240-260 mm at Wilby Way. On the present project there were no clear functional differences between shell- and grog-tempered pots since the same forms of pot occur in both fabric groups. However, it may be significant that large jars, with diameters over 280 mm, were most common at Silverstone Fields Farm, with a few also present at Silverstone 2 and Biddlesden Road Bridge. They were absent from Silverstone 3 where only small vessels, in both wares, occurred. It is possible that this reflects a greater emphasis on storage at Silverstone Fields Farm than at the other sites.

Crop husbandry

Charred plant remains were not particularly common on any of the Iron Age sites although all, except Biddlesden Road Bridge, had evidence for the cultivation of cereals. Emmer and spelt wheats were dominant at Silverstone 3 and Silverstone Fields Farm, while at Silverstone 2 hulled barley was more abundant. It is probable that barley was predominantly a fodder crop and its greater presence may reflect the importance of livestock on this site. Grain and chaff of wheat were also present at Silverstone 2, probably deriving from the processing of semi-cleaned wheat spikelets. The generally low ratio of weeds suggests that primary processing might not have been undertaken.

At Silverstone Fields Farm, barley was the least abundant of the two cereals (although present in small quantities in most samples). Spelt wheat was dominant and weeds present in all samples, although mostly as background domestic waste. Weeds were as abundant as grain and chaff on this site, with chess, a common weed of arable at this time, dominant among them. One pit contained equal amounts of grain and chaff and a high proportion of chess, which may represent the burnt remains of stored grain still in spikelet form, or the charred waste from processing. The material was not *in situ* so the latter is probably more likely. At Silverstone 3 the fairly small assemblages yielded wheat, barley and weeds of cultivated/disturbed ground. These probably represent background scatters of domestic waste and there was no direct evidence of crop processing. Biddlesden Road Bridge provided a clear contrast with the other sites. The almost complete absence of cereals suggests that any cereal-based foods had been prepared elsewhere. The weed species were generally those of disturbed and waste ground. It is likely that they were growing around industrial and domestic refuse and may have derived from burning hay and domestic waste as tinder, rather than from crop processing.

Animal husbandry

The faunal remains were generally typical of Iron Age sites, showing the usual dominance of the main domesticates, cattle and sheep, and smaller numbers of pig and horse. Biddlesden Road Bridge was again unusual in the very low proportion of sheep. Silverstone 2 and Silverstone 3 were very similar in the slight dominance of cattle over sheep, but the dominance of sheep at Silverstone Fields Farm was quite strong. It is interesting that different patterns of consumption were detectable on sites so close together. It is likely that the differences between the sites reflect slightly different animal husbandry activities and it suggests that the settlements were distinctive, and did not share their animal products to an extent that blurred any differences in their productive specialisms.

The slightly higher proportion of cattle at Silverstone 2 and Silverstone 3 is quite within the character of sites in eastern England and the Midlands which tend to show a similar balance of cow and sheep (Hambleton 1999, figs. 20c and 20e), but there are exceptions. Silverstone Fields Farm has a similar husbandry pattern to sites in Wessex which tend to have a dominance of sheep, within the 40-70% range. While earlier studies have drawn attention to this contrast with the Upper Thames Valley, where cattle are more common (Grant 1984), it does not seem that the emphasis on sheep in other parts of the country can be accounted for by elevation or underlying geology, and the trend is not visible more widely. Haddenham, Cambridgeshire, a low wetland site, also had a high percentage of sheep (ibid, 46), as did Wardy Hill (Evans 2003, 127). This may relate to the poor quality of grazing, but it is possible that the high proportion of sheep was rather connected with the dominance of the arable component. It is suggested that the sheep-based animal economies of Wessex helped to maintain large scale arable production, and that there was a symbiotic relationship between sheep and fertile arable land (Hambleton 1999, 46). Hambleton has suggested a husbandry regime whereby sheep could have been grazed in late autumn on land surrounding settlement so as to

manure the land directly, or stalled close to the settlement to allow the collection of manure. There is evidence from the arable weed assemblage, for the use of nitrogen-rich soils, and it seems likely that this was achieved through manuring (Carruthers this volume). Having the animals close to the settlement in autumn, which is the breeding season, may have been a deliberate policy to facilitate selective culling of yearlings and keep an eye on pregnant ewes (Hambleton 1999, 70). It is possible that this pattern is more widely applicable to the East Midlands, and it is noteworthy that the combination of grain-storage pits and the dominance of sheep was found at Twywell (Jackson 1975). However, other sites where sheep are the main domestic animal do not necessarily have a large number of pits (eg Weekley, Phase 1 (Jackson and Dix 1986-7)). There is also no necessary link between sheep and arable fertility, since cattle manure could also have been used, and, indeed, cattle would have been necessary for ploughing. It can be argued that older cattle would have been more prevalent if they were used primarily for traction. Since the age at death data were quite limited at all sites there was insufficient information to enable analyses of herd structures (Deighton this volume).

Patterns of meat consumption have been considered without conclusive results. It is thought possible that Silverstone 3 showed an over-representation of cattle bones with a high meat yield, suggesting that it may have had a bias towards consuming as opposed to producing beef (Polizzotti Greis 2002, 23). This suggestion must be tempered by the observation that this meat would have had to be acquired on the bone, rather than on the hoof (when no selection would be evident), and that the producer site ought to show the reverse pattern of excessive butchery waste. This was not evident on the other sites, and it is possible that the over-representation is a bias of preservation, or reflects patterns of consumption within the site itself (ie butchery waste was disposed of on an unexcavated part of the site). It should further be emphasised that meat selection was a cultural choice and the parts of the animal considered to be 'optimal' and 'waste' may not have fitted modern concepts of those categories.

It is possible that the variations in animal husbandry reflect the importance of secondary products, such as wool at Silverstone Fields Farm. This is not supported by the artefact assemblage and there is little evidence that spinning or weaving were important activities, although it appears they were undertaken. A single spindle whorl was recovered, made from a Roman potsherd (and this therefore must have been very late), together with a possible bone pin-beater used in weaving. No loom weights were found. The other Silverstone sites yielded nothing associated with domestic crafts.

At Biddlesden Road Bridge the smaller animal bone assemblage is in keeping with the generally low density of material from the site. The charred plant remains may suggest that the cereal component of the diet was acquired elsewhere. This site seems to have specialised

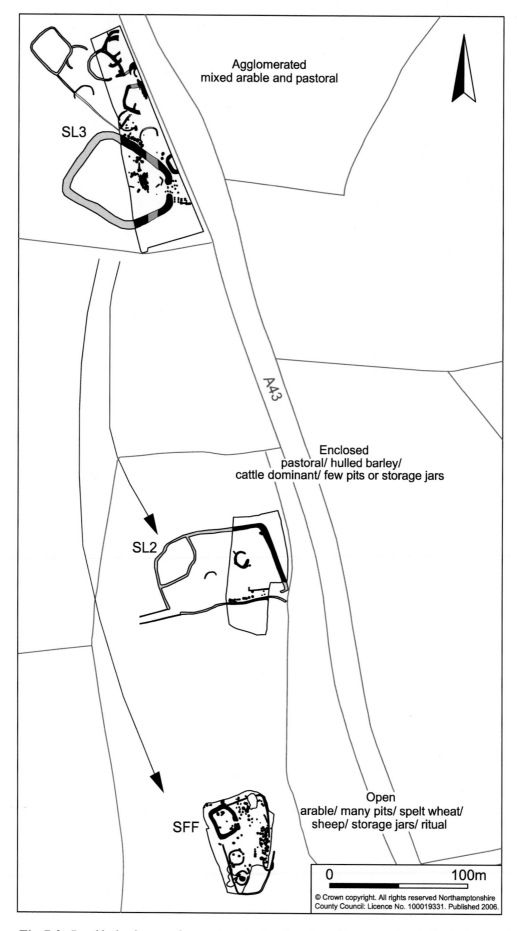

Fig. 7.2: *Possible development from agglomerated settlement at Silverstone 3 to individual pastoral and arable settlements at Silverstone 2 and Silverstone Fields Farm.*

in iron smelting to the extent that arable farming was not undertaken, and indeed the two activities may have entailed incompatible workloads (Carruthers this volume). However, the presence of calf and neonatal sheep elements suggests that animals were bred on the site. Since ewes give birth in early spring it seems unlikely that the settlement was a seasonal one, but it was presumably occupied by very few people. The preponderance of cattle over sheep may have been due to a greater presence of woodland where cattle's ability to browse would have been an advantage. While the numbers of bones are low, it may be significant that four of the six cattle mandibles suitable for tooth-wear estimates indicated senile animals. It seems that cattle were kept to the end of their working lives. The pattern of both old and very young animals is actually one which might be expected from a specialist stock-breeding site, since the trade on the hoof would deplete animals of optimal meat yield leaving the older breeding animals and casualties of infant mortality or culling (Polizzotti Greis 2002, 22). This would also be characteristic of dairying. The numbers of bones are too low to make this suggestion anything other than tentative, but it would make sense to engage in a strategy of exchanging animals for cereals if the latter could not be cultivated.

CONCLUSIONS

The results of the archaeological work on the 18 km stretch of new road have added a significant body of new information for an area of the country which has received relatively little attention. The south-western part of Northamptonshire has not had the development-led pressures of mineral extraction and housing/industry which have fuelled archaeological work in the Nene Valley and the ironstone areas of the county, and the same can be said of the north-eastern corner of Oxfordshire. Both areas have yielded archaeological results of one sort or another, but it is perhaps unexpected that parts of no fewer than eight Iron Age and Roman settlement sites came to light in the predominantly Boulder Clay land north-east of Brackley, while the stretch of road corridor on the limestone uplands between Barley Mow roundabout and the M40 revealed just a single Iron Age pit at Juniper Hill, an Iron Age pit alignment at Cottisford Turn and an Iron Age and Roman settlement at Tusmore. If this transect of road corridor can be considered to be a representative sample of these two distinct topographies, the pattern of early settlement would seem to be the reverse of what might be expected from traditional models of prehistoric and Roman land exploitation which saw the permeable, light soils of the Jurassic ridge as having been preferred to the claylands. It is probable that this distribution favouring the claylands reflects the attraction to early settlement of water sources, features which are notably sparse in this part of the Oxfordshire uplands (Paul Smith, pers. com.). This limitation would favour the repeated occupation of preferred locations, as against a more mobile settlement

pattern, something which is illustrated by the discovery of a Roman settlement partly under the medieval village at Tusmore, and traces of early Iron Age occupation in the same area.

The absence of any features positively dated to the earlier prehistoric period from any part of the route, gives an indication that settlement at this time was rare. This should come as no surprise since settlement sites of this date are uncommon in Northamptonshire, even in the Nene Valley where burial and ceremonial centres are reasonably common (Chapman 1999). The recovery of small quantities of residual flintwork suggests that the land was exploited to some extent, but the total quantity of flint was low, even allowing for the fact that superficial finds were not collected on a systematic basis after the initial fieldwalking surveys. Notwithstanding the body of evidence from Leicestershire, which suggests that claylands were exploited to a far greater extent than previously envisaged (Clay 2002), the increasing attention paid to Boulder Clay areas of Northamptonshire has not indicated the presence of 'core areas' of occupation during the Neolithic and Bronze Age. The small collection of mainly earlier Neolithic flintwork from Silverstone 3 is further evidence of light and probably transient settlement in this area. The upper valley side location may be typical of sites in both Leicestershire and Northamptonshire (ibid, 82).

More intensive exploitation of the landscape took place in the Iron Age. The single earlier Iron Age ditch at Tusmore may have been related to a settlement here, but elsewhere the first indication of activity would appear to be the pit alignments at Cottisford Turn, Silverstone 2 and Silverstone 3. That at Cottisford Turn was not associated with settlement but a radiocarbon date in the third-fourth century BC is consistent with the fabric from the meagre pottery assemblage. The snails indicated a generally open environment with some scrub vegetation, which may have come from a local hedge, or perhaps the tree which the pits may have been aligned upon, although it could have been more widespread. The partial recutting of the pit alignment to form a segmented ditch indicates some maintenance of this boundary in a slightly different form, although it is not clear when this was undertaken or for how long the boundary was maintained. The pit alignments at Silverstone 2 and Silverstone 3 appear to have been the immediate precursors to settlements in the middle Iron Age. The pottery from the pits was not diagnostically earlier than that from the settlements themselves. The snails from one of the pits at Silverstone 2 indicated an open landscape. A pattern of landscape development, where pit alignments form the earliest evidence of land division, is a common one in Northamptonshire. Where dating evidence is forthcoming they tend to be a phenomenon of the earlier Iron Age, and the dating on the current project is therefore relatively late. This may reflect a later concern with boundary definition in this region due to its more marginal position with respect to the centres of population. The reason why boundaries were defined by pits is still a matter for debate and speculation. Pit alignments are sometimes seen as features linking the earlier prehistoric ritual landscapes and the domestic/agricultural landscapes of the Iron Age. They appear, therefore, to have a significant symbolic content which is not easily explained by purely practical considerations. There is no doubt that pit alignments varied in form. The square or rectangular form may have been a distinctive earlier type in Northamptonshire while posthole alignments were a different but probably related expression (Barber 1985). The notable feature of the pits at Silverstone 2 and Silverstone 3 was that most were of a similar size and shape to the pits interpreted as grain stores at Silverstone Field Farm, which is to say they were circular, about 1.5 m in diameter with almost vertical sides and flat bases. It has been argued that these were deliberately designed and different from other pits, such as the 'quarry pits', on that site. It is also noticeable that all these pits tended to lack weathered edges and any depth of naturally accumulated silts, and it seems they were not left open for any great length of time. From these observations it is possible to suggest that the aligned pits held the same sort of symbolic significance as grain-storage pits did, and it is not impossible that, in these settlement contexts, they were used for the same purpose.

The presence of three middle Iron Age settlements on the limestone ridge between Towcester and Silverstone, lying within 500 m of each other and occupied more or less concurrently, has presented obvious questions about their relatedness (Fig 7.2). Each settlement was of a notably different form and it was thought possible that each might have distinctive social and economic orientations. Morphological classifications of Iron Age settlements have been around for some years (eg Knight 1984), but there has been little advance in understanding functional and social differences between them, or indeed in establishing whether site form was closely linked to social and economic practices at all. At a basic level, there were three questions posed which can be identified with different models of settlement. These can be called models of sequential, independent and interdependent settlement.

1   Were the sites occupied simultaneously, or was there settlement movement and development? Differences in settlement form and material distinctions may have been the result of social and economic changes over time.

2   Were the settlements independent entities, each with their own broad-based subsistence economy? Differences in settlement form would have little detectable correlation with material remains. Socially there may be little interaction on a day to day basis. Their proximity is largely coincidental.

3   Did the settlements represent elements of essentially the same economic unit, each with a different economic orientation and perhaps

occupied by a different social group? In this case differences should be apparent in the material record. Each settlement may therefore be seen as a 'modular unit' with the potential to be recognised either within larger agglomerated settlements, or in more dispersed patterns across the landscape.

In practice, the options are not so clear cut, and inevitably the archaeological record provided no unequivocal answers.

The settlements at Silverstone 3, Silverstone 2 and Silverstone Fields Farm were occupied more or less concurrently. Despite some early Iron Age traits on the occasional sherd of the pottery, there was no early Iron Age phase recognisable at any of the sites and occupation at each probably started in the third or fourth century BC. The high precision radiocarbon dates, which were chosen from relatively late phases on each site, were very consistent (see Appendix 1), if surprisingly early. They suggested the main occupation occurred in the third or second centuries BC, although given the inherent difficulties of calibrating dates in this period there is some scope for alternative interpretations. The small numbers of early Roman sherds in the latest phases of each site suggests that the sites were not finally abandoned until the first century AD. The nature of this latest activity has proved enigmatic on each site. At Silverstone 2 there is little doubt that the main enclosure ditch was either still being used or was eventually backfilled in the first century AD (or potentially a little later), while the roundhouse had clearly gone out of use much earlier. At Silverstone Fields Farm there were a few Roman sherds from the latest fill of the inner enclosure, but not from elsewhere on the site, and there were only two Roman sherds from the large enclosure at Silverstone 3, both of which may have been intrusive. The pottery assemblage from Silverstone 3 furthermore lacked diagnostically late Iron Age forms and it is suggested that this site may have been abandoned earlier than the others (Timby this volume). Nothwithstanding a certain complexity to the phasing, it is possible that the site was generally earlier than the other two, with perhaps only the later phases, such as the large enclosure, contemporary with the other sites. It is therefore possible that the 'agglomerated' settlement at Silverstone 3 developed into two separate components, which were the open and enclosed settlements at Silverstone Fields Farm and Silverstone 2. If the large enclosure at Silverstone 3 had been part of this development, rather than related to the earlier settlement, it is possible that this expressed a developing hierarchy in the later part of the middle Iron Age, perhaps linked to economic specialisation at the other sites (Fig 7.2).

An inter-site comparison of the economic evidence does suggest subtle differences. While each settlement shows the broad-based mixed economy so typical of the Iron Age, the dominance of hulled barley at Silverstone

2 is perhaps due to its use as animal fodder rather than for human consumption. This supports initial impressions that this enclosed site, with few pits, was concerned with livestock. At Silverstone Fields Farm the contrasting dominance of spelt wheat, storage pits and sheep suggests a link between sheep and arable farming in the way that has been suggested for the Iron Age 'Wessex economy', with sheep grazing and manuring fields after the harvest. Silverstone 3 had an intermediate charred plant profile, with a less pronounced dominance of wheat and a more or less equal representation of sheep and cattle. Evidence from comparable sites in the region is needed in order to explore this model. It can be noted, however, that this suggests that regional generalisations concerning animal economies may be inappropriate, since there are variations at the micro-level which reflect differing economic strategies between adjacent sites unrelated to broader environmental considerations of climate, topography or natural resources. This variation, moreover, implies that these sites were not so closely integrated as to share the same patterns of meat consumption, which would have resulted in very similar bone assemblages at each site. On this evidence the sites were somewhere between Model 2 and Model 3, which is to say that they were not completely independent nor fully integrated. This is not to say that the inhabitants would not have had strong social ties, but they did not share animal resources on the hoof, and the slaughter and butchery of livestock may have been an individual rather than communal affair. It proved impossible to investigate herd structures due to the small size of bone assemblages at each site and the lack of information on mortality patterns. Neonatal bones came from each site, suggesting that animals were bred there to a certain extent. Similarly, there was no particular indication from the bone assemblages, of 'producer' and 'consumer' sites (cf Polizzotti Greis 2002, 22-3; Hambleton 1999, 21-3). The bones generally represented all parts of the animals and slight biases, such as the possible over-representation of meat-yielding bones at Silverstone 3, may be a result of taphonomic or sampling biases, rather than indicating its consumer orientation.

Inter-site variations in ceramic assemblages are slight and it is difficult to be sure that they reflect significantly different practices. There was a greater number of larger vessels at Silverstone Fields Farm than at the other sites, both absolutely and in percentage terms, which may relate to the importance of storage. Vessels for the storage of grain for consumption would be expected on a grain-producing site, particularly since it appeared to lack above-ground granaries. The contrast with Silverstone 3, where jars above 280 mm in diameter were absent, is particularly marked. It is tempting see this as indicative of consumer orientation at Silverstone 3, but rather it may be a chronological variation, with larger jars, particularly in grog fabric, becoming more popular later on. This may reflect a greater need for storage or a different method of storage. The small sample sizes and the less complete archaeological examination of Silverstone 3 may also mean that sampling biases distort the true picture.

Other artefacts gave little indication of inter-site variation, and there was no strong indication of craft specialism or of social status. While it has been suggested that so-called 'defended enclosures' may have been of high status, there was no suggestion of this from the finds from Silverstone 3 which were quite mundane. The nature and significance of the large enclosure therefore remain unclear. The tentative indications of this being a 'consumer site' must be regarded as undemonstrated unless similar and firmer evidence is found elsewhere. Two Iron Age coins from Silverstone 2 have an uncertain significance with regard to the site's function or status.

The burial of five perinatal infants in the ditch of the small enclosure at Silverstone Fields Farm suggests that this site, and the enclosure in particular, were the focus of ritual for a wider social group than those occupying the site itself. The enclosure was probably a corral for livestock. A cattle skull came from the northern ditch terminal and one of the infant burials was closely associated with a partial cattle carcass. It is possible that there was some sort of conceptual link between the infants and cattle relating to fertility and regeneration. While sheep dominated the bone assemblage at this site, cattle would presumably have been used for ploughing the fields. The use of cattle may also have served as an integrative mechanism with the pastorally orientated inhabitants of Silverstone 2. It has been suggested that this enclosure also acted as a focus for unusual depositions later on because of the quantity of finds, particularly from the northern ditch terminal. The finds included the only iron artefacts from the site, among which was a spearhead. Infant burials are not known to be common in the Iron Age, but a closely similar example comes from Wakerley where infants were buried within an enclosure ditch. Other potentially special deposits in the ditch have been noted by Gwilt, who sees the enclosure there playing a symbolic role as a place for infant burials and the deposition of material culture, linked to its function as a livestock enclosure (Gwilt 1997, 160). The connection between livestock enclosures, infants and other special deposits may be part of a regional pattern of symbolic expression. The blue glass ring is one exceptional artefact from Silverstone Fields Farm (Fig 4.21). It is not known whether it was in some way associated with the symbolic role of the enclosure. It came from a shallow pit outside the entrance but it is not clear that it was intentionally deposited and its position there may have been fortuitous. Its rarity (it is likely to have come ultimately from the continent) suggests that it would have had a particular significance for its owner. It may have had a ritual connection drawing participants from a wide area, again serving as a unifying mechanism for the social group beyond the site itself.

This comparison between the Silverstone sites suggests that there were differences in their economies and social practices undertaken, which can be read in the archaeological record. At the risk of overstretching the evidence, it is possible to see a link between arable cultivation, storage and sheep at Silverstone Fields Farm which contrasted with and complemented the cattle and barley dominated economy at Silverstone 2. The slight differences do not seem to indicate exclusive specialisation within a single economic unit, but rather different emphases within mixed economies, and it seems that each site had a degree of independence. Silverstone 3 occupies a somewhat intermediate position in this comparison, although in the virtual absence of large jars it shows a greater contrast to Silverstone Field Farm than does Silverstone 2. It is unclear whether this reflects functional or social differences, or the fact that Silverstone 3 was earlier when storage was undertaken differently.

The archaeological evidence from the settlement at Biddlesden Road Bridge suggests that it may have had a greater degree of specialisation than the Silverstone sites. At 4 km distant from those sites it may not have had contact on a daily basis, but it would have been well within range for the exchange of subsistence goods and it is highly likely that there were closer settlements as well. The iron-smelting here is unusual in regional terms. Although it does not seem to have been on a large scale, and would not have precluded other activities, the absence of evidence for cereal cultivation suggests that this was not part of the subsistence strategy. The dominance of cattle over sheep was far more pronounced than at any of the other sites. It is possible that this related to the greater extent of woodland. Woodland would have been a necessary resource for iron production, but it is impossible to judge the amount which would have been required at this site. However, neonatal ovicaprid bones were present, suggesting that sheep were bred. The animal bones hint that specialist stock-breeding may have been undertaken, but this needs support from similar sites with larger bone assemblages. The apparently open form of the settlement would argue against a strong emphasis on livestock.

Two other Iron Age enclosures, one at Shacks Barn Farm and the other at Area G, Syresham may be examples of smaller and more isolated settlements. These were relatively invisible and the type may be more common than is presently realised. They may have been seasonally- or intermittently-occupied components of settlements such as that at Biddlesden Road Bridge.

The Iron Age sites examined were all abandoned in or before the first century AD and there is no indication of continuity in settlement location into the Roman period. This change in settlement pattern presumably resulted in social and economic dislocation, but it appears that the iron smelting tradition continued for a while in the Syresham area and the production of local wheel-thrown pottery was also undertaken here in the first to early second century. These were practised in and around new enclosures and land divisions. Pottery production at Brackley Hatch 4 was probably related to a settlement founded in the first century AD as there are no known Iron Age antecedents. The settlement was, however, very extensive and its true

size and nature have not been fully defined. It is unclear whether it might be a nucleated village of some sort, or a scatter of activity set among fields and enclosures. While it was occupied in the second and third centuries, and possibly later, the layout indicates a very disorderly arrangement of ditches and enclosures which appears to lack any formal planning or other recognisably Roman elements. There is more structure evident in the second-third century settlement at Tusmore, although the plan shows 'native' characteristics, such as sub-circular enclosures, within the tightly defined limits of the enclosure. More ill-defined Roman activity came from Shacks Barn Farm, and this may represent a scatter of occupation set among fields.

No clear late Roman occupation was defined. Most of the later Roman pottery, and a few coins, came from the midden at Great Ouse Culvert. This doubtless relates to an undefined site lying outside the road corridor. Some unstratified pottery and coins also came from Brackley Hatch 4. The lack of well-defined Roman sites on the project undoubtedly reflects the processes of settlement agglomeration recorded elsewhere in the region (Dawson 2000; Taylor 1999), rather than any contraction of settlement as a whole. There were therefore probably fewer small farmsteads, whose former inhabitants may have been drawn to villa estates or to the small towns and villages which grew up as a consequence of the development of the *cursus publicus*. Little detail is known of these developments in the immediate area, although Towcester is known to have expanded to include an extensive extra-mural settlement, particularly in the third and fourth centuries (Brown and Woodfield 1983), while at Croughton the villa itself occupied the margin of an extensive settlement of about 5 ha which may fairly be called a village (Blore 1996).

Saxon finds were limited to three sherds of early-middle Saxon pottery from the surface at Brackley Hatch 4. Their significance is unclear. They may relate to occupation of this period somewhere in the field, or alternatively may belong to a manuring scatter from a nearby settlement, which would presumably have been in the vicinity of Whitfield. Intensive fieldwalking surveys, such as the Raunds Area Survey (Parry 2006), have suggested that small numbers of early-middle Saxon sherds do not seem to reflect settlement. The post-Roman development in this region is poorly understood, but it is generally held that there was a retraction of settlement from the Boulder Clay onto areas of permeable geology in the early Saxon period (Foard 1999). This need not mean that land was unused, but it is currently unclear to what extent unsettled areas may have been grazed or put to other uses. Settlement retraction seems to have led to an expansion or regeneration of woodland in the Boulder Clay areas of this part of south-west Northamptonshire, much of which was subsequently to become part of Whittlewood Forest. It has been argued that the woodland in the Rockingham Forest area was deliberately maintained and managed in the Saxon period to support the iron industry which must be regarded as having been nationally important at this time (Foard 2001). Whether the Whittlewood Forest area also had some significance which led to the maintenance, or even encouragement of woodland at this time, or if it was more or less left to its own devices, is currently a matter of debate which requires more research.

APPENDIX ONE
SCIENTIFIC DATING

1.1 RADIOCARBON DATING

Radiocarbon dating was carried out on five samples of animal bone from each of the sites Silverstone 2, Silverstone 3, Silverstone Fields Farm, Biddlesden Road Bridge and Cottisford Turn. They were all 'enhanced precision' AMS dates, using the weighted mean of three determinations on the same sample, and were undertaken by the Rafter Laboratory, New Zealand (Lab. Nos. NZA 16358-16352). Calibrations were undertaken using the INTCAL98 programme. The results are summarised in Table 1.1.

Silverstone 3

The sample was a cattle radius (c 70 g) from the upper fill of the large Enclosure 1 ditch 2051 (context 1020). The deposit contained a large quantity of cultural material which was interpreted as having been deposited after the internal enclosure bank had been demolished and partly filled the ditch. It was therefore one of the latest phases of occupation. The pottery is generally within the middle to late Iron Age tradition and two Roman sherds are thought most probably intrusive (Timby, Chapter 4). In view of this, the mean radiocarbon determination of 2176+/-21 BP (95% confidence, 357-280 plus 257-182 cal BC, NZA 16358) is surprisingly early. There is no reason to doubt the validity of the date, and it is thought probable that the bone had been redeposited from nearby midden material.

Silverstone 2

The sample was a cattle axis (99 g) from the main fill of the later phase of Structure 1 ditch 1082 (context 1064). This deposit contained a large assemblage of pottery, mostly of middle Iron Age character, although with some later Iron Age material. The sherd sizes were fairly large (Timby, Chapter 4). The mean radiocarbon determination of 2214+/-24 BP (95% confidence, 278-196 cal BC, NZA 16359) is earlier than might be expected from the latest pottery from the ditch. It is considered likely that either the ditch was a long-lived feature, or that there was a significant amount of redeposited material in it.

Silverstone Fields Farm

The sample was a cattle tibia (256 g) from a partial skeleton in the central fill of Enclosure 1 ditch 44, Phase 2 (context 45). There was shell-, sand- and grog-tempered Iron Age pottery from this deposit. The mean radiocarbon determination of 2128+/-24 BP (95% confidence, 339-326 cal BC plus 202-60 cal BC, NZA 16360) appears to be earlier than expected in view of the Roman pottery from the upper fill of this feature. The bone is, however, unlikely to have been redeposited.

Biddlesden Road Bridge

The sample was a cattle axis (74 g) from ditch 17 of a relatively late phase (context 1030). The mean radiocarbon determination of 1987+/-36 BP (95% confidence, 52 BC to AD 84, NZA 16361) is much as expected from the pottery assemblage, with a date earlier in this range more likely based on the absence of Roman pottery from the site.

Cottisford Turn

The sample was a cattle astragulus (32 g) from pit 160 (context 161). The mean determination of 2232+/-24 BP (95% confidence, 386-200 cal BC, NZA 16362) is considered to be reliable although it is possible that the bone itself had been redeposited. The date makes it unlikely that the Neolithic date obtained from luminescence dating the sediment in one of the pits (below) is correct.

Comments on results

The samples were all contextually sound and were, as far as possible, judged unlikely to be redeposited because of their unbroken condition. The exception was the astragulus from Cottisford Turn, which was eroded, but was the most suitable dating material from the site. The cattle axes from Silverstone 2 and Biddlesden Road Bridge were unbroken although inherently fragile bones. The cattle tibia from Silverstone Fields Farm was part of what appeared to be a deposit of butcher's waste found in situ. The replicated

Laboratory number	Context number/type	Material	Conventional Radiocarbon Age (BP)	$d^{13}C$ per thousand	Calibrated date range (95% confidence)
SILVERSTONE 3					
NZA 16358	1020, upper fill of enclosure ditch 2051	cattle radius	2191+/-40	-21	
			2181+/-40	-21	
			2155+/-40	-20.8	
			2176+/-21★		357-280 cal BC plus 257-182 cal BC
SILVERSTONE 2					
NZA 16359	1064, upper fill of ring ditch 1063	cattle axis	2215+/-40	-21.2	
			2234+/-40	-21.2	
			2188+/-45	-21.2	
			2214+/-24★		378-196 cal BC
SILVERSTONE FIELDS FARM					
NZA 16360	45, middle fill of enclosure ditch 1	cattle tibia	2126+/-40	-21.2	
			2161+/-45	-21.4	
			2105+/-40	-21.4	
			2128+/-24★		339-326 cal BC plus 202-60 cal BC
BIDDLESDEN ROAD BRIDGE					
NZA 16361	1030, gully 17 cutting ironfurnace	cattle axis	1988+/-40	-21.8	
			1928+/-45	-21.7	
			2034+/-40	-21.5	
			1987+/-36★		52 cal BC- cal AD 84
COTTISFORD TURN					
NZA 16362	161, pit 60	Cattle astragulus	2227+/-40	-21.4	
			2262+/-45	-21.5	
			2211+/-40	-21.5	
			2232+/-24★		386-200 cal BC

Table 1.1: *Radiocarbon dates.*   ★ weighted mean

Field Code	Lab. Code	Sample depth	D_e (Gy)	Dose rate (mGy/a)	Age estimate code	Age (years BC)
TCT01-1	X615	33 cm	13.9 +/- 0.6	2.15 +/- 0.21	OxL -1217	4450 +/- 680
TCT01-2	X616	45 cm	17.6 +/- 6.9	1.92 +/- 0.18	OxL - 1218	7170 +/- 3700
TCT01-3	X617	63 cm	10.8 +/- 1.6	1.61 +/- 0.15	OxL - 1219	4690 +/- 1190
TCT01-4	X618	76 cm	10.1 +/- 1.1	1.84 +/- 0.18	OxL - 1220	3490 +/- 830

Table 1.2: *Results of Optically Stimulated Luminescence Dating.*

dates produced no inconsistencies and there is no reason to suspect their validity.

The samples from the Silverstone sites were chosen from similar contexts, in other words they related to activity of the later phases on those sites. The dates are quite consistent, but they indicate a date in the second or third century BC and all appear to be early compared with the direct or indirect ceramic evidence, which suggests that sites were finally abandoned around the first century AD.

1.2 Optically Stimulated Luminescence Dating from Cottisford Turn pit alignment

Four samples were taken from the sediment fill pit 158 for OSL dating. The field sampling and analysis was undertaken by Dr Ed Rhodes of the Luminescence Dating Laboratory at the University of Oxford. The following is a summary of the results, the full report of which is retained in archive (Laboratory OSL Dating Report P082, April 2002).

The samples were collected in a sequence from a single pit and the associated gamma spectrometer measurements made. Despite the fine-grained nature of the sediment, significant uncertainties were associated with the age estimates for two of the samples (X616 and X617, Table 1.2). This probably results from the incomplete zeroing of the luminescence signal at the time of deposition. This effect would lead to age over-estimation. On the other hand, the results are all internally consistent at 1 sigma at a combined date of around 4220 BC (+/- 780 years) approximately. This situation is considered unlikely to arise coincidentally, as different degrees of incomplete zeroing would be expected for each sample, and therefore represents an argument in favour of the validity of these results.

APPENDIX TWO

INFANT BURIALS FROM SILVERSTONE FIELDS FARM

Skeleton	maximum length (mm)		age range*
	R	**L**	**(weeks)**
SKELETON 1A			
Humerus	65.3	–	36.3-40.9
Radius	–	52.8	36.3-40.9
Ulna	–	–	–
Femur	78.3	78.2	37.3-41.5
Tibia	66.7	67.1	37.4-41.8
SKELETON 1B			
Humerus	–	60.9	34.2-38.9
Radius	–	–	–
Ulna	–	54.3	33.2-37.6
Femur	66.7	67.6	33.5-38.0
Tibia	–	60.2	34.7-38.9
SKELETON 2			
Humerus	69.8	–	38.3-43.0
Radius	56.5	57.1	38.5-43.4
Ulna	63.5	–	37.8-42.2
Femur	77.4	–	37.0-41.2
Tibia	–	–	–
SKELETON 3			
Humerus	63.7	63.1	35.3-40.1
Radius	–	–	–
Ulna	–	–	–
Femur	74.6	73.8	35.9-40.3
Tibia	64.5	–	36.5-40.7
SKELETON 5			
Humerus	–	–	–
Radius	–	–	–
Ulna	–	–	–
Femur	–	77.6	37.1-41.2
Tibia	–	66.9	37.5-41.7

Table 2.1: *Infant burials; age estimation based on diaphysial bone lengths.*
    ★ based on Scheuer et al (1980).

Skeleton	Brachial I		Brachial II		Crural		Humero-femoral		Humero-tibial	
	R	L	R	L	R	L	R	L	R	L
1a	-	-	-	80.95	85.19	85.81	83.40	-	97.90	-
1b	-	89.16	-	-	-	89.05	-	90.09	-	101.16
2	90.97	-	-	81.18	-	-	89.92	-	-	-
3	-	-	-	-	86.46	-	85.39	85.50	98.76	-
5	-	-	-	-	-	86.21	-	-	-	-

Foetal Age*	Brachial I Sex?	Brachial II Sex?	Crural Sex?	Humero-femoral Sex?	Humero-tibial sex?
26	93.0	83.7	90.5	95.2	105.3
28	91.0	80.5	88.6	93.2	105.2
30	93.4	83.4	90.1	94.0	104.3
32	92.7	81.0	86.8	90.8	104.6
34	91.9	81.5	88.1	88.8	100.8
36	91.9	82.3	87.7	88.8	101.3
38	91.2	79.6	86.9	89.0	102.3
40	91.4	79.8	87.6	87.3	99.7
40~	92.8	80.7	84.7	85.4	100.8

Age**	Brachial I		Brachial II		Crural		Humero-femoral		Humero-tibial	
	M	F	M	F	M	F	M	F	M	F
6.5	92.5	90.9	82.5	80.5	82.3	80.6	84.2	82.3	102.3	102.1
13.0	91.6	88.8	81.9	79.1	81.3	80.2	80.0	79.6	98.4	99.3
26.0	89.5	87.2	80.8	77.9	81.1	80.0	78.8	78.1	97.1	97.6
52.0	87.8	85.9	78.3	76.2	80.7	80.6	77.2	77.0	96.5	95.5

Table 2.2: *Infant burials; long bone indices.*

Definition of the indices

Brachial I	(ulnar length X 100) divided by humeral length.
Brachial II	(radial length X 100) divided by humeral length.
Crural	(tibial length X 100) divided by femoral length.
Humero-femoral	(humeral length X 100) divided by femoral length.
Humero-tibial	(humeral length X 100) divided by femoral length.

* Based on Fazekas & Kósa (1978, Table 144) and 40~ based on Scheuer et al (1980).

Maxilla	Crown length			Mesio–distal width			Labio–lingual width		
	R	Mean	L	R	Mean	L	R	Mean	L
SECOND MOLAR (e)									
Modern Dimensions		5.7			8.4			10.0	
SK 1a	3.5		–	8.1		–	6.7		–
SK 2	–		3.6	–		7.2	–		8.0
FIRST MOLAR (d)									
Modern Dimensions		5.1			7.1			8.5	
SK 1a	4.9		–	7.0		–	7.2		–
SK 2	–		4.6	–		6.1	–		7.0
CANINE (c)									
Modern Dimensions		6.5			6.8			7.0	
LATERAL INCISOR (b)									
Modern Dimensions		5.6			5.2			4.0	
SK 1a	–		5.3	–		5.6	–		4.3
SK 2	–		5.6	–		4.5	–		3.9
CENTRAL INCISOR (a)									
Modern Dimensions		6.0			6.5			6.0	
SK 1a	–		7.1	–		7.0	–		4.8
SK 2	–		6.3	–		6.1	–		4.5
Mandible	R	Mean	L	R	Mean	L	R	Mean	L
SECOND MOLAR (e)									
Modern Dimensions		5.5			9.7			8.7	
SK 1a	3.7		3.6	9.0		8.8	6.5		7.0
FIRST MOLAR (d)									
Modern Dimensions		6.0			7.7			7.0	
SK 2	5.0		–	7.0		–	5.0		–
CANINE (c)									
Modern Dimensions		6.0			5.5			4.9	
SK 1a	–		3.6	–		5.1	–		2.6
SK 2	3.8		–	4.9		–	2.9		–
LATERAL INCISOR (b)									
Modern Dimensions		5.2			4.5			4.0	
SK 1a	4.7		5.4	4.9		4.9	3.1		4.4
SK 2	–		5.0	–		3.8	–		3.0
CENTRAL INCISOR (a)									
Modern Dimensions		5.0			4.0			4.0	
SK 1a	5.6		5.5	4.2		4.2	3.7		3.7
SK 2	–		5.6	–		3.7	–		3.1

Table 2.3: *Infant burials; dimensions of the unerupted deciduous teeth.*

Modern data based on mean dimensions of fully formed deciduous teeth adapted from van Beek (1983, Table 2) all measurements are in mm.

SCIATIC NOTCH DEPTH/LENGTH

	SK 1a	SEX	SK 1b	SEX	SK 2	SEX	SK 3	SEX	SK 5	SEX
R	37.14	M	–		–		35.79	M	36.27	M
L	37.38	M	–		–		33.00	M	40.00	M

SCIATIC NOTCH LENGTH/ILIAL LENGTH

	SK 1a	SEX	SK 1b	SEX	SK 2	SEX	SK 3	SEX	SK 5	SEX
R	–		–		–		28.70	?	30.45	?
L	28.16	?	–		–		–		27.38	?

SCIATIC NOTCH LENGTH/FEMORAL LENGTH INDEX

	SK 1a	SEX	SK 1b	SEX	SK 2	SEX	SK 3	SEX	SK 5	SEX
R	13.41	?	–		–		12.73	?	–	
L	13.68	?	–		–		13.14	?	12.24	?

SCIATIC NOTCH DEPTH/ILIAL LENGTH INDEX

	SK 1a	SEX	SK 1b	SEX	SK 2	SEX	SK 3	SEX	SK 5	SEX
R	–		–		–		10.27	M	11.04	M
L	10.53	M	–		–		–		10.95	M

SCIATIC NOTCH DEPTH/FEMORAL LENGTH INDEX

	SK 1a	SEX	SK 1b	SEX	SK 2	SEX	SK 3	SEX	SK 5	SEX
R	4.98	M	–		–		4.58	M? –		
L	5.11	M	–		–		4.34	?	4.90	M

ILIAL BREADTH/ILIAL LENGTH INDEX

	SK 1a	SEX	SK 1b	SEX	SK 2	SEX	SK 3	SEX	SK 5	SEX
R	–		–		–		94.56	? –		
L	–		–		–		–		–	

ILIAL LENGTH/FEMORAL LENGTH INDEX

	SK 1a	SEX	SK 1b	SEX	SK 2	SEX	SK 3	SEX	SK 5	SEX
R	–		–		–		44.37	?	–	
L	48.59	?	–		–		–		44.72	?

Table 2.4: *Infant burials; sexing criteria: pelvic indices.*

Key: SCIATIC NOTCH DEPTH/LENGTH INDEX (22d/22c)
Male range: 27.67 – 36.99
Female range: 26.30 – 29.14

SCIATIC NOTCH LENGTH/ILIAL LENGTH INDEX (22c/22a)
Male range: 24.81 – 32.03
Female range: 27.52 – 33.52

SCIATIC NOTCH LENGTH/FEMORAL LENGTH INDEX (22c/28a)
Male range: 11.40 – 14.58
Female range: 12.48 – 15.58

SCIATIC NOTCH DEPTH/ILIAL LENGTH INDEX (22d/22a)
Male range: 8.02 – 10.14
Female range: 6.98 – 9.98

SCIATIC NOTCH DEPTH/FEMORAL LENGTH INDEX (22d/28a)
Male range: 3.57 – 4.81
Female range: 3.17 – 4.59

ILIAL BREADTH/ILIAL LENGTH INDEX (22b/22a)
Male range: 80.44 – 89.90
Female range: 81.12 – 90.82

ILIAL LENGTH/FEMORAL LENGTH INDEX (22a/28a)
Male range: 44.18 – 47.96
Female range: 43.97 – 47.81

HUMERAL ROBUSTICITY

SK	mid-shaft	proximal	distal
1a	16.23		36.29
1b	14.61	34.48	35.30
2	17.57	36.25	
3	15.23 15.69	40.03 39.94	
5			

FEMORAL ROBUSTICITY

SK	mid-shaft	proximal	distal
1a	17.24 16.11	39.59	
1b	16.49 15.53	36.58 37.57	38.38 37.72
2	17.44	40.18	
3	16.62 15.99	43.30 40.51	42.36 40.79
5	16.11	38.79	0.08

TIBIAL ROBUSTICITY

SK	nutrient-foramen	proximal	distal
1a	24.29 23.34		33.58 33.83
1b	18.94	41.38	29.40
2			
3			31.32
5	21.52	40.96	33.33

Table 2.5: *Infant burials; limb bone robusticity.*

Key: HUMERUS
MID SHAFT ROBUSTICITY: calculated by the sum of the maximum (25d) and minimum (25e) mid-shaft diaphyseal diameters, multiplied by 100; divided by the diaphyseal length (25a).
PROXIMAL ROBUSTICITY: calculated by the sum of the medio-lateral (25g) and a-p (25h) widths of the proximal diaphysis, multiplied by 100; divided by the diaphyseal length (25a).
DISTAL ROBUSTICITY: calculated by the sum of the medio-lateral (25b) and a-p (25f) widths of the proximal diaphysis, multiplied by 100; divided by the diaphyseal length (25a).

FEMUR
MID SHAFT ROBUSTICITY: calculated by the sum of the a-p (28d) and transverse (28e) mid-shaft diaphyseal diameters, multiplied by 100; divided by the diaphyseal length (28a).
PROXIMAL ROBUSTICITY: calculated by the sum of the medio-lateral (28g) and a-p (28h) widths of the proximal diaphysis, multiplied by 100; divided by the diaphyseal length (28a).
DISTAL ROBUSTICITY: calculated by the sum of the medio-lateral (28b) and a-p (28f) widths of the proximal diaphysis, multiplied by 100; divided by the diaphyseal length (28a).

TIBIA
NUTRIENT FORAMEN ROBUSTICITY: calculated by the sum of the a-p (29b) and transverse (29c) diameters taken at the distal extent of the nutrient foramen (location of the cnemic index) multiplied by 100; divided by the diaphyseal length (29a).
PROXIMAL ROBUSTICITY: calculated by the sum of the medio-lateral (29d) and a-p (29e) widths of the proximal diaphysis, multiplied by 100; divided by the diaphyseal length (29a).
DISTAL ROBUSTICITY: calculated by the sum of the medio-lateral (29f) and a-p (29g) widths of the proximal diaphysis, multiplied by 100; divided by the diaphyseal length (29a).

SKELETON

Metric		1a		1b		2	
	F&K	*R*	*L*	*R*	*L*	*R*	*L*
2a	25.4	–	–	–	–	29.3	31.7
2b	32.6	–	42.8	–	–	33.7	34.2
4aA	86.8	–	–	–	–	–	92.0
4aC	65.8	–	–	–	–	–	79.4
4bA	82.0	–	–	–	–	87.0	86.0
4bC	72.4	–	–	–	–	77.3	77.5
7a	31.0	31.7	–	–	–	35.0	34.7
7b	17.5	21.4	–	–	19.2	22.8	23.0
8a	11.7	9.4		–		–	
8b	17.9	20.0		–		–	–
9a	38.3	42.7	42.1	–	–	43.6	42.9
9b	17.5	15.4	18.7	–	–	18.0	19.3
10a	13.1	12.8		–		13.8	
10b	15.2	16.1		–		15.9	
11a	26.5	29.1	–	–	–	29.8	29.7
11b	14.0	16.2	–	–	–	–	–
14a	30.6	27.4		–		–	
16a	25.8	–	–	–	20.8	30.4	–
16b	20.2	–	–	–	18.4	24.5	–
17a	24.6	–	–	–	–	–	24.0
17b	24.5	–	–	–	–	–	30.3
17c	25.1	–	–	–	–	–	28.9
17d	34.5	–	–	–	–	–	39.5
18a	36.5	40.6	37.8	–	35.0	43.3	–
18b	18.0	–	19.6	–	–	20.8	–
18c	41.7	–	52.8	–	42.6	54.1	–

Table 2.6: *Infant burials; the cranial metrics.*

F&K: The full-term (40 weeks) bone dimensions are based on Fazekas & Kósa (1978, Tables 27, 45, 66).
No cranial measurements were available for SK3 and 5.

SKELETON

Metric		1a		1b		2		3		5	
	F&K	*R*	*L*	*R*	*L*	*R*	*L*	*R*	*L*	*R*	*L*
19aI	24.0	–	26.4	–	–	26.1	–	–	–	–	–
20a	44.1	–	–	38.9	–	–	–	–	–	–	–
21a	35.5	–	–	30.6	–	–	–	35.6	–	–	35.8
21b	29.5	–	–	25.4	–	–	–	28.9	29.5	–	28.5
21c	31.6	–	–	27.6	–	–	–	–	32.0	–	30.5
22a	34.5	–	38.0	–	–	–	–	33.1	–	33.5	34.7
22b	30.4	–	–	–	–	–	–	31.3	–	–	–
22c	–	10.5	10.7	–	–	–	–	9.5	9.7	10.2	9.5
22d	–	3.9	4.0	–	–	–	–	3.4	3.2	3.7	3.8
23a	18.5	–	–	–	–	–	20.3	–	–	–	–
23b	12.4	–	–	–	–	–	12.8	–	–	–	–
24a	16.6	–	–	–	–	15.2	–	–	–	–	–
25a	64.9	65.3	–	–	60.9	69.8	–	63.7	63.1	–	–
25b	16.8	17.0	–	–	15.3	18.1	18.5	17.4	17.2	–	16.0
25c	–	19.0	19.5	–	16.0	19.0	19.0	17.5	17.5	–	19.0
25d	–	5.6	5.9	–	4.7	5.7	5.6	5.0	5.1	–	5.5
25e	–	5.0	5.3	–	4.2	5.0	5.0	4.7	4.8	–	5.0
25f	–	6.7	–	–	6.2	7.2	7.4	8.1	8.0	–	6.5
25g	–	13.1	–	11.6	11.0	–	–	–	–	–	–
25h	–	–	–	10.2	10.0	–	–	–	–	–	–
26a	–	–	–	–	54.3	63.5	–	–	–	–	–
27a	51.8	–	52.8	–	–	56.5	57.1	–	–	–	–
28a	74.3	78.3	78.2	66.7	67.6	77.4	–	74.6	73.8	–	77.6

Metric	F&K	1a		1b		2		3		5	
		R	L	R	L	R	L	R	L	R	L
28b	19.9	–	–	16.4	16.2	21.1	–	20.2	19.0	–	21.0
28c	–	23.0	22.0	18.5	18.5	23.5	–	21.5	20.0	–	22.0
28d	–	6.4	5.7	5.2	4.9	6.4	–	6.0	5.7	–	5.8
28e	–	7.1	6.9	5.8	5.6	7.1	–	6.4	6.1	–	6.7
28f	–	11.2	–	9.2	9.3	11.0	–	11.4	11.1	–	11.1
28g	–	19.0	19.7	14.6	14.8	19.8	–	18.9	17.5	19.3	18.1
28h	–	12.0	–	9.8	10.6	–	–	13.4	12.4	12.2	12.0
29a	65.1	66.7	67.1	–	60.2	–	–	64.5	–	–	66.9
29b	–	9.1	8.6	–	5.9	–	8.2	–	–	–	7.9
29c	–	7.1	7.1	–	5.5	–	7.1	–	–	–	6.5
29d	–	–	–	13.5	15.4	–	–	–	–	–	15.4
29e	–	–	–	9.8	9.8	–	–	–	–	–	12.0
29f	–	12.1	11.9	–	9.4	–	–	10.4	–	–	11.4
29g	–	10.3	10.8	–	8.3	–	–	9.8	–	–	10.9
30a	62.3	–	62.2	–	–	–	–	–	–	–	–
31a	15.0	–	–	–	–	16.8	16.5	–	–	–	–
32a	18.2	19.2	19.3	–	–	19.6	19.6	–	–	–	–
33a	9.3	–	–	–	–	10.1	10.1	–	–	–	–
35a	7.9	9.2	–	–	–	8.3	–	–	–	–	–
36a	6.9	6.1	–	–	–	6.4	6.2	–	–	–	–
36b	5.5	4.9	–	–	–	5.0	5.0	–	–	–	–

Table 2.7: Infant burials; the post-cranial metrics.

The full-term bone dimensions are based on Fazekas & Kósa (1978, Tables 86, 107, 144, 162).

Cranial Metrics: The Definitions

1a	length of the squamous portion of the frontal bone.
1b	width of the squamous portion of the frontal bone.
2a	height of the squamous portion of the temporal bone.
2b	width of the squamous portion of the temporal bone.
2c	length of the squamous portion of the temporal bone.
3a	diameter of the tympanic ring.
4aA	height of the parietal bone (arc measurement).
4aC	height of the parietal bone (chord measurement).
4bA	width of the parietal bone (arc measurement).
4bC	width of the parietal bone (chord measurement).
5a	height of the squamous portion of the occipital bone.
5b	width of the squamous portion of the occipital bone.
6a	length of the lesser wing of the sphenoid.
6b	width of the lesser wing of the sphenoid.
7a	length of the greater wing of the sphenoid.
7b	width of the greater wing of the sphenoid.
8a	length of the body of the sphenoid.
8b	width of the body of the sphenoid.
9a	length of the petromastoid portion of the temporal bone.
9b	width of the petromastoid portion of the temporal bone.
10a	length of the basilar portion of the occipital bone.
10b	width of the basilar portion of the occipital bone.
11a	length of the lateral portion of the occipital bone.
11b	width of the lateral portion of the occipital bone.
12a	length of the nasal bone.
12b	width of the nasal bone.

13a	length of the inferior concha.
14a	length of the vomer.
15a	height of the palatine bone.
16a	length of the zygomatic bone.
16b	width of the zygomatic bone.
17a	length of the maxilla.
17b	height of the maxilla.
17c	width of the maxilla.
17d	oblique length of the maxilla.
18a	length of the mandible body.
18b	width of the mandibular arc.
18c	oblique length of the mandible.

All the cranial metrics are based on the definitions in Fazekas & Kósa (1978).

Post-Cranial Metrics: The Definitions

19a	length of the rib (I–XII).
20a	length of the clavicle.
21a	length of the scapula.
21b	width of the scapula.
21c	length of the acromial spine.
22a	length of the ilium.
22b	width of the ilium.
22c	length of the greater sciatic notch (Schutkowski 1989).
22d	depth of the greater sciatic notch (Schutkowski 1989).
23a	length of the ischium.
23b	width of the ischium.
24a	length of the pubis.
25a	diaphyseal length of the humerus.
25b	medio-lateral width of the humeral distal diaphysis.
25c	mid-diaphyseal circumference of the humerus (Anderson unpublished).
25d	mid-diaphyseal maximum diameter of the humerus (Bass 1987: 147-8).
25e	mid-diaphyseal minimum diameter of the humerus (Bass 1987: 147-8).
25f	a-p width of the humeral distal diaphysis (Anderson unpublished).
25g	medio-lateral width of the humeral proximal diaphysis (Anderson unpublished).
25h	a-p width of the humeral proximal diaphysis (Anderson unpublished).
26a	diaphyseal length of the ulna.
27a	diaphyseal length of the radius.
28a	diaphyseal length of the femur.
28b	medio-lateral width of the distal femoral diaphysis.
28c	mid-diaphyseal circumference of the femur (Bass 1987: 212-13).
28d	mid-diaphyseal a-p diameter of the femur (Bass 1987: 212-13).
28e	mid-diaphyseal transverse diameter of the femur (Bass 1987: 212-13).
28f	a-p width of the femoral distal diaphysis (Anderson unpublished).
28g	medio-lateral width of the femoral proximal diaphysis (Anderson unpublished).
28h	a-p width of the femoral proximal diaphysis (Anderson unpublished).
29a	diaphyseal length of the tibia.
29b	nutrient-foramen a-p diameter of the tibia (Bass 1987: 233).
29c	nutrient-foramen transverse diameter of the tibia (Bass 1987: 233).
29d	medio-lateral width of the tibial proximal diaphysis (Anderson unpublished).
29e	a-p width of the tibial proximal diaphysis (Anderson unpublished).
29f	medio-lateral width of the tibial distal diaphysis (Anderson unpublished).
29g	a-p width of the tibial distal diaphysis (Anderson unpublished).
30a	diaphyseal length of the fibula.
31a	length of the vertebral arch of the atlas.

32a	length of the vertebral arch of the axis.
33a	diaphyseal length of the first metacarpal.
34a	diaphyseal length of the first metatarsal.
35a	length of the malleus.
36a	length of the incus.
36b	width of the incus.
37a	length of the incus.
37b	width of the incus.

Unless otherwise stated the post-cranial metrics are based on the definitions in Fazekas & Kósa (1978); 22c,d (Schutkowski 1989); 25d,e; 28c,d,e; 29b,c (Bass,1987) or 25c,f,g,h; 28,f,g,h; 29d,e,f,g (Anderson, unpub). The latter are defined below:

Mid-diaphyseal circumference taken with a narrow tape at the mid-diaphysis (25c); maximum a-p and medio-lateral widths taken with a sliding calliper at the border of the proximal (25f; 28f; 29d,e) or distal (25g,h; 28g,h; 29f,g) diaphyseal surface.

APPENDIX THREE

BONE QUANTIFICATION AND MEASUREMENT

Element	*Equus* horse	*Bos* cattle	*Ovicaprid* sheep/goat	*Sus* pig	*Cervid* deer	*Canid* dog
Scapula	1	6		1		
Phumerus		9	1	1		
Dhumerus		11	2	1		
Pradius		7	7			
Dradius		4	7	1		
Ulna		3	1			1
Pmetacarpal	2	4	4			
Dmetacarpal	2	3	4			
Pelvis		8	1	1		
Pfemer		4	4	1		
Dfemer		2	3	1		
Ptibia		9	14			
Dtibia		8	14			
Pmetatarsal	1	6	11		1	
Dmetatarsal	1	5	11		1	
Astragulus	1		1			
Calcaneum		3	1			
Phalanx1		1	2	1		
Phalanx2	1					
Phalanx3	1					
Mandible		5	2	1		
Teeth	4	4	6	2		
Horn core		1	1			
Pmetapodial		1	2	1		
Dmetapodial		1	3	1		
Atlas		1	1	1		
Axis		2				
Total	**14**	**108**	**102**	**13**	**2**	**1**
Percentage	5.8	45	42.5	5.4	0.8	0.4

Table 3.1: *Animal bone: Silverstone 2, species by element.*

Key: P = proximal; D = distal.

Element	*Equus* horse	*Bos* cattle	*Ovicaprid* sheep/goat	*Sus* pig	*Canid* dog	*Ovic/Capreolus* sheep/goat/roe
Scapula		4				
Phumerus		9	2	1		
Dhumerus		12	5	3		
Pradius	1	19	11			
Dradius	1	13	10			
Ulna		2		1		
PmetaCarpal	1	4	6			
DmetaCarpal	1	6	6			
Pelvis		3	2	1		
Pfemer	2	4	7			
Dfemer	2	6	7			
Ptibia	1	9	23	2		
Dtibia	1	12	23	2		
Astragulas		5				
Calcanuem		1	1			
Pmetatarsal		8	10			
Dmetatarsal		8	10			
Phalanx1	1	1				
Phalanx2		3				
Phalanx3		2				
Horn core		3	1			
Mandible		6	13		1	1
Teeth	1	9	1	6		
Pmetapodial		1	3			
Dmetapodial	1	1	4			
Atlas		1				
Total	**13**	**152**	**145**	**17**	**1**	**1**
Percentage	3.9	46.2	44	5.1	0.3	0.3

Table 3.2: Animal bone: Silverstone 3, species by element.

Key: P = proximal; D = distal; Ovic/Capreolus = Ovicaprid/Capreolus capreolus.

Element	*Equus* horse	*Bos* cattle	*Ovicaprid* sheep/goat	*Sus* pig	*Cervid* deer	*Canid* dog	*Ovic/Capreolus* sheep/goat/roe
Scapula		2	7	3			1
Phumerus	1	5	11	2			
Dhumerus	1	10	13	5			
Pradius	3	14	37				3
Dradius	3	13	38				3
Ulna		1	2	3			1
Pmetacarpal	4	8	12		1		
Dmetacarpal	3	6	12		1		
Pelvis		7	4				1
Pfemer		7	11	2			
Dfemer		6	10	2			1
Ptibia	2	15	48	6	1	2	4
Dtibia	3	14	49	7	1	1	4
Pmetatarsal		4	34				2
Dmetatarsal		4	33				2
Astragulus		3	2				
Calcanuem		5	5	3			
Phalanx1		5		1			
Phalanx2		3					
Phalanx3		1			1		
Mandible	1	6	26	6		1	
Teeth	8	4	6				
Horn core		3	3				
Pmetapodial		2	6	2			6
Dmetapodial		3	6	1			6
Atlas				1			
Axis		1					
Total	**29**	**152**	**375**	**52**	**5**	**4**	**34**
Percentage	4.45	23.3	57.6	7.9	0.6	0.6	5.2

Table 3.3: *Animal bone: Silverstone Fields Farm, species by element.*

Key: P = proximal; D = distal; Ovic/Capreolus = Ovicaprid/Capreolus capreolus.

Element	*Equus* horse	*Bos* cattle	*Ovicaprid* sheep/goat	*Sus* pig	*Canid* dog
Scapula		2			
Phumerus		1		1	
Dhumerus		1		1	
Pradius			5		
Dradius			5		
Pmetacarpal			3		
Dmetacarpal			3		
Pelvis		4			
Pfemer		2			
Dfemer		2			
Ptibia		1			
Dtibia		1			
Pmetatarsal		2			
Dmetatarsal		2			
Calcaneum		1			
Phalanx1		1			
Mandible	5	4	1		1
Horn core			1		
Atlas				1	
Total	**5**	**24**	**18**	**3**	**1**
Percentage	9.8	47	35.3	5.8	2

Table 3.4: *Animal bone:Brackley Hatch 4, species by element.*

Key: P = proximal; D = distal.

Element	*Equus* horse	*Bos* cattle	*Ovicaprid* sheep/goat	*Sus* pig	*Cervid* deer	*Canid* dog	*Ovic/Capreolus* sheep/goat/roe
Scapula		5					
Phumerus		2		3			
Dhumerus		5		2			
Pradius		17					
Dradius		9	4				
Ulna		4	4				
Pmetacarpal	1	6	3				
Dmetacarpal		5	3				
Pelvis	1	9					
Pfemer		3	2	1			
Dfemer		2	2	1			
Ptibia	1	3	5			1	1
Dtibia	1	5	5			1	1
Calcaneum		3					
Pmetatarsal	1	6	2				
Dmetatarsal	1	5	1				
Phalanx1		2					
Pmetapodial		1	1		1		
Dmetapodial		3	1		1		
Horn core		5					1
Mandible		10	3	5		1	
Teeth	11	6	3	2			
Total	**17**	**116**	**39**	**14**		**3**	**3**
Percentage	8.76	59.7	20	7.2	1.3	1.5	1.5

Table 3.5: *Animal bone: Biddlesdon Road Bridge, species by element.*

Key: P = proximal; D = distal; Ovic/Capreolus = Ovicaprid/Capreolus capreolus.

Context/feature	Wear stage	Approximate age
404	I	Senile
1129/ ditch 7, structure 1	D	18-30 months
1168	I	Senile
1254	G	Adult
1315	I	Senile
1326/ ditch 7, structure 1	I	Senile

Table 3.6: *Toothwear for cattle from Biddlesden Road Bridge.*

Context/feature	Wear stage	Approximate age
1002 / ditch 2010	C	6-12 months
1020 / enclosure ditch 2057	G	4-6 years
1036 / enclosure ditch 2051	E	2-3 years
1036 / enclosure ditch 2051	H	6-8 years
1104	I	8-10 years
1264	F	3-4 years

Table 3.7: *Toothwear for sheep/goat from Silverstone 3.*

Context/feature	Wearstage	Approximate age
15	E	2-3 years
15	C-I	6 months-10years
15	C-I	
18	F	3-4years
31 / ditch 107, enclosure 1	D-I	1-10 years
32 / ditch 107, enclosure 1	D	1-2 years
32 / ditch 107, enclosure 1	D-I	1-10 years
33 / ditch 107, enclosure 1	G	4-6 years
41 / ditch 39, enclosure 1	E	2-3years
45 / ditch 44, enclosure 1	C	6 –12 months
54	D-I	1-10 years
54	D-I	
83	E	2-3 years
101 / ditch terminal enclosure 1	C	6-12months
101/ ditch terminal enclosure 1	G	4-6 years
101 / ditch terminal enclosure 1	G	
101 / ditch terminal enclosure 1	D-I	1-10 years
101 /,ditch terminal enclosure 1	D	1-2years
101 / ditch terminal enclosure 1	D	
101 / ditch terminal enclosure 1	C-I	6months-10years
101 / ditch terminal enclosure 1	C-I	
101 / ditch terminal enclosure 1	C-I	
101 / ditch terminal enclosure 1	E-I	2-10years
104 / pit 75	B	2-6 months
104 / pit 75	C-I	6months-10years
104 / pit 75	D	1-2years
144 / pit 142, enclosure 1	G	4-6 years
148 / pit 146	C	6-12 months
148 / pit 146	D-I	1-10 years

Table 3.8: *Toothwear for sheep/goat at Silverstone Fields Farm.*

Measurement	Tibia	Radius
Bp	65.1	69
Sd	33.2	32.9
Bd	54	N/A

Table 3.9: *Measurements from Silverstone Fields Farm cattle skeleton.*

Key: Bp = Greatest breadth of proximal end; Sd = Smallest breadth of diaphysis; Bd = Greatest breadth of distal end.

	Stage 1		Stage 2		Stage 3		Stage 4	
	No.	*%*	*No.*	*%*	*No.*	*%*	*No*	*%*
Fused	13	22.	8	88.8	2	8.3	8	20
Unfused	3		1	11.1	2	8.3	2	2
Indet	42	62.5			20	83.3	30	75

Table 3.10: *Percentage survival for Ovicaprids from Silverstone Fields Farm.*

	Stage 1		Stage 2		Stage 3		Stage 4	
	No	*%*	*No.*	*%*	*No*	*%*	*No*	*%*
Fused	2	13.3	0	0	4	10.3	1	2.4
Unfused	1	5.5	0	0	2	5.1	2	4.8
Indet	15	83.2	0	0	33	84.6	39	92.9

Table 3.11: *Percentage survival for Ovicaprids from Silverstone 3.*

	Stage 1		Stage 2		Stage 3		Stage 4	
	No	*%*	*No*	*%*	*No*	*%*	*No*	*%*
Fused	26	74.3	1	50	4	20	0	0
Unfused	1	2.9	0	0	0	0	2	9
Indet	8	22.8	1	50	16	80	20	91

Table 3.12: *Percentage survival for cattle from Biddlesdon Road Bridge.*

Stage	Elements	Approx age *(ovicaprids)*	Approx age *(Bos)*
1	Scapula Distal humerus Proximal radius Pelvis	6-12 months	7-10months
2	Phalanx1 Phalanx2	13-16 months	18 months
3	Distal tibia Distal metacarpal Distal metatarsal	18-28 months	18-28months
4	Proximal humerus Distal radius Ulna Proximal femur Proximal tibia	30-42 months	30-42 months

Table 3.13: *Bone elements used in defining fusion stages and ages at which fusion occurs.*

BIBLIOGRAPHY

Anderson, A S, and Anderson, A C, 1981 *Roman Pottery Research in Britain and North-west Europe*, British Archaeological Reports, International Series, **123**, Oxford.

Anderson, S, and Boyle, K, (eds) 1996 *Ritual Treatment of human and animal remains*, Proceedings of the first meeting of the Osteoarchaeological Research Group held in Cambridge on 8th October 1994, Oxbow Books.

Anderson, T, and Andrews, J, (n d) *The Roman burials at Monkton, Mount Pleasant, Kent*, archive report.

Ashcroft, D, 1934 Report on the excavation of a Romano-British villa at Saunderton, Buckinghamshire, *Records of Buckinghamshire* 13, 398-426.

Atkins, R, Parry, S, Holmes, M, and Meadows, I, 2001 Excavations of Iron Age settlements at Sywell Aerodrome (1996) and at Ecton (1992-3), *Northamptonshire Archaeol*, **29**, 43-72.

Atkins, R, and Mudd, A, 2003 An Iron Age and Romano-British settlement at Prickwillow Road, Ely, Cambridgeshire: Excavations 1999-2000, *Proceedings Cambridgeshire Antiq. Soc*, **92**.

Audouy, M, and Sharman, T, 1993 *A43 Trunk Road Whitfield Turn to Brackley Hatch Dualling: Initial Archaeological Evaluation*, Northamptonshire Archaeology Report.

Baker, J, and Brothwell, D, 1980 *Animal Diseases in Archaeology*, London: Academic Press.

Bamford, H M, 1985 *Briar Hill Excavations, 1974-78*, Northampton Development Corporation, Archaeol Monog, **3**.

Barber, J, 1985 The Pit Alignment at Eskbank Nurseries, *Proceedings Prehistoric Soc*, **51**, 149-66.

Barrett, J, 1994 *Fragments from Antiquity*, Oxford: Blackwell.

Bass, W M, 1987 *Human Osteology: A Laboratory and Field Manual of the Human Skeleton*, 3rd ed Special Publication, **2**, Missouri Archaeol Soc, Columbia.

Bassett, S, (ed) 1995 *Death in Towns Urban Responses to the Dying and the Dead, 100-1600*, Leicester University Press.

Bates, S, 2000 Excavations at Quidney Farm, Saham Tony, Norfolk, 1995, *Britannia, 31*.

Bellamy, B, Jackson, D A, and Johnston, G, 2000-1 Early Iron Smelting in the Rockingham Forest Area: a Survey of the Evidence, *Northamptonshire Archaeol*., **29**, 103-128.

Bidwell, P T, and Croom, A, 1999 The Camulodunum/ Colchester type series, in R Symonds and S Wade, 468-87.

Binford, L, 1978 *Nunamuit Ethnoarchaeology*, New York: Academic Press.

Binford, L, 1981 *Bones: Ancient man and modern myths*, New York: Academic Press.

Birbeck, V, 2001 Excavations at Watchfield, Shrivenham, Oxfordshire, 1998, *Oxoniensia*, **66**.

Blinkhorn, P, and Jackson, D, 2003 The Pottery, in A Thomas and D Enright, 32-42.

Blore, Fm 1996 *A Report on the Archaeological Evaluation undertaken at Croughton Roman Settlement, Northamptonshire*, Central Archaeology Service Project Report, **492**.

Boardman, S, and Jones, G, 1990 Experiments on the Effects of Charring on Cereal Plant Components, *Journal Archaeol Science*, **17**, 1-11.

Boswell, J, 1988 *The Kindness of Strangers The Abandonment of Children in Western Europe from Late Antiquity to the Renaissance*, Penguin: London.

Boucher, B J, 1955 Sex differences in the foetal sciatic notch, *Journal of Forensic Medicine*, **2**, 51-54.

Boucher, B J, 1957 Sex differences in the foetal pelvis, *American Journal of Physical Anthropology*, **15**, 581-600.

Brain, C, 1981 *The Hunters or the hunted?* Chicago: University of Chicago Press.

Brothwell, D, and Higgs, E, (eds) 1969 *Science in Archaeology*,. London Thames and Hudson.

Brown, A, 1994 Romano-British shell-gritted pottery and the manufacturing site at Harrold, Beds, *Bedfordshire Archaeol*, **21**, 19-107.

Brown, A E, and Woodfield, C, with Mynard, D C, 1983 Excavations at Towcester, Northamptonshire: the Alchester Road Suburb, *Northamptonshire Archaeol*, **18**, 43-140.

BUFAU 1998 *The excavation of an Iron Age Settlement at Covert Farm (DIRFT East), Crick, Northamptonshire*.

Post excavation assessment and updated research design, Birmingham University Field Archaeology Unit, Project, **468**.

Bunch, B, and Corder, P, 1954 A Romano-British kiln at Weston Favell, near Northampton, *Antiq. Journal,* **34**, 218-24.

Campbell, G, 2000 Plant utilisation: the evidence from charred plant remains, in B Cunliffe, 45-59.

Carr, G, and Knusel, C, 1997 The ritual framework of excarnation by exposure as the mortuary practice of the early and middle Iron Ages of central southern Britain, in A Gwilt and C Haselgrove (eds), 167-173.

Carruthers, W J, 1989 for 1988 Mystery object no. 2 – animal, mineral or vegetable? *Circaea,* **6** (1), 20.

Carruthers, W J, 1995 Plant remains; Medieval plant remains, in P J Fasham *et al*, 56-60, 139-42.

Carruthers, W J 2000 The mineralised plant remains, in A J Lawson and C J Gingell, 72-84, 91-95.

Carruthers, Wendy J 2003 The charred plant remains, in R Atkins and A Mudd, 5-55.

Chapman, A 1985 Crick, *South Midlands Archaeol,* **25**, 37-9, Council British Archaeol, South Midlands Group.

Chapman, A, 1999 *An Archaeological Resource Assessment of the Neolithic and Bronze Age in Northamptonshire,* East Midlands Research Frameworks http:/www.le.ac.uk/archaeology/pdf_files/14nhneba.pdf.

Chapman, A, 2000-01 Excavation of an Iron Age Settlement and Middle Saxon cemetery at Great Houghton, Northampton, *Northamptonshire Archaeol.* **29**, 1-42.

Chapman, A, forthcoming A Bronze Age Barrow Cemetery and Iron Age Pit Alignments and Enclosures at Gayhurst, Buckinghamshire, 1998-2000, *Records of Buckinghamshire.*

Clarke, G, 1979 *The Roman cemetery at Lankhills,* Winchester Studies, **3**, pre-Roman and Roman Winchester, Part II, Oxford.

Clay, P, 2002 *The Prehistory of the East Midlands Claylands,* Leicester Archaeology Monog, **9**

Cocks, A H, 1921 A Romano-British homestead in the Hambleden valley, Bucks, *Archaeologia,* **71**, 141-198.

Collis, J, 1977a Pre-Roman burial rites in North-Western Europe, in R Reece (ed), 1-13.

Collis, J, 1977b Owslebury (Hants) and the problem of burials on rural settlements, in R Reece (ed), 26-34.

Condron, F 1997 Iron production in Leicestershire, Rutland and Northamptonshire in antiquity, *Transactions Leicestershire Archaeol Historical Soc,* **71**, 1-18.

Cool, H E M, and Philo, C, 1998 *Roman Castleford, Excavations 1974-1985, Volume 1, The Small Finds,* Yorkshire Archaeology, **4**, Exeter.

Cowgill, J, in prep *An Iron Age and Romano-British smelting site at Creeton Quarry, Lincolnshire and a survey of local smelting sites.*

Cox, M, 1989 *The Human Bones from Ancaster,* Ancient Monuments Laboratory, Historic Buildings and Monuments Commission for England, AML Report, **93/89**.

Crew, P, 1986 Bryn y Castell Hillfort – a Late Prehistoric Iron Working Settlement in north-west Wales, in B G Scott, and H Cleere (eds), 91-99.

Crew, P 1991 The experimental production of prehistoric bar iron, *Journal of the Historical Metallurgy Society,* **25.1(1)**, 21-36.

Crew, P and Salter, C J 1997 High phosphorus steel from experimentally smelted bog-iron ore, in P Crew and S Crew, (eds), 83-84.

Crew, P and Crew, S (eds) 1997 *Abstracts of the International Conference, Early Ironworking in Europe: archaeology and experiment,* Plas Tan y Bwlch Occasional Paper, Maentwrog.

Cromarty, A M, Foreman, S, and Murray, P, 1999 The excavation of a Late Iron Age enclosed settlement at Bicester Fields Farm, Bicester, Oxon, *Oxoniensia,* **64**, 153-233.

Cumberpatch, C G, and Blinkhorn, P W, (eds) 1997 *Not so much a pot, more a way of life,* Oxbow Monog, **83**.

Cunliffe B 1984 *Danebury: an Iron Age Hillfort in Hampshire. Vol. 2:The Excavations, 1969-78: the finds,* Council British Archaeology Research Report, British Series, **52**.

Cunliffe, B, 1985 *Excavations at Porchester Castle. volume I: Roman,* Society of Antiquaries Research Report, **22**.

Cunliffe, B W, 1995 *Iron Age Britain,* London: Batsford.

Cunliffe, B, 2000 *The Danebury Environs Programme The prehistory of a Wessex Landscape Volume 1: Introduction,* English Heritage and Oxford University Committee for Archaeology Monog, **48**, Oxford: Institute of Archaeology.

Cunliffe, B W, and Miles, D, (eds) 1984 *Aspects of the Iron Age in Central Southern Britain,* Oxford University Community Archaeol, Monog, **2**, Oxford.

Cunliffe, B, and Poole, C, 1991 *Danebury, an Iron Age Hillfort in Hampshire. Vol. 5 The Excavations 1979-88: the finds,* Council British Archaeol Research Reports, **73**.

Dawson, M, 2000 The Ouse Valley in the Iron Age and Roman periods: a landscape in transition, in M Dawson (ed), 107-130.

Dawson, M, (ed) 2000 *Prehistoric, Roman and post-Roman landscapes of the Great Ouse Valley,* Council British Archaeol Research Reports, **119**.

Deighton, K, 2001 The Animal Bone, in A Chapman, 26-28.

Deighton, K 2002 The Animal Bone, in NA 2002.

Dix, B, and Jackson, D A, 1989 Some Late-Iron Age Defended Enclosures in Northamptonshire, in A Gibson (ed), 158-179.

Dolby, M 1969 Wormersley, in E R Radley, 237-249.

Downes, J, and Pollard, T, (eds) 1999 *The Loved Body's Corruption: Archaeological Contributions to the Study of Human Society,* Cruithne Press, Glasgow.

Ehrenreich, R M, 1985 *Trade, Technology and the Ironworking Community in the Iron Age of Southern Britain,* British Archaeol Reports British Series, **144**.

Ehrenreich, R M, 1994 Ironworking in Iron Age Wessex, in A Fitzpatrick and E Morris (eds).

Evans, C, 2003 *Power and Island Communities: Excavations at the Wardy Hill Ringwork, Coveney, Ely,* East Anglian Archaeol. Monog, **103**.

Farwell, D E, and Molleson, T I, 1993 *Excavations at Poundbury 1966-80 volume II: The Cemeteries,* Dorset Natural History and Archaeol Soc Monog, **11**, Dorchester.

Fasham, P J, and G Keevill, with Coe, D, 1995 *Brighton Hill South: an Iron Age Farmstead and Deserted Medieval Village in Hampshire,* Wessex Archaeol Report, **7**.

Fazekas, I G, and Kósa, F, 1978 *Forensic Fetal Osteology,* Akadémiai Kiadó, Budapest.

Fell, C I, 1936 The Hunsbury Hill-Fort, Northants: a new survey of the material, *Archaeol Journal,* **93**, 57-100.

Field, D 1982 Animal bones from areas 1 and 2, in D A Jackson, 19.

Field, D 1983 The animal bone, in D A Jackson, 17-32.

Fieller, N R J, Gilbertson, D D, and Ralph, N G A, (eds) 1985 *Palaeobiological investigations,* British Archaeology Reports, International Series, **266**, Oxford.

Fitzpatrick, A, and Morris, E, (eds) 1994 *The Iron Age in Wessex: recent trends,* Assoc. Française D'Etude de l'Age du Fer/Wessex Archaeology.

Foard, G, 1999 *An Archaeological Resource Assessment of Anglo-Saxon Northamptonshire (400-1066),* East Midlands Research Frameworks, http:/www.le.ac. uk/archaeology/pdf_files/29nhas.pdf.

Foard, G, 2001 Medieval Woodland, Agriculture and Industry in Rockingham Forest, Northamptonshire, *Medieval Archaeol,* **45**, 41-95.

Ford, S, and Taylor, K, 2001 Iron Age and Roman settlements with prehistoric and saxon features at Fenny Lock, Milton Keynes, Buckinghamshire, *Records of Buckinghamshire,* **41**, 79-123.

Foster, P, 1994 The Brigstock Survey: an intensive field survey on upland Boulder Clay in Northamptonshire, in M Parker Pearson and T Schadla-Hall, 46-50.

Foundations Archaeology 1999 Crick Hotel Site Northamptonshire: Post Excavation Assessment report.

Frere, S S, 1984 Roman Britain in 1983. I. Sites explored, *Britannia,* **14**, 266-332.

Frere, S S, 1988 Roman Britain in 1987. I. Sites explored, *Britannia,* **19**, 267-338.

Gale, R, 1991-93 Identification of charcoal, in S J Lobb, and E L Morris, microfiche M2: E13-F9.

Gale, R, 2000 Charcoal, in S Bates, 231-3.

Gale, R, and Cutler, D, 2000 *Plants in Archaeology,* Westbury and Royal Botanic Gardens, Kew.

Gale, R, 2001 Charcoal, in V Birbeck, 284-7.

Gibson, A, (ed) 1989 *Midlands Prehistory: some recent and current researches into the prehistory of central England,* British Archaeology Reports British Series, **204**.

Gilbert-Barnes, E, (ed) 1997 *Potter's Pathology of the Fetus and Infant,* St Louis: Mosby.

Gilmore, F, 1969 The animal and human skeletal remains, in P J Woods, 43-56.

Godwin, H, 1956 The History of the British Flora, Cambridge.

Godwin, Sir H, 1975 *History of the British Flora,* Cambridge University Press.

Goodburn, R, 1979 Roman Britain in 1978: I. Sites Explored, *Britannia,* **10**, 267-338.

Grant, A, 1984 Animal husbandry in Wessex and the Thames Valley, in B W Cunliffe and D Miles (eds), 102-19.

Green, Miranda Aldhouse 2001 *Dying for the Gods: Human Sacrifice in Iron Age and Roman Europe,* Tempus.

Greig, J R A, 1991 The British Isles, in W van Zeist *et al,* 299-334.

Guido, M, 1978 *The glass beads of the prehistoric and Roman periods in Britain and Ireland,* Soc of Antiq Research Reports, **35**, London: Thames and Hudson.

Gwilt, A, 1997 Popular practices from material culture: a case study of the Iron Age settlement at Wakerley, in Gwilt, A and Haselgrove, C (eds), 153-66.

Gwilt, A, and Haselgrove, C, (eds) 1997 *Reconstructing Iron Age Societies: New Approaches to the British Iron Age,* Oxbow Monog, **71**.

Hains, B A, and Horton, A, 1969 *British Regional Geology: Central Region,* London: HMSO.

Halkon, P, 1997 Fieldwork on early iron working sites in East Yorkshire, *Journal Historical Metallurgy Society,* **31**, 12-16.

Hall, D N, 1982 The countryside of the SE Midlands and Cambridgeshire, in D Miles (ed), 337-50.

Hall, D N, 2000 *Forest Enterprise Woodlands in Northamptonshire: Whittlewood Forest and Other Woods. Archaeological Survey Part 3,* Forest Enterprise and Northamptonshire County Council unpub report.

Halstead, P, 1985 A study of mandibular teeth from Romano-British contexts at Maxey, *East Anglian Archaeol,* **27,** 219-24.

Hambleton, E, 1999 *Animal Husbandry Regimes in Iron Age Britain,* British Archaeological Reports, British Series, **282,** Oxford: Archaeopress.

Harcourt, R A, 1975 Appendix 2: The Animal Bones, in D A Jackson, 88-89.

Harding, D, 1975 The Pottery, in D Jackson, 69-84.

Helbaek, H, 1953 Early crops in Southern England, *Proceedings Prehistoric Soc,* **18,** 194-233.

Hill, J D, 1996 The identification of ritual deposits of animal bone. A general perspective from a specific study of 'special animal deposits' from the Southern English Iron Age, in S Anderson and K Boyle (eds), 17-32.

Hill, M O, Mountford, J O, Roy, D B, and Bunce, R G H, 1999 *Ellenberg's indicator values for British plants,* ECOFACT , Volume **2:** Technical Annex, HMSO.

Hillman, G 1981 Reconstructing Crop Husbandry Practices from Charred Remains of Crops, in R Mercer (ed).

Holbrook, N, Watts, M, and Bateman, C, 2002 Finmere: an Iron Age settlement in north-east Oxfordshire, *Current Archaeology,* **177,** Vol **15** No. **9,** 394.

Holcomb, S M C, and Konigsberg, L W, 1995 Statistical study of sexual dimorphism in the human fetal sciatic notch, *American Journal of Physical Anthropology,* **97,** 113-125.

Holden, T G, 1986 Preliminary report on the detailed analyses of the macroscopic remains from the gut of Lindow Man, in I M Stead *et al,* 116-125.

Hooper, B, 1985 The human bones, in B Cunliffe, 375-377.

Hubbard, R N L B, 1975 Assessing the Botanical Components of Human Paleo-Economies, *Bulletin Institute Archaeol,* **12,** 197-205.

Jackson, D A, 1974 Two New Pit Alignments and a Hoard of Currency Bars from Northamptonshire, *Northamptonshire Archaeol,* **9,** 13-46.

Jackson, D A, 1975 An Iron Age site at Twywell, Northamptonshire, *Northamptonshire Archaeol,* **10,** 31-93.

Jackson, D A, 1977 Further excavations at Aldwincle, Northamptonshire, 1969-71, *Northamptonshire Archaeol,* **12,** 9-54.

Jackson, D A, 1978 A late Bronze Age-early Iron Age vessel from a pit alignment at Ringstead, Northants, *Northants Archaeol,* **13,** 168.

Jackson, D A, 1979 Roman Iron Working at Bulwick and Gretton, *Northamptonshire Archaeol,* **14,** 31-7.

Jackson, D A, 1981 Archaeology at an ironstone quarry in the Harringworth-Wakerley area, 1968-79, *Northamptonshire Archaeol,* **16,** 14-33.

Jackson, D A, 1982 Great Oakley and other Iron Age Sites in the Corby Area, *Northamptonshire Archaeol,* **17,** 3-23.

Jackson, D A, 1983 The excavation of an Iron Age site at Brigstock, Northants 1979-81, *Northamptonshire Archaeol,* **18,** 7-32.

Jackson, D A, 1988-9 An Iron Age Enclosure at Wootton Hill Farm, Northampton, *Northamptonshire Archaeol,* **22,** 2-21.

Jackson, D A, 1993-4a Excavation of the hillfort defences at Hunsbury, Northampton, in 1952 and 1988, *Northamptonshire Archaeol,* **25,** 5-20.

Jackson, D A, 1993-4b Iron Age and Anglo-Saxon Settlement and Activity Around the Hunsbury Hillfort, Northampton, *Northamptonshire Archaeol,* **25,** 35-46.

Jackson, D A, Pacitto, A L, Tylecote, R F, and Biek, L, 1978 The iron-working features, in Jackson D A and Ambrose T M.

Jackson, D A and Ambrose, T M 1978 Excavations at Wakerley, Northants, 1972-75, *Britannia,* **9,** 115-288.

Jackson, D A, and Dix, B, 1986-7 Late Iron Age and Roman settlement at Weekley, Northants, *Northamptonshire Archaeol,* **21,** 41-94.

Jackson, D A, and Knight, D, 1985 An Early Iron Age and Beaker site near Gretton, Northamptonshire, *Northamptonshire Archaeol,* **20,** 67-86.

Johnston, D E, 1972 A Roman building at Chalk, near Gravesend, *Britannia,* **3,** 112-148.

Jones, R, 1978 The animal bones, in D A Jackson and T M Ambrose, 235-241.

Jones, R, 2003 *The Whittlewood Forest Project,* http://www.le.ac.uk/elh/whittlewood/index.htm.

Kalousek, D K, and Gilbert-Barnes, E, 1997 Causes of stillbirth and neonatal death, in E Gilbert-Barnes (ed), 128-162.

Kenyon, K M, 1938 Excavations at Viroconicum, 1936-7, *Archaeologia,* **88,** 175-227.

Kerney, M P, 1999 *Atlas of the land and freshwater molluscs of Britain and Ireland,* Colchester: Harley Books.

Kidd, A, 1999 *Northamptonshire: The First Millennium BC, A Resource Assessment,* East Midlands Regional Research Frameworks http://www.le.ac.uk/archaeology/pdf_files/19nh1stmill.pdf.

Kjølbye-Biddle, B, 1995 Dispersal or concentration: the disposal of the Winchester dead over 2000 years, in S Bassett (ed).

Knight, D, 1984 *Late Bronze Age and Iron Age Settlement in the Nene and Great Ouse Basins*, British Archaeol Reports, British Series, **130**.

Knight, D, 1986-7 An Iron Age Hillfort at Castle Yard, Farthingstone, Northamptonshire, *Northamptonshire Archaeol,* **21**, 31-40.

Knight, D, 1993 Late Bronze Age and Iron Age pottery from Pennyland and Hartigans, in R J Williams, 219-38.

Lawson, A J, and Gingell, C J, 2000 *Potterne 1982-5: animal husbandry in later prehistoric Wiltshire*, Wessex Archaeol Report, **17**.

Leech, R, 1981 The excavation of a Romano-British farmstead and cemetery on Bradley Hill, Somerton, Somerset, *Britannia,* **12**, 177-252.

Levine, M, 1982 The use of crown height measurements and eruption sequences to age horse teeth, in B Wilson *et al*, 155-204.

Lewis, C, Mitchell-Fox, P, and Dyer, C, 1997 *Village, Hamlet and Field: Changing medieval settlements in central England,* Manchester University Press.

Lobb, S J, and Morris, E L, 1991-93 *Investigation of Bronze Age and Iron Age features at Riseley Farm, Swallowfield,* Berkshire Archaeol Journal, **74.**

Manning, W H, 1985 *Catalogue of the Romano-British Iron Tools, Fittings and Weapons in the British Museum,* British Museum Publications.

Margary, I, 1973 *Roman Roads of Britain,* 3 edn, London.

Marney, P T, 1989 *Roman and Belgic Pottery from excavations in Milton Keynes 1972-82,* Buckinghamshire Archaeol Soc Monog, **2.**

Marren, P, 1992 *The Wild Woods: a Regional Guide to Britain's Ancient Woodland,* David and Charles.

Masters, P, and Shaw, M, 1997 *A43 Silverstone Bypass Evaluation: Stage 2. Fieldwalking and Geophysical Surveys, November 1996 – January 1997,* Northamptonshire Archaeology Report, March 1997.

Mays, S, 1993 Infanticide in Roman Britain, *Antiquity,* **67**, 883-888.

Meadows, I, 1995 Wollaston, *South Midlands Archaeol,* **25**, 41-44, Council British Archaeol, South Midlands Group.

Mercer, R, (ed) 1981 *Farming Practice in British Prehistory,* Edinburgh University Press.

Miles, D, (ed) 1982 *The Romano-British Countryside,* British Archaeology Reports, British Series, **103**, 337-50.

Millett, M, 1990 *The Romanization of Britain: an essay in archaeological interpretation,* Cambridge University Press.

Mitchell, A, 1974 *A Field Guide to the Trees of Britain and Northern Europe,* London: Collins.

Mittler, D M, and Sheridan, S G, 1992 Sex determination in subadults using auricular surface morphology: a forensic science perspective, *Journal of Forensic Science,* **37**, 1068-1075.

Moffett, L C, 1987 *The macro-botanical evidence from Late Saxon and Early Medieval Stafford,* Ancient Monuments Laboratory, Historic Buildings and Monuments Commission for England, AML Rep. **169/87.**

Molleson, T I, 1993 The human remains, in D E Farwell and T I Molleson, 142-214.

Morton, G R, and Wingrove, J, 1969 The constitution of Bloomery slags: Part 1: Roman, *Journal of the Iron and Steel Institute,* **207**, 1556-1564.

Morton, G R, and Wingrove, J, 1972 The constitution of Bloomery slags: Part II: Medieval, *Journal of the Iron and Steel Institute,* **210**, 478-488.

Mudd, A, 1993 Excavations at Whitehouse Road, Oxford, 1992, *Oxoniensia,* **58**, 33-85.

NA 2000a *A43 Road Improvement: Silverstone and Brackley Hatch Sections. Archaeological Evaluations: Stage 3, January – March 2000,* Northamptonshire Archaeology Report, April 2000.

NA 2000b *A43 Road Improvement: Silverstone Sites SL1 and SL3. Archaeological Evaluations: Stage 3, September 2000,* Northamptonshire Archaeology Report, September 2000.

NA 2000c *A43 Road Improvement: Biddlesden Road Bridge, Syresham. Archaeological Evaluations: Stage 3, September 2000,* Northamptonshire Archaeology Report, October 2000.

NA 2000d *A43 Road Improvement: Juniper Hill, Evenley, Northamptonshire. Archaeological Evaluations : Stage 3, September 2000,* Northamptonshire Archaeology Report, October 2000.

NA 2001a *A43 Towcester to M40 Dualling Project. Soil Disposal and Landscaping Areas. Archaeological Desk-Based Assessment* (2 Vols.), Northamptonshire Archaeology Report, March 2001.

NA 2001b *A43 Towcester to M40 Dualling Project. Soil Disposal and Landscaping Areas. Archaeological Evaluation at Area G (Pimlico), Syresham, Northamptonshire,* Northamptonshire Archaeology Report, July 2001.

NA 2001c *A43 Towcester to M40 Dualling Project. Soil Disposal and Landscaping Areas. Archaeological Evaluation at Shacks Barn Farm, Silverstone, Northamptonshire,* Northamptonshire Archaeology Report, April 2001.

NA 2001d *A43 M40 to Towcester Dualling. Proposed Drainage Outfall: Tusmore Park DMV (SAM 103) Proposed Mitigation Strategy,* Northamptonshire Archaeology Report, rev. 18 May 2001.

NA 2002 *A43 Towcester to M40 Dualling Project: Northamptonshire and Oxfordshire. Post-Excavation Assessment and Updated Project Design,* Northamptonshire Archaeology Report, February 2002.

NA 2003 *An archaeological trial excavation at Earls Barton Quarry Western Extension, Northamptonshire,* Northamptonshire Archaeology unpublished report, May 2003.

NH 2000 *A43 Road Improvement Scheme: Silverstone and Brackley Hatch Sections. Brief for Archaeological Recording Action,* Northamptonshire Heritage, Northamptonshire County Council, May 2000.

Oliver, M, and Applin, B, 1978 Excavations at Ructstalls Hill, Basingstoke, *Proceedings of the Hampshire Field Club and Archaeological Society,* **35**, 41-92.

Orton, C, Tyers, P, and Vince, A G, 1993 *Pottery in archaeology,* Cambridge Manuals in Archaeology, Cambridge University Press.

Oswald, A, 1997 A doorway on the past: practical and mystic concerns in the orientation of roundhouse doorways, in A Gwilt and C Haselgrove (eds), 87-95.

Palmer, C, and Jones, M, 1991 Plant resources, in N M Sharples, 129-139.

Parker Pearson, M, and Schadla-Hall, T, 1994 *Looking at the Land. Archaeological Landscapes in Eastern England,* Leicester Museums, Arts and Records Service.

Parry, S J, 2006 *Raunds Area Survey. An archaeological study of the landscape of Raunds, Northamptonshire 1985-94,* Oxbow monog, English Heritage.

Payne, S, 1973 Kill off patterns in sheep and goats: the mandibles from Asvan Kale, *Anatolian Studies,* **23**, 281-303.

PCRG 1997 *The Study of Later Prehistoric Pottery: general policies and guidelines for analysis and publication,* Prehistoric Ceramics Research Group Occasional Papers, **1** and **2**.

Penn, W S, 1960 Springhead: Temples III & IV, *Archaeologia Cantiana,* **74**, 113-40.

Phillips, G, 1999 *An Archaeological Assessment of the Mesolithic in Northamptonshire,* East Midlands Research Frameworks, http://www.le.ac.uk/archaeology/pdf_files/nhmeso.pdf.

Philp, B J, 1966 Ritual burials at Reculver, *Kent Archaeol Review,* **6**, 7-8.

Philpott, R, 1991 *Burial Practices in Roman Britain,* British Archaeological Report, British Series, **219**, Oxford: Tempus Reparatum.

Pliny the Elder, *Historia Naturalis, Book VII, 15,* (trans W H S Jones, 1963 London: Heinemann).

Polizzotti, Greis, G, 2002 *Relations of Production: Social Networks, Social Change and the Organisation of Agriculture in Late Prehistoric Southern Britain,* British Archaeological Reports, British Series, **330**, Oxford.

Price, J, and Cottam, S, 1998 *Romano-British Glass Vessels: a Handbook,* Council British Archaeology, Practical Handbook in Archaeology, **14**, York.

Price, R, and Watts, L, 1980 Rescue excavation at Combe Hay, Somerset 1968-73, *Somerset Archaeol & Natural History,* **124**, 1-50.

Rackham, D J, Giorgi, J A, and Gale, R, 1999 Hatton to Silk Willoughby Gas Pipeline, HWP98 Environmental Archaeology Report, in *Hatton to Silk Willoughby 1050mm Gas Pipeline. Archaeological evaluation, excavation and watching brief,* 2, Network Archaeology Report Ltd, Report, **143**, August 1999.

Rackham, O, 1993 *Trees and Woodland in the British Landscape,* revised edn, London: Dent.

Radley, E R, 1969 The Yorkshire Archaeological Register 1968, *Yorkshire Archaeol Journal,* **42**.

RCHME 1982 *County of Northampton Archaeological Sites, South-West,* **4**, Royal Commission on Historical Monuments, England.

Reece, R, (ed) *Burial in the Roman World,* Council British Archaeology Research Report, **22**.

Reynolds, P J, 1974 Experimental Iron Age Storage Pits: an Interim Report, *Proceedings Prehistoric Soc,* **40**, 118-31.

Reynolds, P J, 1979 *Iron Age Farm: The Butser Experiment,* British Museum Publications Ltd, London.

Reynolds, P J, 1981 Deadstock and Livestock, in R Mercer (ed), 97-122.

Robinson, M, and Wilson, R, 1983 *A Survey of the Environmental Archaeology of the South Midlands,* unpub typescript.

Salter, C J, 1991 Metallurgical aspects of the ironworking debris, in B Cunliffe and C Poole, 412-416.

Salter, C.J, 2002 *Assessment of the metal-working debris from the Biddlesden Road Bridge Site, Syresham, Northamptonshire.* Report for Northamptonshire Archaeology, Northamptonshire County Council.

Sharples, N M, 1991 *Maiden Castle; excavation and field survey 1985-6,* English Heritage Archaeol Report, **19**.

Scheuer, J L, and Black, S, 2000 *Developmental Juvenile Osteology,* London: Academic Press.

Scheuer, J L, Musgrave, J H, and Evans, S P, 1980 The estimation of late fetal and perinatal age from limb bone length by linear and logarithmic regression, *Annals of Human Biology,* **7**, 257-265.

Schmidt, E, 1972 *Atlas of Animal Bones,* London: Elsevier.

Schrufer-Kolb, I, 1999 Roman Iron Production in the East Midlands, England, in S M M Young *et al,* 227-33.

Schutkowski, H, 1989 Beitrag zur Alters- und Geschlechtsdiagnose am Skelett nichterwachsener Individuen, *Anthrop Anzeiger,* **47**, 1-9.

Schutkowski, H, 1993 Sex determination of infant and juvenile skeletons: I morphognostic features, *American Journal of Physical Anthropology,* **90**, 199-205.

Scott, B G, and Cleere, H, (eds) 1986 *The Crafts of the Blacksmith,* Comité pour la Sidérugie ancienne/Ulster Museum, Belfast.

Scott, E, 1999 *The Archaeology of Infancy and Infant Death,* British Archaeol Report, International Series, **819**, Archaeopress, Oxford.

Sellwood, L, 1984 Objects of Iron, in B Cunliffe, 346-71.

Serjeantson, D, and Cohen, A, 1996 *A manual for the identification of Bird bones from Archaeological sites,* revised edn, London: Archetype Publications Ltd.

Silver, I, 1969 The ageing of domestic animals, in D Brothwell and E Higgs (eds), 283-302.

Sim, D, and Ridge, I, 2002 *Iron for the Eagles: The Iron Industry of Roman Britain,* Tempus.

Smith, P, and Kahlia, G, 1992 Identification of infanticide in archaeological sites: a case study from the late Roman-early Byzantine periods at Ashkelon, Israel, *Journal of Archaeol Science,* **19**, 667-675.

Stace, Clive, 1997 *New Flora of the British Isles,* 2 edn, Cambridge University Press.

Stallibrass, S, 1985 Some effects of preservation biases on interpretations of animal bones, in N R J Fieller *et al,* 266, 65-73.

Stead, I, and Rigby, V, 1986 *Baldock: The Excavation of a Roman and Pre-Roman Settlement 1968-72,* Society for the Promotion of Roman Studies, London.

Stead, I M, Bourke, J B, and Brothwell, D, (eds) 1986 *Lindow Man, the body in the bog,* London, British Museum.

Stevens, C J, 2003 An Investigation of Agricultural Consumption and Production Models for Prehistoric and Roman Britain, *Environmental Archaeol,* **8**, 61-76.

Swan, V G, 1984 *The Pottery Kilns of Roman Britain,* Royal Commission on Historical Monuments Supplement Series **5**, London: HMSO.

Symonds, R, and Wade, S, 1999 *Roman pottery from excavations in Colchester, 1971-86,* Colchester Archaeological Report, **10**.

Taylor, J, 1999 *The Roman Period Resource Assessment, Northamptonshire.* East Midlands Archaeological Research Frameworks, http://www.ac.le.uk/archaeology/pdf_files/24nhrom.pdf.

Thomas, A, and Enright, D, 2003 Excavation of an Iron Age Settlement at Wilby Way, Great Doddington, *Northamptonshire Archaeol,* **31**, 15-70.

Thompson, I, 1982 *Grog-tempered 'Belgic' pottery of South-Eastern England,* British Archaeological Reports, British Series, **108**, Oxford.

Tomber, R, and Dore, J, 1998 *The National Roman Reference Collection: a handbook,* English Heritage/Museum of London/British Museum.

Thompson, P, 2001 Animal bone from Sywell, in R Atkins *et al,* 67-8.

Turland, R E, 1977 Towcester, Wood Burcote, *Northamptonshire Archaeol,* **12**, 218-223.

Tutin, T G, Heywood, V H, et al, 1964-80 Flora Europaea, 1-5, Cambridge.

van Beek, G C, 1983 *Dental Morphology an illustrated guide,* 2 edn, (Wright PSG) Bristol.

van Zeist, W, Wasylikowa, K, and Behre, K-E, 1991 *Progress in Old World Palaeoethnobotany,* A A Balkema, Rotterdam.

WA 1993 *A43: M40 to B4031 Improvement. Preliminary Archaeological Investigation,* Trust for Wessex Archaeology Ltd, Ref. No. 36176.

Watson, J P N, 1979 The estimation of the relative frequencies of mammalian species: Khirokitia 1972, *Journal Archaeol. Science,* **6**, 127-37.

Waugh, H, Mynard, D C, and Cain, R, 1974 Some Iron Age pottery from mid and north Bucks with a gazetteer of associated sites and finds, *Records of Buckinghamshire,* **19/4**, 373-421.

Weaver, D S, 1980 Sex differences in the ilia of a known sex and age sample of fetal and infant skeletons, *American Journal of Physical Anthropology,* **52**, 191-195.

Whatrup, C, and Jones, R T, 1986-7 Animal bones, in D Jackson and B Dix, M109 (microfiche).

Wheeler, R E M, and Wheeler, T V, 1936 *Verulamium: A Belgic and Two Roman Cities,* Reports of the Research Committee of the Society of Antiquaries of London, **11**.

Whimster, R, 1981 *Burial Practices in Iron Age Britain: A Discussion and Gazetteer of the Evidence c. 700 B.C - A.D 43,* British Archaeological Report, British Series, **90**, Oxford.

Whytehead, R, 1986 The excavation of an area within a Roman Cemetery at West Tenter Street, London E1, *Transactions of the London and Middlesex Archaeol Soc,* **37**, 23-124.

Wicker, N, 1999 Infanticide in late-Iron-Age Scandinavia, in J Downes and T Pollard (eds).

Williams, J H, 1974 *Two Iron Age sites in Northampton,* Northampton Development Corporation, Archaeol Monog, **1**.

Williams, R J, 1993 *Pennyland and Hartigans: Two Iron Age and Saxon sites in Milton Keynes,* Buckinghamshire Archaeol Society Monog, **4**.

Williams, R J, Hart, P J, and Williams, A T L, 1996 *Wavendon Gate: a late Iron Age and Roman settlement in Milton Keynes,* Buckinghamshire Archaeol Society Monog, **10**.

Williams, R J, and Zeepvat, R J, 1994 *Bancroft: A late Bronze Age/Iron Age settlement, Roman villa and temple-mausoleum,* Buckinghamshire Archaeol Society Monog, **7**.

Wilson, B 1985 Degraded bones, feature types and spatial patterning on an Iron Age site in Oxfordshire, England, in N R J Fieller *et al,* 81-100.

Wilson, B, Grigson, C, and Payne, S, (eds) 1982 *Ageing and sexing animal bones from archaeological sites,* British Archaeological Reports, British Series, **87**, Oxford.

Windell, D, 1981 Great Doddington: an Iron Age enclosure, *Northamptonshire Archaeol,* **16**, 65-72.

Windell, D, 1983 Clay Lane 1980: Interim Report, *Northamptonshire Archaeol,* **18**, 33-42.

Woods, P J, 1969 *Excavations at Hardingstone, Northants 1967-8,* Northamptonshire County Council.

Woods, P J, 1974 Types of Late Belgic and Early Romano-British Pottery Kilns in the Nene Valley, *Britannia,* **5**, 262-81.

Woods, P J, Turland, R, and Hastings, S, 1981 Romano-British kilns at Biddlesden, Buckinghamshire, in A S and A C Anderson, 369-95.

Woods, P, and Hastings, S, 1984 *Rushden: the early fine wares,* Northamptonshire County Council.

Woodward, A, and Blinkhorn, P, 1997 Size is important: Iron Age vessel capacities in central and southern England, in C G Cumberpatch and P W Blinkhorn (eds), 153-62.

Woodward, A M, and Steer, K A, 1936 The Roman villa at Rudston (E. Yorks). Third interim report: The excavations of 1935, *Yorkshire Archaeological Journal,* **33**, 81-86.

Young, C J, 1977 *Oxfordshire Roman pottery,* British Archaeology Reports, British Series, **43**, Oxford.

Young, C J, 2000 *Oxfordshire Roman pottery,* British Archaeology Reports, British Series, **43**, Oxford (reprint).

Young, S M M, Pollard, A M, Budd, P, and Ixer, R A, 1999 *Metals in Antiquity,* British Archaeology Reports, International Series, **792**.

Zienkiewicz, J D, 1987 *Roman Gems from Caerleon,* Cardiff.

I n d e x

Alchester   6, 41–42, 47, 166
Aldwincle (Northamptonshire)   166–168, 173
antler   133, 135, 167
Ardley (Oxfordshire)   1, 85
Ash   158
'Belgic'   91, 104, 108, 111, 115, 117, 164, 166–168, 177
badger sett   25, 26
Bancroft, Milton Keynes   173
Bandbrook Bridge   1
bank   6, 7, 24–25, 27, 76, 79, 80, 83, 164, 166–169, 172, 187
barley   147–157, 178–179, 182, 184
Barley Mow roundabout   85, 163, 181
beaker   93–95, 97, 107, 111, 114, 117, 165
Bicester (Oxfordshire)   115
Biddlesden (Buckinghamshire)   6–9, 50–53, 55–61, 85–87, 89–93, 95, 103–104, 115–118, 123, 125–128, 130–131, 135, 141–143, 145–147, 149, 153, 155–158, 164–166, 172–179, 184, 187–188, 205
Biddlesden Road Bridge   6–9, 50, 51–53, 55–60, 85–89, 90–93, 95, 103–104, 115–118, 123, 125–128, 130, 135, 141–143, 145–147, 149, 153, 155–158, 164–166, 172–176, 178–179, 184, 187–188, 205, 211–212
bird   141–142, 145–147
black burnished ware   94, 105, 107, 110–111, 114
blackthorn   157–158, 161
Blackthorn (Northampton)   115, 117
blinks   148–149, 151, 154–155
bowl   31, 71, 93–95, 97, 101–103, 105–109, 111, 114–115, 135–136, 174
Brackley (Northamptonshire)   1, 6–9, 67–70, 85–87, 89–91, 93, 94–95, 108, 110, 112–113, 117–123, 125, 137, 141–142, 145–147, 154–159, 162, 166, 176–177, 181, 184, 204
Brackley Hatch   91, 93
Brackley Hatch 2   6
Brackley Hatch 4   6–9, 67–70, 85–87, 89–91, 93–95, 108, 110, 112–113, 117–123, 125, 137, 141–142, 145–147, 154–159, 162, 166, 176–177, 184, 204
Brackley Hatch 5   6
Briar Hill (Northamptom)   175
Brighton Hill South, Basingstoke   155
Brigstock (Northamptonshire)   146, 166
Bronze Age   9, 88, 115, 155, 163–164, 181
brooch   47, 122–123, 165
Bryn y Castell, Gwynedd   175
Buckingham Thick Copse   159
carinated vessels   90
Castle Yard, Farthingstone (Northamptonshire)   174

cattle   31, 38, 76, 137, 141–146, 164–165, 170, 173, 179, 181, 183–184, 187–188, 201–206
Catuvellauni   121
cereal   29, 39, 149–150, 152–153, 155–157, 179, 184
chess   17, 39, 148, 150–157, 178–179
Chinnor-Wandlebury   115
Clay Lane (Earls Barton, Northamptonshire)   167, 173
cleavers   148–154
cobbles   39, 42, 47, 52, 60–61
collar   101, 125
colour-coated ware   94, 106, 108–109, 111, 114
Costain Skanska   1, 3, 7
Cottisford Turn   1, 7–9, 72–75, 84, 87–88, 90, 159–162, 164, 181, 187–189
crab apple   159
Creeton, (Lincolnshire)   159
Crick (Northamptonshire)   165–166, 173
Croughton (Northamptonshire)   184
cup   54, 104–105, 107–108, 115, 125, 164, 173
Danebury (Northamptonshire)   150, 153, 175
deer   135, 142, 145, 147, 201, 203–204
desk-based assessment   3, 42
dishes   90, 93–94, 107, 111, 114, 117
Dobunni   121
dog   125, 142–143, 145, 147, 170, 201–204
dumping   26–27, 60, 84, 158
ear-ring   122
Earls Barton Quarry   166
elm   157–158, 161
Emberton   90
Evenley   121
fat hen   155
fence   22
Fenny Lock   115
fieldwalking   3, 6–7, 9, 47, 79, 84–86, 118, 163, 165–166, 181, 184
finger-tip decoration   115
Finmere (Oxfordshire)   166
fired clay   95, 98–99, 102–103, 109, 114, 119–120, 130, 133
flagon   95, 97, 107, 111
flints   9, 61, 87–88, 163
furnace   54, 56, 60, 64, 66, 104, 126–133, 155, 173–175, 176–177
gateway   25, 29, 167
Gayhurst Buckinghamshire)   164
geophysical survey   3, 6–7, 9, 12, 18, 24–25, 42–43, 54, 61, 63–64, 66, 77, 85, 164, 167, 172
glass   39, 63, 129, 133, 135–136, 172, 183

graffiti   109
Great Doddington (Northamptonshire)   167, 168
Great Houghton (Northamptonshire)   146–147
Great Oakley (Northamptonshire)   173–174
Great Ouse   47, 61
Great Ouse Culvert   7–9, 49, 84, 93–95, 108–109, 117, 120–123, 125–126, 166, 184
Gretton (Northamptonshire)   115, 164
Haddenham, Cambridgeshire   179
Hardingstone (Northampton)   146
Harringworth (Northamptonshire)   174
Harrold (Bedfordshire)   90
Hartigans (Milton Keynes)   115, 168–169, 172
Hatton-Silk Willoughby   159
hawthorn   153–155, 158, 161
hazel   158–159
Hazelborough Wood   1, 6–7, 79–82, 159
hearth   27, 43, 49, 51, 128, 130, 132–133, 157, 174
henbane   148, 150, 152, 155
Highways Agency   1, 3, 7, 8
hillfort   115, 174–175
Hobby Close (Northampton)   175
hobnails   48, 125–126
hollow-way   39–40, 42, 77–78, 84
horse   70, 126, 142, 145, 147, 156, 179, 201–204
Hunsbury   175
Hunsbury Hill Farm (Northampton)   175
hypocaust   101
imbrex   101, 109, 120
infant burials   31, 138, 170, 183
infanticide   138–139, 170
intaglio   63, 135
iron smelting   9, 48, 52, 54, 60, 64, 66, 127–128, 131–133, 145, 155–158, 173,–178, 181, 184
jar   22, 61, 89–92, 94–95, 97–99, 101–111, 114
Juniper Hill (Oxfordshire)   1, 6–7, 87, 90–91, 181
kiln   56, 60, 64, 66, 70–71, 77, 93, 108, 110–111, 114, 117–120, 156–157, 176–177
knife   125, 135, 141
Lindow Man   156
Lordsfields Farm   6
Maiden Castle, Dorset   155
maple   159, 176
medieval   6–7, 12, 16, 19–20, 25, 40, 42–43, 47, 54, 61, 71, 77, 79–80, 81, 83–86, 95, 98–99, 101, 104, 106, 114, 118, 120, 122–123, 125–126, 131, 157–160, 175–176, 181
Mesolithic   88, 163
microliths   88, 163
Millstone Grit   43, 135, 170
Milton Keynes   93, 115, 168, 173
mortarium   43, 106, 114
Moulton Park (Northampton)   115, 117
nail   40, 106, 125, 126
needle   135
Nene Valley   93–94, 105–108, 110–111, 114, 181
Neolithic   9, 88, 163, 181, 187
Netherends   6, 42
Northamptonshire Archaeology   1, 3, 147
Northamptonshire County Council   3, 84

Northamptonshire Heritage   3, 7
oak   56, 60, 157–159, 161, 176–177
oats   150, 152, 156
ore   52, 60, 126–128, 131–133, 174–176
Owslebury   170
Palaeolithic   88
Pennyland (Milton Keynes)   115, 168–169
pig   142–143, 145–147, 179, 201–204
pin beater   31, 135
pit alignment   8–9, 19, 73, 75, 99, 102, 164, 166, 172, 181, 189
Pits Farm   6
post-medieval   6, 12, 16, 19, 20, 25, 40, 42–43, 47, 71, 79, 83–84, 86, 95, 98–99, 104, 106, 114, 118, 120, 122–123, 125–126
Potterne, Wiltshire   155
pottery making   9, 145
Poundbury (Dorset)   138
Prehistoric Ceramics Research Group   89
quarry   6, 31, 35, 39–40, 42, 47, 71, 77, 111, 169, 174–175, 182
quern   43, 135, 170
Quidney Farm, Norfolk   159
ridge and furrow   6–7, 43, 79–80, 84–86
Ringstead (Northamptonshire)   164
Riseley Farm, Hampshire   159
Rockingham Forest   128, 159, 175–177, 184
rod   125
Roman road   6–7, 39–42, 47, 84
roundhouse   9, 11, 16, 18–20, 24–26, 30–31, 35, 49, 52, 53–54, 95, 103, 160, 165–167, 172–173, 182
Rushden (Northamptonshire)   111, 117, 177
rye   148–149, 154, 156
saggar   111
Salcey Forest   159
samian   19, 94–95, 97–98, 101–102, 105–111, 117, 165
Saxon   7, 166, 175, 184,
sedge   148–149, 150–151, 154–156
Shacks Barn Farm   1, 3, 6–7, 9, 42, 44–46, 85, 90–91, 93–95, 109, 115, 117, 122, 135, 165–166, 174, 184
sheep   142–146, 179, 181, 183–184, 201–205
sheep/goat   142–146, 201–205
Silverstone (Northamptonshire)   145–147, 156–157
Silverstone 1   6–7, 41–42, 79, 84, 126
Silverstone 2   3, 6–10, 26–30, 41, 85–87, 89–95, 100–101, 115–118, 120–123, 125, 141–143, 145–150, 152–153, 155–156, 159–160, 162, 164–167, 172, 178–184, 187–188, 201
Silverstone 3   3, 6–15, 17–24, 79, 83–95, 98, 100, 115–118, 120, 122–123, 125–126, 134–135, 141–143, 145–147, 149–150, 152–153, 155–156, 161, 163–168, 178–184, 187–188, 202, 205–206
Silverstone 4   3, 6–7, 48, 90–91, 93–94
Silverstone Brook   1, 83, 149
Silverstone Fields   1, 8–9, 32–38, 40–41, 85–94, 96, 115–118, 122–123, 125, 134–135, 137, 141–147, 149–152, 155–156, 162–172, 178–180, 182–184, 187–188, 203, 205–206
Sites and Monuments Record   42
skeleton   7, 31, 137–139, 142, 187, 206

slag   52, 54, 56, 60–61, 64, 66, 76, 78, 85, 127–133, 164,
      17–176
smelting   9, 48, 52, 54, 57, 60, 64, 66, 126–128, 130–133,
      145, 147, 155–159, 173–178, 181, 184
spearhead   31, 125, 170, 183
spike-rush   150, 154, 156
spindle whorl   13–135, 179
Springhead (Kent)   138
Stanwell Spinney (Northamptonshire)   167, 169
staple   125–126, 170
storage vessels   89
sweet chestnut   159
Swinneyford Farm (Towcester)   6
Syresham (Northamptonshire)   1, 3, 6–7, 9, 47, 61–66,
      81, 85–95, 105, 109, 115, 117–118, 120, 123–127,
      132–133, 135, 158, 165–166, 174, 176–177, 184
Sywell (Northamptonshire)   146
terra nigra   117
Thames Valley   106, 179
The Brook   1, 61
tile   40, 48, 98, 101–104, 126
Towcester   1, 6, 39–42, 47, 83, 85, 117, 166, 177, 182,
      184
trackway   6, 19, 20, 25, 42, 79, 83–84
trial trenching   3, 6, 42, 47, 61
Trinovantes   121
Tusmore (Oxfordshire)   1, 6–8
Tusmore Drain Outfall   7–9, 77, 90–94, 109, 115, 126,
      163–164
tuyère   130, 133

Twywell (Northamptonshire)   115, 117, 146–147, 165,
      168–169, 172, 179
Upper Nene   93, 177
Wakerley   146, 165, 167–168, 170, 172–174, 183
Walters UK Ltd   3, 7, 42
Wardy Hill (Cambridgeshire)   179
Watchfield, Oxfordshire)   159
Watching Brief   1, 3, 7–8, 47, 71, 83, 85, 118, 122
Watling Street   166
weaving   31, 135, 179
weed   17, 39, 71, 147–157, 178–179
Weekley (Northamptonshire)   111, 115, 117, 146, 165,
      167–168, 177, 179
Welsh Lane   1, 7
Wessex Archaeology   1, 6
Weston Favell (Northampton)   117
wheat   47, 147–157, 178–179, 183
Whitfield (Northamptonshire)   1, 6–7, 42, 61, 85–86, 158,
      184
Whittlewood Forest   6, 42, 81–85, 86, 159, 184–185
Wilby Way (Wellingborough Northamptonshire)   115,
      118, 165–166, 168, 178
Wollaston (Northamptonshire)   164, 166
Wood Burcote Bridge   1, 79, 83–85, 118, 126
woodland   3, 6, 79, 81–82, 86, 158–160, 162, 176–177,
      181, 184–185
Wootton Hill Farm (Northampton)   166–168,
Wroxeter   138
Yardley Chase   159
Yarnton (Oxfordshire)   106